Deep Change

Cases and Commentary on Reform in High Stakes States

a volume in
Research in Curriculum and Instruction

Series Editor:
O. L. Davis, Jr., *University of Texas at Austin*

Research in Curriculum and Instruction

O. L. Davis, Jr., Series Editor

Narrative Inquiries of School Reform: Storied Lives, Storied Landscapes, Storied Metaphors (2003)
edited by Cheryl J. Craig

Explorations in Curriculum History Research (2004)
edited by Lynn M. Burlbaw & Sherry L. Field

Exposing a Culture of Neglect: Herschel T. Manual and Mexican American Schooling (2005)
by Matthew D. Davis

Wise Social Studies in an Age of High-Stakes Testing (2005)
edited by Elizabeth A. Yeager and O. L. Davis, Jr.

Deep Change

Cases and Commentary on Reform in High Stakes States

edited by

Gerald Ponder

University of North Carolina at Greensboro

and

David Strahan

Western Carolina University

Greenwich, Connecticut • www.infoagepub.com

Library of Congress Cataloging-in-Publication Data

Deep change : cases and commentary on reform in high stakes states / edited
by Gerald Ponder, David Strahan.
p. cm. — (Research in curriculum and instruction)
Includes bibliographical references.
ISBN 1-59311-189-4 (pbk.) — ISBN 1-59311-190-8 (hardcover)
1. School improvement programs—United States--Case studies. 2. Educational change—United States—Case studies. 3. Educational accountability—United States—Case studies. 4. Academic achievement—United States—Case studies. I. Ponder, Gerald. II. Strahan,
David B. III. Series.
LB2822.82.D44 2005
371.2'00973—dc22

2005013181

Printed in the United States of America

CONTENTS

FOREWORD

These times are not the best that American schooling has known. However, neither are they the worst. Without a doubt, they are ambiguous, uncertain, maybe even fragile, and contentious—not terribly unlike times known earlier. Still, these present times have a special character, something educators and other citizens know as particularly different from other periods. Some observers recognize these differences under various names like *accountability, the era of real educational standards, high stakes testing,* and *true, not ersatz educational reform*. Still, reform is not reform is not reform.

Throughout the history of American education, reform or change has been a consistant operational advocacy. Some of the touted reforms simply substituted one slogan for another. Other changes were heavy fisted; they shattered excellent practices as well as tawdry and mindless practices. Some reforms were superficial, only skin deep. Characterizing some changes were efforts to create uniformity of curriculum and teaching and organization across entire states or within all schools of very large cities. In the schooling of the moment, advocacy of and insistence that educational reforms of certain types occur and that they occur rapidly have emanated mainly from state legislatures and governors and only recently from the nation's President and Congress and the federal Department of Education. This present advocacy and insistence constitute a profound and historic shift in the development, enactment, and enforcement of reformed educational policy and practice. Even so, reform is not just reform. Some reforms are deep, truly deep, not just those top-down mandated, not just those that promise and exact penalties when required targets are missed, and not those that depend more on slogans than on thought and action and revision.

This book is about deep change. In a series of research reports and commentaries, it mainly features case studies of powerful reform for the most part in local districts and in individual schools. They are set within the constraints of obvious political realities, essentially the recently legislated and bureaucratically enforced dimensions of high-stakes accountability. In this book, educational practice does not flow only from theory; neither does theory evolve only from educational practice. Rather, practice and theory fruitfully interact, not just some of the time, but most of the time. These accounts of deep change, moreover, are written gracefully, in understandable prose, and largely absent the barnacles of breathless advocacy. To be sure, the accounts are uneven, not as a function of their quality which uncommonly is high, but as a function of their foci and perceived attractiveness

I find much to like about this book. I certainly like the accounts of practice. They are stories of ordinary teachers and principals and students in real, not imaginary, schools. I also like the interpretations of these accounts. Some of them evoke expressions of comfort like, "Of course, the point is obvious. Doesn't everyone know this?" I find others to spring onto my consciousness when I least expect them. Additionally, I know that others are uncommon to my experience. In those instances, I have struggled to slash a trail through my previous perceptions and understandings and, from time to time, to retrace my steps until I find a path to new or freshened meanings.

Also, I like the new concept names used by the authors. They add meaning as well as they express common experience so very uncommonly. *Dailiness* is an example. When I first read this term, I did not need a dictionary to find its meaning. Immediately, I recognized the notions that it captured. Especially important, of course, was that a researcher/author had heard a teacher at one of the schools use the word, surely a personal invention, and had found it precise and particularly valuable in crafting the resultant report.

Most of all, I am buoyed to know how some American teachers are seeking deeper change than legislatively expected by high-stakes accountability requirements. The new standards and tests are concerned about only one thing: increased scores on the statewide tests. The reported scores are important, but they represent only a very modest surrogate for substantial school achievement. The case studies in this book offer clear evidence that to attain even the thin gruel of increased scores, especially in schools that serve seriously at-risk students, more than mandates and requirements are necessary. How very refreshing to note that, with competent and sensitive leadership, school faculties really can develop an explicit sense of vital community, a freshened school culture, as well as they can employ rich conversation about truly important matters related to teaching and to students' productive engagement with subject matter. These case reports remind me that the deliberation employed in the practices of these teachers and administrators never appears to seek *theoretic "solutions" to real problems*. Instead, it seeks *decisions for action* within the multiple particularities of an individual situation. Truly, these case studies, as good as they are, do not represent "best practices," to be used as cookie-cutter patterns for other schools to use. No, they illuminate "wise practices" to be studied by teachers and administrators in other schools as a means of fostering their own culture-building and deliberations.

The authors and editors of this book profess their faith in education, in the possibility of deep reforms in real schools, and in the prospects of increased substantive achievement of students. Furthermore, they illuminate the fact that serious school reform in the present time requires radical cultural change in schools and that this necessary change can be accomplished. What good news!

I commend this excellent book to teachers and administrators. I sincerely hope that they find it as provocative, refreshing, and informing as I have found it to be. Only a few books merit our investment of time to consider how other educators have succeeded ... and failed in their efforts at significant ... and deep ... school reform. This book is one of those few.

O. L. Davis, Jr.
Catherine Mae Parker Centennial
Professor of Curriculum and Instruction
The University of Texas at Austin

PREFACE

Practice improves by learning from experience. Even with good theory or with paradigm shifts, we still have to craft or hone our understandings by using knowledge in particular ways in practice settings. But productive change does not have to come only through trial and error. Bigger vision, an understanding of the networks of chaos or complexity, insights into patterns of promise can come more clearly and quickly from experience in settings linked with reflection and productive conversation. Long traditions of thinking about learning and practice, from John Dewey through Donald Schon to Jean Lave, Etienne Wenger, David Perkins, and Margaret Wheatley support the leveraged power of the combination of experience, reflection, and dialogue.

We have collected in this book sets of cases, reflection, and commentary of schools, leaders, teachers, reformers, and observers in an effort to provide insights into patterns of promise for improving school practice. Our cases share contexts of high stakes accountability and the search for practices that lead to learning—for students, for teachers, for leaders. Some succeeded. Some did not. Some had the scale of a school; some a district or system; some a state. All, we believe, have lessons and meanings that can be developed through reflection and productive conversation. None have recipes. All have hope.

This book is the result of research, conversation, invitation, and collection. As with all big projects, it has taken patience and persistence, and the product is the manifestation of many hands, hearts, and minds. We want to acknowledge and thank O.L. Davis, Jr. for seeing the value in this collection of cases and commentary and for inviting the work to be included in the Research in Curriculum and Instruction Series for Information Age Publishing. We also want to thank George Johnson and his associates at Information Age Publishing for their work in preparing the book and providing a place for these authors and their ideas. Certainly we want to thank our contributors who worked with us to conduct the research or to enhance the collection. And finally, we want to thank our families and our doctoral students, who create and sustain the relationships that result not only in work such as this, but also in deep changes in our own lives. It is to them, our families of birth and of choice, that we dedicate this book.

G.A.P.
D.B.S.
April, 2005

CHAPTER 1

THE DAILINESS, DILEMMAS, AND DIALOGUE OF DEEP CHANGE

Gerald Ponder and David Strahan

ABSTRACT

This chapter presents the concept of "deep change," in which schools and programs use the impetus of high stakes accountability and many of the principles now embodied in the No Child Left Behind rhetoric and legislation to transform their cultures to higher levels of performance. The chapter also serves as the introduction to the book. These high performing cultures have developed largely through conversation and dialogue between teachers and school leaders. The conversations are directed by data from assessments and are concerned with diagnostic teaching practices; they create communities of practice and identities for community members. However, these high performing cultures are fragile and sustainable only with substantial energy and daily attention. These cultures also create their own dilemmas and paradoxes that require continual negotiation.

It was a struggle to meet him where he was. I had to change my expectations. Yes, I have expectations, but you have to be flexible with each individual student. Helping him understand, pulling him, practicing it with him,

Deep Change: Cases and Commentary on Reform in High Stakes States, 1–9

> so that he could explain it to Mom and Dad: "This is what setting is ... this is what characters are ..." He has just skyrocketed. He is the success story of my class.... It's a daily thing ... it's not something I did in the beginning of the year and just hoped that it carried. It's an every day, every day thing. (Fourth grade teacher, Hunter Elementary School)

This teacher's description of her practice captures many of the lessons we have learned in the North Carolina Lighthouse Project and in the other studies presented in this book. They are lessons shared, we believe, by still other studies of school reform and school success. There is, in this teacher's description of her work, a focus on the learner and the process of learning, rather than just the intended learning outcomes. The language is diagnostic and analytical, not judgmental nor blaming. The student's parents (in this case, the parents are themselves English Language Learners) are part of the process. There is no mention of tests or other accountability outcomes, yet she is clear and specific about intent, using words like "setting" and "characters" to indicate priority concepts in curriculum, instruction, and assessment. There is concise articulation of "best practice" thinking, of teacher and student efficacy, of the power of persistence and the accumulation of experience. Further, her statement of practice—diagnostic, inclusive, intentional, persistent, deeply optimistic and determined—was common at her school and among her colleagues. What might take researchers and analysts pages and chapters to describe, this teacher says succinctly in a sentence layered with tacit understanding. "It's an every day, every day thing."

The studies presented in *Deep Change: Cases and Commentary on Reform in High Stakes States* represent markers in a current set of journeys in search of the "what works" grail. Work on this book started, in a way, in 2000, when we received a small grant from the North Carolina Center for School Leadership Development to conduct what they named a "Lighthouse Schools Study." Our charge in the Lighthouse Project was to study designated "lighthouse" schools—schools that had succeeded on state accountability measures despite overwhelming challenges from poverty and diversity, and to find lessons that could help other schools, other leaders, other teachers achieve similar results (Strahan, 2002; Strahan & Ware, 2001). Our subsequent multi-year case studies of Hunter and Central Elementary Schools found some usable lessons.

We also found, in our conversations with teachers, principals, and others about this "lighthouse" work, that front-line practitioners in high-performing schools in North Carolina, in Texas, and in Kentucky—three of the states most impacted by high-stakes accountability—all had similar things to say about the test-driven systems under which they worked. While there certainly were reasoned stresses imposed by high-stakes testing, the school leaders—principals and teachers—with whom we talked spent little time complaining. Instead, they framed the accountability systems as mostly productive. The tests and other elements of the systems had given them, they said, a common language of practice. They had made their work more focused, rather than merely limited. They had given them data with which to direct their work, rather than simply a target toward which to drill their students.

We began to find other work occasioned by similar positivistic impulses to include in this collection: the work by Joy Phillips and Cheryl Craig in their studies of an Annenberg project in Houston; Pedro Reyes' and Carol Fletcher's study of migrant education in the Rio Grande Valley; studies of a struggling middle school, rural networks, and relational leadership in North Carolina; and studies of Kentucky schools since KERA. There are lessons for practice from the stories of each of these challenging settings.

There also are reminders of the dailiness and dilemmas of this work. At the end of the day, the students in these schools leave, to return to return to environments that produced the circumstances policymakers define as problems.[1] And next year a new set of challenges will arrive at the school house door, and they will still be 6, 8, 10, or 13 years old. At the end of the day, teachers and principals leave to return to their own homes and neighborhoods, usually very unlike those of their students. And next year a new subset of teachers and principals will arrive to begin anew the tasks of learning to teach well other peoples' children.

They will face the same conceptual, pedagogical, cultural, and political dilemmas in crafting effective schools and quality teaching that many have faced before.[2] Nearly 30 years ago, Ron Edmonds (1979) asserted, "We can, wherever and whenever we choose, successfully teach all children whose schooling is of interest to us. We already know more than we need to do that" (pp. 24-25). Twenty years ago, *A Nation at Risk* focused our attention on the perilous state of public education. Since that time, systematic efforts to improve schools and to advance learning and teaching have become essential elements in the fabric of education. The Bush Administration's strategic plan for education and the No Child Left Behind legislation confirm again that the search for the "what works" grail still is alive and vigorous.

While widespread results have not warranted Edmonds' optimism, inquiry and dialogue about effective schools and classrooms have been lively, and our collective understandings and frameworks have grown (see, e.g., Barth, 1990; Danielson, 2002; Elmore, 1995; Marsh, 1999). We now understand, for example, that those identifying elements of effective schools that correlate highly with student academic success does not mean those elements can be readily replicated or scaled up. Turning the "characteristics of an effective school" into a checklist is fatally reductionsitic.

Creating a school culture and school organization that is high performing and centered on student learning is a complex sociolinguistic and sociocultural **process** that requires daily doses of leadership, capacity building, tough personnel and other human resource decisions, benevolent but hard-edged entrepreneurship in getting support and protecting gains, and a clear vision and persistent focus orchestrated through curriculum, instruction, assessment—and dialogue (Nelson & Burns, 1984; Fullan, 1999; Schlecty, 2001).

The literature on schools and programs that produce academic success among all children, and especially children of color and poverty, yields results that sound sensible, especially to practitioners and others engaged in the dailiness of teaching and leading. We find that active engagement with purposeful academic tasks fuels student achievement. We find that working together as members of professional learning communities increases teachers' knowledge about teaching, their collective feelings of efficacy, and their proven ability to promote active engagement by students. And we find that sound, caring, and collaborative instructional leadership fosters both professional learning communities and active engagement by students (Strahan & Ware, 2001, p. 4).

But we also find that well-intended reforms are often not enacted in ways that achieve the intentions, and, in fact, may produce paradoxical results (Malen, Croninger, Muncey & Redmond-Jones, 2002). We find that structural changes usually precede deeper changes in curriculum and instruction, and that structural changes are not enough to produce results in achievement (Elmore, Peterson, & McCarthy, 1996; Van Tassel-Baska, Hall, & Bailey, 1996). And we find that "beating the odds" and "closing the gap" and other reforms of great interest depend intensely on a well-woven tapestry of relationships and language. In "beat-the-odds" and "close-the-gap" schools, teachers and principals engage in "substantive discussions and extended deliberations ... [about] ... new vocabulary and reform-based practices." They engage in ... "highly organized, connected, and overt effort[s] to increase student performance ... [and] ... to help teachers gain the knowledge to effectively incorporate the new practices into their daily routines" (Langer, 2000; Wolf, Borko, Elliott, & McIver, 2000).

This book offers case-based lessons about what we have termed "deep change." For us, "deep change" in schools means a number of connected things. It means, first, a focus on *learning*, for students, teachers, principals, parents—everyone involved with the work of the school. Not teaching, primarily. Not leadership, primarily. Learning. It means that school leaders, whether teachers, principals, or others, continue to search for better practice, realizing that it takes the right mix of assessment, challenge, and support to reach each kid, each parent, each teacher. For students, deep change learning means that the school and its faculty are focused on broader ideas of development and learning than that represented in mandated tests. Further, "deep change" recognizes the *process* of successful practice. There is no "there," no fixed destination, and the idea of "best practice" exists only in the sense of the caveats of "for this time," "for this task," "for this activity setting," "for this student, here, now." It's an every day, every day thing. A dailiness.

That process frame is a level of understanding born usually of collectively shared and reflected experience. It is largely a matter of *dialogue,* especially dialogue that is about practice and that is directed by data about student learning.

Two pieces—David Perkins' (2003) *King Arthur's Round Table* and Etienne Wenger's (1998) *Communities of Practice*—help inform our meaning of dialogue. Perkins uses the metaphor of King Arthur's Round Table to help explain his ideas of "how collaborative conversations create smart organizations." Perkins defines *intelligence* as "knowing what to do when you don't know what to do." He further suggests that organizations—including schools—are made up of "conversations," some regressive, some progressive. It is through the progressive conversations—open, focused on solving problems and creating visions—that organizations increase their collective intelligence—knowing what to do when you don't know what to do—and become "smart." In his work on social learning, Wenger develops the concept of "communities of practice" to explain how, through processes of participation, negotiation of meaning, and reification, groups of people engaged in common practices—whether offices of claims processors, families, or school faculties—become communities. Productive dialogue—progressive conversations in Perkins' terms—leads to common histories and shared repertoires, providing paths of induction and celebration, along with the possibilities for increased collective intelligence. Communities of practice also lead to *identity* for their members. So teachers and principals in deep change schools become students of learning and of better practice. It is part of their being, not just their doing.

L'Esperance, Strahan, Farrington, and Anderson (2003) describe these places as "schools of significance." Their description is that "schools of significance ... are being transformed and empowered by the collective vision of entire school communities ... their cultures are rich with indicators of broad and deep renewal with data to support (the efforts) ... they are in a constant mode of reflection ... they are data-directed, not data-driven ... and are becoming student-centered communities that promote academic achievement for all children."

At their best, "professional learning communities" embody these process-centered, dialogic features. At their best, professional learning communities offer ways to sustain reform and anchor schools in better practice in the ebbs, flows, and power surges of district and state policy. At their best, professional learning communities keep schools—still the most important unit of quality performance—on good headings. But "professional learning community" is still more concept than commonplace. School boards and policymakers still look too often to hero superintendents and turnaround principals to compel change, rather than to dialogue and development as ways to invite, induce, and sustain it.

There is an old story of a conversation between a wizened veteran of the school wars and a novice teacher. The novice teacher wonders aloud to the older veteran whether the complex and compelling changes required by real reform can ever be done. The veteran educator replies to the question by saying, "Of course they can. In fact, there are two ways for such significant change to occur—the normal way and the miraculous way." "Two ways?" the novice replied. "Tell me about them. Start with the 'normal way,' please." The wise old veteran looked into the distant skies and said, "The normal way is for a band of angels to descend on a beam of light from a darkened sky and, when they reach the ground, to transport themselves each to a different school. Once there, they raise their wings and stretch their arms, causing all good reform to happen in an instant." "That's the *normal* way?" the young teacher asked incredulously. "I can hardly wait to hear the miraculous way." The veteran looked intently at the novice and said, "The miraculous way—is for us to do it ourselves."

Dailiness. Dialogue. Data. Negotiating dilemmas. Determination. There is no magic, only collective intelligence and communities of practice that can sustain progress and maintain a moral center.

The stories of and struggles toward deep change in this book are presented in two parts. *Part One, Journeys Toward Deep Change: Reports From Schools,* contains case studies of schools that have accomplished or attempted deep change. Most of the cases have another, paired chapter, to provide different perspectives and voice. Chapter 2, "Success Cycles at Hunter Elementary" describes the role of school conversations in developing collective culture and improving the quality of instruction Chapter 3, "Sustaining School Reform at Hunter" extends the story of Hunter by describing the role of Professional Development School elements and the tripartite diagnostic model of instruction in sustaining success. Chapters 4 and 5 tell two sides of Central Elementary School. Four relates the development of a school culture that resulted in a communal sense of responsibility, strengthened instructional norms, and a crafted data-directed process of dialogue that sustains the other elements of school culture. Five reports two ways teachers responded to district mandates by adapting or selective "shelving," while they collaborated to gather information and craft their own core practices. Chapters 6 and 7 describe ways teachers in a middle school engaged their own powerful learning through narrative practice and learning communities to create innovative curriculum and raise student achievement.

Chapter 8 provides another story: the struggles of one grade level team in an urban, under-resourced middle school without the boost of external funding or district attention to form a learning community, improve student performance, and enhance achievement. Ann Lieberman's commentary draws threads of reflection and learning and links these cases to the broader landscape of school reform.

In *Part Two, Programs of Significance and Deep Change,* five chapters report cases of district, state, or larger programs of importance. Chapter 10, "That Dog Won't Hunt!" confirms the importance of collaboration and determination within Kentucky's Education Reform Act. Chapter 11 presents an example of a phenomenon underrepresented in the literature but nonetheless crucial for collaboration, relational leadership. Chapter 12 reports the process of developing and using collaborative dialogue-based school improvement networks in a low-wealth, rural school district. Chapter 13 tells of the researchers' intent to identify successful instructional strategies in mathematics programs for migrant students, only to discover that the less tangible but more powerful elements of workplace cultures focused on instructional improvement held the real lessons for scalable sustainability in the Rio Grande Valley. Chapter 14 relates six features of higher performing schools in reading, writing, and English. And Michael Fullan comments on programs of significance in Chapter 15.

We close the book with a postscript chapter on patterns of promise, first steps in initiating deep change.

Deep change reform is not born of "what works" grails, structural changes, and one-shot workshops. Deep change comes from daily practice in different and effective ways of saying and doing until the new ways become ways of being and thinking. Deep change comes from imperfect but persistent records of negotiating the dilemmas of culture, pedagogy, and politics. Deep change reform comes from deep beliefs that "together we can," and a diagnostic and task-focused dialogue among teachers, principals, and families. The stories in the cases in this volume provide some pieces of color and texture in the tapestry of successful school reform. But like the lighthouses that inspired our studies, they provide beacons that show some hazards and light some channels. They don't show the way. Each school and program must find its own. It's an every day, every day thing.

NOTES

1. See especially the discussion on the social construction of educational and social problems in Scheurich (1997, pp. 97-98).
2. This framework of dilemmas is from Windschitl (2002).

REFERENCES

Barth, R. (1990). *Improving schools from within*. San Francisco: Jossey-Bass.

Danielson, C. (2002). *Enhancing student achievement: A framework for school improvement*. Alexandria VA: ASCD Publications.

Edmonds, R. (1979, September). Effective schools for the urban poor. *Educational Leadership, 37*, 24-25.

Elmore, R. (1995, Fall). Getting to scale with good educational practice. *Harvard Educational Review, 66*, 1-26.

Elmore, R., Peterson, P., & McCarthy, S. (1996). *Restructuring in the classroom: Teaching, learning, and school organization*. San Francisco: Jossey-Bass.

Fullan, M. (1999). *Change forces: The sequel*. London: Falmer Press.

Langer, J. (2000, Winter). Excellence in English in middle and high school: How teachers' professional lives support student achievement. *American Educational Research Journal, 37*, 397-440.

L'Esperance, M., Strahan, D., Farrington, V., & Anderson, P. (2003). *Raising achievement: Project Genesis—A significant school model.* Westerville, OH: National Middle School Association.

Malen, B., Croninger, R., Muncey, D., & Redmond-Jones, D. (2002, Summer). Reconstituting schools: 'Testing' the 'theory of action'. *Educational Evaluation and Policy Analysis, 24,* 113-132.

Marsh, D.D. (Ed.). (1999). *Preparing our schools for the 21st century: 1999 ASCD yearbook*. Alexandria, VA: ASCD Publications.

Nelson, L., & Burns, F.L. (1984). High-performance programming: A framework for transforming organizations. In J.D. Adams (Ed.), *Transforming work*. Alexandria, VA: Miles River Press.

Perkins, D. (2003). *King Arthur's round table: How collaborative conversations create smart organizations*. Hoboken, NJ: John Wiley and Sons.

Scheurich, J. (1997). *Research method in the postmodern.* London: Falmer Press.

Schlecty, P.C. (2001). *Shaking up the school house: How to support and sustain educational innovation*. San Francisco: Jossey-Bass.

Strahan, D. (2002). *Achieving success in the North Carolina Lighthouse Schools: Patterns of performance in elementary schools that have beaten the odds.* Phase II Report. (Principals' Executive Program, Center for School Leadership Development, The University of North Carolina, 2002, available at http://www.ga.unc.edu/pep/).

Strahan, D., & Ware, A. (2001). *Achieving success in the North Carolina Lighthouse Schools: An analysis of the dynamics of meaningful reform*. Phase I Report. (Principals' Executive Program, Center for School Leadership Development, The University of North Carolina, 2001, available at http://www.ga.unc.edu/pep/);

Van Tassel-Baska, J., Hall, K., & Bailey, J. (1996, Winter). Case studies of promising change schools. *Research in Middle Level Education Quarterly,19*, 89-116.

Wenger, E. (1998). *Communities of practice: Learning, meaning, and identity.* New York: Cambridge University Press.

Windschitl, M. (2002, Summer). Framing constructivism in practice as the negotiation of dilemmas: An analysis of the conceptual, pedagogical, cultural, and political challenges facing teachers. *Review of Educational Research, 72*, 131-175.

Wolf, S., Borko, H., Elliot, R., & McIver, M. (2000, Winter). 'That dog won't hunt!': Exemplary school change efforts within the Kentucky reform. *American Educational Research Journal, 37*, 349-396.

PART I

JOURNEYS TOWARD SIGNIFICANCE: REPORTS FROM SCHOOLS

CHAPTER 2

SUCCESS CYCLES AT HUNTER ELEMENTARY

Collaboration, Culture, Commitment, and Continuity

Gerald Ponder and Sandra M. Webb

ABSTRACT

This case study described how teachers and administrators have responded to pressures for accountability by articulating a unique, two-dimensional vision that links their words and actions. By comparing observations and interviews, the researchers showed that this dual vision of meeting children's needs and getting them ready for testing "was a *lived* vision and extended beyond the customary goals written for a school improvement plan." This dual vision has enabled participants to integrate moral purpose ("teach the whole child") with practical accountability (strategies for improving test scores). The examples reported, such as the EOG Camp, demonstrated how participants simultaneously prepare for exams and engage students in meaningful, responsive instruction. By examining the nature of participants' conversations in planning sessions, the researchers highlighted the process of "enabling dialogue," which captures "the continual emphasis

Deep Change: Cases and Commentary on Reform in High Stakes States, 13–35

on assessment, instruction, and *individual* student attention, as well as the collaborative give and take that occurred as classroom teachers, interns, volunteers, specialists, and the principal compared notes and formulated action plans for students." This "value-added quality of talk at Hunter" helps us better understand the role of school conversations in improving the quality of instruction and in creating more supportive professional learning communities. [adapted from a manuscript published in *Journal of Curriculum and Supervision*, 18 (3) Spring 2003, 222-239.]

INTRODUCTION

The gabled roof, central cupola, and red brick façade are all architectural markers of another era, decades ago, when the school first began serving the children of workers from a nearby textile mill. The mill and its children have long since disappeared. Now the school serves a far different group of kids and their families, and the current demographics read like a cacophony of challenge. More than 80% of the students qualify for free or reduced-price lunch—schooling proxy for poverty. More than half of the students who begin any given year at this school will move to another before the year is through. Some will move three, four, or even five times during the year. Children speak nearly twenty languages at the school, and for one in every five students, English is not his or her first language.

The age of the building and the urban character of the student body do not prepare visitors for crossing the front threshold. Inside, colorful murals grace the plaster walls of the front halls. The school's motto, "Together We Can," is a central feature of the murals and a visible reminder in hallways, classrooms, and offices. Outside the main office, video segments loop continuously during the day, showcasing events, activities, and students. The hum of energy is palpable, as small groups of students work actively on their lessons or move purposefully from one place to another. Here and there are scenes of one-on-one tutoring; while in one room, the school's curriculum facilitator works with the first-grade teachers during a weekly staff development session, made possible by creative scheduling and caring volunteers.

This is Hunter Elementary, a Lighthouse school in North Carolina. A small number of these centrally located schools were designated to "light the way" for other highly impacted schools in the state. Hunter fit the state's demonstration profile as it has, with a high poverty, high diversity student population, shown significant growth and steady improvement on the state's accountability system for each of the last five years. The tested grades, third through fifth, achieve scores on standardized reading, math, and writing exams that are *twenty-five points higher* (almost two standard deviations) than demographics-based formulas predict they should be. Nor is test performance the sole—or even the primary—criterion for results at this school. Teachers and other school personnel are quick to say that their focus is the "whole child." They work to provide a safe and caring environment, to wrap the children in a web of high expectation and high support, so that the kids believe they *are* readers and writers and that they can *do* math, not just perform on a test. The faculty and administration intend to establish successful academic identities in the students, not to engage them in the annual peaks and valleys of testing and forgetting for the sake of meeting the goals of an accountability program.

Table 2.1. End-of-Grade (EOG) Score Tables for Hunter Elementary School

Percentage of Proficient Students on Reading EOG for Hunter Elementary, 1997-2003

Year	*3rd Grade*	*4th Grade*	*5th Grade*
1997	47.3	44.0	43.6
1998	60.7	56.5	61.0
1999	77.8	40.0	75.0
2000	64.8	68.8	75.6
2001	62.5	59.6	87.2
2002	75.9	78.9	77.4
2003	88.9	83.3	84.9

Percentage of Proficient Students on Math EOG for Hunter Elementary, 1997-2003

Year	*3rd Grade*	*4th Grade*	*5th Grade*
1997	58.2	48.0	43.6
1998	51.8	65.2	58.5
1999	77.8	60.0	76.9
2000	59.3	89.6	87.8
2001	77.1	92.7	92.3
2002	77.5	94.8	89.1
2003	92.1	92.2	87.7

Proficiency in Reading by Ethnic Group at Hunter, 2000-2003

Year	*All*	*White*	*Black*	*Asian*	*Hispanic*	*Multiracial*
2000	58.0	57.0	59.0	50.0	100.0	50.0
2001	69.8	79.7	68.6	57.6	55.6	63.9
2002	77.2	83.1	76.8	70.0	83.3	70.9
2003	85.7	88.8	86.2	80.0	NA	89.2

Proficiency in Math by Ethnic Group at Hunter, 2000-2003

Year	*All*	*White*	*Black*	*Asian*	*Hispanic*	*Multiracial*
2000	77.0	79.0	76.0	68.0	100.0	82.0
2001	87.4	97.4	82.9	85.0	83.3	77.8
2002	85.6	93.3	83.3	94.4	100.0	88.2

In Spring 2001, a research team from the University of North Carolina at Greensboro began conducting a case study at Hunter Elementary to examine and to describe the ways that the school's faculty effectively supports student achievement.[1] The study continued for more than two years. Four research questions guided this study: (1) How do participants define success? (2) How do participants collaborate toward continued growth in achievement? (3) How do participants promote success? and (4) What types of support are necessary to sustain growth?

METHOD

The case study was a part of the North Carolina Lighthouse Schools Project, which identified three elementary schools demonstrating high performance on statewide achievement tests among students who are traditionally poor test takers. During phase one of the project, researchers collected demographic and achievement data, interviewed teachers and administrators, and generated school profiles and performance patterns (Strahan & Ware, 2001). The study we report was conducted during phases two and three of the project, when research teams were sent to each of the three schools to interview teachers, conduct classroom observations, and attend planning sessions to better understand the working of educational reform at each school location.

Our methods were guided by an ethnographic approach that focused on cultural meanings of participants (e.g., what they said, what they did, what artifacts they produced) (Spradley, 1979). Whenever possible, we retained the folk terms used by the participants to preserve their cultural meanings.

Setting and Participants

Hunter Elementary School is located in the Piedmont of North Carolina, a K-5 school serving a population of approximately 400 students. Ninety-one percent of the students are members of an ethnic minority; 20% speak a language other than English as their first language. In addition, 85% qualify for free and/or reduced lunch, and 50% live in a single parent family or in a blended family that includes a stepparent.

The primary participants at Hunter Elementary during phase two of the study were the principal, a Caucasian male, and four teachers: a first-grade teacher (African-American female), two fourth-grade teachers (Caucasian female and African-American male), and a fifth-grade teacher (Caucasian male). At the request of the research team, the principal nominated these four teachers based on two criteria: (1) they possessed qualities valued in the school community, and (2) their students scored high pass rates on the statewide achievement tests. Although students were not interviewed, they were observed, along with their teacher, within classroom instructional settings. During grade level planning meetings and focus sessions, several additional faculty members also participated. Phase three of the study was conducted in the late spring of 2003, nearly a year after the principal who had helped build the culture of the school was transferred—a price for success—to a high school. Phase three participants included four other teachers (K, 3,4,5) and the curriculum facilitator. The same questions and similar procedures were used in phase three, and the data thus became, in part, an examination of the continuity and permanence of the school's culture and capacity.

Data Collection

Primary sources of data included transcripts of interviews and focus group sessions as well as observations during classroom instruction and grade level planning sessions. Each research team interviewed the principal and teachers separately using a semi-structured protocol. The teachers were observed in two authentic settings: (1) during classroom instruction, and (2) meeting with grade level teachers during a planning session. During observations, notes were recorded on a template at five-minute intervals, using six guiding questions.[2] A second interview was conducted with teachers following the classroom observation to discuss issues relating to the lesson. Finally, artifacts were gathered in the form of planning materials, lesson plans, curricular documents, and minutes of grade level meetings.

Data Analysis

Analysis began during data collection using the constant comparative method (Strauss & Corbin, 1990). During the first round of analysis, we conducted an open coding of transcripts of interviews and field notes of observations. We then met to align our coding categories and discuss emerging themes. In the second round of analysis, we recoded the data and as new data were acquired, we compared these data to previously coded data, expanding properties of categories and developing emerging themes. During the final phase of data analysis, we conducted selective coding of the data to refine our categories and elaborate emergent themes. To address issues of trustworthiness, our team shared the themes of our study with representatives from Hunter during a focus group session as a member check. We also participated in peer debriefings within our team and with members of other teams in the Lighthouse Project. Finally, as we coded and analyzed data, we were conscious of attending to confirming as well as disconfirming evidence in generating our findings. Negative cases were used to clarify and expand our categories and themes.

RESULTS

As a result of our data analysis, four themes emerged that described the school community, shared beliefs, common values, and instructional practices that contributed to success cycles for Hunter students, its staff, and a transition in leadership. The first theme explained the way Hunter participants conceptualized success as a two-dimensional definition. The second theme focused on the collaboration within this school community focused on a shared definition of purpose, embodied in Hunter's vision. The third theme was a shared purpose that guided instruction for the academic improvement of all students. Theme four depicted the support needed from internal and external resources to promote community collaboration and continued growth. In the following sections, we describe each theme in more detail and provide illustrative accounts from participants as supporting evidence.

Theme 1. "Time to Shine": Defining School Success

We found that participants believed Hunter was successful if two conditions were satisfied: "whole child" needs and state mandated accountability goals. First and foremost, participants indicated that it was of primary importance that "whole child" needs were met, giving each child a "time to shine," and cultivating a love of learning in their students. The principal told us that emphasizing programs and activities other than those directly related to improvements in test scores at first met with critical reactions from central office staff.

> (W)hen we first started doing this we got a little bit of flack for saying, "Well, we need to have a 100 Day Celebration, we need to take time to go to the Outer Banks, we need to take time to go to Washington." There was a lot of, well, if you're a low-performing school, why aren't you spending time with specific instruction?" Seeing the hope, not losing focus on what the whole child is about, that you have to make it inviting and fun and stimulating, and you do that by all those extra things you do.... Even though it's not spe-

> cific classroom instruction. (It) charges kids up, and invigorates the school and adds to the setting. And we haven't lost sight of that. (Hunter principal)

The participants believed strongly that the success Hunter students experienced came from creating learning environments and life experiences that "motivated" and "excited" students about learning, and did not focus only on academic skills embodied in standardized tests. In the principal's words, hooking students into learning and calling attention to positive experiences in academic settings began a new cycle, a cycle of success.

> Our teachers know that the kids have to experience some success. And when they experience a little success they want more. And so that's a cycle, but it's not a vicious cycle of despair that goes on and on. But it's the success cycle that kids want to come back for more. (Hunter principal)

A second, mutually respected condition of school success was to prepare every student to meet the demands of state wide accountability tests that are administered at the end of each year. While test scores are important to all schools in the current climate of accountability, we found that Hunter participants interpreted this success as helping *every* child prepare for the academic challenges of testing. Preparation for annual testing was a major focus of student assessment and individualized instruction for tested grades. Further, non-tested grades, particularly first and second, played crucial roles in contributing to the school wide efforts for improving academic achievement measured through testing. A fourth grade teacher explained:

> So, it's like you have a whole team of people working toward a common goal, one common vision. One of those is to have at least 80% of all students on grade level, at least. That starts all the way down to our pre-K program. The reading, the types of activities that the students are involved in. The literacy carries on to kindergarten, first, and impacts the upper grades as they move along.

School success at Hunter had two elements. One captured holistic visions of meeting the developmental, social, and learning needs of each child. The second element addressed the political demands of accountability testing by focusing on the academic progress of each child as measured by these assessments. Both were equally respected. A unique tradition at Hunter, Camp EOG (named for the state-mandated tests, or "End-Of-Grade" tests), creatively integrated these potentially conflicted conditions into a uniform purpose and exemplified the way staff at

Hunter designed learning environments to honor the "whole child," while addressing focused, policy-directed goals.

> The week before EOG tests, the kids are grouped by ability in reading and math, and they can come to school and dress in anything they want. We all wear camp clothes, and they can wear hats. And in the morning they rotate through stations with a teacher, five kids in a group, and that teacher works with those kids with what they need, and we do ninety minutes of reading, ninety minutes of math, and in the afternoon we hope they can sign up for the class they want to go to.... They did so well that year, and we had a great test. (Fourth grade teacher)

Theme 2. "Together We Can": Collaborating for Success

"Together We Can," the school motto, served as a unifying vision and a slogan that communicated the values associated with relationships, responsibility, and results-oriented efficacy. The first word, "together," conveyed to staff and students that they were not alone in meeting the challenges of change, complexity, and accountability. Participants reported numerous examples of the ways in which this sense of community was fostered. Within the Hunter community, "together" had an inclusive base of support that not only connected staff, but also extended to students, parents, volunteers, and members of external professional communities.

> [T]he kids know they have to work together, even starting at the primary grades as partners, and then you build them up a little bit and they're still working together. Even sometimes when you don't say, "Can you help so-and-so?", the kids just go over and they help and they see the other student struggling and they step in. It's built their independence up. They're willing to step out of their comfort box to help somebody else. And it's spread out through the community-through our lunch buddies, through our tutors. I recently had my husband coming here for one of my students as a lunch buddy because the child needs the attention.... We're just spread out. (Teacher focus group).

Within a school culture, values often are built into a school slogan to communicate the defining character of the school (Deal & Peterson, 1999). The tacit meanings within "together" further shaped Hunter school culture as a community of learners. Teachers as well as students were considered learners, deserving support from others in the tasks and challenges that they faced. One participant commented on the meaning that this community support had for her.

> Two years ago when I was teaching writing, it was three weeks before the writing test and—I do not cry, I am not a crier—but I was almost in tears, so afraid. I said, "I can not do this by myself. I do not know what to do." And I said it to ________ at the buses. I said, "I need help." I usually do not ask for help.... By the time I got back to my room, the room had 14 people in it asking, "What can we do?" That is the kind of people working here. (First grade teacher)

This kind of community support was made possible by promoting meaningful relationships, which emerged as another important value within the shared meanings of "together." Participants described these relationships as both professional and personal, and found them to be instrumental in making the kinds of improvements needed at Hunter. A fourth grade teacher said it this way.

> Our relationship has gone beyond just Hunter School, and that is also part of the vision. We do a lot of social functions at the school that are outside of school. Every month we have a social event. We go to a restaurant and get to know each other on more than just a professional level, because working together goes beyond just the Standard Course of Study [the state-mandated curriculum guide] or the prioritized curriculum [a local district interpretation of the state guide, placing emphases on certain objectives and priority order on sequence]. You have to factor in personalities, like you said. I have to know Amanda well enough to say, "Well, we can do this" and not offend her, and if I didn't then I would probably have to bite my tongue and not share that. So, I think that that is really important. Trying to build meaningful relationships. Not only professional, but also that goes beyond the school building.

"We"

Within the Hunter school community, we found a network of interwoven and interdependent roles that were embedded in the shared definition of school success. Hunter's "we" included the roles of student, teacher, teacher assistant, parent, specialist, intern, volunteer, and principal. Although these roles contained some traditional expectations that can be found in all schools, we highlight in this section roles that uniquely reflected Hunter's school culture and were reported by participants as contributing significantly to school success: *students as resources; teachers as leaders and resource managers; assistants, interns, and volunteers as valued collaborators; and the principal as "visionary" and "yes man."*

Students as resources. At Hunter, students are valued as resources and take on the roles of volunteers, tutors, and role models for other students. Participants reported that as students were celebrated for the contributions that they made to the school community, they began to view themselves as part of the "we" that made the school successful, increasing their own sense of belonging, independence, and self-esteem.

> We're constantly rewarded, but more than that, we constantly reward the kids. Verbal praise, I think, is the biggest way: "Lucy, I love how you just helped your neighbor. Michael, you're going to get a talk-it-up because you just picked up the trash." It's like every little thing we see them doing, we want to praise them for it. Before you know it, they are working together. (Teacher focus group)

Teachers as leaders and resource managers. In addition to the traditional role of instructional leader, Hunter teachers assumed school wide leadership roles. Participants agreed that all teachers collaborated in various ways to help each other accomplish the challenging tasks of working with a student population of poverty and academic need. We found that teachers worked together in several structured settings: professional development, grade level planning, and school-wide organization and programs. The principal promoted collaboration and leadership among staff through administrative support.

> We have set up a schedule, an environment that put people in planned situations and that made, not made but, a push for, encouraged, enhanced team interaction. With a resource teacher, literacy facilitator, and the grade level team, our schedules [provide] at least an hour a week [when] they are together, with no kids. They are there during school time.... To really focus on where we're at, where we're going and what we need to do. So that's been a key. (Hunter principal)

Beyond the more formal collaborative structures, participants informed us that teachers also frequently support each other in a myriad of daily, informal encounters facilitated by the relationships that are promoted by the school culture, which "makes the load easier" for all.

> We rely heavily on each other.... We have a new teacher now on the 3rd-grade level, and she feels really burned out, but we meet together, our 3rd-grade team does, every week for two days after school. And we plan our lessons together, and we share the responsibilities. If one teacher is having a hard time, we try to take on the load and help that teacher out. And we try to divvy up responsibility so each person doesn't have to do the same thing. We share things. And that makes the load easier. (Third Grade teacher)

Another critical role of teachers was resource manager of additional manpower in the classroom. Teachers must effectively plan, direct, and supervise the efforts of the many volunteers, tutors, and assistant teachers that provide the small group and individualized instruction important to the academic achievement of Hunter students. Although the principal found the human resources, it is the responsibility of teachers to assume the leadership that will efficiently utilize these extra adults in the best interests of their students. The principal explained that this was a new role that teachers had to learn.

> But by using the manpower, by using a tutor effectively, by getting feedback and planning your assessment, by using the IMS [Instructional Management system] manager that we have, that focuses testing and assessment and using those results, that all took a lot of work on individuals' parts to grow and (to) put in a lot of time before and after and realizing that if you don't put in that before time and after time to coordinate these things it will be a hodgepodge mess. (Hunter principal)

Assistants, interns, and volunteers as valued collaborators. Participants repeatedly advised us that they could not accomplish what was necessary for student success without the support of other adults. Assistants, interns [pre-service students in a Professional Development School program from a local university], and volunteers who serve as tutors, guided reading teachers, lunch buddies, writing buddies, and math buddies are integral to the instructional programs and resulting student progress. In one teacher's words:

> And for you to say, "What do I do just in my classroom?" It's hard to say because it goes so far beyond.... There has to be a level of support. I couldn't do it on my own. I couldn't do it without my assistant. I couldn't do it without my student teacher. There is a level of support, and I think the good things that we do, I know the good things that we do for our students even in our classrooms are attributed to not just the teacher and the assistant, or even the teacher, the assistant, and the student teacher, but to outside factors. (Fourth grade teacher)

Another participant directly presented the impact that these adults have on instruction and meeting students' needs in this way:

> I have four adults in my room three mornings a week. I can meet everybody's needs at the level they're at, having the four adults in the room. I don't know of any other school that can do that. (Teacher focus group)

Principal as "visionary" and "yes man." Participants informed us that the principal not only "set the course" of Hunter's vision, but continues to "stay the course" of school success. The principal's paramount responsibility as a visionary was collaborating with stakeholders to keep the "big picture" of Hunter a viable and vibrant vision. His role comprised numerous expectations, routines, and practices, several of which included: communicating and maintaining high expectations, advocating for the school, nurturing a school climate responding to change but consistent with core values, and "bringing on board" staff that honor the vision. During an interview, the principal gave us a glimpse of the impact of his role.

> But one of the things we do, is I tell people all the time, "I want you here heart and soul, but to be here heart and soul you've got to know what the expectations are.... And that's not [my] expectations, but these are expectations that [the] Leadership [Committee] has said we need to be doing at Hunter Elementary School.... And letting people know what that vision is and saying, 'Do you want to be a part of this? ... When I interview someone, I don't come after school, I don't come on a Saturday to do the whole interview. I want them to see what we're about. I want them to see in a classroom how you manage three different people and that you don't do it by yourself. That's all part of getting them to buy into what we do. (Hunter principal)

Another primary role of the principal was described by participants as that of a resource generator, procuring and committing time and money, but also recruiting extra human resources to make the instructional programs requiring small group and individualized instruction possible. The principal referred to himself as the "yes man," and within his description of this role is a relationship of trust in his staff that further illustrated the respect for staff leadership and professionalism that he cultivated.

> So, you know, I'm their "yes man." And that's a good thing, because I want to create an environment for them where we have the resources that they believe they need. And I trust their judgment, that's a key point. Because that's part of being a professional and treating them as professionals. And if you don't have that, you don't have that growth. It's little things like not locking the supply closet and saying you have to get a requisition for those things. It's respecting others to say, "I need this," and "I need more of this," and "Can you get it for me?"... Now, that doesn't mean I'm always going to agree with them, and it doesn't mean that I'm always going to do it, but I'll listen to them. (Hunter principal)

"Can"

The final word in the slogan "Together We Can" communicated the collaborative will and support of all community members, evidenced in the motivation and drive participants reported for meeting school goals and in the trust they had in the collaborative process, which unified the school community.

Things being in print. Reaching children where they are. Presenting material in several different ways, not just lecture. We try to be—what we do is plan as a grade level and with just that planning and dialogue, we bounce off so many different ideas and so many different ways to introduce things and to get students involved. And that's not just at grade level. Every other week at our leadership meetings we share our best practices.... So reaching students where they are, coming up with as many different, creative ways to present material as possible, because I think that learning is as fun as the teacher makes it. (Fourth grade teacher)

Theme 3. "First Things First": Promoting and Continuing Success

A consistent theme that evolved was the common understanding of certain school priorities that participants shared and which informed their practices as they interacted with each other and with students and delivered instructional programs. These priorities also were identified as critical factors in promoting success in student achievement. In the following section, we report "first things" followed by a passage that represents this priority in participant language.

- *Communal sense of purpose*: An overarching moral purpose to address the needs of each child.

It's not our *mission* for EOG goals, because we want the child to be a well-rounded person. We don't want them just to perform on the EOG. We want what we teach to be useful throughout their life. We're not teaching to the EOG; we're teaching to the student. (Teacher focus group)

- *High expectations*: An "every day thing" that applied a positive challenge throughout the school community to "do your personal best."

High expectations. That's something that we see every single day.... And that is expected of you. There is pressure, not in a negative sense, but there is pressure at Hunter to be a good teacher. You know if you are being slack that that is not acceptable from your students, from your colleagues, from the assistant in your classroom, or from [the principal] himself.... Because if you don't have high expectations for yourself and if he doesn't have high expectations for the staff, how can we expect the students to rise to the occasion? (Fourth grade teacher)

- *Focused curriculum, assessment, and instruction*: Assessment was reported as guiding instruction, which addressed a prioritized curriculum and individual needs.

I do *a lot* of assessment. One or two assessments a week.... If a child is not doing so well with a certain concept with Geometry then they will be tutored in that area. Then at the end of the year we will continue to work with the child. But we have a check off sheet as well. If that child is doing fine in that concept, then you get checked off. But if they continue to struggle,... when we start reviewing that's when we pull students that are having trouble,... and we will put them in a group and work with them. (Second grade teacher)

- *Student engagement*: A variety of instructional strategies, such as small groups, pacing, hands-on activities, creative lesson design, and modeling, were used to capture and sustain student participation.

Basically I am like a coach ... I am just constantly talking and constantly giving them feedback, having them doing different things all the time. I don't waste time; we are always doing something. When they finish one activity they are doing something else. For the faster finishers, when they finish, they know exactly what they need to do when they finish. (Fifth grade teacher)

- *Success for all*: Continuous attention to each child's academic progress so that every child is nurtured toward academic achievement.

I had a folder for every student, and I would personalize it for each student so they knew what they needed to work on. Sometimes they had just taken a practice test, and I would take a little check list and write on there what that student needed to be talked to about today—"Please help them do that." (Third grade teacher)

- *Building meaningful relationships*: Caring relationships were intentionally nurtured within the community to support members in striving toward shared goals.

I have a lot of interaction with them where I mess with them and they mess back.... The one girl that wanted to question me, I just grabbed her hand and let her wait. I had her *with* me ... if they're there and you don't get any closer well that's about all ... you keep that relationship, and you don't really care to do anything extra for them. And for these kids, it's hard to get them to realize that we're doing it just for them. (Third grade teacher, explaining her efforts to build mutually beneficial relationships among her, her students, and the school's accountability system).

Theme 4. "Whatever it Takes": Supporting and Sustaining Growth

The final theme, "Whatever It Takes," described the support mechanisms that participants at Hunter believed were necessary to continue to make progress and sustain the improvements that had been achieved. We found that sustaining growth and improvement according to our participants involved (1) *the development of a school identity,* (2) *access to educational innovations and human resources,* and (3) *collaboration with a larger professional community.*

Development of a school identity. Within the larger school district system, Hunter was able to carve out its own school identity. The principal advised us that establishing this identity and setting the school's agenda was a crucial step in working within a larger school system and still implementing educational innovations through the leadership efforts of the local school community. Sources of support needed from the central administration were described as resources to keep their programs viable and the professional respect to adapt system-required programs to meet the needs of Hunter's student community and instructional programs. In the principal's words:

> One of my favorite committees that I got put on was the [district-wide] Out-of-the-Box Committee. And so, I think they [teachers] see me set a tone of, we will operate under [the district guidelines], but we will operate out of the box when it needs to be done. (Hunter principal)

> And it's not that we don't worry about Downtown because we do, but it doesn't mean that we have to agree with everything or implement everything the way they say it because I don't think anyone can come in here and tell us better about what we need and how to get there.... What Central Office should do is provide resources, trust our judgment to get us there. (Hunter principal)

Access to instructional innovation and human resources. A second major source of support for sustaining growth was access to sources that provided information about instructional innovations and the supplementary human resources necessary for introducing these new ideas and maintaining small group and individualized instruction. A teacher told us about the impact of this support in his classroom:

> This is one of the great things that I like about this school, well about the administration, because he allows us to do things for the kids as long as it is working. He allows us to try things. We will come to him and say we want to try this and he will say, "OK, try it, just give me feedback on it." We wanted to try and individualize work more. In the mornings right after guided

> reading for 45 minutes we'll have a little math session, called GIG. Meaning, "Get In Gear." What I have done is basically grouped the kids.... We have teachers, we have ESOL teachers, the assistant to ESOL, our assistant, interns that come in ... and they are working with three maybe 2-4 kids on different activities. (Second grade teacher)

Collaboration with a larger professional community. Partnerships with professional communities were viewed as valued relationships for improving the level of leadership and instruction already in place at Hunter. One participant reflected on the benefits of leadership training:

> And just in the last couple of weeks, there has been such a turn around, even with our weekly team meetings. We were talking about that yesterday at Leadership (Committee). And every grade level had something positive to say just from what Lighthouse did for us on that one day, deciding what our needs were and breaking it down, understanding it ... everybody getting on the same page. So that now, when we have our team meetings it's more of, "What do you need from us? I will tell you what I have to tell you. But, what do you need help with?" (Fourth grade teacher)

When participants addressed ways that success at Hunter was supported and sustained, they referred to material needs in the form of instructional aides, supplies and equipment, and additional manpower in their classrooms. In addition, participants also informed us that professional development, recognition, and encouragement (i.e., the principal trusting their judgment in trying new ideas in the classroom) created a climate of further growth and improvement in instruction. Finally, development of a school identity created a mechanism for building coherence by focusing on what was working well and adapting educational innovations or mandates into this already existing framework.

DISCUSSION

The case study of Hunter Elementary School portrays a school community that has achieved success by joining together in a shared purpose. Hunter's common goals put children first, promote collaboration among members of the school community, focus instruction simultaneously on the prioritized curriculum and learner needs, and marshal the resources necessary for teachers to address learner needs in the classroom on an ongoing basis and to assume leadership roles that contribute to further improvement. Hunter's shared purpose bonds members of the community in relationships that provide the support necessary to work with children that come to school with different needs and from diverse backgrounds. In the words of the principal, the members of this school community strive to begin "the success cycle [so] that the kids come back for more."

In the previous sections we described Hunter's definition of success, the collaboration among members of the school community to meet common goals, the priorities and practices that contribute to student achievement, and the resources necessary to support and sustain this growth. In the following sections, we highlight three qualities of the Hunter school culture that evolved as important factors facilitating the cycle of success: *the dual vision of success, enabling dialogue, and the golden rule of leadership.* We end the discussion by taking a more critical look at the *dailiness and dilemmas of high performing school cultures.*

Hunter's Dual Vision: A Cycle of Success

While it is typical and expected that schools within public education contexts that mandate accountability measures adopt goals to address testing and goals to meet the developmental needs of students, we believe that Hunter's two-dimensional vision is unusual in several important ways. First, Hunter's dual vision of meeting children's needs and getting them ready for testing was a *lived* vision, and extended beyond the customary goals written for a school improvement plan. Hunter staff entered a social agreement that supported their vision and created what Sergiovanni (2000) describes as a covenantal community, shaping a shared purpose, shared commitment, and communal support. "This community inspires deep loyalty, and compels members to work together for the common good" (Sergiovanni, 1996, p. 66).

A second distinguishing quality of Hunter's dual vision is that both purposes (e.g., whole child needs and accountability scores) were equally respected. In the political debates surrounding accountability programs and mandated testing, the holistic needs of children and the standards defined by accountability programs and measured by standardized tests are often framed as competing or contradictory purposes. We suggest that because the Hunter principal and teachers viewed these as dual purposes that were uniformly respected, they were at times flawlessly integrated. An example of this integration was EOG Camp, which has become a Hunter tradition each spring. In a festival atmosphere that combined the fun and interest of a "Survivor" television show with the skill practice for test preparation, students rotated through small group settings for final instruction and practice before the end of the year achievement tests. In the words of one participant, "It's really one of the best things we have ever thought of ..."

A final implication of Hunter's dual vision is that it presents both the moral purpose and the pressure (i.e., in the form of accountability goals) that are considered co-catalysts for initiating and continuing change forces in educational reform (Fullan, 2001). Throughout our study participants made connections between a moral purpose and Hunter's vision. The ever-present accountability goal of 80% at grade level provided the pressure to persist with change and innovations that resulted in focused teaching and student achievement.

Enabling Dialogue

Critical to the high performance at Hunter were the structured and supported opportunities for professional development and collaboration during the school day. These times of learning and conversation created a complex system of teacher collaboration and development that converted tacit knowledge into explicit and procedural knowledge on an ongoing basis (Fullan, 1999). Other researchers and change advocates have examined such talk and claim that it improves teaching (McGreal, 1988; see also, Wolf, Borko, Elliott, & McIver, 2000), builds collective efficacy (Goddard, Hoy, & Hoy, 2000), cultivates relationships and a sense of community (Lewis, Schaps, & Watson, 1996), and, ultimately improves student learning. Our experience at Hunter is consistent with this body of research. One implication of our study is that the conversations guided by enabling dialogue, both formal and informal, contributed in varied and supportive ways to creating effective learning environments for the successful achievement of Hunter students.

The term *enabling dialogue* further allows us to capture the continual emphasis on assessment, instruction, and *individual* student attention, as well as the collaborative give and take that occurred as classroom teachers, interns, volunteers, specialists, and the principal compared notes and formulated action plans for students. The "enabling" that took place was not only of academic-need, but also encompassed dialogue about families, health, self-esteem, and special ways that particular child could "shine." Whereas school conversations typically address teaching and school improvement, we found that this value-added quality of talk at Hunter, focusing on the needs of individual students, contributed to ongoing student achievement.

Golden Rule of Leadership

One striking quality of Hunter was high expectations, and as one teacher remarked, "That's something that we see every single day."

Accompanying these expectations, however, was a deeply committed respect for and trust in the teaching staff. Administrators acted with the same respect for teachers that the teachers demonstrated for students. We were reminded of the "Golden Rule" of leadership: Do unto teachers, as you would have teachers do unto students.

During one focus session, the facilitator engaged the participants in a discussion of the influences of high expectations and the challenging needs of Hunter students. How did these participants find the energy and enthusiasm to manage from day to day? The response was that these teachers felt valued as a "whole" person, just as each student is valued as a "whole" child. At Hunter we found that teachers and students alike were considered multifaceted individuals with their own talents and needs that deserved recognition.

The Dailiness and Dilemmas of High Performing School Cultures: The Costs of Commitment and Success

The stories, events, and effects we found at Hunter Elementary School are characteristic of the dailiness—the every day, every day demands on energy and resilience required to produce effective and relevant instruction—and dilemmas of this work. In our phase three observations and interviews, we found that the culture at Hunter had experienced another success—that of continuation. The elements of "Together We Can" and the other themes that brought success to the school had survived the transfer of the visionary principal who started them. In some cases, they even had been enhanced or adapted to meet the disaggregation and other requirements of the No Child Left Behind legislation.

But at the end of the day, Hunter students still left the school to return to the environments that produced the circumstances policymakers have defined as problems and that teachers and principals are charged with overcoming. And next year, a new set of students with the same characteristics but with different names will arrive to challenge the teachers and principals with the same conceptual, pedagogical, cultural, and political dilemmas in crafting effective schools and quality, culturally relevant teaching as many have faced in the past. Hunter Elementary is marked by a pervasive local advocacy that puts the diagnosed needs of their students above the demands of educational policy at the district, state, or national levels. They really do believe in a functional culture of leaving no child behind, and they advocated for their students by placing them in a network of significant relationships, advocating for families, mediating between the larger institution of schooling and their building, and educating parents in the kinds of practices their child needs for school success. That kind of advocacy and energized resources was an everyday thing.

Edmondson (2004) recently cautioned that, while policy-driven research that responds to functionalist "what works" questions is a good and necessary beginning, we as researchers, practitioners, and citizens need to move beyond these politically constructed views. We should also ask the critical questions about the consequences of accountability systems laden with school ratings and teacher evaluations. What are the costs of success for schools of significance in a policy environment of heavy accountability?

When we reexamined the Hunter data through a lens of more critical questions, we found the school's high performance came at a price, a price paid disproportionately by the teachers and administrators at the school. Teachers came early and stayed late, often putting in twelve hour days at the school. They sometimes returned on Saturdays or Sundays to finish the week's work or to prepare special materials for one or two of their students or to produce communications for the parents. The principal was at the school routinely from 6:30 in the morning until 6:30 or 7:00 at night, and he frequently returned on weekends. The teachers and administrators at Hunter expended enormous effort to redress the historic marginalizing effects of poverty and racism.

In so doing, they created, as one teacher said, a "poster child" school for the state's accountability system. Their substantial efforts to create academic identities—as students who *were* writers or readers or math kids rather than as students who *did* writing or reading or math on End-of-Grade tests; their continuing advocacy and local agency; their culture and collaborative identity went largely unnoticed as exceptional and child-centered endeavors that enabled student performance. They were known first as proof that a school with these demographics could experience test success, and thus an affirmation for the policies that produced the tests.

And in the 2003-2004 school year, Hunter was honored as North Carolina's Title I Distinguished School for its efforts at closing the achievement gap—one of only thirty-two such schools in the nation to be so recognized by the National Association of State Title I Directors and the U.S. Department of Education.

The dailiness of the work produced other dilemmas. Teachers and administrators worried about life after Hunter. They worried that they had produced a protected environment for students that could not continue beyond the walls of the school and after the fifth grade. The "M Factor"—mobility or moving on induced by parents' inability to pay the rent or sustain a job has always been a problem at Hunter and schools like Hunter. Good tests and good lives are difficult to produce and sustain when half or more of the faces in the classrooms and schools in May are different from the ones in September. And the dailiness of the work—the everyday demands of high energy and high performance—also produced an "M Factor" among teachers. Despite all efforts to recruit and inform new teachers of the commitment and performance expected and supported at Hunter, some tired or transferred after a year or two. In our Phase Three data collection, we learned that the second grade teachers had started a book club and study group at 6:30 A.M. two mornings per week because two of the four grade level teachers were new and "needed the help."

Stories of the stress and shortages induced by accountability-driven performance demands are now common in school reform. But even successful and significant schools are subject to the energy costs of high performance. The distance between the challenges of politics and policy and the support for good practice and high performance continue to grow. And front-line practitioners—teachers and principals—in schools of significance bear disproportionately the consequences of the capacity gap—the distance between accountability system expectations and the intellectual, human, social, community, and material resources required to produce an adequate functioning capability—while they are attacking the achievement gap.

Lessons for Cycles of Success

How does a school begin the cycles of success? As the former principal at Hunter considered the question, he listed several critical pieces. "Know the history of the setting." By listening carefully to others in the beginning stages of change, he came to understand the politics and culture of the school. His next piece was "to create an environment that is conducive to learning ... It has to be inviting. And it has to be neat and orderly. And it's got to be consistent." As a final piece, he presented "the bottom line":

> The bottom line is that you have to have good people—that have the same vision, passion, and energies and that want to be there ... and they have to be trained. I mean, you've got to give them the resources, but they've got to be good and care about kids. And then comes patience.... You've got to revel in the small successes that you have. And really celebrate that and continue to grow.

Hunter Elementary School has grown a strong culture of cycles of success. It is a culture with personal costs in time, energy, commitment, and life balance, and with elements of paradox and dilemma. But Hunter also is a place of consequence and growth for those who work and study there. It is a lighthouse of contextualized lessons in will, skill, and relationships, deep change, and continual tweaking, not a scalable roadmap for certain success. It is, like a handful of other stories of achievement in this time of high stakes accountability and reform, a school of significance, a testament to the power of relational leadership and an unwavering focus on developing identities of capability through assessment, challenge, dialogue, and support.

The school has survived a change in principals, turnover among the teachers, and the continued mobility among students. The culture of the school has its keepers—most notably the curriculum facilitator who remained when the principal was moved. But the culture of the school has its own power to continue, to teach, and to transform each day and each year into another cycle of success.

NOTES

1. Data and description are summarized from the original report of the Lighthouse Schools Project. For more detailed information regarding this project, see Strahan (2002).
2. Interview and observation protocols and forms appear in the appendices of Strahan (2002).

REFERENCES

Deal, T., & Peterson, K. (1999). *Shaping school culture: The heart of leadership*. San Francisco: Jossey-Bass.

Edmondson, J. (2004). Reading policies: Ideologies and strategies for political engagement. *The Reading Teacher, 57*(5), 418-429.

Fullan, M. (2001). *The new meaning of educational change* (3rd ed.). New York: Teachers College Press.

Fullan, M. (1999). *Change forces: The sequel*. London: Falmer Press.

Goddard, R., Hoy, W., & Hoy, A. (2000, Summer). Collective teacher efficacy: Its meaning, measure, and impact on student achievement. *American Educational Research Journal, 37*, 479-507.

Lewis, C., Schaps, E., & Watson, M. (1996, September). The caring classroom's academic edge. *Educational Leadership, 54*, 16-21.

McGreal, T. (1988). Evaluation for enhancing instruction: Linking teacher evaluation and staff development. In S. Stanley & W.J. Popham (Eds.), *Teacher evaluation: Six prescriptions for success*. Alexandria, VA: ASCD.

Sergiovanni, T. (2000). *The lifeworld of leadership: Creating culture, community, and personal meaning in our schools*. San Francisco: Jossey-Bass.

Sergiovanni, T. (1996). *Leadership for the schoolhouse*. San Francisco: Jossey-Bass.

Spradley, J. (1979). *The ethnographic interview*. New York: Harcourt Brace Jovanovich College.

Strahan, D. (2002). *Achieving success in the North Carolina Lighthouse Schools: Patterns of performance in elementary schools that have beaten the odds*. Chapel Hill, NC: The Center for School Leadership and Development.
Strahan, D., & Ware, A. (2001). *Achieving success in the North Carolina Lighthouse Schools: An analysis of the dynamics of meaningful reform*. Chapel Hill, NC: The Center for School Leadership and Development.
Strauss, A., & Corbin, J. (1990). *Basics of qualitative research* (2nd ed.). Thousand Oaks, CA: Sage.
Wolf, S., Borko, H., Elliott, R., & McIver, M. (2000, Summer). 'That dog won't hunt!': Exemplary school change efforts within the Kentucky reform. *American Educational Research Journal, 37*, 349-393.

CHAPTER 3

SUSTAINING SCHOOL REFORM AT HUNTER ELEMENTARY

The Role of University-School Partnerships

Robert Gasparello and Sue Mercier
with Samuel Miller, Jean Rohr, and Gerald G. Duffy

ABSTRACT

This chapter extends the findings of the case report in Chapter 2 by (1) elaborating the key and collaborative role of the university Professional Development School partnership in the success of Hunter Elementary, and by (2) basing the continued success of the school on a constantly refreshed culture that invites strong participation by university faculty and pre-service interns. School and university educators participate in collaborative staff development, and the school hires new teachers from the PDS program who are already inducted into the ways of the school and who have emerging identities as "success cycle" teachers. In addition, the cornerstone of school success, its guided reading program, operates on a tripartite diagnostic model of instruction that includes problem-driven instruction, judgment-

Deep Change: Cases and Commentary on Reform in High Stakes States, 37–46

focused teaching, and practice-based learning for students, teachers, and pre-service interns.

INTRODUCTION

As noted in Chapter 2, the collaborative sense of commitment embodied in the "Together We Can" motto is a driving force behind our success at Hunter Elementary School. Part of the "Together We Can" motto included working with a university (Miller, Duffy, Rohr, Gasparello, & Mercier, 2005). Consequently, this chapter has two purposes: (1) to describe our partnership with the university and its role in our success at Hunter and (2) to describe how we at Hunter and our university partners are strengthening this long-standing arrangement in order to sustain our success over the long haul.

THE UNIVERSITY-SCHOOL PARTNERSHIP

In fall 1996, we at Hunter Elementary entered into a partnership with the University of North Carolina-Greensboro. At the core of the partnership was the agreement that we would offer field experiences for a full cohort of approximately 25 pre-service teachers during both their junior and their senior years. The immediate advantage to us was that the added "person power" allowed us to lower our teacher-pupil ratio so we could provide more focused instruction for our high poverty students. The immediate advantage to the university was that they could more closely supervise their pre-service teachers' progress in a highly diverse student environment. For both of us, it was an opportunity to work with dedicated educators in a collaborative effort to make a difference—a difference with children in our case, a difference with teacher candidates in the case of the university.

The partnership was modeled on the concept of the "Professional Development School" (Holmes Group, 1986, 1990, 1995; Teitel, 2003). The Professional Development School (PDS) concept is a major departure from standard approaches to teacher education and to school-university relationships. In traditional teacher education, the typical practice is to provide pre-service teachers with student teaching experience for a semester in widely-separated schools, with university supervisors who have little direct responsibility in the ongoing teacher education curriculum traveling from school to school to visit students. In this traditional model, there is typically little congruence between what methods course instructors emphasize and what either the teachers in the schools or the field supervisors emphasize, and the school's role is limited to agreeing to take a student teacher for a semester. The result is all too often a scattered, weakly supervised and conceptually mixed pre-service teacher education program.

In contrast, the PDS concept is a collaborative partnership with significant advantages to both partners. For us at Hunter, for instance, the partnership markedly increases the number of people available to teach our high poverty children while also providing us with the professional stimulation that comes with close association with a teacher education program. For our partners at the university, who now have methods course instructors intensely involved in supervising their students at Hunter, the arrangement increases the conceptual congruence between the methods classes and what student teachers experience at Hunter. As a result, they have a much stronger teacher education program.

Of course, it is not easy to accomplish this partnership. Over the years, both we at Hunter and our partners at the university have struggled with what "collaboration" really entails.

For us at the school, for instance, we have sometimes found it difficult to give up our classrooms to student teachers; supervising student teachers is sometimes an added chore, the added adults in the schools seemed at first to make life more difficult rather than less difficult and, of course, it is always difficult when a student teacher struggles and has to be removed. However, for us the most difficult aspect of collaboration is finding common ground with a university whose mission is often quite different from ours. We serve a high poverty and needy clientele and, as such, we have many immediate needs that we wish the university could help us with, and it is frustrating when the university's agenda makes it impossible for them to provide a specific resource. For instance, we often wish we could make more frequent use of professors as in-classroom consultants helping teachers with specific instructional problems. However, university demands often limit professors' availability.

For our partners at the university, the difficulties are different but no less vexing. For instance, as noted above, professors always feel pressured by the time demands, and the tension between being in our school and attending to competing university duties. Not all professors are willing to make such accommodations. Similarly, not all professors are comfortable with the fact that collaboration requires that the university cannot simply tell us what they want but, instead, must first develop new ideas with us and then modify (and sometimes abandon) their requests to fit our constraints. Finally, not all professors like giving up the role of being experts who disseminate "answers" and then leave. Collaboration means being equal partners in our community, and working side-by-side with us year-after-year, a concept that is not easy for professors who work in a culture that values scholarship more than hands-on application.

In sum, as is the case with all partnerships, both partners must make accommodations and learn new things. We at the school have to make room for professors and their needs; professors have to abandon the "ivory tower" in favor of our day-to-day classroom needs. Patience and understanding are essential on both sides. We at the school must try to understand the constraints the university is working under and make accommodations accordingly, and the university must try to understand the constraints we are working under and make accommodations accordingly. The result is often a situation that is less than perfect for both partners, especially initially. However, we have also learned the importance and value of mutual trust. When both parties are willing to make compromises and accommodations over time, trust develops and a partnership is possible.

While it is difficult to achieve this trust, it has been worth the effort. Currently, we host two cohorts of students whose teacher education preparation emphasizes literacy. One cohort is a set of junior students who are just beginning their professional education, are taking literacy methods courses, and applying what they learned at Hunter on three half-days a week throughout their junior year. The other cohort is a set of seniors who are in their second year at Hunter; they spend three half days a week at our school in the fall and then are here full time for the spring semester. Consequently, at any given time we now host upwards of 50 pre-service teachers, all of whom are involved in teaching children, sometimes in 1-on-1 situations, sometimes in small groups, and sometimes in whole class situations.

Perhaps the most dramatic impact of this arrangement is seen in our guided reading program. Guided reading is a highly recommended technique for improving students' reading achievement (Fountas & Pinnell, 1996). For guided reading to be successful, however, students must read at their instructional reading level—that is, the material they read can be neither too difficult nor too easy. However, because of the wide ability range in any given classroom at Hunter Elementary (i.e., the wide range of instructional reading levels in any one classroom), each teacher has to form multiple small groups. As is typical in many high poverty schools, children are often difficult to manage, making small group instruction hard to do with only one adult in the classroom. Children not in the group working directly with the teacher are often inattentive and disruptive. With the advent of our partnership with the university, however, teacher candidates are on site several days a week, which gives us several adults in each classroom. As a result, intensive guided reading is now an instructional fixture at Hunter Elementary, with small groups receiving instruction under direct supervision and for longer periods of time.

The guided reading program has been supplemented by a tutorial program, which, again, was made possible by our partnership with the university. Third grade is a crucial year in North Carolina schools because policy mandates that if students do not pass the state End-of-Grade Test (EOG), they cannot move on to fourth grade. Because two or three students in every class are in danger of failing the EOG, we used our student teachers as tutors for at-risk children. Three times a week, for up to 30 to 40 minutes each over an entire year, students in danger of failing the EOG received intensive help.

As noted in Chapter 2, the guided reading and tutoring have resulted in dramatic achievement gains. Students have made steady progress in reading over the years and, as is evident in the deportment of our children, our goal of developing the "whole child" has also been achieved.

We at Hunter attribute this success, in large part, to our partnership with the university. As our former principal has said, "The role played by the university professors, interns, and graduate students and the collaboration that takes place was and still is a crucial piece [of our success]." Similarly, our curriculum facilitator reports that the relationship with the university creates a stronger sense of professionalism among our Hunter teachers, supports our staff development efforts, and provides valuable resources we would otherwise not have, among other advantages.

And, of course, the university benefits also. A much more programmatically cohesive teacher education program results because professors can provide their teacher candidates with frequent field experiences supervised by personnel who are closely involved in both the teacher education curriculum and in the instructional practices at Hunter. For instance, in developing both the guided reading and the tutoring program, teacher candidates received intensive instruction and supervision from both school and university personnel. This was of immense value to teacher education candidates who were able to make substantive connections between their methods courses and their field experience. The fact that they were able to work at different grade levels in different semesters further helped them adapt their understandings to different children in different grades. The result is the development of excellent teachers. In fact, we have hired a number of the university's student teachers because we have had an opportunity to see what strong, qualified candidates they are. Other principals in the district often seek the ones we do not hire.

In sum, there are many components that explain our success at Hunter. We have focused goals, we have a unified vision, we utilize community people, we have a spirit of mutual support, we set high expectations, and we have strong leadership, all of which are documented in Chapter Two.

However, it is also fair to say that much of our progress is because of our partnership with the university. While the most obvious benefit of that partnership is the increased number of people in the school and the resulting achievement score gains, a less obvious but perhaps more important benefit is that the partnership is a mutually generative arrangement that is a source of strength and vision for both the university and us as we look to the future.

SUSTAINING THE HUNTER MODEL

It is difficult to sustain a model such as ours. As detailed in Chapter 2, we pay a price for our success. We work extraordinarily long hours, the collaboration with the university requires frequent meetings and consultations to ensure coordination, and the "dailiness" of the energy demands wears some of us down so much that we request transfers to other schools. Similarly, our university partners continue to find it difficult to balance the demands of PDS-based teacher education with the university's expectation for scholarly research.

Sustaining progress was made more difficult in 2002 when the principal who guided our efforts during the first eight years was transferred to another school, and a new principal came on board. Often, when the leader of a particularly successful educational innovation leaves, the project flounders. The fact that it didn't in this case is attributable to two factors.

First, of course, is the fact that, despite the change, the leadership in the building remained strong. The curriculum facilitator who had been instrumental in creating and cultivating the Hunter model in partnership with the original principal continued her duties at Hunter. Her commitment to the model provided a continuity that helped sustain it during the leadership transition. Second, the new principal embraced the model, adapted his leadership style to the requirements of the model, and worked to maintain it. Finally, individual teacher leaders in the building continued to support the model, and worked hard to ensure its continuation. Together, this leadership team ensured that, despite the change in leadership, the model would continue.

The second factor in sustaining the Hunter model is that we work hard to create a dynamic situation that is accepting of new conceptual ideas. That is, rather than simply settle for what we were doing, we have consciously tried to improve it. This effort, and the new ideas associated with it, are energizing, serve to keep us looking ahead rather than settling for the status quo, and help us sustain our success. Here again our partnership with the university has been important.

For instance, our university partners have pointed out that the PDS model as we know it has potential for increased collaboration that will result in additional benefits for both partners. Three examples are illustrative. First, by teaching methods courses at Hunter rather than on campus, collaboration can be expanded to involve classroom teachers in the teaching of methods courses. Reciprocally, university personnel can spend more of their time in classrooms helping not only pre-service interns but also helping teachers themselves. Second, the school can be viewed as a research site, and the practices at the school, both at the classroom level and at the teacher education level, can be a source of scholarly study. This not only serves the needs of professors who must do research but, also, is professionally stimulating to teachers who are subjects of study or close observers of studies being conducted in the school. Finally, the teacher education function can be expanded beyond service to pre-service teachers to include professional development for teachers as well. That is, university personnel assigned to the school can be involved in the school's ongoing staff development efforts, providing expertise and longitudinal assistance in developing curriculum and in improving instruction.

These efforts have the advantage of enlivening still further the professional spirit that we at Hunter Elementary already experience. We are stimulated by being closely associated with a teacher education program that makes use of our expertise, by being able to have access to professors and advanced graduate students who can assist us in our staff development efforts, and by having a close association with research efforts. For our university colleagues, of course, this elaboration on the concept not only strengthens their teacher education program and the preparation of their teacher candidates but also makes it possible for them to do the scholarly work essential to survival in the university.

These recent innovations have been guided by a conceptual model that highlights the three main themes of our work (see Figure 3.1). As the figure shows, we believe that student achievement depends upon judgment-focused teaching, problem-driven instruction, and practice-based learning.

Judgment-focused teaching means that we put a high priority on teachers being proactive in adapting instruction to fit the demands of the situation, often on a case-by-case basis. That is, teachers are not merely knowledgeable; they thoughtfully transform professional knowledge to accommodate the special needs of the children at Hunter.

Problem-driven instruction means that a primary goal at Hunter is that we cast instruction in academic work that represents genuine literacy activity that, in turn, helps children persevere. In doing so, we emphasize high-challenge comprehension abilities as well as basic skills.

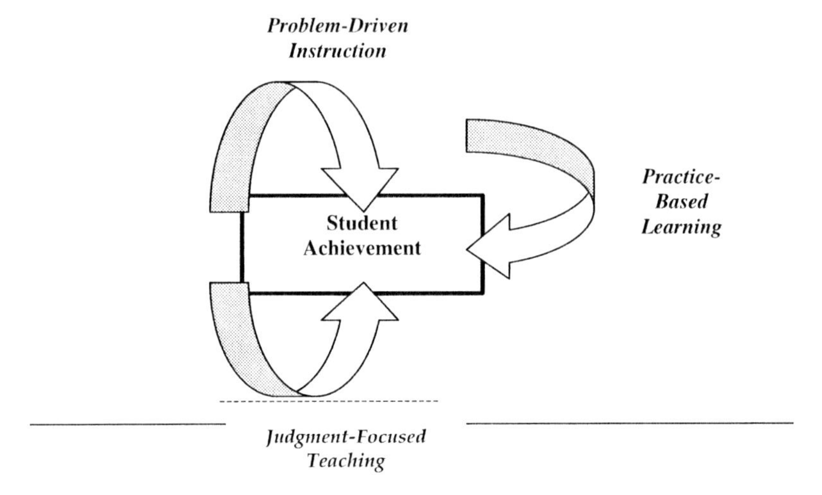

Figure 3.1. Public school-university collaborative professional development school reform and teacher education model.

Practice-based learning means that learning is activity-based. We work to actively engage children in extensive and intensive experiences that help them apply what they learn in real situations.

The three elements of the model represent the three conceptual forces that we believe are key to our continuing success with our high poverty clientele. The model guides teachers as they work with children, and our student teachers as they work under our supervision.

However, the model's usefulness is not limited to that. It is useful in guiding the efforts of professors as they work with teacher candidates and the efforts of researchers as they pursue studies at Hunter Elementary. From the teacher education perspective, for instance, the three elements of the model are prevalent themes throughout teacher candidates' professional education. Judgment-focused teaching means that, while the teacher education program emphasizes the usual forms of professional knowledge (i.e., text-rich environments, classroom management, high time-on-task, explicit teaching and various best practices, among others), a major curricular goal is to prepare future teachers who are able to transform professional knowledge to fit the various situations faced in classrooms; problem-driven instruction means that the teacher education program strives to develop teachers who are committed to involving children in academic tasks that go beyond basic skills to include genuine literacy and high-level thought; and practice-based learning means that the teacher education effort is committed to providing teacher candidates with extensive and intensive experiences in teaching children of poverty, and in ensuring that professors closely supervise such experiences.

Similarly, the model guides the research efforts undertaken at Hunter Elementary. For instance, in line with the judgment-focused emphasis, some studies examine teacher decision-making, the way teachers transform knowledge "on-the-fly" during instruction, and how they manage to do so. Consistent with the problem-driven emphasis, some studies examine the relationship between high-challenge tasks and student motivation, the relationship between authentic literacy activity and students' conceptual understandings about reading, and teachers' professional thinking as they attempt to engage children of poverty in authentic literacy tasks, especially in the context of the pressure to produce high scores on state assessment tests. In the area of practice-based learning, studies examine children's learning during experience-based classroom activities and the impact of a two-year field experience on the developmental progress of teacher candidates.

In sum, the model is multi-leveled, and it permeates all phases of our work, both at Hunter and in our collaboration with the university. One example is illustrative. Consistent with our judgment-based emphasis, classroom teachers and teacher candidates put a heavy emphasis on assessment. In support of this, university and school personnel work together to develop assessment procedures that are then put to work in classrooms. Classroom teachers receive practical support in response to needs they have expressed, teacher candidates stop thinking that what they do in their methods courses is all they have to do to learn to be professional teachers, and children receive differentiated instruction geared to their particular needs. Hence, everyone benefits.

Our vision for the future is that we will maintain this system of mutual benefits. The above model represents our current thinking about how we conceptualize our work. It serves as a vehicle to help school and university "stay on the same page," as a touchstone regarding what it is we stand for, as a goal that we can continue to achieve as we work to improve the educational opportunities for our children, and as a way to help us sustain our efforts. However, we fully expect that the model is temporary. As we continue to work together, we will continue to modify the model based on what we learn about how to improve the quality of the education we provide for children and teacher candidates.

However, we have no illusions about the difficulty of doing so. The problems associated with collaboration noted earlier have not gone away. Each year we encounter new problems, new tensions, and new difficulties. However, we now have a foundation of trust, tangible evidence of benefits for children and to teacher candidates, and an understanding that sustaining our success means continuing our efforts to improve the model.

CONCLUSION

These are times when all of education is under fire. Teachers in high poverty schools such as ours are under tremendous pressure to generate high scores on standardized tests, often at the expense of higher-level thinking and education of the whole child.

Similarly, our university colleagues are under pressure. Federal officials make increasingly more threatening announcements about the failures of teacher education while providing unprecedented support for alternatives to teacher certification that circumvent teacher education.

Given these events, this is not a time for "going it alone." If we are to establish that classroom teachers can prepare students from high poverty backgrounds to be literate in all senses of that word, and if we are to establish that good teacher preparation is essential in creating teaches who can develop such literacy, we must work together. Our collaboration with our university colleagues is an example of an effort to do so.

Consequently, we believe that sustaining our success is not only important to us at Hunter and to the teacher educators at the University of North Carolina-Greensboro. Sustaining our success is also important because it is important to establish that America is best served (a) by schools like Hunter that take a comprehensive approach to school reform and (b) by teacher education programs that work closely with schools to develop teachers and to create new professional knowledge. We believe that "together we can."

REFERENCES

Fountas, I.C., & Pinnell, G.S. (1996). *Guided reading: Good first teaching for all children*. Portsmouth, NH: Heinemann.

Holmes Group. (1986). *Tomorrow's teachers*. East Lansing , MI: Author.

Holmes Group. (1990). *Tomorrow's schools*. East Lansing,MI: Author.

Holmes Group. (1995). *Tomorrow's schools of education*. East Lansing, MI: Author.

Miller, S., Duffy, G., Rohr, J., Gasparello, R., & Mercier, S. (2005). Preparing teachers for high-poverty schools. *Educational Leadership, 62*(8), 62-65.

Teitel, L. (2003). *Professional development schools handbook*. Thousand Oaks, CA: Corwin Press.

CHAPTER 4

BEATING THE ODDS AT CENTRAL ELEMENTARY SCHOOL

Developing a Shared Stance toward Learning

David Strahan, Heidi Carlone, Suzanne Horn, Fern Dallas, and Anita Ware

ABSTRACT

This case study describes how teachers and administrators at Central Elementary School have created a more supportive school climate. Results from state-mandated achievement tests show that student performance at Central has improved steadily in recent years. Interviews with teachers and administrators and observations of lessons and planning meetings conducted over a two-year period document three major changes in school culture that have contributed to these accomplishments. During this time, teachers and administrators have developed a shared stance toward learning that link values and beliefs into a communal sense of responsibility. This shared stance has strengthened instructional norms that emphasize more active student engagement, infusing lessons with higher levels of cooperation and student involvement. Grade-level planning sessions and site-based staff

Deep Change: Cases and Commentary on Reform in High Stakes States, 47–64

development feature a process of data-directed dialogue that nurtures the other two changes. Results show how these cultural dynamics are sustaining school renewal, student accomplishment, and teacher development.

INTRODUCTION

Teachers and administrators in almost every community are involved in some type of school improvement initiative. Some of these initiatives are responses to state-level or district-level mandates. Others may be grass-roots efforts to respond to the changing needs of students and families. As school reform initiatives have multiplied, researchers have explored the complexity of educational change (see, e.g., Brown, 1999; Fullan, 1990; Strahan, 1994; Van Tassel-Baska, Hall, & Bailey, 1996; Wolf, Borko, Elliott, & McIver, 2000). These studies document many of the ways that interpersonal and contextual dynamics shape school reform, showing that the visible outcomes of school improvement are often the result of deep-seated changes in school culture.

Understanding the dynamics of school reform is the goal of the North Carolina Lighthouse Project. Initiated in 1999 by the North Carolina General Assembly, the Lighthouse Schools Project seeks to identify characteristics of successful schools and to highlight certain practices, called "lighthouse" practices, so that teachers and principals across the state can study and learn from one another and serve as catalysts for school improvement. This article presents a case study of one of the three Lighthouse Schools based on two years of observations and interviews.

SCHOOL CULTURE AS A FRAMEWORK FOR UNDERSTANDING SCHOOL REFORM

A growing number of studies of school reform have chronicled ways that efforts to enhance teaching and learning are intertwined with efforts to improve school culture. Fullan (1990) found that meaningful changes occur when participants develop "collaborative work cultures" in which everyone studies the complexities of school change (p. 22). To examine these dynamics as they evolve, several researchers have conducted long-term, descriptive studies of schools immersed in reform (see Elmore, Peterson, & McCarthy, 1996; Van Tassel-Baska et al., 1996; Wolf et al., 2000). In their case studies of three middle schools "deemed promising in respect to education reform initiatives," Van Tassel-Baska, Hall, and Bailey (1996) found that the major challenge at all three sites was to address the "gulf between the articulation of practice and actual practice itself" (p. 110).

> One lesson that emerged is that changing a school's philosophy and/or mission is only one step toward systemic change. Having a coherent mission, even under the guidance of a visionary leader, does not complete the school reform process. The level of change necessary needs to trickle into each classroom. This will not happen until curriculum and instruction are reformed in the same manner that structural organization has been reformed. (Van Tassel-Baska et al., 1996, p. 111)

Using "an exemplary sampling procedure," Wolf et al. (2000) examined four schools within Kentucky's reform movement "where good things were happening" (p. 357). The research team invited state officials to nominate schools with diverse populations of students and then selected four sites that represented urban and rural locations. Two of these were elementary schools; two were middle schools. Team members conducted three site visits at each school across two different school years. Researchers interviewed students, teachers, and administrators; observed lessons; and gathered work samples from teachers and students. They found that successful change efforts occurred "in a larger web of connection and [were] dependent on their collaborative and consistently positive stance toward learning as well as their principal's leadership" (p. 349). Although each faculty accomplished reform in a unique fashion, teachers' responses shared four "commonalities": an appreciation for the history and heritage of their school, an efficacy of cooperative leadership, careful reflection on reform, and their dedication to students (p. 350). Researchers concluded that:

> giving words to teachers and children so they could internalize critical concepts was the driving force in the Kentucky reform. It is true that the schools were poised to listen well to the new vocabulary and enact the reform-based practices the words defined. However, the teachers took these words and practices to heart through substantive discussions that occurred formally on core days and in weekly professional development sessions as well as more informally in daily team meetings and hall conversations. These extended deliberations strengthened the positive and trusting relationships that had already existed among participants, as they rolled up their sleeves to do the work of the reform. (p. 390)

The results of these studies reveal that meaningful improvements in teaching and learning require a "reculturing" of teaching, meaning the development of new notions of whom we are and how we teach. The central focus of that reculturing is student learning.

In their review of school culture and leadership studies, Peterson and Deal identified five recurring characteristics of schools that have become learning communities:

- Staff have a shared sense of purpose; they pour their hearts into teaching.
- Norms of collegiality, improvement, and hard work underlie relationships.
- Rituals and traditions celebrate student accomplishments, teacher innovation, and parental commitment.
- Informal networks of storytellers, heroes, and heroines provide a social web of information, support, and history.
- Success, joy, and humor abound (Peterson & Deal, 2002, p. 29).

Based on their research, Peterson and Deal (2002) have generated a framework for analyzing school culture. Their fundamental premise is that:

> over time, all schools develop a unique personality built up as people solve problems, cope with tragedies, and celebrate successes. This personality, or culture, is manifested in people's patterns of behavior, mental maps, and social norms. (p. 9)

Key concepts in the study of culture are:

- Values—the standards set for what is "good";
- Beliefs and assumptions—systems of perceptions that guide behavior; and
- Norms—unstated rules and prescriptions that staff and students are supposed to follow (p. 12).

Peterson and Deal conclude that school culture is the key to productivity, noting that "teachers and students are more likely to succeed in a culture that fosters hard work, commitment to valued ends, an attention to problem solving, and a focus on learning for all students" (p. 11).

To examine these dynamics in greater detail, our case study describes how one particular elementary school has developed a more supportive school culture over a two-year period. The following questions have guided this investigation:

- What values do teachers and administrators share regarding "good" teaching?

- What beliefs and assumptions guide their instructional decisions?
- What are the instructional norms that shape shared teaching practices?

THE RESEARCH PROCESS

Central Elementary School

Central Elementary, a K-5 elementary school in a mid-sized city, serves more than 600 students. The demographics of the student body are challenging, with 66% of the students on free or reduced lunch, a proxy for poverty. Ninety percent of the students are minority, and 20% speak English as a second language. Since 1997, students at Central have successfully increased their levels of academic achievement (see Figure 1).

As depicted in Figure 4.1, the 3rd, 4th, and 5th graders have gradually improved in both reading and math. In 1997, only 49.4% of Central students in grades 3 through 5 were proficient in reading and math, as measured by state assessments. The school was unsuccessful in meeting state-established academic growth targets, meaning Central was low performing. Since then, students have exceeded growth targets, earning recognition for exemplary growth, and by 2002, 74.6% of students in grades 3 through 5 were proficient in both reading and math. The principal described the school before the turnaround:

> I used to hear a lot of excuses. It was "but these children can't, and these parents can't." Teachers would ask, "How can you expect us to do better?" Now they believe that they can do it. We've seen that if we give them our best, we can do it the right way. Now they believe it's possible.

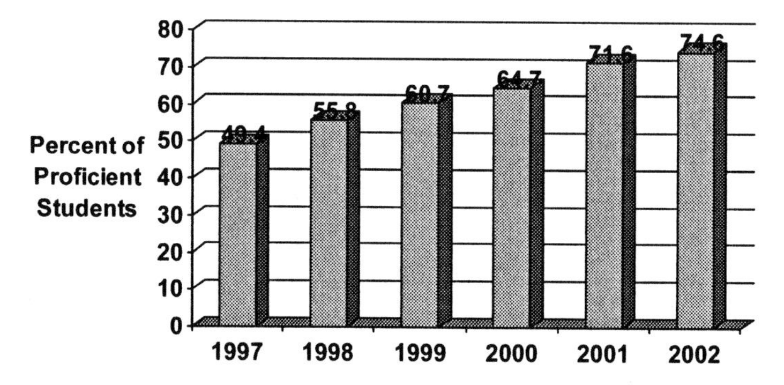

Figure 4.1. Third, fourth, and fifth graders at or above grade level in reading and math at Central Elementary School.

This turnaround is one of the reasons that project directors invited Central Elementary School to participate in the North Carolina Lighthouse Schools project. Working with teachers and administrators, researchers from the Lighthouse project have explored some of the dynamics that have contributed to this success.

DATA COLLECTION AND ANALYSIS

In the spring and fall of 2000, representatives from the Lighthouse Project interviewed 17 administrators, teachers, parents, and support personnel at Central Elementary School. The purpose of these interviews was to explore participants' views of how their schools have become more successful in promoting student performance on state-mandated assessments. These interviews generated more than 70 pages of single-spaced transcripts. The research team analyzed these transcripts to generate themes that guided the Phase One Summary Report (Strahan & Ware, 2001).

Data for the next phase of the study included interviews, classroom observations, observations of grade-level meetings, and focus groups. Researchers asked the principal to nominate four teachers who possessed characteristics the school valued and whose students had high passing rates on the state's standardized tests. A member of the research team interviewed each teacher separately. Researchers recorded comments in a narrative fashion during the interviews and tape-recorded comments. Following this initial interview, a researcher observed the participant in two authentic situations: teaching a lesson and participating in a meeting with colleagues. Observers recorded notes on a template, jotting down the time every five minutes. Following the observations, researchers conducted a second interview with each teacher to discuss issues related to the lesson itself. The team also collected archival records, including planning documents and minutes from grade-level team meetings.

To analyze the data, the research group used the constant comparative method, coding transcripts from the interviews and the notes from the classroom and meeting observations to identify the principal themes that emerged from the data and selecting illustrative examples to use in the initial summary reports (Strauss & Corbin, 1990). In fall 2002, the team conducted a focus group with new participants from each school. These interviews provided an opportunity for teachers to review carefully the findings of the preliminary report for three purposes: to assess the report's validity from their viewpoint, to recommend any necessary revisions or clarifications, and to add insights and illustrations that might enhance the report. Team members randomly selected participants for this group interview from a list of teachers who had been at the school the year before and who had not participated in the classroom observations and individual interviews.

During the group interview, research team members asked participants to "go over each of the themes in detail" and asked, "What do you think about this? Please comment." The responses were tape-recorded and transcribed. Participants affirmed each of the major themes and suggested minor changes in wording. Participants also provided additional examples and illustrations of the themes. After incorporating those clarifications and illustrations into a final report, team members shared the report with teachers and administrators. The participants read the report carefully for accuracy and agreed that the report captured an accurate picture of their school. The Center for School Leadership Development has published this detailed case report (Carlone & Horn, 2002). The report identified 20 specific themes and 3 general patterns of data that describe how teachers and administrators at Central Elementary School have achieved success.

Based on those themes, the team began a reanalysis of data to identify the dynamics of school culture that underlie these descriptions. Team members examined interviews and observations collected over the past two years and generated patterns of cultural growth that characterize the values that teachers and administrators share regarding "good" teaching, the beliefs and assumptions that guide their instructional decisions, and the instructional norms that shape shared teaching practices. These patterns provided a basis for an additional round of interviews and observations with 10 teachers and administrators in the spring of 2002. Citations at the end of each quotation in this report identify the participant's role (T = teacher, P = principal) and the time frame of the quotation (year and semester). The citation for the first quotation, for example, is T01S, signifying a teacher interview from the spring semester of 2001. All names used in this report are pseudonyms, as is the name of the school.

RESULTS

Interviews and observations at Central Elementary document three major changes in school culture over the past two years. First, teachers and administrators have developed *a shared stance toward learning*. This stance links shared values and beliefs into a communal attitude and posture. Just as a golfer or a tennis player assumes a stance for action, teachers and administrators assume a stance for action in the classroom. Over the past few years, teachers and administrators at Central have developed a stance of shared responsibility. Students learn that they are responsible for their own learning, for pushing themselves, and for helping their classmates. Teachers demonstrate and express strong feelings of responsibility to promote all students' learning and positive feelings about themselves as successful learners and as important people. The principal demonstrates responsibility to her teachers to secure much needed resources, to access and translate information about current initiatives and research, and to build confidence in the community.

This shared stance toward learning has contributed to the second major change in school culture: *strengthened instructional norms that emphasize more active student engagement.* In their lessons, teachers promote high levels of cooperation and involve students in assessing their own understanding. They emphasize a shared commitment to respond to individual needs and to make learning as active as possible.

The shared stance has also contributed to the third major change: *teachers and administrators have developed stronger procedures for promoting data-directed dialogue regarding school reform.* Grade-level planning sessions and site-based staff development feature discussions on students' progress on formal and informal assessments of achievement. Teachers and administrators assess their own success based on student learning.

Shared Stance Toward Learning

In their interviews over the past two years, teachers and administrators have more clearly articulated a stance of shared responsibility. This stance links underlying values and beliefs into a communal attitude and posture that emphasizes everyone's stake in the learning process. Participants repeatedly defined success as going beyond state mandates to reach the whole child:

> There are mandates that we have to satisfy. But there are things beyond those mandates that I try to expose the children to in 1st grade.... [I look] at the child as a whole person.... I want to become aware of their physical, psychological, emotional, and academic needs.... You can't teach their head until you reach their heart. (Ms. Innes, T01S)

> [My definition of good teaching means] to reach every student. I try to reach everybody... . A good lesson to me means that you encourage every child, that you make every child feel like, "Yeah,I saw that light bulb come on!" (Ms. Edwards, T01S)

> I think here at Central we have to go above and beyond the mandates in order to reach our population of children, meaning going the extra step, teaching in a variety of ways. Maybe teaching something a little bit longer [than would otherwise be the case]. (Ms. Wilson, T01S)

Knowing the stress that the high-stakes accountability testing has placed on administrators, teachers, and students at Central Elementary School, one might assume that talk of test performance pervades the school and classroom culture. Though talk of testing (how to improve performance, how to prepare students, how to handle students who are at risk of failing) is present, it does not solely determine teachers' and administrators' definitions of success.

A clear message in all classrooms the researchers observed and in all interviews is that students need to take responsibility for their own learning. In classroom activities, students were asked to communicate their understanding of the subject matter to whole groups, defend their answers, take responsibility for moving on to the next task, choose the research question they wanted to pursue, and take an active role in their preparation for the end-of-grade test.

> I do make them responsible for their own learning and for each other's learning. If they are working in a group, everybody in the group has to know what they are doing, and they have to be able to explain it. So they have to teach each other, and I use a lot of peer tutoring that way. (Ms. Babbit, T01S)

> Especially with the younger students, you may nurture maybe a little bit more than you would with the older ones, but I do try to challenge them and turn them loose and let them learn on their own and be independent. That's part of 2nd grade—this learning how to be an independent student and an independent worker. They resist that a lot, but I have to wean them off sometime and it's hard to get that message sometimes across to their parents.... I do a lot of tough love. I let them fall on their face sometimes and learn from their mistakes. (Ms. Lancaster, T01S)

A teacher who transferred to Central after eight years at another school described this sense of student responsibility as follows:

> One of the things that I like about this school is that the kids that have been in this school are well trained. I've actually gone back to other teachers and said that I had fragile children at the school that I was at before, and I'm used to a little bit more controversial behavior and that kind of thing. But these students, you can really tell, are confident and they have some skills—how to deal with different situations that they come up with behaviorally in school and social situations. (Ms. Smith, T01F)

During lessons, students are responsible for facilitating class discussion by proving, or discussing, why they or their group reached a specific conclusion to a problem and explaining the journey they navigated to arrive at the answer they decided was best. The following excerpt from a lesson observation illustrates this dynamic:

> Rick's group came up with the answer. "How did you group that?" Ms. Owens asks. He explains the different ways they added weights and guessed. Ms. Owens re-explained the strategy to the class. "If I had you do this on your own, I would ask you to do this in a circle map." (Observation notes, Ms. Owens's classroom, 01S).

In talking about their instruction, teachers emphasized learning as a social activity. Group work, partnering, and peer teaching are common practices.

> They need to be able to work collaboratively with other students because that is what they are going to need to do in the future—to be able to work well with others and be able to come up with ideas together. (Ms. Lancaster, T01S)

> We do a lot of small-group, in-class assignments where they work in a group so that it's not so much dependent on what they know as an individual but what their group can put together, and that gives them some degree of confidence of success. (Ms. Owens, T01S)

According to the teachers, the key to group work was often to step out of the way and allow the children to struggle with issues to discover answers.

> But a lot of times to just kind of step back and say, "Try it. Do what you think will work." And even if that means that [the] group may not be successful on that task, kind of praising them for whatever efforts they made and explaining to them, you know, that was a good thought, that was a good idea. Now if this was the goal that we were trying to reach, what could you have done differently? So kind of even if it means having some moments of not being successful, kind of pushing them to really try things on their own and realizing that it if didn't work, it's still going to be OK. (Ms. Owens, T01S)

Teachers stressed the importance of cooperation rather than competition. They focused on team building:

> While we are doing [group work] I am also doing team building with them. I do a lot of activities where they are not competitive, where they have to cooperate to succeed. And probably the first three months of the year, we do those daily to try to get them to work as a team. (Ms. Owens, T01S)

> A lot of my students, they like to come in and try to compete with each other, and they get stressed when their competition hasn't gone the way they wanted, or if they haven't won, or whatever. We're all in this together, and we know we have to cooperate and it doesn't matter who wins or loses.

> We're not there to beat the person in whatever the case may be. (Ms. Lancaster, T01S)

Teachers believe that students who take responsibility for their learning will be actively engaged in lessons. This belief was evident in the classrooms the research team observed. There was little down time, and a lot of time was spent on task. Students engaged in problems that went beyond surface-level answers and were asked to solve problems, interpret information, share differing views, and synthesize information.

> We do a lot of group work as far as the tougher, higher-order-thinking problems are concerned. We do a lot of small-group work so that it's not so much dependent on what they know as an individual but what their group can put together, and that gives them some degree of confidence of success. (Ms. Owens, T01S)

> Learning is doing, so they have to do in order to learn. I can't stand up and just feed it to them in a lecture-type form. They have to be engaged. (Ms. Wilson, T01S)

Teachers also emphasized the importance of understanding each student's needs, so they can adjust their instructional strategies:

> I work to teach [with] a holistic approach. I think that it is my philosophy that cognitive and affective learning is very, very important. I always start my year in getting to know the children, and that is somewhat of an informal process to begin with, and then the assessments and the mandates of testing come later, and I think that gives me a good clue as to what learning strategies I can provide in my instructional program, as to how to accommodate their learning. (Ms. Innes, T01S)

Encouragement is an important factor in reaching students, especially those who are having difficulty.

> I also try to ... encourage all of them, no matter what level they are at. But if there is—even if they are struggling with something—whatever success they are having is good, and that's an improvement and they can build on that. (Ms. Owens, T01S)

A teacher who recently joined the Central faculty after teaching her first three years at another school described the essence of the stance toward teaching that she shares with her colleagues:

Interviewer: How do you think your colleagues here would define good teaching?

Teacher: I would say hands-on experience, making learning fun for the students, giving them an opportunity to take part in the lesson, speak out, explain what they are doing, anything that is involving critical thinking, a lot of cooperative learning, structured.

Interviewer: What do you mean by "structured?"

Teacher: Making sure students know what it is they are supposed to be doing. They have an assignment where they're working on something with a group, but still they are not wild. They know that "this is expected of me. This is when it is due." We have high expectations of them. (Ms. Michaels, T01F)

Emphasis on More Active Student Engagement

Based on this shared stance toward learning, teachers' planning sessions feature not only a consideration for content, but also ways to involve students more actively in lessons. Their emphasis on learning as a social activity prompts discussions and reflection about ways to group students (mixed ability, mixed behavior) to promote optimal learning. This emphasis on learning in groups reinforces learning as a social activity, which helps maintain a sense of community.

> I try to include someone at each table that's got the leadership ability and skills and kind of distribute that so that there is somebody around that can kind of help the group, pull them through. A good lesson to me is that you make every child feel like "Yeah!" ... Every day I don't get everybody, but I acknowledge every last one of them every day in some way, in some lesson. (Ms. Edwards, T01S)

Teachers work to build cooperation between themselves and students. They accomplish this through a caring commitment to the students and by trying to establish a comfortable level of learning for all students in the classroom.

> They don't have a problem telling me, "I don't get this" and "You're not teaching me right." Not in those terms, but basically they don't have a problem with telling what they don't understand. (Ms. Babbit, T01S)

> I try to say something positive to everybody to make them feel like, yes, I know what you are doing. I know what you are doing. I am seeing what you are doing. (Ms. Edwards, T01S)

> I want to instill in them that they all can be successful at doing something, you know, and I feel it's kind of part of my job to find out what they are good at and to enrich that within them. (Ms. Innes, T01S)

In describing their planning, teachers said they consider students' prior knowledge and experiences to meet the students where they are in terms of their learning trajectories. They work hard to help students build on that knowledge, and they foster the attitude in all children that they are capable of learning.

> Before you teach them, you have to let them know that you really love and care about them. They have to know that you genuinely care about them, not that it's superficial because they can see through that. Once they know you are there for them and care for them academically as well as for whatever else is going on in their lives and that they can trust you, then they will open up to you. It's a two-way street. It's an open line of communication.... They perform better when they are comforted when they know that. (Ms. Edwards, T01S)

Individualizing instruction in ways that this diverse population demands requires teachers to find multiple ways of providing students with extra help. They provide this help by recruiting student interns, offering tutoring, structuring small-group work, and involving parents.

> We have a guided reading teacher, like a tutor, who provides extra help and works with two other groups. We have all the groups meet with every student every day in a small group. We also have computer programs with reading that provide students an opportunity to improve reading skills, who do not necessarily like to read a book, but they'll go read it on a computer because they like the computer. It gets them motivated to actually go and to be able to enjoy reading books. (Ms. Silva, T01S)

In the lessons we have observed, the teachers presented material enthusiastically, used active learning strategies to teach (e.g., use of manipulatives, problem solving), sustained a brisk pace in the classroom, and maintained a work ethic in their classrooms.

> You have to take into account the learning styles of the children as well as attention spans. You have to be really willing, make it fun. Sometimes I dance, I sing, whatever I have to do. They come in the mornings, they're tired, and you just have to be prepared for that. They know it's a day of learning and you're here to do a job. (Ms. Wilson, T01S)

In an interview that preceded a lesson observation, one of the 5th grade teachers described some of the ways she promotes problem solving:

> A lot of times with hands-on-type things we will be working with geoboards. We will be working with shapes in geometry, and an area of this like creating shapes on the geoboard and calculating the area and the perimeter. Also, I use it for graphing to learn coordinate planes. In small groups, they will take the manipulatives and have an assignment to complete. (Ms. Wilson, T01S)

On the day of the observation, she asked her students to practice graphing by analyzing the scores of hypothetical students on reading tests and hypothesizing how their grades may have fluctuated. Students worked in small groups to generate hypotheses and then presented these to the class. Another 5th grade teacher structured a problem-solving activity that required students to identify five coins of the same value that would weigh 25 grams. Students worked together to list the information they needed and then tested their estimates with calculators. After the lesson, the teacher noted that students were making progress on applying the strategies she had been teaching, choosing key words out of the problem statement, and then proving their answers. Teachers reported that they were using these types of problem-solving strategies more often and requiring students to "think through" the problems on their own rather than showing the students how to solve them. These shared strategies and others (concept maps, guided reading) reflect teachers' collective emphasis on active student involvement.

Data-Directed Dialogue Regarding School Reform

As suggested earlier, performing well on end-of-grade tests is only one part of Central's definition of success. Even so, talk about testing took place during grade-level meetings, teacher interviews, and the principal interview. Although they have to pay attention to achievement on end-of-grade tests, annual testing is only one source of information that teachers utilize.

> It's almost as if I'm programmed to look at test results and say, "Wow, I'm a good teacher because I have *3*s and *4*s" [higher scores] or, "I really stink because I have *1*s and *2*s" [lower scores]. It's hard on me, but I know I'm in there teaching very hard every day, trying to reach every child. To ... reach those children, take the extra time, I may not get to the whole content that's on the end-of-grade test. (Ms. Wilson, T01S)

> Just because [the students] pass [the test] doesn't mean they're successful. Some students can perform well on tests and test great. Other students will freeze up, but they are on grade level or they do a good job. I don't think

that should be the only thing we look for to define that they are successful. (Ms. Silva, T01S)

I try to find ways to focus on the things they have improved on throughout the year as well. In the past, we have taken criterion-referenced test (CRT) results and looked at the results and set goals for the next CRT, for what they want their achievement level to be; not achievement level, but their mastery, their mastery to be at the next one and so on, so that they can see as they are improving, as they are getting better. (Ms. Owens, T01S)

At Central, the grade-level meetings feature a great deal of discussion about student progress. A teacher described this process as follows:

We, as a grade level, you know, we sit down with, like, every nine weeks, you know, look at the whole year, but then every nine weeks you clarify your goals to be taught during that time, and then, but we write our goals for the day on the board, what we're doing that day, what our agenda is, so that if she [the principal] were to glance up there, she could see what that is. We have really taken this to heart to try to be sure that we have those things in place and that we are working toward those goals. (Ms. Albert, T00S)

Discussions about students' progress also take place across grade levels:

But it's also as far as curriculum goes, like our writing program. We're really trying to make sure that each grade level can follow up on what the previous grade level did, so we're working together on the communication between grade levels to make sure that we're consistent as well as being able to build on what the previous grade level did. We're really doing a good job at that. (Ms. Jones, T00S)

School-based staff development also features discussions about student performance and ways to enhance it. A teacher noted:

I think the thing that stands out to me is implementing the literacy plan. I've heard that we're ahead of some other schools in the district as far as that goes. And she [the principal] introduced it to us last year. And we learned about the different parts. I think we learned, in some form or another, we learned about all the different parts of the literacy plan, and we're expected to be doing all of them. Not necessarily be doing all them perfectly, but to be giving each of them a try. And she provided the materials we needed, you know, and let us at least know how we could get hold of them, you know, for guided reading, for example. And expected us to be working on that and to be informing ourselves about it and to be knowing what all the different parts are. (Ms. Kennedy, T00S)

Although performance on the end-of-grade tests provides one source of information about students' learning and teachers' teaching, the teachers also use criterion-referenced tests, classroom products, previous teachers' evaluations, and group discussions about best practices as sources of data to inform their instruction in an ongoing attempt to meet students' developmental needs.

CONCLUSIONS

Over the past few years, instruction at Central has focused more on student performance through shared commitment to student learning, more engaging instruction, and ongoing curriculum articulation. Results from this investigation suggest that three major changes in school culture have enabled these accomplishments. In their interviews over the past two years, teachers and administrators have more clearly articulated a stance of shared responsibility. This stance links underlying values and beliefs into a disposition that energizes instruction. Teachers share a commitment to the students and families of the Central community. Although they might choose to teach in less challenging settings, these teachers have resolved instead to work with the students at Central to make a difference. This creates a community of caring, which permeates the school culture. Students have shown more responsibility for their own learning, for pushing themselves, and for helping their classmates. This shared stance toward learning has strengthened instructional norms that emphasize more active student engagement. Lessons feature higher levels of cooperation and student involvement. These two changes are nurtured by data-directed dialogue that guides grade-level planning sessions and site-based staff development.

At this point in their school improvement journey, teachers and administrators at Central Elementary School have created a culture characterized by values that define "good" teaching as meeting the needs of their students, by beliefs that all students can learn and share responsibility for their learning, and by instructional norms that feature active, collaborative lessons. This shared stance toward learning and teaching gives direction to their discussions about how best to improve their school, discussions fueled by data-directed dialogue. These dynamics have produced a climate that sustains continued growth and development. Our notes from an end-of-the-year planning session show these dynamics in action and provide a concluding illustration to this analysis of cultural growth at Central Elementary School:

> On a sunny morning at the beginning of summer, nine teachers and two administrators gather in a quiet room to review the school improvement plan and develop an organizational structure for the next school year. After

exchanging greetings and comparing notes on the day's agenda, they launch into the business at hand. The principal distributes summaries of recent test scores by grade level and asks, "When you look over these percentages, what jumps out at you?" One teacher notes the breakout of scores comparing results for students who had been there since kindergarten with the general population. "This shows higher pass rates for the students who have been here longer." Another teacher emphasizes that all of the pass rates are high. "Four years ago, we thought we could never reach 90% proficiency. Look at these 5th grade scores—94% in math and 93% in reading."

"What other patterns do you see?" asks the principal. A teacher notes that the retest scores showed a huge jump. "This shows that some of our students need more time." Another teacher expresses a concern that the 4th grade passing rate for reading (76%) is not as high as it is for math (90%). This prompts an animated discussion of the frustrations students express when faced with the long passages on the test. One teacher says, "I watch the students as they thumb through their test booklets. Some of them whisper, 'This is so long!' Others groan. On the math tests they keep moving. On the reading tests, I can see them drift and fade. This is so different from their reading during independent reading time. They stay with their books, and I know they understand them from what they say and write." (Ms. Albert, T02S)

Other teachers agree. Several share stories of times when their students have shown great excitement and persistence with trade books that challenge them to read at higher levels. As the discussion progresses, participants agree that they need to address the issue of students' endurance as readers. Several teachers suggest ways to increase the length of practice passages. Others propose lengthening the amount of independent reading time during the school day. After almost 45 minutes of discussion, the principal proposes that they make independent reading a higher priority next year and suggests that they gather research to find ways to do so more productively. Several teachers offer suggestions for studies to read. A volunteer agrees to compile a set of studies. Another wonders if it is possible to put together more useful diagnostic profiles to give next year's teachers more than just the test score summaries. The discussion continues. (Observation notes, leadership team, 02S).

These notes capture some of the process of data-directed dialogue in action. Participants began their discussion with a review of recent scores from state-mandated achievement tests. Trends in the data suggested a pattern related to test-retest performance. Several participants personalized this pattern with illustrations and shared stories from their observations of students. This dialogue resulted in the identification of a central goal for improving instruction—helping students extend their endurance as readers. With this goal in mind, participants worked together to generate suggestions that will guide the next round of professional development efforts. As conversations like this one continue, they will strengthen Central's shared stance toward teaching and extend the cycle of school reform.

AUTHORS' NOTE

This report was written with the sponsorship and approval of the Center for School Leadership Development. It was originally published in *The Journal of Curriculum and Supervision* (2003, volume 18, number 3, pages 204-221) and is reprinted with the permission of the publisher (ASCD).

REFERENCES

Brown, R. (1991). *Schools of thought*. San Francisco: Jossey-Bass.

Carlone, H., & Horn, S. (2002). Results from Central Elementary School. In D. Strahan & A. Ware (Eds.), *Achieving success in the North Carolina Lighthouse Schools: An analysis of the dynamics of meaningful reform* (pp. 44-68). Chapel Hill, NC: Center for School Leadership Development.

Elmore, R., Peterson, P., & McCarthy, S. (1996). *Restructuring in the classroom: Teaching, learning, and school organization*. San Francisco: Jossey-Bass.

Fullan, M. (1990). Staff development, innovation, and institutional development. In B. Joyce (Ed.), *Changing school culture through staff development* (pp. 3-25). Alexandria, VA: ASCD.

Peterson, K., & Deal, T. (2002). *The shaping school culture fieldbook*. San Francisco: Jossey-Bass.

Strahan, D. (1994, Spring). Putting middle level perspectives into practice: Creating school cultures that promote caring. *Midpoints, 5*, 1–12.

Strahan, D., & Ware, A. (2001). *Achieving success in the North Carolina Lighthouse Schools: An analysis of the dynamics of meaningful reform*. Chapel Hill, NC: The Center for School Leadership Development.

Strauss, A., & Corbin, J. (1990). *Basics of qualitative research*. Thousand Oaks, CA: Sage.

Van Tassel-Baska, J., Hall, K., & Bailey, J. (1996, Winter). Case studies of promising change schools. *Research in Middle Level Education Quarterly, 19*, 89–116.

Wolf, S., Borko, H., Elliott, R., & McIver, M. (2000, Summer). 'That dog won't hunt!': Exemplary school change efforts within the Kentucky reform. *American Educational Research Journal, 37*, 349–396.

CHAPTER 5

CONTINUING A JOURNEY TOWARD SIGNIFICANCE AT CENTRAL ELEMENTARY SCHOOL

David Strahan and Jennifer Mangrum

ABSTRACT

This case study examined the responses of teachers from the same school to two different types of professional development. Kindergarten and second grade teachers participated in mandated workshops. Fifth grade teachers developed their own agenda for collaboration. Researchers participated in grade-level meetings and conducted interviews across two school years. Results showed that participants responded to professional development initiatives in ways that reflected the nature of these experiences. Teachers questioned the basic values of the mandated program and worked together to adapt core practices to meet their needs. In the non-mandated setting, participants collaborated to gather information and generate ideas for enhancing student engagement. In both settings, participants reported improvements in instruction but accomplished them in different ways.

Deep Change: Cases and Commentary on Reform in High Stakes States, 65–85

INTRODUCTION

In the preceding chapter, we presented a summary of the ways that teachers and administrators at Central Elementary School created a more supportive school culture over the first two years of the North Carolina Lighthouse Schools partnership. During that time period, participants developed a shared stance toward learning that linked values and beliefs into a communal sense of responsibility. This shared stance strengthened instructional norms that emphasized more active student engagement, infusing lessons with higher levels of cooperation and student involvement. Grade-level planning sessions played a powerful role in that reculturing, featuring a process of data-directed dialogue that helped sustain school renewal, student accomplishment, and teacher development. To learn more about how teachers worked together in professional development communities, this study examined ways that grade level teams at Central Elementary school responded to mandated and non-mandated reform initiatives during the third and fourth years of our partnership.

BACKGROUND

In recent years, a growing number of studies have provided rich descriptions of schools that successfully promote student achievement (Langer, 2001; Spillane, 1999; Wolf, Borko, Elliott, & McIver, 2000). As Fullan suggested, the pictures that have emerged from these studies are fairly consistent. In successful schools, teachers work collaboratively with their colleagues to enhance instruction (Fullan, 1999). As they do so, they develop stronger instructional strategies, and these strategies enhance student achievement. At the same time, teachers develop a stronger professional community, enabling them to provide even more social support for learning. This "spiral of reform activity" links ongoing assessment and instructional improvement to enhance student accomplishment (Fullan, 1999, p. 34).

In their analysis of the dynamics of school improvement, L'Esperance, Strahan, Farrington, and Anderson (2003) defined a "school of significance" as one that "has been transformed from its previous condition and is empowered by the collective vision of the entire school community. In a school of significance, the culture is rich with indicators of broad and deep renewal with data to support the school's focus on both academics and community" (p. 6). In contrast to "schools of success" that promote high test scores in a technical fashion, schools of significance achieved their success in ways that are *data-directed rather than data driven.* Teachers and administrators worked collaboratively to provide instruction that is engaging and focused. They used data to guide their decisions but their actions were driven by purpose: to make a difference in the lives of their students (p. 6). This sense of moral purpose helped transform the culture of the school.

Our case studies with the North Carolina Lighthouse schools have documented ways that this moral purpose inspired teachers and administrators to accomplish school improvement in a meaningful fashion (Carlone & Horn, 2002; Strahan, 2003; Strahan & Ware, 2001). While these schools have accomplished technical improvements such as aligning assignments to tests and developing more systematic efforts to increase test-taking skills, they have also pursued a higher vision. Their primary focus has been creating classroom learning communities with their students and professional learning communities with each other. These communities nurtured student engagement and professional growth.

Other case studies have suggested teachers' conversations help shape these dynamics. Spillane (1999) conducted systematic observations of lessons with 25 elementary and middle-level math teachers who had participated in district-wide reform initiatives and reported high levels of implementation on surveys. He found that only four of these teachers demonstrated teaching practices consistent with the reform. In contrast to their colleagues who tended to work individually, these four had created "enactment zones" which Spillane defined as "the spaces where the world of policy meets the world of practice" (p. 407). Enactment zones featured ongoing deliberations with colleagues and facilitators, reading and discussing documents related to the reforms, and watching and discussing videotapes.

In a year-long case study of reform in a California elementary school, Coburn (2001) found that teachers made sense of reform initiatives through conversations. These conversations occurred formally in grade level meetings and informally with clusters of their closest colleagues. The most meaningful of these conversations were those that promoted engagement and reflection (pp. 151-152). Coburn described a process of "sensemaking," which characterized much of this discussion and enabled participants to integrate new ideas into their work in their classrooms. Coburn concluded, "Work with other teachers helped them grapple with multiple and sometimes conflicting messages" (p. 162).

Based on their studies of *The National Writing Project*, Lieberman and Wood (2003) concluded that the most meaningful professional development occurred in the learning communities characterized by the giving and receiving of critical support. Learning communities nurtured teachers' growth in three key ways: teachers learned from each other, teachers made their work public and opened up for critiques, and teachers learned from taking different roles and seeing the world through different perspectives.

This study reexamined data from our earlier studies at one of the North Carolina Lighthouse schools and conducted follow-up interviews with participants to learn more about how professional development communities continued to evolve. In particular, this study examined ways that grade level teams at this school responded to mandated and non-mandated reform initiatives. The following questions guided this investigation:

1. How have professional learning communities evolved at Central Elementary School over the past four years?
2. What issues do participants currently face in their efforts to sustain successful reform and how are they addressing these issues?

METHODS

In the spring of 2000, district administrators nominated Central Elementary School for a study of "beating the odds" schools because students' scores on statewide assessments had risen dramatically over the preceding three years. A K-5 elementary school in a mid-sized city, Central serves more than 600 students. Two thirds of the students qualify for free or reduced lunch, a proxy for poverty. Ninety percent of students are minority, and 20% speak English as a second language. In 1997, only 49.4% of Central students in grades 3 through 5 were proficient in reading and math, and the school was unsuccessful in meeting state-established aca-

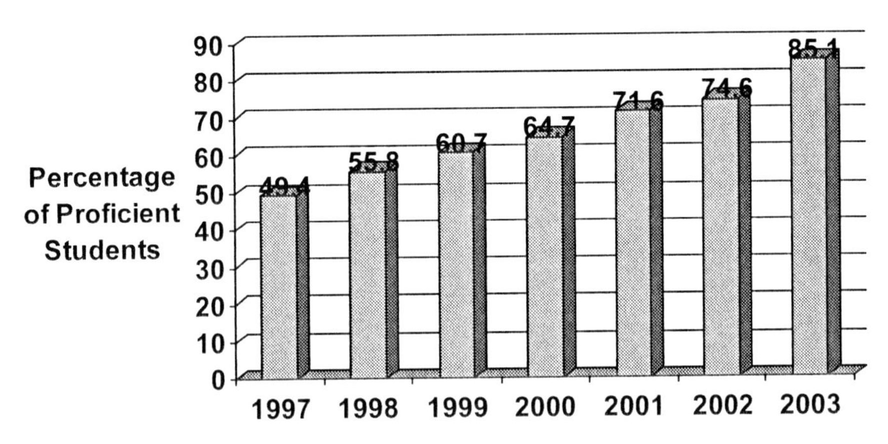

Figure 5.1. Third, fourth, and fifth graders at or above grade level in reading and math at Central Elementary School on North Carolina End-of-Grade tests

demic growth targets. Since then, students have exceeded growth targets, earning exemplary growth recognition. Today more than 75% of students in grades 3 through 5 are proficient in both reading and math.

Researchers began working with grade level teams at Central Elementary School in the summer of 2002 as part of a collaborative study of school reform. As university representatives to this partnership, the researchers met with the school leadership team to identify priorities for collaboration for the 2002-03 school year. Based on their examination of research reports and achievement test data from the preceding year, participants agreed that their major focus would be to improve the level of "academic learning time" in lessons, especially among students who had not previously experienced academic success. Teachers from three grade level teams volunteered to work with university researchers to identify strategies for improving academic learning time and to study the impact of these strategies. Two of these grade level teams (kindergarten and second grade) began mandated staff development on literacy strategies in the fall of 2002 and those "mandated" strategies became the focus of inquiry. Teachers on the other grade level (fifth) were not required to attend these workshops and were invited to develop their own agenda for improving academic learning time.

During the 2002-03 school year, researchers functioned as participant observers in grade level meetings, attending monthly discussions and conducting semi-structured interviews. One of the researchers attended mandated staff development workshops with kindergarten and second grade teachers and conducted debriefing interviews with them about these workshops. Across the year, researchers tape-recorded and transcribed at total of 21 interviews. Using data analysis procedures suggested by Creswell (1994), researchers read the transcripts to get a sense of the whole and wrote down initial reactions along the margins. Researchers then listed of all the topics, generated categories, and began looking for emerging themes. Following this initial analysis, researchers conducted "member checks" with participants to elicit their responses to categories and themes.

In the fall of 2003, we met with participants in grade level groups for follow-up discussions. In these focus group interviews, we revisited themes from the first draft of our report and asked participants to reflect on changes at Central during the fall semester. To prepare this chapter, the researchers examined these new data in relationship with data from the early investigations to present a summary of the key aspects of teacher development at Central. Citations at the end of each quotation in this report identify the participant's role (T = teacher, P = principal) and the time frame of the quotation (year and season). The citation for the first quotation, for example, is T035, signifying an interview with a teacher from the spring of 2003. All names used in this report are pseudonyms.

RESULTS

Instructional norms and moral purposes have grown stronger over the past four years as teachers at Central Elementary have continued to enact their shared stance that links values and beliefs into a communal sense of responsibility. The values regarding "good teaching" that participants have enacted often center on understanding the needs of students as individuals. In the most recent round of interviews, a teacher described how she viewed these connections:

> I just like to watch them for a little bit and kind of see what I can from them, learn from them first before I assume anything. When, there's a little girl who never speaks in class but here (in guided reading) she talks all the time. So observation is my first thing and then I would ask, it sounds like a silly question but, "What do you like?" and "Do you have brothers and sisters?" and then they look at me like I'm crazy but then later on it helps me. So when I can say, "oh we're dividing and I know so-and-so loves Pokemon" they're excited. So just like, finding out about them, more than their academics, has helped me to help them in the end. (T03S)

This commitment to understand students as individuals and respond to their needs has become an instructional norm at Central. Teachers consistently defined "good teaching" as engaging students actively, promoting collaboration, and creating community. By expressing their values in this fashion, participants articulated a vision that focuses on both academics and community, suggesting a desire to make a significant difference in the lives of students. While embracing a responsibility to improve test scores, teachers and administrators have pursued this goal in ways that fit their moral purposes of collaboration and community. They have extended these ideals to include their work with each other as well as with their students.

Conversations that have occurred in the grade level meetings have enriched this shared stance. One of the major priorities of the principal has been to develop strong professional learning communities in each of the grade level teams.

> I think there are a lot of things that the principal has started to really show that the staff here matters. Where it could be like that planning session for each grade level, you know, if, if she didn't set that up, and organize that,

> and say let's do this then we wouldn't have it, and I think that's really important. (T025)

At Central, grade level meetings have featured a great deal of discussion about student progress. Teachers and administrators have developed stronger procedures for promoting data-directed dialogue regarding school reform. Grade level planning sessions and site-based staff development feature discussions on students' progress on formal and informal assessments of achievement. Teachers and administrators assess their own success based on student learning.

> We've looked more at test data, tried to analyze that a little more this year. We found that a lot of the test data information we get from the district is not very reliable. So we've really had to dig into it to see what we were missing, like the CRT test for instance, they're not very reliable. It influences re-teaching. We use those to go back and re-teach from. (T025)

During the 2002-03 school year, grade level teams worked together to address the new expectations for accountability mandated by the federal "No Child Left Behind" legislation.

> I think that really meeting the needs of the kids this year has been our focus. To be good teachers we've been focusing on individuals small groups and as a whole and so differentiation has got to be, even though it's a buzzword, has got to be part of what we're doing and that's made us a good teacher in that sense. Being consistent in all of our classrooms I think also has helped our kids greatly. They're not use to that, and having that has been wonderful. Utilizing our time better this year has made us better teachers and just the communication that we have with one another. (T03S)

Over time, grade level teams have evolved to serve two connected functions at Central. They now serve as instructional organizations that facilitate collaborative planning and also as sources of personal support for teachers. In the final year of the study, a teacher described how the recent multicultural festival reflected the underlying nature of the professional learning community:

> We just did the multicultural week and I think it was just like 37 different countries represented here. It was amazing and we focused on that this year, the whole school looking at who do you have in your room and where did they come from, do research, do projects, let people know about these things, so we're extremely diverse, in kids and in teachers we found out which we really didn't know that much, that our backgrounds, we may have been born here but many of us have relatives or siblings or distant cousins that are from somewhere else. We're all different age levels. It has always

> been peers, it's not a hierarchy kind of situation with anyone here. There's not principal versus teachers, there's not teachers versus assistant teachers, everyone input as equal importance into perspective. (T03S)

These efforts to promote collaboration and teamwork nurtured a strong commitment to grade level teams as professional learning communities. In their dialogue with colleagues, teachers shared ideas for teaching and strengthened the professional bonds with each other. These professional bonds represented another dimension of the culture of accomplishment that has grown at Central over the past four years.

During the 2002-2003 school year, teachers and administrators faced two major challenges as they worked to sustain successful reform in ways that were significant as well as successful. Teachers at the primary grades struggled to implement a new literacy program mandated by the school district. At the intermediate grades, teachers intensified their efforts to reach individual students who were not showing signs of academic progress. Both of these efforts demonstrate how participants are working to sustain successful reform by identifying students' learning needs and engaging in collaborative problem solving to address those needs.

The mandate to implement a new literacy program at the primary grades resulted from the school district's efforts to improve achievement test scores at all of the elementary schools with high percentages of students on free-and-reduced lunch. Central office administrators viewed this as a means of providing more support. They gave each school a choice: develop their own research-based program or adopt the one the district had selected. As one of the teachers explained,

> We had to vote. We had a choice to do that or come up with an alternative program and were given very little time. So basically we opted to do this because we didn't have time to do our research. (TS03)

Kindergarten and second grade teachers attended training sessions in which a consultant from Literacy for All (a pseudonym) presented workshops to forty-five teachers from three different schools. The teachers sat with their grade level teams and most of the interaction during the workshop was with their colleagues. Kindergarten and second grade teachers also met informally with a researcher to discuss their perceptions of the workshops, both individually and collectively. Primary grades teachers soon discovered that the new program required much more detailed assessments than those that they had been using did.

> We had worked out our own grade level assessment and that works great for us. We know what these children know. And it is much faster. It is probably not as refined as some of theirs, exactly like what she (the consultant) is talk-

> ing about with the rhyming words. You know it is whether they know rhyming words but not whether they know the nonsense words. And they left out the concepts of print assessment for two of the grade levels. (TS03).

These new assessments required much more time to administer, which proved to be a major source of frustration.

> We've done nothing but assess. We are doing it constantly. It's almost like you do it for 4 weeks, teach 2 weeks and do it for 4 more weeks. You don't get a chance to focus on the things you know they need help with because you are so busy assessing. (TS03)

For some of the teachers, these additional assessments created more than just a time conflict—they were out of synch with their personal and professional beliefs about teaching.

> I strongly believe that those assessments are unnecessary because the spelling assessment just has everything you need to know about your students. If the student knows the beginning consonant, the ending consonant, and that's all it is. And the vowels, the digraphs, all of that stuff and you're running records. That's all you need. I think it is unnecessary and it is too much work for us and too much for the children. (TS03)

> They (kindergartners) are not developmentally ready for some of this stuff. Some of ours are absolutely not ready. They were lost when we were trying, and frustrated to the hilt, when we were asking some of those questions on that test at the beginning of the year. There were some children who didn't know their colors and we're asking them to talk about vowels ... I think my kids are missing out on some of the fun things that we used to do to help them learn skills. We don't have time anymore. I actually think we've taken away their childhood. (TS03)

While their initial reactions to the workshops focused on their concerns regarding assessments, conversations in grade level meetings soon began to reveal more deep-seated resistance to the philosophy and practice of the program itself. Before the workshops began, participants described literacy in a broad sense and advocated an integrated approach. Kindergarten teachers suggested that this new program was out of synch with that philosophy:

> **Teacher 1:** We've been doing balanced literacy and so therefore this was *supposed* to be a boost for us to really fine tune some areas that we think would really help our students quite a bit. And we were kind of at a loss.
>
> **Teacher 2:** I'm frustrated because I can't get around to some of the things I want to do because I don't have the time. I just

think my kids are missing out on some of the fun things that we used to do to help them learn skills. We don't have time anymore. I actually think we've taken away their childhood.

Teacher 1: I do too. And I think we're leaving out a lot of developmental things. They are requiring us to go beyond where they should be for five-year-olds. (Group agrees).

Interviewer: What does a kindergartner's day look like?

Teacher 2: Reading and writing.

Teacher 4: You feel compelled to do everything to get them ready for the next level.

Interviewer: When I think back to the fall, I asked you to describe your best literacy lesson, and tell me about how you teach reading. You guys said puppets, music, and role playing ... and are you telling me that Literacy for All restricts you from doing as much of that as you... .

Group: Yes! (Everyone agrees.) (TS03)

During the first few weeks of training, participants identified the primary philosophy of the program to be that students in grades Kindergarten through second grades must have decoding skills to become successful readers. Several times during the year, the teachers came together with the researcher to share what they were learning in the workshops. In this setting the teachers responded by helping each other make sense of the experience and to relate it to their individual needs as teachers and learners.

Teacher 1: (One teacher referring to another) She can do it. It's just when it is thrown at her, she's just probably feeling massively overwhelmed with everything else..... And it's a new dance and you're still dancing like you have been dancing. You're just gonna learn a couple of steps to a new dance and blend it and roll with it.

Interviewer: Do you think the workshops have been meaningful for you?

Teacher 2: Not from the workshop, but like I said reading the books that I researched on my own. I have been able to apply it to what I already know about phonics and all the other components of the program.

Teacher 4: You're right. The resources are really good. They are very, very good.

Interviewer: Are you learning anything more about your children because of the assessments?

Teacher 1: I think it has heightened our awareness of when we are teaching reading skills that we can parallel (our reading adoption) with that. We know "aha" that's something that's on that particular assessment and that's something we really need to focus on. So I think it does heighten that.

Teacher 2: And it is also a visual, because you keep up with charts that you can look at them and tell exactly where the kids are and the kids that you need to work with so that you can keep them together.

Teacher 3: It reaffirms because teachers know. Basically when they come in you work with them one on one you basically know their skill level. And it reaffirms a lot of things that you already know.

In these conversations, participants were able to take some aspects of the program, make sense of them, and help each another find ways to adapt them in their classroom.

Interviewer: Has everyone completed the spelling assessments and just had to figure it out on your own?

Teacher 4: Yes and according to each student, each group what do they need to work on. That is supposed to be based on your phonics (assessment). I say no! That means I am supposed to have eight groups during my guided reading time! 8 groups? 8 groups, I said "NOOOO!" No, no, no."

Teacher 1: Wait. She (the consultant) wanted you to do 8 reading groups?

Teacher 4: 8 groups. 4 reading groups and 4 skill groups. That's what she told me.

Teacher 1: ... You're going to have to work out a way, blend a way that'll work with what you did before and try to blend with what they are asking you to do now.

Teacher 4: Exactly.

Teacher 1: And do the best you can do with it.

For all of the teachers, implementing this new program required a great deal of discussion and planning.

Teacher 1: What we immediately saw that day (the first day of the training) was that we were going to have to take it a step farther and if we were going to get more out of in we were going to have to put the time into it and that's what we did. We have definitely used the word sorts and a lot of the different things that have been helpful. (TS03)

Interviewer: How would you finish this sentence? When I face a problem implementing Literacy For All, I ...?

Teacher 2: I discuss it with my teammates. If I encounter a problem, I go to them to find out if they are encountering that same problem. Is it Literacy for All or is it me? Or my class? And if they tell me that they are having the problem then we get together and sit down and discuss the problem and ways to get around it or what to do about it.

Teacher 4: I just work on it. A couple of attempts until I think, "Okay, I need help." ... and then I go to my pod and we do it our *own way*. [Under her breath she giggles] (SP03).

These discussions continued informally during the 2003-2004 school year. When we met with participants for follow-up discussions in the fall of 2003, they reported that staff development sessions for Literacy for All had featured fewer lectures and more times for grade level teams to plan together. Kindergarten and second grade teachers continued to be frustrated with the amount of time they were required to devote to assessments. Kindergarten teachers were especially concerned that some of the assessments were not appropriate for their students.

> You feel like it's a waste of time to do a spelling inventory on students who cannot recognize the letters of the alphabet, not even their name, nor sounds, so you just feel like some of the assessments that we have to do the first nine weeks of school are very unnecessary and a waste of time when we could be spending more time with the kids teaching them the skills that they need to learn. (TF04)

One of the second grade teachers had become so frustrated with giving so many tests that she referred to herself as "a test queen."

> I used to give a spelling test and I used to give a math test a lot of the time. Now I am giving a science and social studies test almost every week. I am giving a language, grammar type test almost every week and so I look at Fridays and I am going, "Oh my gosh, I am testing them all day long." Where is Friday Fun day, what in the world, where did that go? I am testing them all day long. And I tell them, I keep telling them, okay look if we can just get past the test, we can get out of here. Finish the test and literally last Friday afternoon it was dismissal time, they were packed up and we were in the middle of the science test and I was like, "You guys there's no way. We cannot finish it." (TF03)

Grade level team meetings and informal conversations with colleagues continued to be a source of support and a means for tailoring the program to the culture at Central.

As their colleagues in the primary grades struggled to implement a new literacy program, teachers in the intermediate grades decided to intensify their efforts to engage all of their students in lesson activity. Fifth grade teachers responded to their opportunity to identify their own priorities for collaboration by initiating an action research study to learn more about the levels of Academic Learning Time during lessons. With faculty and interns from the university, they developed a procedure for observing individual students during lessons and charting levels of engagement. In this collaborative effort, participants had an opportunity to generate their own data collection procedures. Conceptually, they chose to focus on individual students and their responses to lessons. Working with the researchers, they constructed a procedure for understanding student responses. Observers recorded notations of each student's level of engagement during three-minute intervals. If the student appeared to be engaged in the activity, the observer recorded a check mark. If the student appeared to be off-task, the observer recorded a code, which summarized the type of off-task behavior (LO for "looking around," LE for "leaving the room," TA for talking—not about the task, etc.). In their conversations about these observations, teachers identified patterns of student responses. For example,

Interviewer: What have you learned from your observations of Academic Learning Time?

Teacher 3: The ones who don't know the material are the ones who don't focus and pay attention.

Teacher 1: The quiet ones surprised me. They are ones who blend in and I didn't realize how much they were off task.

Teacher 3: We tend to overlook the quiet ones.

Teacher 4: There are some we're just losing after 10 minutes. They look like they're getting into it and then before you know it they are gone.

Teacher 2: One I didn't expect was sharpening her pencil, messing with things in her desk. I took the data to that child and said, "Look at this. Look at how many times you were out of your seat or not paying attention." It made a difference with her.

Interviewer: What types of lesson activities seem to be the most engaging?

Teacher: Current events and topical things seem to really hold their interest. When Casey read with them they weren't very into it but once the discussion opened up they really were engaged.

Teacher 3: Social studies and discussion keep them interested.

Teacher 1: We did a lesson on how McDonald's was being sued. They really related and were so interested in talking about the issue.

Teacher 2: Hands on activities as well.

Interviewer: Are you saying that choosing topics they are interested in and relate to as well as allowing them to have dialogue motivates your students?

Group: Yes. (TS03)

These observations have confirmed their suspicions that some of their students were not as engaged in lessons at they would like and identified a few others that were less engaged than they thought.

> There was one surprise. I mean I had one child that surprised me—a really quiet boy that was off task almost the entire lesson and I never noticed. But I think with us doing the observation sometimes we are cued into the ones who are not on task anyway and our eyes kind of go to them. (TS03)

Based on these observations, teachers are discussing ways to increase levels of engagement.

Teacher 3: I want to pull in "Time for Kids" (current event magazine for children).

Teacher 1: Using simulations in the classroom works well. I'd like to do more of those. I did one where I told the children "You are the teacher. Here's your data. Analyze it." The data were graphs of student information like number of AR points, grade level. I also asked them to conference with parents about the data.

Teacher 2: Teaching reading through science and social studies. I'd like to see us do more themes/units that would be of interest to students. That was a goal of ours for this year, to design more units but we haven't gotten to it. (TS03)

Fifth grade teachers also collaborated with researchers to develop a task interview procedure that might help them obtain more detailed observations of students who did not show much engagement with the Academic Learning Time observations. The first step of this process was to meet together to discuss ways to follow-up. For example, the following discussion occurred in March.

Interviewer: Last time you talked about the academic learning time observations, you talked about some students who were on task and some students who were maybe not so much on task and it was helpful to me to read your notes. What are some things you have noticed now that you have looked at these observation patterns?

Teacher 1: Predictable. I did my first one and I was not surprised. The ones who are typically … do not know where we are if we talk to them, they are the ones who are flitting around, looking at desks, turning around.

Teacher 3: I think we can all say the same thing. It is the same kids who are struggling this year.

Interviewer: Please give me a highlight of your most challenging cases. I just want to get a sense of what are the issues. Pick one, each person just pick one and we will go around. You can use first names but not last.

Teacher 1: Bobby. Very low with reading but can do things when he chooses to do things. As far as being engaged during a lesson, he is doing everything but paying attention. His biggest interest is having my attention or my student-teacher's attention constantly. As long as he has our attention he is okay, but when he loses that attention then he goes.

Interviewer: When you see those brief bright spots, when you really feel like he is with you, is it because of the subject matter?

Teacher 1: It is when we are sitting with him one-on-one doing something.

Researchers then met with Bobby individually and conducted a task interview. They asked him to describe an assignment (word problems in math) and "walk us through it."

When they met with the teachers again in April, the researchers reported on the task interviews they had conducted with Bobby and two other students. They reviewed the general procedures for the task interviews with the consent form that parents had signed and then gave a summary of their observations. Teachers interjected comments and suggestions. For example, the following exchanges occurred during the discussion of Bobby's interview:

Interviewer: Let's just walk through and look at Bobby's responses. The first thing we said was, "Tell us about, tell me about this assignment." And he said he was to underline and he knew it was about division and addition. He didn't use the term averaging. Then he told us that everyday they do some problems like this. We said, "Well, what's the purpose of this?" and he said, "It's to learn the teacher's way of dividing," and I asked him, I said, "Well, do you have your own way?" and he said, "Yeah." And I said, "Well when you do it your way, do you get the right answer?" and he said, "Yeah, but I need to learn her way too." Then we gave a list of activities and we asked him to rate each one of these in terms of the extent to which they were helpful. The things he highlighted as helpful were small group lessons, social studies, conferencing with the teacher, he loves that.

Teacher 1: Oh yes he does.

Interviewer: We asked him to select the two or three that he liked and we said, "Well what is there about these activities that are helpful?" He said that the main thing for him is that the teacher can correct his problems and give him feedback. He likes to be in a group because people in the group will help him answer the problems and get feedback. And then we said, "Well, what about the lowest two or three?" and he said, "Worksheets seem hard to me and they aren't always interesting." So my sense as the interviewer is he's really struggling to establish some confidence and he's teacher dependent at this point.

Teacher 1: Very.

Interviewer: In terms of what he relies on for that confidence, is that a fair read?

Teacher 1: Right on.

Interviewer: Okay, then the rest of the interview.... We started the real nuts and bolts of the task interview with the word problem. I said, "I want you be the teacher and tell me how to do this," so this is what he did: he set it up and we checked the addition, he got that part right, and then he told me to divide by twelve, "Are you sure 12?" "Yes." So we divided by 12 and the answer, he said, was 4.33. At that point I said, "Does that make sense?" and he said, "Yeah." And I said "Well, look back at the problem, this was one about rebounding. This kid is a good rebounder. One quarter he had 18 rebounds, would it make sense that his average would be 4?" And he said, "No." So then he said, "Well, okay how many quarters?" and then he liked the answer 13 because there was no remainder. "Oh I like that."

All: [laughter]

Interviewer: So my inference, just based on that problem, was he hasn't internalized this idea of asking himself "does this make sense?"

Teacher 1: No he has not.....

Interviewer: Then we said, "What should we recommend to your teacher to help you with these kinds of assignments?" He says, "Well I need to work more with other people and with her." So that's where we are. Does this add anything to our knowledge of Bobby?

Teacher 1: The social studies thing kind of surprised me. The rest of it doesn't because Bobby is by my side every minute of the day and if he could go home with me, he would. But he doesn't work well on his own at all.

Interviewer: Well, let me ask you this, I'm not trying to push us too far too fast but what's going to happen to Bobby on the end of the year test?

Teacher 1: This year he has to take the paper pencil because they don't have a computer. So he's going to have to take the paper pencil test. He'll get extended time testing in small group and then separate room, but he still has to read it and answer questions. What I'm working on with him, actually the whole group with math right now, is not really solving the problems yet, just setting them up. And we did it four at a time, "Okay Bobby go do the first four for me, okay go do the next four for me." Trying to get him to look at those problems, figure out the questions; figure out what he needs to know, and how to do it, because he has a chance on the math test if he can figure those things out.

When we met with fifth grade teachers the following fall semester, they reported that they had implemented an interdisciplinary unit on "businesses," in which students created "junior achievement type ideas, formed their own businesses and marketed their product" (TF03). This unit had been very successful and they had been able to use student work during this unit to assess their students' progress with reading comprehension:

> I've found that a lot of my students can comprehend and can talk to me about a book and can fully understand what they've read or what they've, and but when they have to put their answers on paper is where they run into

> problems. And that's what I am finding with a lot of mine who can answer questions but can't put it down on paper. And they can do the same, even multiple choice, even if it's a multiple-choice type question, be it fill in the blank, be it give a detailed answer to a question, an open-ended question, be it multiple choice. If I asked them that question orally they can get to the answer. If I have them put it on paper, they can't. (TF03)

At the time of our meeting with them, they were trying to find ways to help students to transfer their understanding of oral tasks to pencil-and-paper assessments. They identified this as a major goal for the rest of the year.

Although the teachers in both the primary and intermediate grade groups engaged in collaborative problem solving, the nature of conversations in these two settings was thus very different. Given an opportunity to collaborate to improve Academic Learning Time in their own ways, fifth grade teachers defined their problem as a matter of individual engagement, generated ways to gather data, and shared ideas for improving lessons. In contrast, their colleagues in the primary grades were required to participate in a mandatory staff development program. In their discussions regarding these experiences, kindergarten and second grade teachers shared frustrations with the workshops and expressed value systems that questioned the basic philosophy and core practices of the professional development program that had been mandated for them. They worked together to find ways to modify these core practices to meet the needs of their students that reflected shared values and established practices.

During the following year, as intermediate grade teachers were required to implement Literacy for All, they began to experience some of the same frustrations as their primary grades colleagues.

> My concern is that with one individual teacher in the classroom and having to do three or four different spelling groups or phonics groups, okay, that becomes overwhelming for me. And that's on an individual basis, and I don't know if my colleagues feel the same, but it is overwhelming for me to sit down and plan how I am going to do this with four different groups of children and maintain classroom management while I am working with a group over here and I have three other groups that might be making words, that might be doing word sorts or you know, that's my concern. (TF03).

Our conversations with teachers during the fall of 2003 suggested that they were concerned about sustaining the momentum of the reforms they had accomplished. A new elementary school opened nearby. Their principal and many of their teachers were transferred to this school. Consequently, they experienced an influx of new teachers as well as a change in leadership. One of the biggest challenges they had experienced was the loss of much of their team planning time. Scheduling changes and reallocation of teaching assistants made it more difficult for teams to have extended blocks of time to meet. When we met in early November, grade level had only met once or twice for extended planning in contrast to the monthly meetings they had experienced in the preceding years.

> Not having the team planning time is a big change. It's not just team planning time. It's planning time-period. If there is something that we need to get done on Mondays, Tuesdays, and Wednesdays, the only time we have is that "specialist" time (art, music, physical education). (TF03)

In spite of these new challenges, teachers continued to express their commitment to the core principles that had guided their reform.

> I feel like what we expect of the students, for the most part, that has not changed. We still follow the Central pride. We still use our brags and our school-wide policies and procedures. (TF03)

CONCLUSIONS

In their interviews over the past four years, teachers and administrators have emphasized active student engagement, collaboration, and community. In their work with students and with each other, teachers have strengthened a community of caring, which has permeated the school culture. This community has demonstrated many of the characteristics of "significance" that L'Esperance, Strahan, Farrington, and Anderson (2003) have described. The culture at Central has grown rich with indicators of broad and deep renewal with data to support the school's focus on both academics and community. Students have shown more responsibility for their own learning, for pushing themselves, and for helping their classmates. Lessons have featured higher levels of cooperation and student involvement. Teachers and administrators have developed and enhanced instructional norms by developing strong professional learning communities at each grade level. They have used data to guide their decisions but their actions are driven by purpose: to make a difference in the lives of their students.

Continuing interviews with participants have suggested that recent initiatives to improve instruction are testing these grade level communities. Like the teachers in Coburn's (2001) study of efforts to reform reading instruction, the teachers at Central grappled with "multiple and sometimes conflicting messages." Teachers at the primary grades worked together to try to adapt the mandated literacy program with their own best practices. The amount of time devoted to assessments and the extent to which activities are developmentally appropriate appear to be the biggest issues. Unlike the four teachers in Spillane's (1999) study who created enactment zones, the K-2 teachers at Central did not have a structure in place to make sense of the mandated initiative. While they participated in informal discussions with colleagues, their conversations seemed to become more reflective and purposeful when they met with the researcher. The fact that the interviews were conducted as vertical conversations in which the varying grade levels involved spoke with each other may have helped structure these conversations. At the intermediate grades, teachers have extended their collaborative efforts to focus more specifically on students who are not showing progress. Their biggest concern has been the amount of time and energy it takes to make these individual connections. These concerns have grown during the past year as teachers have had less time to meet in their grade level groups.

The spiral of reform activity in professional learning communities links ongoing assessment with instructional improvement to enhance student accomplishment. Both groups of teachers exhibited what Fullan (1999) referred to as a moral purpose. The goal for these teachers has been to collectively make a difference in the lives of all students and to reduce the gap between high and low performers. The K-2 teachers struggled with the mandated program because it did not always align with their goals. They struggled to find a balance between what they believed about good teaching and what the program required. On the other hand, the fifth grade teachers created their own initiative and felt comfortable that it aligned with their goals for children. The tone of the conversations in the two groups was different because of these different levels of congruence with their moral purpose.

As they attempt to sustain successful reform over time, teachers and administrators must find ways to address the issues that have emerged. The shared beliefs and instructional norms that they have developed over the past four years may not be fully embedded in the culture of the school. As teachers and administrators have been reassigned, new colleagues may or may not automatically share these norms and values.

Without as much time to meet on a regular basis, grade level teams may not continue to evolve as professional learning communities.

Our evidence suggests that Central has achieved "moments" of significance. Whether or not these moments grow or fade remains to be seen. It may well be that cultural growth is a fragile enterprise, one that needs constant nurture and support. In their efforts toward significance, teachers and administrators have demonstrated the complexity of school reform and the degree of human energy it takes to make it work.

AUTHORS' NOTE

This report was written with the sponsorship and approval of the Center for School Leadership Development at the University of North Carolina at Chapel Hill. Portions of the article originally appeared in the Phase Three Report of the North Carolina Lighthouse Project and are published here with permission.

REFERENCES

Carlone, H., & Horn, S. (2002). Results from Central Elementary School. In D. Strahan & A. Ware (Eds.), *Achieving success in the North Carolina Lighthouse Schools: An analysis of the dynamics of meaningful reform* (pp. 44-68). Chapel Hill, NC: the Center for School Leadership Development.

Coburn, C. (2001). Collective sense making about reading: How teachers mediate reading policy in their professional communities. *Educational Evaluation and Policy Analysis, 23*, 145-170.

Creswell, J.W. (1994). *Research design: Qualitative & quantitative approaches*. London: Sage.

Fullan, M. (1999). *Change forces: The sequel*. London: Falmer Press.

Langer. J. (2001). Beating the odds: Teaching middle and high school students to read and write well. *American Educational Research Journal, 38*(4), 837-880.

L'Esperance, M., Strahan, D., Farrington, V., & Anderson, P. (2003). *Raising achievement: Project Genesis—A significant school model*. Westerville, OH: National Middle School Association.

Lieberman, A., & Wood, D. (2003). When teachers write: Of networks and learning. In A. Lieberman & L. Miller (Eds.), *Teachers caught in the action* (pp. 174-187). New York: Teachers College, Columbia University.

Spillane, J. (1999). External reform initiatives and teachers' efforts to reconstruct their practice: The mediating role of teachers' zones of enactment. *Journal of Curriculum Studies, 31*(2), 143-175.

Strahan, D. (2003). Promoting a collaborative professional culture in three elementary schools that have beaten the odds. *Elementary School Journal, 104*(2), 127-146.

Strahan, D., & Ware, A. (2001). *Achieving success in the North Carolina Lighthouse Schools: An analysis of the dynamics of meaningful reform*. Chapel Hill, NC: the Center for School Leadership Development.

Wolf, S., Borko, H., Elliott, R., & McIver, M. (2000). 'That dog won't hunt!': Exemplary school change efforts within the Kentucky reform. *American Educational Research Journal, 37*, 349-396, 2000.

CHAPTER 6

POWERFUL LEARNING

Creating Learning Communities in Urban School Reform

Joy C. Phillips

ABSTRACT

This paper focuses on one urban middle school's response to a major school reform initiative. Data for this paper were drawn from a larger research and evaluation study of this reform initiative located in a large city in the southwestern US. Funded schools invested heavily in high-quality professional development for teachers. Reformers believe that increasing teacher learning will improve student academic achievement. In the middle school presented here as a case study, administrators and teachers chose to focus on improving "regular" (nonmagnet) students' academic achievement by increasing opportunities for their teachers to participate in high-quality professional development. By engaging in their own powerful learning, teachers created a set of innovative curriculum programs targeted toward previously low or underachieving students. As a result of these new curriculum programs, student achievement over all socioeconomic and academic groups increased dramatically during the five-year reform effort.

Deep Change: Cases and Commentary on Reform in High Stakes States, 87–106

INTRODUCTION

This article uses qualitative data to describe how administrators and teachers in one urban middle school, T. P. Callaghan,[1] shared leadership tasks to develop an authentic learning community. This middle school was one of 88 schools participating in a school-based reform initiative in a major city in the southwestern United States. The reform focused dollars on high-quality professional development for administrators and teachers. By engaging in their own powerful learning, teachers at T. P. Callaghan created a set of innovative curriculum programs targeted toward previously low or underachieving students. T. P. Callaghan Middle School serves a multiethnic student population representing extremes of the economic spectrum. The new programs described in this paper focus on previously underachieving students or on blending students across socioeconomic, ethnic, and academic groups. As a result of these new curriculum programs, student achievement over all socioeconomic and academic groups increased dramatically during the five-year reform effort.

CREATING A LEARNING COMMUNITY

Often teachers believe that conventional district or campus training programs do not meet their needs. Traditional staff development offerings consist typically of "one-shot" presentations or workshops with little follow-up or support in which experts transmit knowledge to novices (Spillane, 2000). This training is inadequate for those participants requiring more challenging advanced instruction. Researchers agree, judging most current staff development to be intellectually superficial, disconnected from deep issues of curriculum and learning, fragmented, and noncumulative (Ball & Cohen, 1999).

This traditional view of staff development is outdated and incompatible with the prevailing vision of school reform. Today's educational reformers expect teachers to help diverse student learners become competent and skilled. Schools are urged to connect with their communities. Reformers expect students to succeed in ways unprecedented in the history of U.S. public education (Ball & Cohen, 1999).

Today's educational reformers expect teachers to know meanings and connections, not just procedures and information. Teachers are required to connect ideas across disciplinary fields and to students' everyday lives. Teachers must understand children's interests and needs. Furthermore, teachers need to understand cultural differences, including differences in language, class, family, community, and gender. Ultimately, teachers have to expand their ideas about learning. Teachers must know pedagogy so that they can connect children effectively with content, adapting and shifting teaching modes in response to students. In effect, teachers are now expected to develop and adapt their teaching practices in response to their everyday classroom experiences (Ball & Cohen, 1999).

Gradually a concept of teacher *professional* development has emerged from the more limited notion of *staff* development. In order for teachers and schools to deliver excellent instruction that promotes high academic achievement for all students, sustained professional development is necessary. Some educators suggest that implementation of the new vision of professional development represents a paradigm shift. According to this new paradigm, teacher professional development occurs every day on the job among teams of teachers who share responsibility for high levels of learning for all students. While this paradigm includes formal training programs, it also recognizes the power of informal learning. To implement this new paradigm, school leaders must change organizational structures to create new school cultures that foster experimentation, collaboration, and continuous improvement (Sparks, 2000).

Ball and Cohen (1999) have called the new paradigm "a pedagogy of professional development." They have described it as a dynamic interaction between teachers, students, curriculum content, and environment. In this complex interaction, *teaching* is defined as what teachers do, say, and think *with* students, about curriculum content, using particular methods of instruction, in specific environments, over time. Researchers and master teachers see teaching as a collection of practices, including pedagogy, learning, instructional design, and managing instructional organization. Research also suggests that when teachers' knowledge, skills, and strategic actions are seen as resources, student achievement rises significantly (Cohen, Raudenbush, & Ball, 2000). Teachers learning from their day-to-day teaching practice constantly improvise, conjecture, experiment, and assess as they adapt and develop their practice (Ball & Cohen, 1999).

Schools participating in the reform initiative highlighted in this paper support this emerging vision of educational reform. Administrators and teachers in these schools view professional development as necessary to maintain and refine implemented reforms. In this environment, professional development serves many functions, including new staff orientation and training. Professional development also creates forums for teachers to have collegial conversations about curriculum programs and instructional problems and solutions. Teachers participating in professional development gain a common knowledge base of reforms and their underlying philosophies. Teachers engage in active inquiry into current beliefs and practices. Finally, professional development keeps teachers current on district, regional, state, and national issues and guidelines. Teachers at reform schools report that prior to this reform their greatest need was for intellectual and professional resources. Teachers say the reform funding gives them necessary role models, research literature, and collegial support to implement reforms.

An academically rich environment begins with teachers who are deeply knowledgeable about their discipline area, about how children learn, and about which pedagogical strategies best support student learning. This special teacher knowledge is called "pedagogical content knowledge"—a form of knowledge that combines subject matter (content) knowledge with an understanding of instruction, producing a highly specialized type of knowledge unique to teachers (Shulman, 1987).

As teachers in these reforming schools engage in professional development activities, they create peer networks within schools, between schools in the same district, and among schools in the region, state, and nation. Reform funding has enabled teachers to develop mechanisms that allow them to collaborate effectively with their peers. Through collaboration, teachers observe each other's classroom instruction, videotape lessons, analyze student needs, investigate teaching problems, and generate ideas for new teaching strategies.

Teachers in participating schools collaborate actively in Critical Friends Groups,[2] Literature Study Circles, Professional Academies, Teacher Writing Groups, and Teacher Action Research Teams. Study groups read such literature as *What's Worth Fighting for in Your School?, The Seven Habits of Highly Effective People, A Framework for Understanding Poverty, Nonfiction Matters, The First Day of School*, and *Strategies That Work*. Literature study groups enable faculties to engage in long-term literature studies. With ongoing groups, teachers have more time to be reflective about the topics, their own practice, and how to implement new approaches.

Expert teachers emerge from these activities as peer leaders in roles such as Critical Friends Group Coaches, Content Specialists, and Reading Learning Facilitators. Furthermore, a number of teachers have become certified as curriculum trainers in national programs, including the Coalition of Essential Schools (CES) and the New Jersey Writing Project (NJWP).

Research details ways in which the professional community of teachers plays a vital role in school reform and improvement. Learning communities create "spaces" for teachers to form professional relationships, share information, and provide collegial support. The creation of small, collegial communities of practice contrasts sharply with the traditional approach to staff development. An extensive body of research (Liberman, 1988; Little, 1993; McLaughlin, Talbert, & Bascia, 1990; Westheimer, 1998) supports the power of such learning communities.

Additionally, teachers in reform schools learn how to infuse art across the curriculum. When teachers integrate art into their teaching, they draw upon an emerging body of research that supports their efforts. Emerging research suggests that formal education systems have two purposes: expanding and deepening students' understanding and developing students' cognitive ability. In this view literacy is considered much more than simply reading and writing. Theorists conceptualize literacy as ways of constructing and communicating meaning. Students learn to read and write, but they also learn to communicate through poetry, music, visual art, and dance (Eisner, 1998).

By infusing art into the curriculum, teachers give students multiple opportunities to develop and perfect methods of expression. Furthermore, by drawing upon the arts, teachers expose students to complex processes not based upon specific rules or procedures. Consequently, students must develop the cognitive ability to judge quality or "rightness of fit" (Goodman, 1978). To judge rightness of fit, students must pay attention to patterns and configurations and whole items or work products rather than discrete elements. These complex tasks help students develop sophisticated cognitive skills. Students use these well-developed cognitive skills to learn across the curriculum, and they also use them in their daily lives outside of school.

RESULTS

This section begins with a description of the larger research study from which the T. P. Callaghan case study was drawn. Next, an overview of the reform initiative along with a snapshot of T. P. Callaghan Middle School is provided. To illustrate the findings, vignettes are presented of three innovative programs T. P. Callaghan teachers developed as a result of participating in high quality professional development largely funded by the reform initiative. Two language arts teachers participated actively in long-term study groups focused on previously low-achieving students. One history teacher created a program to develop student leaders—representing a cross-section of the student population—after visiting a model program in Canada. These teachers and programs contributed significantly to a dramatic improvement in student academic achievement across all student groups.

RESEARCH STUDY

This paper draws data from a large research and evaluation study in a major urban city in the southwestern United States. This city is one of 18 sites across the country that received dollars from a private foundation to serve as seed money for local initiatives based on the foundations' reform imperatives. Each national project site was implemented uniquely based upon local conditions, funding, and politics. All 18 projects were expected to target public and private dollars toward three reform imperatives: enhancing teacher learning, reducing isolation within schools and between schools and communities, and personalizing the student learning environment. This paper focuses on one urban middle school's response to the localized reform: enhancing teacher learning.

Data were collected data for this paper from principal and teacher interviews, classroom observations, teacher focus groups, and reporting documentation.[3] Additionally, student work products, including student-authored anthologies, artwork, and skits were examined.

SETTING

The school featured in this paper, T. P. Callaghan Middle School, was one of 88 schools funded in this southwestern city. T. P. Callaghan, a 76-year-old public school, has educated many distinguished graduates—some have gone on to achieve national prominence. T. P. Callaghan has had only 10 principals; turnover occurred mainly due to retirement or promotion to the district office. During its history, T. P. Callaghan has evolved from a school located on the edge of a newly developing town to an inner-city school in the middle of one of the nation's largest cities.

In 1973 T. P. Callaghan was designated a magnet school campus in a move designed to aid in desegregation of the cities' public schools. Two-thirds of the school's current student population is enrolled in the magnet program. The remaining one-third of the student population is "zoned" to the school from surrounding neighborhoods. The T. P. Callaghan school community is ethnically, socioeconomically, and academically diverse. During the 2001-2002 school year, 45% of the students were White, 32% Hispanic, 15% African American, and 8% Asian. Presently, 1425 students are enrolled in sixth, seventh, and eighth grades. Approximately 556 students (one-third) are enrolled as "regular" (nonmagnet) students.

Until 1998 the magnet students benefitted most from instructional programs and resources available at T. P. Callaghan Middle School. With implementation of the reform initiative, T. P. Callaghan administrators decided to focus on improving the "regular" (nonmagnet) students' academic achievement by addressing one of the three national reform imperatives: teacher learning.

TEACHER STUDY GROUPS

At T. P. Callaghan Middle School, teachers participating in study groups have developed a number of impressive curriculum innovations. This school used reform dollars to hire university-based faculty to help them develop new instructional strategies. Several university faculty used study groups to engage teachers in the planning process. One faculty-led study group has evolved into a post-baccalaureate course focused on teaching reading in middle school. This group has studied *The Art of Teaching Reading* by Lucy Calkins, *Mosaic of Thought* by Ellin Keene, and *Strategic Reading* by Jeffrey Willhelm. In the two examples that follow, language arts teachers developed strategies for helping "reluctant readers" strengthen their literacy skills.

Imagining Classic Literature

The first example focuses on a sixth grade language arts teacher, Jennifer,[4] and her class of regular students. As she explained to me, many of these primarily Hispanic and African American students were reading below grade level when they entered her class. However, watching Jennifer and the students in action, no one would ever know that these were initially considered struggling or "reluctant" readers.

Jennifer—a young, Anglo woman—threw herself into her teaching practice by using her considerable performing and fine arts talent to guide her students. Building upon her knowledge of Writer's Workshop and other strategies, she dramatically read aloud classic literature passages to the class while they followed along using their own copies. She began by guiding the students to consider "prompting" questions about the story. She wrote the questions on a dry-erase board surrounding two sides of the room.

As the story progressed, Jennifer encouraged students to draw images to illustrate what they imagined the story narrator was imagining. She provided the students with colored construction paper and chalk. Later, she instructed the students to go back to the story and find the words or passage they were illustrating, cut out the words, and use the text as a caption for their illustration. The students used scissors and paste to finish the assignment.

The students (and the observers) were clearly captivated by the teacher's reading. As the students worked into the assignment, they appeared lost in their thoughts. The teacher selected a gory Edgar Allen Poe story, "The Tell Tale Heart," which was particularly appropriate to capture the attention and imagination of young adolescents. The students' resulting artwork centered in impressive graphic detail on elements of the tale and was eventually displayed in the classroom along with artwork from previous lessons.

By reading aloud, Jennifer modeled an enthusiastic reader. By using art, she engaged the students in the story. And by directing them back to the printed text, she connected their artwork directly to the literature. With her animated instructional style and student-centered work assignments, she demonstrated instructional practice more typically seen in magnet classes. She certainly did not treat the students as low-achieving academic performers. Rather, she demonstrated high expectations for the students and set high academic standards for their work. These high standards can be seen in the rubrics she developed for her regular, nonmagnet students.

Using standards established by the International Baccalaureate Middle Years Program (IBMYP), Jennifer created a set of learning objectives for her regular students based on standards usually reserved for high-achieving magnet students. She designed and implemented this alternative assessment strategy by combining information from her long-term study group and her personal knowledge with the IBMYP standards. With this rubric she evaluates not only her students' work but also assesses the student during the process of doing the work.

Jennifer assesses student knowledge, skills, and critical thinking ability by using the rubric she created from nine IBMYP objectives:

1. Express a personal response to literature and demonstrate the ability to approach works in an independent fashion;
2. Demonstrate some awareness of the effects of style and techniques employed by authors (such as figures of speech, plot devices, and characterization);
3. Demonstrate knowledge and understanding of the works studied;
4. Demonstrate the ability to comment on the language, content, structure, meaning, and significance of both familiar and unfamiliar pieces of writing;
5. Demonstrate the ability to express ideas with clarity and coherence in both oral and written communication;
6. Demonstrate the ability to use language to describe, analyze, explain, narrate, entertain, and express feelings;
7. Demonstrate a critical awareness of differing media of communication;
8. Demonstrate competence in the general skills and strategies of the writing process; and
9. Evaluate own writing and the writing of others.

The teacher uses the rubric by measuring student progress on a scale of 0 to 8. She has clearly defined each criterion and provided descriptors of proficiency at each of the eight levels. The eight criteria are Writer's Notebook, Writing Process, Content of Writing, Mechanics of Writing, Genre Studies, Media/Visual Literacy, Approaches to Learning, and Evaluation/Reflection of Processes.

For instance, a student demonstrating high achievement with the Writer's Notebook is assessed with the following standard:

> The student's notebook is incorporated into his/her daily life in a way that demonstrates a truly personal response to life as a writer. It contains evidence of serious reflection, many writing strategies (personal responses to literature, narratives, observations, etc.), and a variety of media (mementos, photos, quotations, etc.). The student has maintained more than one notebook throughout the year.[5]

Jennifer uses a variety of assessment techniques to evaluate students' progress on the rubric. In addition to using running records, grades, and tests, she also reviews student portfolios. Portfolios include Works in Progress folders, Pieces Completed folders, and Student Written Reflections. Her assessment approach is very labor intensive, but it enables her to stay student-centered, focusing on the unique needs of each student.

Latino Boys Writing Group

Another language arts teacher at this middle school, Carlos, participated in several teacher study groups led by university faculty. A young Latino, he was especially concerned about adolescent Hispanic boys considered at high risk of dropping out of school. Using grant money, this seventh grade teacher developed a plan for an extracurricular boys writing group. Initially intended for young Hispanic boys, the group quickly became known as the Latino Boys Writing Group. The program began as a summer experiment; when Carlos secured extra support, he continued the group throughout the year as an after-school program.

Carlos recruited a local Latino writer to work with him on the project. Together, they reached out to boys that might have felt disconnected from school. As mentors and teachers, they tried to connect the boys' experiences outside school with their writing experiences in the group. Carlos describes the group:

> We meet weekly for an hour or more. I always order a couple of pizzas and the local pizza guy gives us a discount. If I don't have money for pizza, I'll buy some Popsicles or something, or bags of chips. We come in and we

write. Sometimes we don't have anything to eat, which is ok, because the kids still come.

Mario and I always have a piece of our own writing, either a poem or a story. We read our work to them, and we talk about the work. Then the kids will try to write something similar. Or they'll write in their notebook and share that with the group, because we focus on writer's notebooks throughout middle school. We read aloud daily in class, and we've even published an anthology of class writings.

The goal with Latino boys is to draw them into the school community. The boys who participate in the Latino Boys Writing Group are those kids who sit in the back in the classroom, the ones who kind of fade into the background if you don't engage them. They are not necessarily on a sports team or in a club or the chosen leaders. But these kids are part of our school population. They're valuable. So we invite them to the Latino Boys Writing Group to connect them with the school setting, to make them a part of the school. I'll call the parents if I have any questions or concerns. They have my number, and they'll call me at home sometimes.

Sometimes we don't even get to writing or reading poetry in our Latino Boys Writing Group because we're talking about things that happen during the day. Or we are talking about making good choices. Mario and I always try to serve as springboards for their thinking about making good choices, thinking about their lives and the stories they can tell through their writing. There have also been times right before or after the holidays when only two boys come to the Group. But Mario and I still meet with them because, you know, they came. We don't want to say, "No, we're not going to meet today because there's only two boys here." We want them to know that they are all important to us.

Carlos reaches out to students who in other urban middle schools might be ignored. As a result of the teacher's dedicated effort, obvious caring concern, and effective mentoring, these boys engage more with school in general and the writing process in particular. He encourages the boys to write from their own experiences, to write about things that matter to them. All writing is important, he tells them. Moreover, he helps them become more comfortable with reading aloud by having them read their work to the group. Everyone's work is honored and taken very seriously as he teaches the boys to respect themselves and each other. This group has published two anthologies and some boys have read their work publicly in the community.

In this example, Carlos contextualized learning by building upon students' pre-existing knowledge. He consciously used students' prior knowledge, skills, beliefs, language, and culture as a starting place for instruction. With contextualized instruction, teachers use familiar materials and illustrations to introduce students of new knowledge and to validate students' experiences as meaningful.

Developing Student Leaders

Teachers at this middle school also contextualize instruction by encouraging students to examine complex social issues. For example, one teacher, Elizabeth, trains students to serve as peer leaders in their guided advisory classes. This approach deliberately mixes magnet and regular students from across sixth, seventh, and eighth grades. The magnet students are primarily White and middle class, while the regular students tend to be African American or first- or second-generation Mexican immigrants from working class families.

Previously, the magnet and regular students rarely interacted or attended classes together. T. P. Callaghan teachers learned of this innovative guided advisory approach by visiting a Canadian school. Teachers thought this approach would not only help students get to know each other, but would also provide a way for students from different grade levels to interact in a meaningful way. They devised a curricular design called "Guidance Support Groups"—commonly known as GSG. Administrators and teachers formed student groups composed of a mix of magnet and regular students from three grade levels. The GSGs, which substitute for the old "homeroom" concept, support all students through structured activities designed to build character, to develop leadership, and to increase world awareness.

Ninth-grade students—including regular and magnet students from all socioeconomic groups—are selected as GSG leaders. These student leaders are trained in facilitation skills and group activities. Student-led group activities focus on complex social issues such as bigotry, stereotyping, and racism. These middle school students have shown a remarkable ability to openly discuss complicated issues.

While working with ethnically, economically, and academically diverse students, Elizabeth contextualizes instruction by devising lessons about prejudice and stereotyping. She described one lesson:

> In this lesson I wanted students to become aware of things they see every day: People being made fun of because they are different, people not being accepted for who they are, prejudice, racism, bigotry, anti-Semitism. I ask the students to work in groups to come up with a basic definition of these terms describing prejudice. Then I give them a short amount of time to develop a skit to illustrate the word. Using a skit, the students present the information in a visual way. It's much more powerful than just talking about the words.
>
> The students use their own ideas about prejudice based on what they've seen, heard, and experienced. After these student leaders become comfortable with the topic and the lesson, then they teach it to the other kids in their advisory class.

> It was hard at the beginning to get our student leaders comfortable with the idea of talking about heavy topics. We started off small, talking about little things, things that make you happy and sad, things that are good in your life, things that are frustrating. Eventually, the students begin to bond since they see each other four days a week. But they also see each other in the halls, since their lockers are all together. There's constant interaction throughout the school day. It makes them become like a family.

DISCUSSION

The reform funders required participating schools to develop a unique theory of action to focus their school development work. According to their theory of action, T. P. Callaghan's designated leaders decided to focus their reform effort on improving teacher learning for the express purpose of improving student learning. The leaders focused their reform even more closely upon the nonmagnet students. The principal, Brian Patrick, described their initial thinking about the disparity among student groups as a "notion of discomfort."

> I would say there was a notion of discomfort regarding—not the big picture at T. P. Callaghan—the big picture looked beautiful. It was wonderful. All of our VanGuard (magnet) students were doing great. But we began to talk a bit about the regular program, the five different socioeconomic groups, the economically disadvantaged.
>
> And we talked about how there are different ways to learn. Forget the teaching aspect. To learn and get kids to maximize their potential in a way that's innovative, certainly rigorous, but very interesting to the kids. Now, heck, how do you get there?

With their early conversations, these reformers put the student at the center. However, they quickly realized that carrying out the plan of improving the regular students' academic achievement required a complex set of tasks involving many of the school's teachers. Thus, they decided to focus their reform dollars on helping the teachers develop new knowledge, skills, and practices.

Initially school leaders created a staff development plan for the teachers. As more teachers became involved in the staff development activities, the teachers developed stronger voices in the planning process. Eventually, teachers essentially took over the process of developing each year's plan. Ultimately, teacher learning occurred in a variety of ways, including departmental study groups, action research teams, and personal learning time.

Study Groups

As teachers took on leadership tasks, the principal, Brian Patrick, continued to be actively involved. He explained how they began with departmental study groups:

> A small group collaborative comprised of three or four teachers, sixth-grade regular teachers, talked about how challenging it was to bring reading alive in their classrooms. And they talked about how they could really reinforce their focus on developing reading stamina, just getting kids to read for x number of minutes.
>
> And then they talked about the possibilities of going to New York, to Columbia Teachers College, for a reading workshop and a writing workshop. And how powerful that would be. My response was to tell them that I certainly encourage that possibility, and I applaud the fact that you guys have not been satisfied with the reading programs we've been using.
>
> Now, by working together as a team, they've taken their 150 kids to a whole new level. They've got their kids putting sticky notes in their books and responding to what they read and trying to relate it to themselves and to the real world.

The current principal, Brian Patrick, who took the reform work forward, formerly served the school in a variety of roles including assistant principal, language arts magnet teacher, and in-school suspension center teacher. After he became principal he decided he needed to develop a more collaborative leadership style. He talked about creating a leadership team using his classroom knowledge as a starting point.

> I say, 'Now guys, don't think I don't know what you're going through, I was there and I'm as guilty as the rest of you. But we've got to make it a priority. Now, let's talk about how we're going to do that. Let's get a plan of action to shift this focus more to the classroom.

In this example of shared leadership, the principal clearly is not abdicating leadership responsibility. By creating a leadership team and guiding the team to develop a student-centered action plan, he is expanding the leadership role to include other administrators (assistant principals) and teachers. Furthermore, the principal models the leadership behaviors he wishes others to emulate, including how to share control.

> I learned a lot as a new principal, because I'm quite controlling. Or, rather, I used to be. And I'm organized. But I've learned that some things are have-to-dos or nonnegotiables on my plate. I've learned that change specific to the culture of a school cannot be mandated. You can't get it to happen in any way other than *you* modeling what it would look like and challenging teachers to change the dynamics, the culture of this school. Because we all feel there is room for improvement. And, then, let's talk about how to go

> about doing it, and I'm going to provide you the support that I can, as well as, a bit of pressure.

With this disclosure, the principal revealed that he, too, had to change his behavior as he continued to learn from his experiences as well as his own professional development.

Personal Learning Time

T. P. Callaghan teachers have benefitted significantly from a second type of individualized professional development they call "personal learning time." As a component of their reform theory of action, T. P. Callaghan administrators and teachers decided to embed regular professional development time into the school day. Together, they made a commitment to dismiss students early on Friday afternoons. Students leave school at 1:15 p.m. every Friday, and teachers meet for professional development from 1:35 to 3:30 p.m.

Initially, this designated weekly time was devoted to group work such as study groups; typically, teachers could select from among a variety of options. As teachers participated more actively in decision making, they began to ask for individualized professional development time. The principal described the process:

> We added a personal learning time on Friday afternoon, but we didn't really define it. I said, "That's your time to do what you think is important. But you must spend it on things other than lesson plans and grading papers." I told them, "This is not time for what you didn't get done earlier in the week, because you already had that time."
>
> I would start the year with my thoughts regarding what personal learning ought to be or what I would envision mine as. And I'd share a bit with the teachers on what I'm doing. I'm not just sitting in some office. And give them some ideas like, "What are some things that you do well?" and then, "What are some things you just do?" I did this to help give them an idea where to start.
>
> Last year we took 10 Friday afternoons for the personal learning or small group collaborative time. I would ask for a reflection,[6] and I gave them a template. But I didn't require them to use the template. I told them, "Ramble if you want, but don't tell me what you did. I want to know what your learning meant to you. Where are you going next? And you may be going nowhere because you're confused. Just know that I don't have all the answers. But I'm happy to chat a bit to see if we can't come up with something."

Turning teacher learning over to the teachers clearly demonstrates the principal's level of trust with his staff. Through this trust, the principal also established accountability systems. He required the teachers to give him written reflections, although he didn't require a standardized form. In essence, he established a system for regular dialogue with each teacher focused on the teacher's individualized learning process. The principal rated the investment in professional development very highly.

> From my perspective, this is what has changed our school community. The ownership the teachers have taken, the learning I have engaged in over the five years of the reform. We went from a model that was very isolated to one that was very meaningful to each person. How powerful this has been for us!

By examining these innovative curriculum programs, we see how leadership tasks in this school have been distributed or "spread over" individuals at T. P. Callaghan Middle School. Initially, the official school leader, the principal, reported experiencing a persistent feeling of discomfort regarding student achievement. Since the magnet students represented two-thirds of the student population, their high academic performance masked the regular students' lower achievement. After disaggregating achievement data, the disparity between students groups became obvious.

The principal worked with his leadership team to create an action plan to address the student achievement disparity. This group understood that teachers were key actors in improving the regular students' academic achievement. Furthermore, the team understood that administrators and teachers needed more knowledge to achieve their goals. Thus, the leadership team focused reform dollars on investing in teacher learning. By investing in teachers, the formal school leaders began to share leadership tasks with teachers, and teachers began to assume leadership roles in creating innovative curriculum strategies.

Finally, this case study demonstrates how teachers and administrators took into account key factors of the environment. For example, Spillane and colleagues have suggested that environment incorporates not only the interactive set of actors but also tools, language, and organizational structures, including structures related to race, class, and gender (Spillane, Halverson, & Diamond, 2002, p. 28). Three aspects of T. P. Callaghan's environment illustrate this dimension especially well.

First, T. P. Callaghan's reform team focused their work on the regular students, who were separated from the magnet students in a number of critical ways. The regular students initially did not benefit from the magnet program's creative curriculum. Furthermore, this group was composed of primarily Hispanic or African American students from working class families. As the Guided Advisory teacher, Elizabeth, pointed out, the magnet students rarely interacted with the regular students before the new structure was put into place at T. P. Callaghan.

A second defining characteristic of T. P. Callaghan's environment is also sociocultural. Two of the three examples of innovative curriculum practices described in this paper expressly address students' background and personal experiences. The Latino Boys Writing Project seeks to connect young boys to reading and writing by having them focus on experiences personally meaningful to them. In doing so, these boys understand that their teacher, Carlos, recognizes their culture as important, and he respects them and their families.

Similarly, the Guided Advisory teacher, Elizabeth, facilitates students across socioeconomic and academic groups to consider complex issues of discrimination and prejudice. She helps students to understand different perspectives and to respect and care for each other. The sixth-grade language arts teacher, Jennifer, also establishes a culturally responsive classroom while introducing students to multiple literature genres. For example, her room is lined with culturally diverse young peoples' literature such as *Happy to Be Nappy* and *Bud, Not Buddy*. Additionally, she conducts extended lessons on cultural topics such as the Jazz Era using diverse music, literature, and art sources.

Third, as a Texas public school, T. P. Callaghan is required to comply with the Texas Education Agency's accountability system. The Texas system, which has received a great deal of recent national attention, requires schools to disaggregate student achievement data by four socioeconomic groups: African American, Hispanic, White, and economically disadvantaged. Prior to data disaggregation, the principal reported, T. P. Callaghan's student achievement looked great. However, upon closer analysis, the gap between student groups became apparent. The principal, Brian Patrick, described their data examining process.

> We have focused on data specific to every child in this school for the last three years now. We pick it apart so that we can know exactly how students are doing when they come to us, instead of not having a clue and not really being concerned because our 900 students (the magnet students) make everything look great.
>
> And we focus on ways to effect kids' success at T. P. Callaghan cognitively and affectively. Forget the magnet program. We look at every socioeconomic group, the economically disadvantaged group. We took the item analysis, and we went through the objectives. We looked at the items kids were getting wrong. We had department meetings and asked ourselves, "What does this mean?" And some teachers realized they hadn't taught the concept before the TAAS test was given in April. So it all comes down to what the state considers mastery. We've got to at least cover that. There's a whole heck of a lot more we want to do. But we do need to at least figure out how we can cover all the material in a meaningful way prior to the test. And so we disaggregate the data and look at longitudinal pieces as well just to see

where our areas of weakness are and some of this came down to teacher learning.

And now the student achievement scores have gone up dramatically in the last three years. I would say that is directly because of the teacher personal learning, the heightened awareness, and the work done in our departmental study groups. It's beyond organizational stuff, beyond pen and papers. Now the teachers never talk about the TAAS. To them it's just another genre.

T. P. Callaghan students have, indeed, shown dramatic academic growth especially in reading and mathematics achievement in the last three years. In 1999-2000, T. P. Callaghan received an *Acceptable* rating from the Texas Education Agency (TEA), a rating indicating that at least 50% of all students passed each subject area (reading, mathematics, writing, science, and social studies) on Texas Assessment of Academic Skills (TAAS). The following year, T. P. Callaghan achieved a *Recognized* rating, meaning a minimum of 80% of all students passed each TAAS subject area. With the data for 2001-2002, T. P. Callaghan moved to the highest rating, *Exemplary*, demonstrating that 90% of all students passed each TAAS subject area.[7]

As discussion of these aspects of T. P. Callaghan's environment illustrates, the situation or context is crucially important in leadership practice. Context is a primary reason why prescriptive or "magic bullet" models of school reform rarely improve student achievement. Only when administrators and teachers take context into account can they create effective strategies for their unique circumstances. As with a theory of action, solutions must be built, not borrowed.

CONCLUSION

From this examination of leadership and instructional practice at T. P. Callaghan Middle School, five key themes emerge: high-quality professional development, research-based literature, shared leadership, collaborative processes, and context. These key themes do not stand alone. Woven together, they represent processes and commitments of practitioners in an authentic learning community. While this case study provides a model of school-based reform, the T. P. Callaghan model cannot be transported to another setting. As the themes collectively demonstrate, effective school change requires customized design at the campus level. However, these themes can serve as a framework for schools interested in developing effective learning communities.

First, T. P. Callaghan put improving teacher learning at the center of their reform work. Initially, the school's formal leaders created staff development plans. As teachers engaged more in the decision-making process, professional development became increasingly individualized. From the outset, these administrators and teachers believed in investing in high-quality professional development that enabled them to become reflective practitioners, to enrich their content knowledge, and to experiment with innovative instructional strategies.

Second, T. P. Callaghan practitioners used research-based literature to guide their work. T. P. Callaghan administrators and teachers were readers who actively sought new idea sources from empirical data. They sought out university faculty to facilitate their learning, to connect them to relevant literature, and to help them connect theory to practice.

Third, T. P. Callaghan transformed into an authentic learning community because leadership was shared, or distributed, among formal and informal leaders. As teachers developed stronger decision-making voices, many took on leadership tasks. This shared leadership created a supportive learning environment in which teachers could experiment with innovative curriculum and instructional strategies. Collectively, they developed innovative programs that transformed student learning.

Fourth, T. P. Callaghan administrators and teachers collaboratively developed and implemented their reform work. They did not work and make decisions in isolation. Teachers collaborated on leadership teams and in study groups. By collaborating, these practitioners offered each other professional and personal support. Additionally, administrators and teachers provided critical feedback on instructional practices as well as on individual learning plans.

Finally, T. P. Callaghan practitioners considered the school context extremely important. They knew their student population well, and they deliberately created culturally relevant programs to make learning more meaningful. The entire T. P. Callaghan reform plan was crafted around the school's circumstances and environment. Although the practitioners studied other curriculum models and strategies, they designed customized programs that suited T. P. Callaghan Middle School students uniquely. Ultimately, I conclude that T. P. Callaghan experienced successful outcomes because they shared leadership, focused on specific outcomes, and collaboratively created an authentic learning community for students and adults.

AUTHOR'S NOTE

This article was first published in the *Journal of Curriculum and Supervision*, 18(3) Spring 2003, 240-258. Reprinted by permission.

NOTES

1. This school name is a pseudonym.
2. Critical Friends Group (CFG) is a form of teacher-led study group that originated in 1995 at the Annenberg Institute for School Reform at Brown University through a program entitled the National School Reform Faculty (NSRF). In 2000 the NSRF moved to the Harmony School Education Center in Bloomington, IN. For more information see http://www.harmony.pvt.k12.in.us/.
3. As a school in the larger research project from which this paper was drawn, T. P. Callaghan Middle School was carefully examined as one of 12 case study schools. I gratefully acknowledge the contributions of the case study research team as helpful in expanding my understanding of the school's history and in serving as validation of my independent findings.
4. All names presented are pseudonyms.
5. Teacher's rubric.
6. Some of these teacher reflections are examined in detail in Cheryl Craig's chapter in this volume, "Inquiry as Stance: An Administrator-Initiated Narrative Practice."
7. For more information about the accountability system, see the Texas Education Agency (TEA) website at http://www.tea.state.tx.us/perfreport/account/. TEA has recently revised the accountability system and developed a new testing standard, the Texas Assessment of Knowledge and Skills (TAKS). The new system went into effect in 2003.

REFERENCES

Ball, D.L., & Cohen, D.K. (1999). Developing practice, developing practitioners: Toward a practice-based theory of professional development. In L. Darling-Hammond & G. Sikes (Eds.), *Teaching as the learning profession: Handbook of policy and practice*. San Francisco: Jossey-Bass.

Cohen, D.K., Raudenbush, S.W., & Ball, D.L. (2000). *Resources, instruction, and research: A CTP Working Paper.* Seattle: University of Washington, Center for the Study of Teaching and Policy.

Eisner, E.W. (1998). *The kind of schools we need: Personal essays*. Portsmouth, NH: Heinemann.

Goodman, N. (1978). *Ways of worldmaking*. Indianapolis, IN: Hackett.

Lieberman, A. (Ed.). (1988). *Building a professional culture in schools*. New York: Teachers College Press.

Little, J.W. (1993). Teachers' professional development in a climate of educational reform. *Educational Evaluation and Policy Analysis, 15*(2), 129-151.

McLaughlin, M., Talbert, J., & Bascia, N. (Eds.). (1990). *The contexts of teaching in secondary schools*. New York: Teachers College Press.

Shulman, L. (1987). Knowledge and teaching: Foundations of the new reform. *Harvard Educational Review, 57*(1), 1-22.

Sparks, D. (2000). Foreword. In T.R. Guskey (Ed.), *Evaluating professional development*. Thousand Oaks, CA: Corwin Press.

Spillane, J.P. (2000). *District leaders' perceptions of teacher learning: CPRE Occasional Paper.* Philadelphia: University of Pennsylvania, Consortium for Policy Research in Education.

Spillane, J.P., Halverson, R., & Diamond, J.B. (2002). *Towards a theory of leadership practice: A distributed perspective*. Working paper, Institute for Policy Research, Northwestern University.

Westheimer, J. (1998). *Among schoolteachers: Community, autonomy, and ideology in teachers' work*. New York: Teachers College Press.

CHAPTER 7

INQUIRY AS STANCE

An Administrator-Initiated Narrative Practice

Cheryl J. Craig

ABSTRACT

This chapter chronicles the development of a narrative practice that grew out of a Critical Friends Group activities underway at T. P. Callaghan Middle School. It reports the use of email and written correspondence between the principal and the teachers in ways that supported the educator's personal professional growth. The work includes the "tests" some teachers devised to gauge the principal's actual engagement and support, and the results of the email and written exchanges.

INTRODUCTION

Over the past two decades, teacher professional development at T. P. Callaghan Middle School,[1] a campus located in a major urban center in a mid-southern state, has changed in how it has been designed, delivered and received. In the 1980s, the Madeline Hunter input-output model dominated. Following that, other forms of school district mandated pro-

Deep Change: Cases and Commentary on Reform in High Stakes States, 107–120

fessional development prevailed. Next, a state-directed, national reform initiative determined that "models of teaching" would form the teacher professional development at Callaghan. When a second major national reform movement set up a local office in the urban center in 1997, the school proposed that it would become a professional development academy for faculty members from other campuses. The school district supported the school's reform plan by allowing the Callaghan teachers to teach extra minutes per day, thus enabling Friday afternoons to be solely dedicated to professional development.

Under the strong leadership of Callaghan's former principal, the essential groundwork for a leading edge, inquiry as stance approach to teacher learning was put in place. The remaining challenge was that the 85 members of the Callaghan faculty had never had the chance to determine their own professional development experiences. Thus, when the opportunity arose, the educators began to plan for one another in the exact same way as people external to the school had always done. Simply put, alternate approaches to teacher learning neither existed, nor had they been imagined.

When the previous principal retired, the Callaghan teachers were no longer content with externally driven teacher professional development. With the funding available from the second reform movement, they wanted to take hold of teacher learning—first for themselves and their school, then for others and their schools—by becoming a model of how high quality professional development could be enacted on a large, urban campus. As can be seen, Callaghan's reform plan changed as the school's relationship with the reform movement took shape. As one faculty member succinctly put it, the proposed changes "changed." With assistance from the reform movement, the Callaghan faculty found space, time, funds and support with which to experiment with how to productively alter the approach to teacher learning at the school.

When Brian Patrick was named principal of T. P. Callaghan Middle School in 1999, he did not initiate campus-designed and supported professional development at the school: the faculty demanded it. The demand naturally grew from the teachers' discontent with the less-than-satisfying approaches that had been tried over time. It also stemmed from that fact that two cohorts of Callaghan educators participated in the original Critical Friends Groups associated with the reform movement (Cushman, 1999). As circumstance would have it, Brian Patrick happened to be one of the original coaches. Not only had Brian, first as a teacher, then as an Assistant Principal, lived the checkered history of professional development at T. P. Callaghan Middle School, he had also facilitated a Critical Friends Group where he met face-to-face the reasons why the mass approach to professional development at Callaghan needed to be changed. In the CFG group meetings, Bob experienced the power of reflective practice and came to value how inquiry as stance approaches met the diverse needs, issues, and interests of individual teachers and small groups of teachers.

In 1999-2000, T. P. Callaghan Middle School became the first campus in the reform movement to engage in full school Critical Friends Group meetings during school hours. This development was highly significant, but Brian Patrick knew it was not enough. He recognized that the Callaghan teachers also needed to engage in personal professional inquiries that would complement and extend what was taking place in the Critical Friends Group meetings. Furthermore, as principal, Bob felt the need to stay in touch with the teachers' concerns and interests and to personally come to know each faculty member better. He additionally knew the school district, the reform movement, and the public at large would hold him accountable for the teachers' growth in what could only be perceived as an unconventional approach to professional development. Against this backdrop, Brian Patrick initiated a narrative practice—email and written communications—with the teachers at T. P. Callaghan as a way to support the personal inquiries that teachers engage in when they pursue their personal professional development interests.

Brian began by publicly declaring that eleven Friday afternoons of the school year would be dedicated to individual and small group personal learning. Patrick prefaced the introduction of his inquiry oriented, narrative practice with the following written explanation:

> We no longer evaluate our profession from the standpoint of becoming a better teacher, rather—improvement with respect to learning. There is a big difference between the two (teaching and learning). We can become better teachers, but our greatest and most meaningful challenge is that of becoming a better learner. It is only through continuous and purposeful learning that we can positively impact the achievement and cognitive and affective growth of our students.

When he first introduced the time for personal/small group inquiry and expressed his desire to be involved in it, the Callaghan teachers dutifully responded. Behind the scenes, however, many questioned whether he actually read their plans, questions and wonders or whether the new form of communication merely became part of another intricate paper trail designed to monitor, not improve, practice. Then one teacher broke the ice. In the middle of a lengthy reflective passage, the teacher wrote that if Brian honestly read his communication, they would meet after school to discuss his professional development interests and concerns. When Patrick promptly accepted the faculty member's invitation, his action conveyed not only to him but also to the Callaghan faculty that the reflective exchanges were being taken seriously. News traveled fast in the rambling old school building. Soon most of the teachers saw the reflective space Brian created as one where each individual could have "one-on-one" time with the school principal. This point was further reinforced when Brian repeatedly shared the purpose of his narrative practice with the teachers in faculty meetings. What follows is a verbatim explanation he offered in one such meeting:

> In your individual focused planning time last week, each of you wrote about something different—as well as something you plan to do in a different way—in order to address our students' needs. I read some phenomenal reflective comments about your practices.

He went on to say:

> I suppose the lingering question for some of you is what does he do with these pieces? (Reads and thinks about them) And are they actually read? The bottom line is that it is a reflective tool for you, as a professional, to document your ever-changing journey. It is a reflective way to look at such things as the influence of culture, the needs of middle school children, and the development of successful school programs.

In the sections that follow, seven examples of how six representative teachers and one group of teachers responded to the narrative practice initiated by their principal are featured. In the exchanges, the diversity of teachers' professional development interests and the nature of classroom challenges at Callaghan bubbled to the surface.

EXAMPLE 1: ASSESSMENT PLAN, MIDDLE YEARS PROGRAM

This first example, written in the form of a letter, explains how one teacher made sense of assessment in the middle years program being implemented at the school.

Dear Brian,

I am giving you a copy of everything I have been working on regarding my assessment plan for this school year. I'm giving it to you for several reasons. I would love to have you question or challenge me on anything you see or wonder about, because I know that a parent or colleague will at some time, and I would like to be able to clear up any "loose ends" or holes in my technique now. I also want you to know what I am up to in my classroom in case I need your support on any matter where parents are concerned.

In a nutshell what I have done is develop a grading rubric for my entire course. The Learning Objectives come straight from the Middle

Years Program, and the design of the rubric does as well. Basically, I've set up an assessment criterion that is MY PLAN for teaching and the student's plan for learning. If you look at the Assessment Descriptors, the highest level of achievement is what I am pushing the student toward. So, I better teach at that level. That is how my approach to assessment works for me. It forces me to think about what I will be teaching on a daily basis to bring my students up to that level. The rubric is used throughout the year to monitor student growth along the way. The rubric is used in the end result as a way to determine where my students are when they leave my class.

I am using various techniques to measure and document this growth (There is a list of Assessment Techniques attached as well). I am pretty clear about what "evidence" is for these areas. Ideally, I should be able to sit with a student, their parent, another teacher, or you, and examine the student's work in my class, along with my running records, etc., against these descriptors and really determine where that student is at any point throughout the year. This is all in the plan—I really think I can make it work.

Some of the premises that brought me to this point are the ones that we have been talking about as a group [as a faculty and in our CFG Groups]—how to really measure student growth—how to move from grading students to really examining student work and learning—how to assess both student work and the student at work, etc.

Anyway when you have an opportunity to read it over, have a "House-of-Pies" moment, and let me know what you think.[2] Like I said—I look forward to discussing any tough concerns or questions.

Sincerely,
6th Grade Teacher

EXAMPLE 2: THINKING SKILLS AND READING PROGRAM

A middle school teacher who teaches thinking skills and reading wrote this second piece that explores her recent feelings of unease.

My recent time was spent considering how to improve my plans for this nine-week period. As I reflected over the past nine weeks, I was unhappy to discover that I had covered much less material than I had planned. I needed to find out what was the cause of my lack of progress. I discovered a couple of reasons.

This year I had a more difficult time dividing my mind into my two subject areas. This was because:

1. I am studying the art of teaching reading more deeply and it is difficult to come out of that way of thinking.
2. I am developing a different curriculum for Thinking Skills and I need to spend more time in the development phase.
3. The people I work with are so smart and so ingenious that I have to work three times as hard as I normally do just to keep up with them.
4. (This is a complaint) The schedules took so long to set and the students were moved around so much that I lost weeks in the presentation of my stuff. Schedules are still being shifted. (A big problem, for me, is the rearranging of thinking skills. Students should not get a choice of their teachers. They get who they get!)

Addressing the problems:

1. The Friday time really helps. I can spend much of that time reading and developing lessons that improve the quality of the information I am presenting. I just need to make sure that I do not waste that time doing nit-picky stuff—like cleaning my room. This has got to be just 'me' time.
2. I have to learn to ask for help. I do not actually know a lot about building and tools and the like, but there is a myriad of resources surrounding me in this school, and I must utilize them. This problem also is a blessing because it ensures that my class is always fresh—that makes me happy.
3. Too bad—so sad—I just have to work harder. What a privilege it is to work with such talented and smart people. This certainly raises the quality of education available to the students in our cluster.
4. I just need to get over this problem, but it would help if people who change schedules would not accommodate students solely on student likes and/or dislikes.

EXAMPLE 3: HEALTH AND PHYSICAL EDUCATION

In this third excerpt, a Health and Physical Education teacher at Callaghan describes an inquiry he embarked on during his self-determined professional development time.

I believe that teachers need to become better learners to promote student learning. With the pool of information available in libraries and electronic databases, I think teachers can become better learners through tapping into these resources and using them effectively.

In conjunction with Friday's individual/small group study, I utilized the time to read, brainstorm and plan ways to incorporate cooperative learning strategies in my classroom. The article, "Cooperative Learning in the Physical Education Classroom," *Journal of Physical Education, Recreation, and Dance* [JOPERD] was used as the foundation of my individual study. Where the reform movement imperatives are concerned, cooperative learning de-emphasizes isolation. The objectives of cooperative learning are to improve group interaction, communication skills, individual teacher time with students, active or engaged learning time, classroom behavior and students' internalization and application of knowledge. This article explains how to implement cooperative learning strategies. By using these strategies, I intend to look at and modify my approaches in the classroom. By continuing to learn existing and new information, I hope to promote student learning at Callaghan. Next session my objective will be to explore the latest research with respect to motivation with the intent of learning some new motivational strategies for Health and Physical Education.

EXAMPLE 4: LEARNING THROUGH THE ARTS

In this fourth example, a teacher describes how she plans to integrate visual art in her English classes. In the process, she describes the purpose the activity serves for her, others, and the students she teaches.

The focus of my study is to integrate visual art into my English classes. Learning will be increased through my participation as a "teacher-in-residence" in the Learning Through Art Program at the Museum of Fine Arts.

This year I will attend a series of lectures, which will familiarize teachers with the museum's permanent works and provide background in the history of these pieces. These lectures occur on Saturdays (approximately one full Saturday a month) and in the evenings (two evenings a month). The time commitment is substantial, but the resulting knowledge will make it more than worthwhile.

The eventual outcome (over the next few years) will be a published book of our units, which the museum will sell to other districts interested in including the study of art in their classrooms. I will measure personal success in this endeavor by observing and evaluating the quality of my students' work when I present the units in class. I will also consider the degree to which students can make connections between literary and visual concepts such as theme, symbolism, characterization, perspective, tone and style.

I feel that this project is invaluable and reflects the areas of interaction prescribed in the International Baccalaureate Middle Years Program, most obviously in my subject area, but also with respect to approaches to learning about health, social education, and environment.

I have always felt that the arts—literary, performing, and visual—should be integrated and have sought to include various works of art into my lessons, including videos of dramatic performances, photographs, prints of painting, songs, examples of sculpture, and crafts. I think an English classroom should provide opportunities for students to experience new cultures through multi-sensory approaches. The state objectives emphasize the importance of viewing, interpreting, analyzing, and producing visual images and messages in the English Classroom (Objectives 7.22,7.23 and 7.24). Objective 7.4 particularly speaks to the importance of gaining an appreciation of one's own culture and that of others. With a world-class art museum merely blocks away from the school, there is really no excuse not to incorporate the works into classroom activities.

This experience will provide me with the additional learning I need to continue to write and teach fresh, innovative lessons that will affect my students' academic, cultural and personal growth.

EXAMPLE 5: HISTORY

In the fifth example, a history teacher tells of how he took advantage of the enormous learning possibilities inherent in a museum visit. He, like the teacher in Example 1, wrote his reflective piece in the form of a letter.

Dear Brian,

On Friday, I went to the Museum of Natural History to view a traveling exhibit. I did so to enhance my knowledge of the subject area and to see if a possible field trip for my students might make sense.

The exhibit was very impressive. It dealt with 'explanation' as a theme then focused on 'British scientific explanations.' The purpose of the exhibit was to highlight the explanations compiled on the British ships: The Endeavor, The Challenger, and The Beagle. The scientific process was featured through presenting dozens of actual species collected by the researchers. There were truly amazing field drawings, scientific and naval tools, cartography, tools, samples of flora and fauna as well as a large exhibit on longitude and latitude. The clashes of culture were effectively displayed. The exhibit additionally made effective use of multimedia display and interactive devices.

My goal is to increase my content knowledge as much as possible and whenever possible. I do not know how to qualify questions like "What will be different about you?" Knowledge is vastly more global than that. All I can say is the more I know, the greater the intellectual authority I carry into the classroom and the broader the perspective available to my students. The same is also true for occasionally stepping off the rather small universe of Callaghan Middle School into the larger universe off campus.

Sincerely,
7th Grade Teacher

EXAMPLE 6: FOREIGN LANGUAGE

In this sixth illustration, a foreign language teacher at Callaghan discusses with Patrick how she adapts her class to meet the needs of Attention Deficit Disorder students.

I have spent the last two months reflecting. I started teaching at Callaghan with a lot of enthusiasm. I love foreign languages and I wanted to make this program accessible to all students. In the beginning I concentrated my efforts on discovering new strategies to help the most disadvantaged group, immigrant Hispanic students, in reaching their academic goals. I noticed that many Hispanic students were happy to understand Latin and Italian and were thrilled with the possibility of learning English. To all of them the goal of attending college is something incredible.

Pretty soon I discovered that some students in all my classes exhibited a level of ATTENTION DEFICIT DISORDER. I concentrated my efforts on developing different strategies in order to hold their attention. I started a program of tutoring in the afternoon from 3:30 p.m. to 5.00 p.m. in order to help my students reach the academic standards in Latin 7; I also started a program of Grammar and Analysis. I noticed that all the students with the attention problem were able to focus better and dramatically increase their potential. Starting this week, the students are beginning to translate English into Latin. This will be very beneficial because it will help them use memory (Vocabulary) and reasoning (Application of Grammar and Latin cases). In my opinion, serious cases of attention deficit disorder can be improved through these activities. I also started to work with Theater in Latin and I noticed that many shy kids improved and acquired a sense of security.

My goal is to focus on each individual student's ability to learn. For that reason, I must adopt different strategies. I believe that LEARNING is the essential key and I need to find different tools in order to connect with my students' minds. I am doing my best to offer classes with a lot of visuals and different sources of information. I know my strengths; I spend a lot of time refining my abilities and improving my weaknesses. I am very maternal and I am providing my students with a great deal of attention. I am quite sure they feel a warm and secure environment in my classes.

I studied adolescent psychology and I am trying my best to help my students in this difficult period of puberty. At the same time, I am focused on strong academic goals. My students' LEARNING is my concern. I was a gifted and talented child; so are my two children. Gifted and talented children need a lot of special attention because they can easily feel very alienated.

I notice that I am growing with my students. My imagination has developed, so has my capacity to adapt. My patience and desire to improve are very solid. I love my students and I love to teach. Of course I have continued passion for LEARNING.

EXAMPLE 7: REFLECTIONS ON LEARNING IN A SMALL GROUP BOOK STUDY

In the seventh example, three reading teachers at Callaghan Middle School wrote a poem to reflect what they learned from reading the following books: The Art of Teacher Reading *by Lucy Calkins and* Mosaic of Thought *by Eileen Keene.*

> *Once or twice she had peeped into the book her sister was reading,*
> *It had no pictures or conversations in it,*
> *"and what is the use of the book" thought Alice, "without pictures or conversations."*
> —from *Alice's Adventures in Wonderland* by Lewis Caroll

And we ask ourselves,
with the art of reading teaching
before our eyes and beyond our reach,
how?
How to teach questioning,
how to teach visualizing,
how to teach wondering,
how to teach connecting,
to the child with no questions,
no wonders,
no connections,
and no pictures or conversations

peeping and whispering
from the pages of the book—

Alice had not a moment to think about stopping herself before she found herself falling down what seemed to be
a very deep well. Either the well was very deep, or she fell very slowly,
for she had plenty of time as she went down to look at her,
And to wonder what was going to happen next.

Flipping back to remembered pages
Gliding our fingers across the lines
We reread
To ourselves
To each other,
Connecting Calkins to classroom,
Kenne to colleagues,
and text to students,
we wonder—
is the data accurate,
or does it become curiousor and curiousor
the closer you look?
Are we teaching a test, a text,
Or a student?—
And we question—
What does Calkins mean by
"a curriculum of talk"
and Keene by
"a mosaic of thought"
and with these questions stirring the air—

She puzzled over this for some time, but at last a bright thought struck her.
"Why, it's a Looking-Glass book, of course!
And if I hold it up to a glass, the words will all go the right way again."

And then we laugh,
And breathe,
And realize—
We will teach them to do
What we do as readers—
To touch the text with our fingers,
To question the text with our curiosity,
To visualize the text with our pictures,
To connect to the text with our lives,

And to enter that Wonderland that is
Reading.

And Alice knelt down and looked along the passage into the loveliest garden you ever saw.

STRENGTHS, CONSIDERATIONS, AND FUTURE POSSIBILITIES OF THE INQUIRY ORIENTED, NARRATIVE PRACTICE

This small slice of a principal-initiated narrative practice within one urban, middle school context clearly shows the plurality of teachers' professional development interests and the richness of their inquiries when they are able to direct their personal and small group learning. What also emerges are the issues with which teachers wrestle daily: the matter of how instruction relates to assessment/evaluation, the needs of special learners, how people learn together, how to merge learning inside and outside of school, and so on. Also highly evident is the nature of knowledge that teachers already hold and express in their practices as well as the generative way their learning unfolds over time when freedom to choose personal professional learning is allowed.

In the featured examples, it is clear the teachers needed to describe their personal professional development in order to inquire into it and to narrate their experiences of it. The question of how to balance description and narrative in texts of this nature arises. So, too, emerges the idea of how the teachers and the principal can move from merely describing personal professional development to illuminating what has been learned from it. These are fundamentally different tasks that are necessarily entwined. However, a danger exists that individuals may hide behind "cover stories" of description while never interrogating their personal professional development experiences (Clandinin & Connelly, 1995; Craig, 2000; Olson & Craig, 2001). For the principal, the question becomes one of how to assist teachers who are uncomfortable and not thriving at the task. Furthermore, given the invitational nature of the practice, a secondary issue has to do with the one or two individuals who refuse to participate in the exchanges. This is a particularly important consideration when an untenured, beginning principal is being held responsible for the professional development of teachers at Callaghan Middle School.

This leads to a second "cover story" caution. Even within this practice, opportunities exist for teachers to respond with what they imagine their principal would like to hear versus an elaboration of what they are actually engaging in and learning in the unassigned time. The notion of how to maintain the authenticity of space and communication emerges. This is true both for the administrator and the participating teachers.

A significant strength of this practice is that it nurtures the relationships between the principal and members of a very large faculty. In many ways, Brian Patrick is personalizing learning for the middle school teachers just like they aim to personalize learning for large numbers of students. Trust between individuals develops. Nevertheless, the hierarchical relationships that sit in the background must never be taken for granted. In both cases, it is critical that information made public to individuals with more institutionally ascribed power in one situation not be used against individuals with less power in other situations, particularly where formal evaluation is concerned. This is a consideration that all educators must constantly keep in mind.

A second consideration is that the principal-teacher ratio, like the student-teacher ratio, is seriously out of balance. A principal, like a teacher, must deal with numbers that far exceed human capacity. As such, response to individuals and groups of teachers may not occur as quickly as anticipated. In the Callaghan situation, a case in point arose with the Language Arts teachers featured in the seventh example. In the midst of another reflective comment, one teacher candidly wrote:

> I am reeling from the fact that you never commented on our incredibly intelligent reflection that included allusions and nods to *Alice in Wonderland*, as well as high degree of creativity and higher level thinking skills. Oh, well. We are working on another one now, wherein the plot twists and turns unexpectedly, yet intriguingly centers on a pan of fudge cooked by my Aunt Barbara.

In Patrick's response, he addressed the issue and legitimately raised another point that bears consideration. We might ask: Is it possible the principal's reply was delayed not only by demands placed on his time, but also by his desire to respond in an equally penetrating manner? Brian's explanation appears to convey this mixture of views:

> Regarding your "incredibly intelligent reflection (*Alice in Wonderland*) with the high degree of creativity and thinking skills...," it is **clearly** at the application and synthesis level ... I do apologize for not commenting promptly on the excellent work you trio did but it has taken me a heck of a long time to figure out the **real meaning** of the work! The **depth and complexity** demonstrated by you high achievers challenged me to some "real" thinking.... You are doing great work together—I really do appreciate your dedication and love for our kids.

This latter caution and consideration gives way to strong possibilities that naturally arise out of Brian Patrick's administrator-initiated narrative practice. Once the reflective exchanges between Callaghan teachers and their principal become firmly established, it is entirely possible that individual teachers and groups of teachers may want to dialogue with one another with Brian Patrick serving in a discussant role to ease time constraints. Furthermore, posting the narrative exchanges on a password-safe section of the school's website would enable teachers who normally do not communicate with one another to respond to one another—not because they feel obligated to—but because they feel compelled to enter into powerful discussions with their peers and administrators. As can be seen, the inquiry oriented, narrative practice featured in this chapter is filled with rich possibilities for future school growth and teacher development. At the same time, it carries with it cautions and considerations to which mindful attention must be paid along the way.

NOTES

1. In all other research reports, the school is identified as T. P. Yeager
2. Brian Patrick was known for his fondness for frequenting this local restaurant for a dessert.

REFERENCES

Clandinin, D.J., & Connelly, F.M. (1995). *Teachers' professional knowledge landscapes.* New York: Teachers College Press.

Craig, C.J. (2000). Stories of school/teacher stories: A two-part invention on the walls theme. *Curriculum Inquiry, 30*(1), 11-41.

Cushman, K. (1999). Educators making portfolios: First results of the national reform faculty. *Phi Delta Kappan, 80*(10), 744-749.

Olson, M., & Craig, C. J. (2001, April). *Uncovering cover stories: Claiming not to know what we know and why we do it.* Paper presented at the American Educational Research Association Annual Meeting, Seattle, WA.

CHAPTER 8

NEGOTIATING TENSIONS IN SCHOOL REFORM

Efforts to Promote a Learning Community in an Urban Middle School

Fern Dallas and David Strahan

ABSTRACT

This chapter documents ways that a group of sixth grade teachers in an urban middle school attempted to form a professional learning community. During the 2002-03 school year, they met once a week to consider ways to implement state and local mandates for improving their reading instruction. Participants describe the challenges they faced as they worked together to improve their own morale and enhance student achievement. Results underscore the complexity of reform initiatives with low performing middle schools.

INTRODUCTION

In the event of an in-flight emergency, oxygen masks will drop from the overhead compartment above your seat. For those of you traveling with

Deep Change: Cases and Commentary on Reform in High Stakes States, 121–140

> small children, first place the oxygen mask on your own face and then place the mask on the child's face.

Although it may stretch the metaphor to suggest that teachers in urban schools are breathing their last gasps, a critical dimension of school reform in challenging settings is caring for the caregivers. Following the flight attendant's instructions, teachers need to preserve themselves so that they can address the needs of their students. Unfortunately, in an era of public and political demands for school reform, retention of qualified teachers has become an issue of major significance. The needs are greatest in schools located in impoverished neighborhoods where teacher turnover, at times, has reached epidemic proportions. Teachers in these environments often encounter many situations that generate daily stress which can affect their physical and psychological health (Olson, 2000).

Some schools have attempted to provide additional support for teachers by creating professional learning communities. Recent research has shown that teachers involved in a professional learning community collaborate more with one another on instruction, are more involved in school reculturing through decision making, have higher teaching efficacy, and have higher student achievement. Teachers involved in this type of professional development have reported a sense of renewal and recommitment to their students. In these studies, collaboration between teachers has strengthened classroom instruction and broadened the professional knowledge of the participants. Professional learning communities have increased communication in faculties where teacher isolation was at one time the norm. Teachers involved have reported a greater sense of collegiality and feeling valued within the education profession (Leonard & Leonard, 1999; Midgley, Feldlaufer, & Eccles, 1989; Langer, 2000; Chester & Beaudin, 1998; Dallas, 2002).

This chapter documents ways that a group of sixth grade teachers in an urban middle school attempted to form a professional learning community. During the 2002-03 school year, they met once a week to consider ways to implement state and local mandates for improving their reading instruction. Based on a dissertation study, this chapter describes the challenges they faced as they worked together to improve their own morale and enhance student achievement (Dallas, 2003).

CONCEPTUAL FRAMEWORK

A growing body of research has suggested that teacher resiliency is a critical factor in teacher retention and in classroom success. Bobek (2002) defined resiliency as the ability to adjust to changing situations and increase one's competence in the face of adverse conditions. As described by Brown, D'Emidio-Caston, and Benard (1996), resilient individuals overcome their circumstances and even "succeed despite risk and adversity" through social competence, problem solving skills, autonomy, and a sense of purpose and future (p. 118). Brown et al. concluded that conditions that foster resiliency include caring and support that links beliefs and actions; positive and high expectations that encourage engagement; and opportunities for meaningful participation in school that create a sense of community and promote personal and shared empowerment (Gordon & Coscarelli, 1996; Bobek, 2000; Brown et al., 1996).

These factors that promote resiliency among adults can be cultivated in middle school teachers through the development of professional learning communities. In their analysis of the complexities inherent in teacher development, Cochran-Smith and Lytle (1996) propose that there are at least three different conceptions of teacher learning that manifest themselves in efforts to promote professional learning communities. In "knowledge for practice" communities, the role of the teacher is to "solve problems by implementing certified procedures" (p. 299). These communities encourage teachers to adopt and implement practices that have been selected for their use in a technical fashion. "Knowledge in practice" communities emphasize the wisdom of practice of experienced teachers and encourage teachers to work together as colleagues to improve teaching collaboratively (p. 263). In the third type of community, "knowledge of practice," participants' knowledge is "socially co-constructed through inquiry and collaboration" (p. 273). Cochran-Smith and Lytle noted the tensions that emerge among these three fundamentally different views of teachers' roles and responsibilities when participants received conflicting messages about the nature and purposes of collaboration.

These conflicting messages can create a need for participants in learning communities to negotiate their work together. Glickman, Gordon, and Ross-Gordon (2004) concluded that successful reform requires teachers to work with their team mates in a fashion that is "collegial," not just "congenial," the distinction being the extent to which their interactions are "purposeful" and directed toward "improving schoolwide teaching and learning" (p. 6). While it is certainly helpful if teachers get along well, it is also important that they form a working community if they are to make substantial improvements in instruction.

Coburn found that teachers involved in school reforms reshaped and even transformed policies within the contexts of their professional communities before they enacted reforms. Formal and informal conversations with colleagues helped teachers "make sense" of policy messages and determine which policies to implement and which policies to reject. Coburn (2001) pointed out that teachers' professional communities are important for sense making, and they highlight "the ways in which local teacher communities can form powerful microcultures that mediate environmental pressures" (p. 145).

Coburn suggested that the key factor in this "sense making" was the nature of the conversations teachers had with one another. "When teachers came into contact with new messages about reading instruction, they often spent time with their colleagues constructing an understanding of what the messages meant." Some messages for the teacher were easily comprehended while others required "quite a bit of conversation" for teachers to understand. Obviously, not all the messages about reading could be incorporated into classroom practice, and so the teachers' professional communities played a crucial gate-keeping role. From their conversations in these communities teachers made sense of the given message and either engaged the idea or dismissed it. "In conversations with their colleagues, teachers rejected messages from the environment for a range of reasons, many of which were linked with their worldviews or shared understandings" (Coburn, 2001, pp. 152, 154).

At Main Street Middle School, teachers were involved in multiple reform initiatives during the 2002-2003 school year, several of which focused entirely on literacy instruction. Teachers received suggestions from many sources including the program consultants, workshops they attended, their literacy facilitator, their local administration, and the district administration. They tried to "make sense" of these suggestions, deciding to adopt, adapt, or reject them based on their beliefs and their conversations with each other. This study examined those dynamics.

THE SETTING

Main Street Middle School is an urban middle school located in a predominately working class neighborhood in a small southeastern United States city. The school serves approximately 700 students in grades six through eight. Students bring a rich cultural mix of languages, customs and values from America and from abroad. The ethnic make-up of the school is approximately 90% minority students. See Table 8.1 for the student demographics at Main Street. There are 14 different languages spoken in the homes of these students.

Since the beginning of the state student assessment system in 1996, they have received no recognition for student achievement. The faculty and staff are placing major emphasis on increasing the proficiency levels of all students. Currently, the principal reports that 59% of the students are performing proficiently by the end-of-grade, standardized state testing program compared to the district average of 69% of the students. The

Table 8.1. Student Demographics at Main Street Middle School 2002-2003

	African American	*Caucasian*	*Asian American*	*Hispanic*	*Other Minorities*
Percentage	73%	10%	8%	4%	5%

Table 8.2. Faculty Demographic Percentages for 2002-2003

African American	*Caucasian*	*First Year Teachers*	*Lateral Entry Teachers*	*New Administrators*
53%	47%	20%	22%	66%

most commonly used indicator of the socioeconomic status of a school is the percentage of students who qualify for free and reduced lunch. At Main Street 83% of the students qualify for this service.

Main Street Middle School has a staff of forty-nine teachers, three administrators, and sixteen support personnel determined to raise achievement scores. Although the school suffers approximately a 24% turnover annually, 35% of the teachers have been teaching at Main Street for more than four years and have earned tenure. Forty-two percent of the faculty is new to Main Street in the last two years. Among these, 22% are uncertified lateral entry teachers, and 20% are beginning or initially licensed teachers. See Table 8.2.

Main Street Middle School experienced a change in administration in the summer of 2002. A new principal and assistant principal replaced two of the three previous administrators. The new principal brought with her a strong leadership style and ideas of how to move students academically to meet the goals set by the state. The staff has joined her with a School Improvement Plan (2002-2003) that focuses on:

- increasing the proficiency levels of students in reading,
- increasing the proficiency levels of students in mathematics,
- providing modification for students in the Exceptional Children Program,
- providing staff development for addressing differentiation,
- establishing quality teaming among teachers to integrate reading and mathematics in all areas,
- continuing literacy training to help increase reading scores,
- addressing the needs of all students (including students in Exceptional Children's Program, 504 & Limited English Proficiency), and

- increasing parental involvement in all educational areas of the school.

All of these initiatives required a great deal of change in classroom schedules, procedures, and structures. The principal introduced flexible grouping as the desired method of instruction. She hired a consultant to provide staff development for all the Language Arts teachers and literacy staff in the school. She created a master schedule so teachers could spend time together planning, and she expected teachers to form professional learning communities to plan intensively to meet the needs of each student.

THE PARTICIPANTS

The 6th grade Language Arts teachers agreed to participate in this study of professional learning communities. As a group they face the greatest challenges for academic growth for their students. Historically the sixth grade has performed lower than the rest of the school on state reading tests. In the previous year, Main Street sixth grade scored 56.6% proficient while the school average was 59.06% proficient. In fact, in the last two years the sixth grade reading scores have seen a marked decline as measured by the state End-of-grade Reading assessment. See Table 8.3 for the reading scores. The principal has mandated the 6th grade goal for growth as "70% of the students reading on grade level by February, 2003" (Personal communication).

During the previous years the Language Arts teachers did not work or plan collaboratively. Because this was their first year to form or participate in a professional learning community, it was an ideal situation to study. This community of teachers comprised a first year, uncertified, lateral entry teacher (Matthew), a first year, elementary certified teacher (Akkia), a third year, middle grades language arts certified teacher (Joy), and an experienced seven year, elementary certified teacher (Ken). Also joining this group were Barbara and Abbey. Barbara was a teacher of exceptional children who met with children of special needs in her class-

Table 8.3. Percentage of Students Scoring at the Proficient level in 6th Grade Reading

	1999-2000	*2000-2001*	*2001-2002*	*2002-2003 Goal*
District Average	70.3	69.7	72.1	
Main Street	53.2	39.6	56.6	61.6

room as well as inclusion in the regular classrooms of the other teachers. Abbey was a middle grades certified language arts teacher who supported the team by providing additional focus for below grade level readers. She provided small group instruction with students from each of the regular classes. Ken, a veteran teacher, has a Master's degree in education and served as the department leader.

PROCEDURES

The first author served as a participant observer in the professional learning community. This year-long study began at the beginning of the 2002-2003 school year when the researcher met with the group and began the task of establishing rapport (Stake, 1995). Individual interviews were conducted at the beginning of the year to elicit the participants' expectations of the professional learning community and the overall school improvement initiatives. The first author attended and took field notes at all group meetings and professional development opportunities involving the sixth grade Language Arts professional learning community, both voluntary by the group or mandated by the principal. After midyear the first author interviewed the teachers again to learn their perceptions of their professional learning community and how these professional relationships contribute to their own professional growth. Teachers also completed a questionnaire about the level of implementation of literacy components since that was the focus of their professional development for the year. Final teacher interviews and classroom observations occurred in the spring semester. Teachers completed another questionnaire about their level of implementation of the literacy components and their confidence with their ability to teach the various components. Observations and informal conversations continued throughout the study between the researcher, teachers, and students.

Qualitative data sources included the researcher's field notes from group meetings and informal conversations with the participants while at the school and emails, individual questionnaires, focus group interviews, class observations, group generated artifacts (lesson plans), and 6th grade quarterly reading assessments. The researchers analyzed, coded, and categorized the data using constant comparative analysis and pattern matching. During the 2003-04 school year, the second author visited Main Street Middle School on several occasions and interviewed three of the remaining participants to elicit their views of their collaboration after the fact (Glaser & Corbin, 1997; Yin, 1994).

RESULTS

While each of the teachers in the professional learning community had his or her unique perspective, collectively they formed a new entity that took on a life of its own. The sixth grade Language Arts professional learning community began meeting before school started during the staff development workdays. They had two instructional goals to accomplish during this time. Their first task was to create a year-long scope and sequence for the language arts curriculum. The second task was to figure out how to teach using flexible groups and IMS (Instructional Management System) passages. They had to accomplish both of these tasks as a group.

The initial meetings were awkward for several reasons. For most of the members, this was the first time they had ever planned collaboratively. Not only were they required to plan together, but they were also asked to work with people they did not know. Ken and Joy both were accustomed to planning by themselves, though Joy welcomed the idea of a professional support system.

Consequently, the sixth grade professional learning community had a difficult start. It was especially challenging for them to make sense of the flexible grouping concept. Akkia, who had some experience with grouping during her student teaching at an elementary school, helped the group with her ideas of how to level the groups based on test scores. They grouped their students by their End-of-Grade scores, but had little knowledge of the specific reading levels of the students in each group or what to do with the groups. Most of the teachers simply continued their old teaching methods of whole group instruction with the students sitting in desks arranged in groups. Ken was especially frustrated because the groups created class discipline problems and management issues for him.

In their initial interviews, participants expressed frustrations with the early meetings of the professional learning community:

> We have met every Tuesday since the start of school for our planning meetings, which have ranged from totally disastrous to meetings that are actually somewhat productive. We have a long way to go. (Joy)

> I think at the beginning of the year we didn't have any idea of what was to be going down.... Been confused, more than anything; it's been a lot of changes, so I think everyone is dealing with a bunch of confusion about where do we go and how do we do this, and I didn't expect that. (Matthew)

At the beginning of the year, the group constructed the year-long plan based on literature genres. When the administrator first reviewed their plan, she instructed the group to rewrite their year-long plan to include reading comprehension skills as the major focus. This change did not sit well with the group, but they reluctantly complied. The literacy facilitator provided them with a list of the reading comprehension skills tested, and Ken and Akkia worked on a schedule and sequence to teach all the skills by March.

The major emphasis for the group's staff development became evident in October when all the Language Arts teachers attended a two-day staff development workshop on balanced literacy. The teachers had the opportunity to clarify issues and see components of the model demonstrated during the workshop. The consultant explained each of the eight components, provided the research base behind the model, and motivated the group to "jump right in."

The sixth grade Language Arts professional learning community met after school on the last day of the workshop to decide how to proceed. As a group they agreed to start with the home reading, self-selected silent reading, conferencing, teacher directed reading instruction, and read alouds. They omitted writing because the state writing test had been postponed a year. They conceded that they thought the school schedule did not allow for small group reading instruction or literature circles. Also, they decided to implement word study. An administrator visited the meeting and emphasized implementing read alouds, silent reading, and conferencing on the next Monday. Participants made a list of materials they would need (folders, baskets, and highlighters).

Implementing the literacy components proved to be difficult for the group. The teaching methods were unfamiliar to the group, and they described their initial attempts as "awkward." At a team planning meeting three weeks later, Joy admitted, "I feel so strange reading and doing the think aloud part of the teacher directed instruction." The group agreed, and Matthew added, "I keep wanting to stop and ask questions while I'm reading just to see if they are listening." Ken expressed a need for more pre-reading activities. Akkia made all the conferencing cards for the group, but did not see how she could be conferencing individually if the rest of the class was being disruptive.

By January the group rated their own levels of implementation of the seven basic components of the literacy model. Table 8.4 presents the teachers' self-reported measures.

The one component that the group thought they were doing adequately was the thirty minutes of self-selected silent reading time. Even so, they were not monitoring the levels of the books to match the reading levels of the students. Few of the teachers had given the computerized test to determine comprehension levels. These issues were addressed in the planning meeting in November, and the teachers discussed ways to be more effective during the silent reading time. Matthew successfully implemented one of the ideas which involved assigning a participation grade to

Table 8.4. Self-Reported Implementation of the Literacy Components as of January, 2003

Balanced Literacy Components	*Not at All*	*Barely*	*Some*	*Much*	*Daily*
Read-alouds		Barbara* Akkia	Ken Joy		Matthew
Sustained silent reading with level text		Barbara		Ken	Joy Akkia Matthew
Conferencing		Barbara	Akkia	Ken, Joy Matthew	
Small groups with leveled text		Akkia Joy		Ken, Barbara Matthew	
Teacher directed reading			Joy	Ken, Barbara, Matthew Akkia	
Word and spelling instruction		Ken, Barbara Matthew	Akkia Joy		
Writing		Ken, Barbara Matthew	Akkia Joy		
Literature circles	Everyone				

*Barbara is an EC teacher who floats to all the classrooms. Abbey chose not to complete this section because she is not responsible for classroom instruction and scheduling.

the reading time. He indicated that really helped him get more conferencing accomplished.

During the spring semester, the group attempted to implement additional components and to do so with more frequency. The levels of usage they reported were corroborated with classroom observations by the researcher (see Table 8.5). In spite of their shaky beginning, the group made a great deal of progress in a short amount of time. By the end of the spring semester, the majority of the teachers had implemented a majority of the components of the literacy program.

NEGOTIATING TENSIONS IN SCHOOL REFORM

The professional learning community progressed through several stages of development. As stated earlier, all of the teachers agreed the early meetings were difficult. However, the group persisted, determined to satisfy the requirements of the principal even though some of the members were not convinced that what they were doing was best for the students. As they began to focus on the things they could change, the first issue

Table 8.5. Implementation of the Balanced Literacy Components as of Spring, 2003

Literacy Components	*Not at All*	*Barely*	*Some*	*Much*	*Daily*
Read-alouds		Matthew Akkia, Abbey*	Ken Barbara*	Joy	
Sustained silent reading with level text			Barbara		Joy, Akkia, Matthew, Abbey, Ken
Conferencing			Barbara	Ken Akkia	Matthew Abbey, Joy
Small groups with leveled text			Joy, Akkia	Ken, Abbey Barbara Matthew	
Teacher directed reading				Ken Barbara Joy	Matthew Abbey Akkia
Word and spelling instruction	Matthew Abbey	Ken	Akkia Joy Barbara		
Writing		Matthew Abbey Barbara, Ken	Joy		Akkia
Literature circles	Matthew Abbey Barbara Ken, Akkia	Joy			

*Barbara visits all the classrooms for EC modification
*Abbey pulls students from the regular classroom for small group tutoring

they addressed was classroom discipline. They began using each other's classrooms for "time outs" for students who were being disruptive.

Another problem the professional learning community addressed was eliminating the isolation among department members, replacing it with collaborative support. Joy, in her second year at Main Street, indicated in an interview that without the relationships built during the planning time, she would feel completely isolated both personally and professionally, especially since she is not on the same floor as the other three members. Akkia and Matthew expressed gratitude toward their colleagues in the community for the new friendships and support provided to them as new teachers. Ken responded that the professional learning community has been a lifesaver for him, an opportunity to vent in a safe environment with people he trusts. Barbara and Abbey, the EC teacher and literacy teacher, both felt very connected to the group and enjoyed the camaraderie as the year progressed. Interestingly, Matthew and Ken put a positive spin on the complaining that characterized some of the meetings, relating in interviews how complaining was "therapeutic of sorts." Matthew elaborated, "They (our students) didn't get to see what we felt and we didn't get to act it out in classroom because we had the opportunity to act it out somewhere else."

During the spring interviews each member noted that the level of support within the professional learning community had been meaningful considering their awkward beginning and the challenging environment of the school:

Joy: As far as people getting along with each other, knowing each other, knowing who everybody is and sort of being supportive of their, our colleagues. I think that has definitely improved.

Ken: It was a huge support. I think we have established relationships. So we were strangers in the beginning and I think we have grown to be close, fairly close group. I think that I feel that I could go to any of them with any professional problem certainly, and some personal things.

Matthew: It's made us, made me feel closer to everyone else, and it just gave me a lot of ideas and everybody more friendly, and I think that actually it's been a big benefit. Because it allowed everybody to get together and share so I actually now can't imagine the year without it.

Akkia: We've gotten closer, that contributes to the relations between each other, because okay we're looking out for each other. As far as getting work together I really haven't had a problem with that because I can go to anyone and get something.

The support that participants received from one another contributed to the resiliency of the group. They were able to overcome their difficult beginning and become a viable and productive learning community. They described the professional learning community at the end of the year like this:

Joy: It has been fun and it's just been fun sharing ideas. Last year any idea I got from anybody was just by accident. This year I just feel like I've been really blessed to hear lot of good ideas, you know and all the wonderful things you've brought in, suggestions, and ideas, and stuff. It's just been a real blessing, so yeah it's been hard, I'd do it all over again even if I knew how it was going to be. It's helped.

Ken: Well its forced me to be flexible because its not always my way. Well, it has certainly unified us in practice, in curriculum matters, which is a good thing.

Matthew: It helped. I think it helped experienced teachers more than it helped me probably. It helped them keep their sanity, because I was one to say, "I'll do whatever you tell me anyway, so I don't … ," whereas they had their own styles and things like that. It helped to be able to get together and vent and share and things like that. It's grown into a great thing and now we get together and laugh and joke.

Akkia: A lot of people around here are like, "You can do it" very encouraging staff, "You'll do great, "if you need anything let me know." It's a lot of that. If I need anything I can go to someone, it's not like I am just out here by myself. But I guess those meetings do help because more than likely, being the type of person that I am, I keep to myself.

Participants expressed more confidence in their teaching at the end of the year. The general consensus was that because they were all teaching the same thing, they were more confident in their lesson preparation. Teachers also completed a self-report survey in the spring, labeling their confidence levels with each of the literacy components (see Table 8.6). Although they expressed confidence in their abilities with certain components, this chart does not represent whether or not they were actually teaching those components. For example, most of the teachers reported feeling confident in their ability to read aloud to their classes, but few of the teachers reported actually doing that consistently due to the discipline problems addressed earlier.

By the end of the year, the professional learning community spent a great deal of their time planning instruction. As they got better at communicating and the expectations were clearer, they became more efficient at lesson planning. Joy described the group's progress toward efficient planning,

> It's less painful. We don't have these long excruciatingly painful silences, where people were just sort of going ughhh, but I think it became an easier thing for us to do and I think the majority of us developed an appreciation for the way in which it did benefit both us and the students.

The collaboration became rich with more talk regarding pedagogy as illustrated in the following vignette from a January planning meeting:

Table 8.6. Participants' Confidence Levels in Instruction of the Balanced Literacy Components

Balanced Literacy Components	*Not at All*	*Barely*	*Somewhat*	*Proficient*	*Got it Down*
Read-alouds			Matthew	Joy, Barbara	Abbey, Akkia, Ken
Sustained silent reading with level text			Barbara	Joy, Matthew, Akkia	Abbey, Ken
Conferencing			Barbara	Joy, Matthew, Akkia	Abbey, Ken
Small groups with leveled text		Joy, Akkia	Barbara	Abbey	Matthew, Ken
Teacher directed reading			Joy, Barbara, Matthew	Akkia	Abbey, Ken
Word and spelling instruction	Matthew		Joy, Barbara, Akkia, Ken	Abbey	
Writing	Barbara	Matthew	Joy, Akkia	Ken	Abbey
Literature circles	Barbara, Matthew, Akkia	Joy, Ken	Abbey		

*Abbey pulled students out of the regular classroom for group tutoring and Barbara went into all the 6th grade Language Arts classrooms for EC modifications.

Akkia: Next is drawing conclusions. Then it's the end of the quarter. We'll need to review, review, review.

Barbara: We need to do literary terms, mood, tone.

Joy: and analogies. I'll copy this analogy resource book for the group.

Ken, Matthew, and Akkia: Thanks!

Joy: Use it as a warm up or for homework. What is the objective for drawing conclusions?

Barbara: SCOS goal 4.02. It's part of the critical thinking section.

Akkia is writing up the plan for the group.

Joy: We are looking for evidence in the text for the conclusions.

Akkia: Use the question stems from the new EOG to look for evidence. I did that with the play and the O. Henry story in groups.

Matthew: I'll get some IMS passages.

Joy: I have an activity that I think will be helpful; it is an interview protocol game for pre-reading. I'll use the play, *Charlie and the Chocolate Factory* and Rod Serling's *Monsters Came to Maple Street*. But I'm worried they haven't done any poetry.

Fern: You can write units and rotate them for the next quarter; maybe you can work on that next week.

Ken: The way to teach all this stuff is to teach all this at the beginning of the year with literature and refer to it all the time. (1-7-03)

By the spring semester the group planned and shared ideas more freely. Akkia was excited that she now has two filing cabinets full of strategies and activities for instruction. Matthew established himself as the literature expert and provided "fresh text" ideas for teaching the various skills. Joy provided classroom activities that motivate and connect to students, and Ken managed the meetings. They planned the units to teach the genres and rotated them over a period of ten weeks.

Even so, they continued to find it difficult to implement some of the literacy components and reverted back to previous modes of teaching. For example, to teach novels, Matthew and Joy both planned a unit on novels as whole class instruction. When asked why they chose a novel for the whole class, they both responded similarly. "That's the only way I know to teach it," said Joy. Matthew added, "The kids pay attention when we do it all together." Each of them said the novel study was the best unit they had done all year. After a few weeks of teaching whole group, classroom observations documented a return to the flexible group model advocated by the literacy program. In informal conversations, several participants suggested that they made this change to satisfy consultants and administrators. Ken, for example, said his return to groups was for the sake of appearance, "In reality, it may look good when you walk into a classroom, at a given time, even my classroom there are days it looks good, whether that's real, I'm not so sure."

Students' scores on state mandated reading tests at the end of the year showed that the sixth graders made some improvements in their reading performance. As indicated in Table 8.7, sixth grade students' scores rose by an average of 1.35 points. Although this increase was lower that the average gains for the other grade levels, sixth grader's scores rose for the first time in several years.

When we returned to Main Street Middle School to talk with participants the following year, we learned that one of the teachers had to take a medical leave and another moved to a different grade level. We were able to interview three of the remaining participants. When we asked them to

Table 8.7. Students' Scores on State Mandated Achievement Tests in Reading at the End of the Year

	2002 Average Reading Score	*2003 Average Reading Score*	*Gain*	*Percentage growth*
Grade 6	153.91	155.26	1.35	0.88%
Grade 7	153.30	158.80	5.50	3.58%
Grade 8	154.65	160.00	5.35	3.46%
School	153.95	158.00	4.05	2.60%

reflect back on the performance of their students the year before, they focused on the progress of individuals.

Matthew: I was pleased with how my students performed. I had some 2's (below average) move up to 3's (above average), and some 3's go to 4's (highest level). I was proud. Not amazed, but proud. All in all though, I try not to put too much emphasis on the test or EOG's. I try to just teach my students skills for taking tests in general and how to keep focused on the task at hand.

Joy: What I really scrutinize are what my team and my individual kids did. I knew that overall the school, we had done well, but I was less concerned with that than I was with just my kids. A lot of our two's have gone up to three's. A lot of the one's we've gone up to two's.

Joy was concerned however that some of the better readers in her classes did not do so well.

Joy: A lot of my fours go back to threes, because we were so busy working with the low kids. We're pouring so much of our energy and effort into targeting the low kids, trying to figure out what their weaknesses were, trying to figure out how to help them, you know, doing all the things to try and get their scores up, that a lot of our bright kids should have stayed fours or even gotten or could have even achieved more, fell back to threes. To me that was a really hard thing.

Participants reported that their grade level team was not working together as often or as closely as they had the year before. Matthew suggested that this year's meetings were less structured.

Matthew: We meet as much as we can, but it isn't often. Like I said before, we try to plan what we are all going to do for the week or next few weeks so we can all be on the same page. We share materials and ideas. As a team we meet informally often, but it might just be for a few minutes. We spend more time in meetings than anything really. We just do the best we can... . We have been doing a lot of workshop work this year. It seems like I never get my planning time. We are always working on some new program or project. I do a lot of planning on my own and not here at school, but we do try to make sure we are all somewhat on the same page.

Participants noted that changes in personnel impacted the way they worked as a grade level group.

Joy: We found a formula finally by the end of last year that allowed us to work together. This year it's been working sort of so-so, but now we're losing language arts teachers. It's a little more frustrating. We're trying to do things the way we did last year and trying to use the same methods. I think we're about to fall back now into our old pattern of coming together, meeting, talking, seeing what everyone else has got and then going our merry way and there's not the cohesiveness that we all had.

Without opportunities to meet as often and without a facilitator, it seemed that participants were finding it difficult to maintain the momentum they had developed the year before. Abby, who moved to another grade level, reported that all of the language arts teachers were still struggling to implement the basic elements of the balanced literacy program.

Abby: I don't know of anybody that really tried literature circles, we're not quite sure still how to do that and how to manage that. We've just been focused so much on small group part and I try to do my silent reading. I try to do that component and conference with the kids, they like that.

Our interviews with these three teachers midway through the following school year suggested that the language arts teachers at Main Street Middle School were still working to implement the literacy reforms initiated the year before and finding it difficult to do so.

CONCLUSIONS

Overall, the professional learning community of the 2002-2003 school year enabled the teachers to interact formally in the planning meetings and informally as friends and colleagues. As a group, their conversations centered on the mandated reforms. They made sense of some of the reforms and made honest attempts to satisfy the requirements. They half-heartedly attempted some practices (word study and small groups) and ignored others (writing, literature circles and differentiation). They insisted to the researchers that they intended to implement these components of literacy but were waiting for the right conditions to do so. Results from the achievement tests at the end of the year showed very slight growth in reading.

In spite of few concrete improvements, qualitative data indicated that participants viewed their experience with the professional learning community during the 2002-03 school year as positive. Teachers reported stronger professional relationships, more collaborative problem solving, collegial support from the members of the group, and more confidence in their abilities to carry out the desired reform initiatives.

In almost all of their interactions, participants demonstrated "deep down desires" to have successful students. They often resorted to teaching strategies that were more controlling than inviting "just to keep order." By the end of the 2002-03 school year, test preparation activities replaced most of the literacy reform efforts. These issues were at the forefront of discussion during the planning time of the professional learning community, and efforts were renewed to keep or return to place mandated reforms.

Even so, participants exhibited professional growth in several areas through the professional learning community. Akkia received ideas, resources, and teaching strategies. She grew out of a "survival mode" and developed her own routines. Joy gained ideas, resources, teaching strategies and greater confidence. She was persistent in her efforts and planning. Matthew gained the ability to put it all together in an "easy going manner," building a positive classroom climate. Matthew's growth was dramatic over the year considering he began with limited pedagogical knowledge. Ken complied with the program mandates, learned new ways to teach literacy and collaborate with colleagues. All four of them agreed that the professional learning community was valuable and made the reform initiatives more possible.

As participants indicated when we returned to visit them the following year, implementing changes at Main Street Middle School will take considerable time. Even though participants seemed to grow professionally, their own reports and our observations indicated that they were able to implement consistently only about half of the components of the new literacy program. Their students' scores on reading achievement tests showed less progress than did seventh and eighth grade students. By the middle of the following year, participants were struggling to maintain their momentum as a professional learning community, responding to changes in personnel and frustrated by less time to meet. Glickman et al. (2004) would describe their interactions as "congenial" with some aspects of "collegial" relationships forming. Joy's concern about falling back "into our old pattern" without the same sense of "cohesiveness" suggests that these gains may be short lived (p. 6). For their working relationships to grow stronger, it is likely that participants will need encouragement and much more tangible support.

These results underscore the complexity of reform initiatives with low performing middle schools. Participants agreed that their biggest accomplishment was the development of more meaningful relationships with each other. This new support structure proved valuable. It may have provided the life sustaining oxygen that enabled participants to end the year with some feelings of accomplishment and a sense that they were developing a professional learning community.

It is likely that participants experienced some of the tensions resulting from conflicting views of learning communities that Cochran-Smith and Lytle (1996) described. Their primary focus in working with each other was to make sense of initiatives and support each other, a "knowledge in practice" perspective. Administrators and curriculum developers wanted them to form a "knowledge for practice" community that would implement the strategies and procedures specified in the program. This tension may have reinforced a "survival" mentality that focused on doing what was needed. If that were so, their work together may have helped them survive the pressures of the school year. For the school to improve, however, participants will need to enrich and extend these relationships, moving beyond a survival mentality toward a more successful posture toward school reform. Administrators will need to find a way to work with grade level teams to create more "collegial" working relationships, interactions that focus on improvements in learning and teaching in ways that are meaningful and grow stronger over time.

REFERENCES

Bobek, B. (2002). Teacher resiliency: A key to career longevity. *The Clearing House, 75* (4), 202-205.

Brown, J., D'Emidio-Caston, M., & Benard, B. (1996). *Resilience education*. Thousand Oaks, CA: Corwin Press.

Chester, M., & Beaudin, B. (1996). Efficacy beliefs of newly hired teachers in urban schools. In M. Tschennan-Morran, A. Hoy, & W. Hoy (Eds.), Teacher efficacy: Its meaning and measure. *Review of Educational Research, 68*(2), 202-249.

Coburn, C. (2001). Collective sensemaking about reading: How teachers mediate reading policy in their professional communities. *Educational Evaluation and Policy Analysis, 23*(2), 145-170.

Cochran-Smith, M., & Lytle, S. (1996). Relationships of knowledge and practice: Teacher learning in communities. *Review of Research in Education, 24*, 249-306.

Dallas, F. (2002). *Enhancing teacher efficacy through peer coaching: A collaborative effort toward supporting teacher quality and middle school improvement*. Paper presented at the meeting of the American Educational Research Association, New Orleans.

Dallas, F. (2003). *Enhancing teacher efficacy and resiliency through professional learning communities: A case study in middle school teacher professional development*. Unpublished doctoral dissertation, University of North Carolina Greensboro.

Glaser, A., & Corbin, J. (1997). *Grounded theory in practice*. Thousand Oaks, CA: Sage.

Glickman, C., Gordon, S., & Ross-Gordon, J. (2004). *SuperVision and instructional leadership: A developmental approach*. Boston: Pearson.

Gordon, K., & Coscarelli, W. (1996). Recognizing and fostering resilience. *Performance Improvement, 35*(9), 14-17.

Langer, J. (2000). How teachers' professional lives support student achievement. *American Educational Research Journal, 37*, 397-440.

Leonard, L., & Leonard, P. (1999). Reculturing for collaboration and leadership. *Journal of Educational Research, 92*(4), 237-242.

Midgley, C., Feldlaufer, H., & Eccles, J. (1989). Change in teacher efficacy and student self-and task-related beliefs during transition to junior high. *Journal of Educational Psychology, 81*, 247-258.

Olson, L. (2000). Finding and keeping competent teachers. *Education Week, 19*, 12-18.

Stake, R. (1995). *The art of case study research*. Thousand Oaks: CA Sage.

Yin, R. (1994). *Case study research designs and methods*. Thousand Oaks, CA: Sage.

CHAPTER 9

SHAPING MANDATES FOR SCHOOL REFORM

Practices, Problems, and Possibilities— A Commentary

Ann Lieberman

ABSTRACT

This commentary chapter uses examples from the case studies in the first part of the book to discuss the tensions and possibilities embedded in the policy and practice discourse about school reform. In particular, this chapter contrasts the decades-long policy/practice dichotomy between the pressures of mandated high-stakes accountability systems such as those in Texas and North Carolina and the culture-changing need to create community and build capacity between the teachers and leaders charged with accomplishing school improvement. Both perspectives are necessary, but there is still too little attention to creating the conditions that will disturb the "social realities" of schools and create local capacity for learning and change. These cases provide lessons and examples of the work it will take to create schools for low income students in which teachers simultaneously work on multiple agendas and develop community commitments that integrate their own

Deep Change: Cases and Commentary on Reform in High Stakes States, 141–150

social learning with the instructional needs of their students in these schools.

INTRODUCTION

The changes in the world have deeply affected every country, bringing with them great challenges for schools. In his little book called *Runaway World,* Anthony Giddens (2003) describes the far reaching economic and social changes that are taking place as he likens the current period to the industrial revolution. These very changes of family structure, the nature of work, a reduced role of government, rapidly changing demographics and a privatization of public life require cosmopolitan responses if public schools are to survive and endure (Hargreaves, 2003). Policymakers' immediate responses to these changes have been to raise academic standards and increase accountability.

It is against this complicated background that the cases of school reform in this book were written, each trying to make important changes in the quality of teaching and learning for students and their teachers. From North Carolina to Texas, these schools sought to change the culture in their schools by supporting a learning community that hopefully would permeate the school encouraging instructional improvements and higher test scores. They were responding to policy initiatives in their states that mandated new external accountability schemes that raised the bar on student learning as a way of pressuring the schools to find ways for students to learn and perform better on statewide tests. The schools described in this book took up the challenge and focused their efforts on serious school-wide learning goals. Their stories teach us much about the joys and trials of trying to change school cultures in a high-stakes environment; about the subtleties and complexities of the social realities in their schools; as well as the vivid reality of the practices, problems and perplexities of schools in the process of change.

THE POLICY DEBATE: HIGH STAKES OR ENABLING CAPACITY

In the early 80s there was much talk about top/down policies to promote bottom/up practices. At that time researchers were struggling with the idea that policies from the top needed to reach the place where changes were to happen, the local school. But this proved problematic. In fact, one noted policy researcher was widely quoted after reporting on a national study of federal school reforms, as saying that: "*it is exceedingly difficult for policy to change practice*" (McLaughlin, 1998, p. 71). She continued to report that what matters most is "local capacity and will" the very things policy can't touch. Local expertise, organizational routines and resources have much to do with how practitioners can actually execute their plans. And will, "the motivation to embrace policy initiatives is essential to generate the effort and energy necessary to make real change happen" (p. 72). McLaughlin further went on to say that *local variability is the rule: uniformity is the exception.*

But a few years later, the federal and state policies shifted once again to other new initiatives. On the one hand *A Nation at Risk* warned people that we were falling behind and many policies were passed that mandated new curriculum, more math and science and a general sense of urgency about what students should know and be able to do (National Commission on Excellence in Education, 1983). More and better curriculum would be needed for our country to compete in the world marketplace. On the other hand, the Carnegie Corporation (1986) offered *A Nation Prepared: Teachers for the Twenty-First Century* which called for teachers to be leaders, to collaborate and learn to work together. It called for a reinvigoration of the profession with teachers as partners in the leadership and improvement of practice. These two perspectives are still with us today—one that mandates change in an attempt to raise standards and hold the schools accountable—and another that attempts to involve teachers and the school community in working on improving the school with them as key participants in deciding how to innovate and change to meet the needs of their students. Today's buzzwords are accountability and testing as well as building the capacity of participants to create learning communities. Both are necessary, but it is the *how* that most concerns us here. Today there is much talk about what schools should be doing, but less about how to get there. These cases describe what it will take to change school cultures and why policies that only deal with ends (accountability schemes) will often disappoint both the policymakers and those for whom the policy is intended (the schools).

Telling schools what to do has never produced improved schools over many decades through many reform movements. Numerous researchers and historians have documented why these assumptions are faulty and why the conditions and supports for local learning are the critical aspects for improving schools for both students and their teachers (see, e.g., Berman & McLaughlin, 1978; Cuban, 1990; Fullan, 2001; Tyack & Tobin, 1994).

But all agree that the first task in improving schools becomes figuring out how to create the conditions for local learning and to understand that any changes will disturb the "regularities" of school cultures (Sarason, 1982). Such starting conditions were named *social realities* by Lieberman and Miller (1984) several decades ago when they described what characterizes the realities of a teacher's life in most school cultures.

TRANSFORMING THE NEW SOCIAL REALITIES OF TEACHING

In 1999 Lieberman and Miller posed a set of propositions which described the realities of the profession from the teacher's perspective. They said:

- Teacher isolation was the norm, leading teachers to develop unique repertoires of teaching strategies that were seldom shared or made public and often defended and protected.
- The reward system often encouraged this isolation by placing responsibility for feedback on students rather than on colleagues or peers.
- A weak knowledge base on learning contributed to individualism and privacy requiring teachers to take on blind faith that what they were doing made a difference for their students.
- Competing and conflicting policies reinforced these norms, leading to teachers having a *personal* rather than a *shared professional* sense of goals and expectations.
- Control was often visible, learning was not.
- Teaching was a flat profession requiring the same of veterans as of novices while offering little support for differences.
- Teaching was deemed technical work requiring skills and techniques to be mastered and evaluated (Lieberman & Miller, 1999).

The schools described in this book appear to have started with these realities. For *Central* it meant bringing the school together and fashioning a set of values and beliefs that all would agree upon and having those values guide the kind of instruction they wanted in the school. Professional development was key to these changes. For some it was a mandated curriculum, while others developed their own ways of improving instruction. For *Hunter* there were not only values, but strong inspiration and vision from a dedicated principal; shared leadership; and a focused curriculum. And, in addition *Hunter* was involved in a school/university partnership that brought many additional adults into classrooms to support the growth of students. For the non-magnet students at *Callaghan Middle School*, it was using teacher study groups as a way of developing curriculum innovations. In all of these schools there was an attempt to create opportunities for teachers to work together, to grow up a shared set of values and ways of working that would create a more collaborative environment—one that would help teachers participate in the transformation of their school from an isolated to a more collective culture.

For all of the schools it meant moving:

- *From individualism to a professional community,* building norms of collegiality, openness, trust and experimentation, in turn building greater professional responsibility and accountability.
- *From teaching at the center to learning at the center* which would translate to such activities as collaboratively looking at student work Designing curriculum together; sharing instructional strategies and constructing alternatives to standardized approaches to learning.
- *From technical and managed work to inquiry and leadership* where teachers view themselves and are viewed by others as constantly inquiring into teaching and learning and where teachers take leadership for part of the core work of their schools (Lieberman & Miller, 2004, p. 11).

Such transformation did indeed occur as the principal at *Hunter* moved the school to creating a vision of promoting and sustaining success which included: high expectations, student engagement, meaningful relationships and a curriculum with focus. For *Central,* although there was a lot of innovation (grade level planning, active student involvement, etc.), and a lot of new knowledge discussed (and even tried), the approach to change might have been too technical and too fragmented to take hold long enough to be sustained. Although there was fragmentary progress in parts of the school, as a whole innovation appears to have faltered. For *Callaghan,* with a history of mandated reform, the principal facilitated Critical Friends Groups (CFG's) as a way to build a more personalized approach to professional development. Culturally relevant curriculum, distributed leadership and a customized professional development were the centerpieces of *Callaghan's* reform efforts. In all the cases, many important practices were developed and many implemented and it is instructive for us to see what different schools with different contexts do, where they start, and what practices engage the teachers in an evolutionary process of change.

SOCIAL PRACTICES AND INSTRUCTIONAL PRACTICES

Wenger (1998) has noted that social learning addresses a critical part of how adults learn in the context of their work. He notes that a social theory of learning has four components. People have to find *meaning* both individually and collectively. They need to talk about their *practice* as they engage in action, and they often do this in the context of *a community of practice*. And when people find meaning and develop practices together in the context of a community, they often change the way they feel about each other and themselves. This kind of learning changes ones' *identity*. "Such participation shapes not only what we do, but also who we are and how we interpret what we do" (p. 4).

Reading these cases and looking for new practices that were developed, we begin to see that one set of practices involved creating greater collaboration, discussion and direction about what school could become. These 'social practices' are what Wenger was talking about and they call our attention to the fact that the school culture must become more accommodating to the adults' learning as well as the students'. Toward that end a number of structures and roles helped the schools develop visions, shape a view toward learning (their own as well as the student's) and nurture a more collaborative approach to improving the school. Such structures included: study groups, critical friends groups, Camp EOG, *(end of grade)*, teachers as leaders, peer helpers, tutors, interns, pre-service students, assistants, university professors, slogans (Together We Can), principal as visionary and self-directed professional development. These groups, along with additional personnel and models of different ways of doing business, all help schools to commit themselves to the struggle to improve. But there were instructional practices too. Teachers were involved in creating a more engaged set of learning opportunities for their students while they learned some new pedagogical practices for themselves. For *Hunter* it was holding high expectations and providing high support and working on literacy and math skills by providing high engagement opportunities. For *Callaghan* it was the starting and maintaining of the Latino Boys Writing Group and making the curriculum relevant to the lives of their students. For *Central* it was coming to see learning as a social activity by doing work in groups, providing active engagement of the students and providing a problem-solving curriculum. When the social learning of the faculty melded with the instructional practices for students, schools improved not only their test scores, but became communities where the struggle to improve was collectively held. This often invisible part of improving schools is critical to any changes that might eventually accrue to what happens in the classroom. Working and learning together for the adults is a necessary prerequisite for schools to improve. But it is not without problems.

THE PROBLEMATIC NATURE OF IMPROVING SCHOOLS

As Sarason (1982) warned us several decades ago, changing the programmatic regularities of schools is very difficult. The social realities must change to build a culture of caring, support and high expectations.

Instructional practices must be more engaging so that students can learn. Different structures must be built and maintained and new roles and relationships need to be developed. And teachers must learn new ways of facilitating learning for their students. The principal needs to orchestrate the symphony while being aware that all players do not need the same things, yet eventually they must learn to play together.

These cases provide a close up look at how problematic situations arise showing us how strong, yet how fragile school improvement initiatives can be. At *Hunter*, which would undoubtedly be called a success in anyone's terms, the commitment and energy to raise all students to a higher level had its costs. Teachers worked exhaustively to maintain the high level of student involvement by putting in 12 hour days, only to be matched by the long days put in by the principal who was playing the roles of visionary, supporter, nurturer, resource getter, cheer leader and more. In a school where commitment and energy are critical components, it is not surprising that some teachers eventually transferred to another school. Burn out in these kinds of schools is inevitable. How can people maintain their commitment in light of the incredible constancy and pressure of sustaining school that works for both students and adults?

For *Central*, which appears not to have had such a strong integrated community as Hunter, problems appeared as the primary teachers were engaged in a mandated literacy program. Teachers balked at the philosophy of the program and the intricacies of the program itself. With little time to practice and less to talk about what they were doing, primary teachers continued to be frustrated. In another part of the school fifth grade teachers created their own professional development focus and worked on literacy in a self-directed program. The examples of these two different approaches to solving the problem of literacy showed not only that some teachers were frustrated and fighting change, but the changes appeared to be fragmented into two different sets of assumptions about professional development. For the primary teachers it was a mandated program, while the fifth grade teachers organized their own program. Lacking a collective vision, some teachers may indeed make progress with their students, but it will be difficult to sustain over time. And when pockets of a school each carry on as if they were different cultures, it will be difficult to build a sense of community—a necessity for improving schools.

POSSIBILITIES AND PERPLEXITIES OF RE-FORMING SCHOOLS

In sum, what we learn from these cases is a richer and deeper understanding of the tensions, perplexities and possibilities of re-forming schools that always exist and are in constant states of negotiation and accommodation. There are the tensions of leadership in a school. Principals need to take a stance that is both collegial and authoritative, neither giving away their authority nor exercising it so much that there is no possibility of sharing it. They need to both *create* a vision and *develop* a vision which means that they need to be visionary, but engage teachers in developing ideas that they can believe in and commit themselves to. Somehow people must get invested in ideas that they can commit themselves to, even if the ideas come from a figure in authority. Leaders need to know the difference between making technical improvements *versus* cultural changes. Both are necessary, yet one without the other probably won't sustain. In our contemporary society, those in leadership must provide a process for learning that leads to results. Yet there are often detours along the way. A results orientation that shortcuts the process will have difficulty gaining the kind of commitment that will be needed to make the kinds of changes that last. Yet, a school that continues to work on a process without gaining results will falter as well. Leaders come to understand the differences between transmitting or transacting the teaching and learning process. (This is a teaching problem as well as a learning problem.) When is the right time to tell and when is it right to let people work out their difficulties and learn from it? Leaders must differentiate between when people need to learn from experts and when they can learn from experience (Lieberman, 2001, p. 160). Learning how to negotiate these tensions is as much a teaching problem as it is a leadership one. Few leaders have had experience juggling these tensions as they work to build learning communities in their schools, yet this complicated set of conditions is what it will take to re-form schools. Only one school with a charismatic and dedicated leader was able to fulfill this view of leadership, doing it with a Herculean effort and leaving structures, values and practices in place for his successor.

These cases also show us the tensions between policies at the top (high stakes testing) and the myriad number of social and instructional practices that go into improving schools at the bottom. Teachers and principals must work on several agendas *at the same time*. They must participate in building a community of learners for the adults while they also have their eyes on the inevitable testing of the practices that are being worked on. Both of these agendas are huge and, as we see in these descriptions, it is difficult to bring all the agendas together.

To date we have mixed reviews on whether high-stakes accountability systems affect both the teachers and their students in desirable ways. A study done by a group of researchers on the effects on professional development in high stakes accountability systems found that in six Southern states high-stakes accountability helped focus professional development efforts on the curricular needs of students, but showed little evidence that it helped teachers change their practice to enhance student learning (Berry, Turchi, Johnson, Hare, Owens, & Clements, 2002). Two other policy researchers in discussing the fit between policy and the realities of practice state: *to realize investment in teachers' learning, policies need not only cohere with one another and make sense in teachers' contexts, but they must also correspond with the needs and circumstances of the teachers who are expected to benefit from them* (Darling-Hammond & McLaughlin, 1999). High-stakes tests may look like an important policy tool, but it appears that this kind of policy oversimplifies the complexities of teaching and learning, particularly in low income schools as they work to sustain both the sense of community and the improvement of student learning.

To create schools that work for students in low income schools, many agree that teachers need to be full participants in professional learning communities—communities that encourage them as learners as well as their students. We cannot expect teachers to create a nourishing community for their students when they have no community of their own. To construct such a community, teachers need to do the "social work" that comes with changing the participation of teachers from solo actors, to community participants. Such community formation comes about when teachers come to understand that forming a community is a process unto itself, one that provides for moving from caring about oneself to members taking responsibility for all in the community (Grossman, Wineburg, & Woolworth, 2001). This is a massive innovation in and of itself!

These cases provide us with the realities of the work it will take to improve low income schools. They describe the complex agenda that requires both the learning of social practices which grow up a community and the importance of changing instructional practices for students. They add to our understanding of the importance of context, leadership and professional development that matters for teachers as they teach us what it will take to embrace a future that supports both the learning and participation of adults and their students in a continued struggle for a more democratic future.

REFERENCES

Berman, P., & McLaughlin, M.W. (1978). *Federal programs supporting educational change, Vol. 8: Implementing and sustaining innovations.* Santa Monica, CA: Rand Corporation.

Berry, B., Turchi, L., Johnson, D., Hare, D., Owens, D.D., & Clements, S. (2002). *The impact of high-stakes accountability on teachers' professional development: Evidence from the south.* Chapel Hill, NC: Southeast Center for Teaching Quality.

Carnegie Corporation of New York. (1986). *A nation prepared: Teachers for the twenty-first century.* New York: Carnegie Corporation.

Cuban, L. (1990). Reforming again and again and again. *Educational Researcher, 19*, 3-13.

Darling-Hammond, L., & McLaughlin, M.W. (1999). Investing in teaching as a learning profession: Policy problems and prospects. In L. Darling-Hammond & G. Sykes (Eds.), *Teaching as the learning profession: Handbook of policy and practice* (pp. 376-411). San Francisco: Jossey-Bass.

Fullan, M. (2001). *The new meaning of educational change* (3rd ed.). New York: Teachers College Press.

Giddens, A. (2003). *Runaway world: How globalization is reshaping our lives.* New York: Routledge.

Grossman, P., Wineburg, S., & Woolworth, S. (2001, December). Toward a theory of teacher community. *Teachers College Record, 103* (6).

Hargreaves, A. (2003). *Teaching in the knowledge society: Education in the age of insecurity.* New York: Teachers College Press.

Lieberman, A. (2001). The professional lives of change agents: What they do and what they know. In F. Rust & H. Freidus (Eds.), *Guiding school change: The role and work of change agents.* New York: Teachers College Press.

Lieberman, A., & Miller, L. (2004). *Teacher leadership.* San Francisco: Jossey-Bass.

Lieberman, A., & Miller, L. (1999). *Teachers—Transforming their world and their work.* New York: Teachers College Press.

Lieberman, A., & Miller, L. (1984). *Teachers: Their world and their work.* New York: Teachers College Press.

McLaughlin, M. (1998). Listening and learning from the field: Tales of policy implementation and situated practice. In A. Hargreaves, A. Liberman, M. Fullan, & D. Hopkins (Eds.), *The International Handbook of Educational Change, Part I.* Dordecht: Kluwer Academic.

National Commission on Excellence in Education. (1983). *A nation at risk: The imperative for educational reform.* Washington, DC: U.S. Department of Education.

Sarason, S. (1982). *The culture of the school and the problem of change.* Needham Heights, MA: Allyn & Bacon.

Tyack, D., & Tobin, W. (1994). The grammar of schooling: Why has it been so hard to change? *American Research Journal, 31*, 453-479.

Wenger, E. (1998). *Communities of practice: Learning, meaning, and identity.* New York: Cambridge University Press.

PART II

PROGRAMS OF SIGNIFICANCE: CASE STUDIES OF INITIATIVES THAT CONNECT SCHOOLS

CHAPTER 10

"THAT DOG WON'T HUNT!"

Exemplary School Change Efforts Within the Kentucky Reform

Shelby A. Wolf, Hilda Borko, Rebekah Elliott, and Monette McIver

ABSTRACT

Our research presents case studies of four exemplary schools as they worked to meet the demands of the Kentucky Education Reform Act (KERA) as well as the system designed to assess results—the Kentucky Instructional Results Information System (KIRIS). Here we argue that the teachers' responses to large-scale reform efforts exist in a larger web of connection and are dependent on their collaborative and consistently positive stance towards learning as well as their principals' leadership. Thus human capital, the knowledge and willingness to learn on the part of individuals, is inextricably linked to social capital, the relationships of trust and willingness to risk among school personnel. How our four schools successfully met the challenge of KERA and KIRIS was unique to each site. Still, there were critical commonalties—their regard for history and heritage, the efficacy of their cooperative leadership, their careful reflection on the reform itself which ultimately allowed them to teach to and well beyond the KIRIS test (particularly in writing), and, most important, their dedication to students.

Deep Change: Cases and Commentary on Reform in High Stakes States, 153–200

> In a certain part of the country called Appalachia you will find dogs named Prince or King living in little towns with names like Coal City and Sally's Backbone. These dogs run free, being country dogs, and their legs are full of muscles from running rabbits up mountains or from following boys who push old bikes against the hill roads they call hollows. These are mostly good dogs and can be trusted. (Rylant, 1991, p. 1)

On one of our initials trips to Kentucky, we sat in the office of the Kentucky Department of Education and discussed our research plans with the administrators who watch over Kentucky's educational reform. In our first interview, we learned an instructive lesson about untrustworthy dogs. We had been explaining our interests in simultaneously conducting a widespread survey of Kentucky teachers of writing and mathematics with case studies of exemplary teachers who were working in the accountability grades (4th and 7th grades for writing, 5th and 8th for mathematics).[1] Moreover, for these cases, we were looking for teachers who were not "stars"—unique to their communities—but hardworking teachers who were well supported by their school contexts.[2]

One administrator was especially pleased with our focus on exemplary sites and suggested that it would be smart to study "sites that are doing things that can be done in other areas." While he was not implying immediate transferability, there was a sense of an "existence proof." He explained, "If you can find a school that has a lot of challenges and see what they've done, then... people say if *they* did it, I can do it, and I'm willing to look for my own solutions." He continued:

> If you want a Kentucky-ism that you can use, a principal I was talking with said that there's a school that's 18 miles down the road from his school that has 80% of the kids on free and reduced ... lunch, and they have made progress and they are at a higher absolute rank. So what he says to his teachers is, "Don't bring up to me about how our kids are disadvantaged. *That dog won't hunt!*" That's the Kentucky-ism. And part of that phrasing from the principal is a characteristic that people in the department talk more about, and this is a "no excuses" approach. That is, you don't say why things can't be done; you say, "What is it that we need to do?" And what the principal was saying was, "If you can show me a place that has done it, I will go talk with them about *how* they did it." It gets us past this belief barrier that we've had for so many years that our kids can't do it. (A96F)

With this lesson in mind, we set out to find schools with good hunting attitudes, schools that could be trusted to ask, "What is it that we need to do?" and then set out to do it. We found two in an urban area and two in the Appalachian coal towns where good dogs chase rabbits up the hollows.

BACKGROUND ON KERA AND KIRIS

Before we lay out a conceptual frame for how schools shift within educational reform efforts, we need to present some background on Kentucky. Indeed, pushing past the "belief barrier...that our kids can't do it" was particularly critical because this state, perhaps more than any other, set out to prove that "all students can learn at high levels" (White, 1999, p. 20), and the reform that they initiated was both complicated and courageous. One Kentucky school superintendent wrote:

> Only Kentucky had been bold enough to ... design an education system that included all of the piecemeal reform efforts in existence in other parts of the country—and then some. Preschool education, site-based management, ungraded primary schools, performance-based teaching and testing, technology integration, rewards and sanctions for schools—all these initiatives ... were part of the state's ambitious overhaul. (Simpson, 1991, p. 29)

The motivation behind all this change was an unprecedented Kentucky Supreme Court decision (*Rose v. Council for Better Education, Inc.*) in 1989 which declared the state's public school system unconstitutional. The "justices gave remarkable weight to student outcomes.... The court concluded that a school system in which a significant number of children receive an inadequate education or ultimately fail is inherently inequitable and unconstitutional" (Foster, 1991, p. 34).

As a result, the legislature created a new school system through the Kentucky Education Reform Act (KERA) of 1990 which brought about substantive changes in *finance*, *governance*, and *curriculum*. In terms of *finance*, KERA was guided by three concepts: "the system must be 'adequate,' it must be 'substantially uniform,' and it must provide 'equal educational opportunity' to all Kentucky children" (Adams & White, 1997, p. 168). In terms of *governance*, school-based decision making became the norm. In fact, five years after KERA began, the Partnership for Kentucky School Reform described school governance as "a two way street. A new, decentralized system is in place, one that relies on and incorporates initiatives, partnerships, and communication between school administrators (from the top down) and those active at the 'point of instruction,' i.e., teachers, parents, and community members (from the bottom up)" (Boston, 1995, p. 18).

Still, in this triumvirate of reform nothing has been more important than *curriculum*, for KERA insisted on accountability, instituting the Kentucky Instructional Results Information System (KIRIS) to make sure teachers got the job done.[3] The influence of this testing system was pervasive: "Ask almost any teacher in Kentucky about KERA, and invariably the response will be about KIRIS. While KERA has resulted in many progressive changes... KIRIS, the assessment and accountability component of KERA, has commanded everyone's attention" (Jones & Whitford, 1997, p. 276). Part of the reason for the attention has been the high-stakes nature of the KIRIS results. Schools that performed well were given rewards (including cash bonuses for teachers), and those that performed poorly were sanctioned, which resulted in a state-mandated improvement plan and/or assistance by one of the state's Distinguished Educators (DE).[4]

Yet, the rewards and sanctions were less important than what KIRIS was actually testing—the impact of innovative curricular changes. In writing, students in the 4th, 7th, and 12th grades were responsible for three assessments: (a) a writing portfolio which contained students' original writing in a variety of genres; (b) open response items in which students read short passages and answered questions through written response; and (c) on demand writing in which students had 90 minutes to craft their response to a specific prompt (Wolf & McIver, 1999). While students crafted their portfolios over the year, open response and on demand writing came in a week of spring testing. The curriculum implied by these assessments emphasized that students should think like writers, writing in varied genres for multiple audiences and purposes. Students were to use the writing process to develop their pieces, whether the piece was a short-term, on demand test item or a long-term portfolio entry. Finally, students were asked to be reflective writers—cognizant not only of their writing processes, but willing to evaluate their products with a critical eye.

In mathematics, KIRIS testing occurred in grades 5, 8, and 12. It was designed to assess students' mathematical literacy—their understanding of concepts and procedures—as well as their ability to use this understanding to solve problems in other disciplines and in real life. It consisted of three types of assessments: (a) open response items in which students demonstrated their ability to apply skills and show understanding of concepts; (b) multiple choice items which tested both computational and problem-solving skills; and (c) mathematics portfolios where students demonstrated their problem solving and communication in several mathematical core content areas. Although mathematics portfolios were included in the Accountability Index through the 1995-96 testing cycle, "a panel of measurement specialists appointed to investigate the technical quality of KIRIS found that the scoring of portfolios was insufficiently reliable to support their use for accountability" (Borko & Elliott, 1999, p. 395). While the panel recommended continuation, they were pulled from the Accountability Index for research and development, and ultimately eliminated. Still, this unsuccessful attempt to have children construct mathematics portfolios demonstrated the state's willingness to work towards creative curriculum.

Writing and mathematics curriculum are only two examples of the kinds of practices KIRIS both *inspired* and *demanded*, which aligns with McDonnell's (1994) portrayal of "assessment policy as persuasion and regulation" (p. 394). McDonnell found that state policymakers:

> intend for the assessment system and the policies linked to its use to shape not just student outcomes, but also what and how students are taught. A state legislator described that intent by saying, "if we have a test of this importance, it will drive the curriculum. I see assessment as accomplishing both accountability and curricular reform." (p. 406)

In a state-wide survey, conducted in parallel to the exemplary site case studies, Kentucky teachers validated the legislator's prediction: "They agreed that the KIRIS assessments and the curriculum materials provided by the state were the most potent influences on instruction in mathematics and writing" (Stecher, Barron, Kaganoff, & Goodwin, 1998, p. 75).

When a test as powerful as KIRIS sets the goal and the pace of curricular reform, with politicians exerting pressure on professionals about what and how to teach, it is helpful to consider the reform in light of McDonnell's (1994) strategies for consensus among professionals and policy makers. First, McDonnell said it is critical for all parties to cast a skeptical eye on the ability of any test—no matter how innovative—to provide data objective enough to ensure that rewards and sanctions are merited. In Kentucky, the shifts in testing requirements (e.g., elimination of the mathematics portfolio) and questions about KIRIS scoring show that professionals did not see the test as infallible. On the contrary, the history of KIRIS exemplifies the struggle to build and administer a set of standardized assessments that were both creative and psychometrically sound.

According to McDonnell, the second strategy to bring diverse views of testing together is to link new assessments with "capacity-building instruments":

> Because many new forms of assessment require that teachers play a key role in their design, administration, scoring, and use, these assessments will not work as intended unless adequate training is provided. The need for major new investments in professional development is even greater for those assessment policies that are expected to change curriculum and instructional practices. (p. 414)

In Kentucky, attention to professional development was high. From the services supplied by the regional centers to the extensive materials (e.g., videotapes, sample prompts) offered by the state, and even to the Distinguished Educators sent to struggling schools, Kentucky worked to build the capacity of its professionals to meet the goals of the new curriculum

(Borko, Elliott, & Uchiyama, 1999). Boston (1996) described the shift in professional development in the following way:

> In pre-reform Kentucky, professional development was the neglected step-child of public education. It encompassed just four days of inservice education a year; statewide funding for keeping teachers professionally up-to-date was limited prior to 1990s.... Today, Kentucky professional development effort has changed from a centralized, state-dominated function to a decentralized model in which local needs dictate what happens. With KERA, funding has moved quickly from an initial $1 per student (1990-91) to $23 per student (1995-96). Overall spending on professional development has increased dramatically, from $1.1 million in 1990-91 to $11.6 million in 1994-95. (pp. 11-12)

McDonnell's (1994) third strategy for consensus is the potential for new assessments to inspire deliberation. Innovative yet imperfect assessments get people talking, weighing the merits and errors, considering the strategies and tips. In Kentucky, KIRIS was on the tip of everyone's tongue, and through talk convictions remained steadfast or opinions were swayed. Still, no matter the outcome, the bottom line in such discussions seemed to be "What do our children need to know?" and "How best can we communicate that knowledge?" (see Boston, 1995, pp. 10-13).

In this brief summary of Kentucky's educational reform, we've tried to outline the areas for systemic change: finance, governance, and curriculum. The curricular implications of KIRIS are critical, for the assessment both regulates and persuades professionals towards curricular reform, in an attempt to change the very nature of teaching and learning in Kentucky. And it rewards those that succeed and sanctions those that don't. In short, it is a powerful tail to wag the dog.

Still, if we consider yet another adage concerning old dogs and new tricks, we know that it will take more than new assessments to change schooling. For that, we need to look beyond Kentucky to the research that reflects the conditions under which reform is not simply rejected or grudgingly accepted, but thoughtfully considered, through a clear-eyed view of the strengths and limitations of testing, through capacity-building opportunities, and through reflective deliberation on what's best for children. Schools that consistently consider children first demonstrate that while change is often *initiated* by outside factors (tests, professional development, and test-inspired talk), what *sustains* and even *strengthens* substantive reform is the *local capacity* of school individuals who are resolutely committed to teaching, learning, and above all, children. Indeed, the importance of professionals' local capacity is an area that we turn to in the theoretical framework to follow.

CONCEPTUAL FRAMEWORK

In their study of school districts involved in change, Spillane and Thompson (1997) leaned on Coleman (1988) to suggest that "local capacity" is based on (a) physical capital (financial resources), (b) human capital (commitment to reform and disposition to learn by teachers and administrators), and (c) social capital (relationships internal and external to the district). Coleman (1990, cited in Ball & Cohen, 1995) described this triad in terms of accessibility: "Physical capital is wholly tangible, being embodied in observable material form; human capital is less tangible, being embodied in the skills and knowledge acquired by an individual; social capital is even less tangible, for it is embodied in the *relations* among persons" (p. 7, emphasis in the original). Although human and social capital are considered less and less tangible, they are not tangential. Instead, they are essential elements in understanding what makes a school exemplary in the face of strong state reform movements.

Looking at the human relationships both within and outside of a school (social capital) is gaining increasing credence in the research literature, as is studying professionals' willingness to learn (human capital). For example, Muncey and McQuillan (1996) concluded that principals were not only "central to the school change process; they were often *the* central person" (p. 270). Still, they cautioned that "the principal's role was often less directive than traditional conceptions of this position would suggest [for it] involved a balancing act, one that required knowing when to be directive and assertive and when to back off and allow faculty to direct change efforts" (p. 270). The principal was less a "top-down" administrator than a "leader of leaders ... who uses power to achieve ends rather than to control people" (Lieberman & Miller, 1990, p. 762). And those ends must be student-oriented goals (Sarason, 1993). As Schmoker (1996) suggested: "Schools improve when purpose and effort unite. One key is leadership that recognizes its most vital function: to keep everyone's eyes on the prize of improved student learning" (p. 103).

Keeping eyes on the prize implies a vision of student learning that school faculty can share, and shared vision is created in an atmosphere of trust. At times this occurs with a principal's longevity: "Principals who remained in their position for an extended tenure were more likely to...generate trust, to adjust school-based initiatives, and to garner the level of grassroots support necessary for change to endure and be refined" (Muncey & McQuillan, 1996, pp. 271-272). This vision implies that school leaders have their eyes wide open to reform realities. While they are advocates for change, their advocacy is not a simple salute to higher powers; instead, it is a reflective appraisal of the reform's pros and cons with a bottom-line view of what will be best for teachers and students.

Still, this reflection is a heavy burden to carry, for implementation is dependent on: "the content of the reform, the faculty's willingness and capacity for change, the strength of the school as an organization, support and training, and leadership. To examine restructuring in light of the first four dimensions is to see that it places an exceptional burden on the fifth" (Evans, 1993, p. 20).

Other research has focused on teachers' attitudes towards learning because "Teachers who see themselves as learners work continuously to develop new understandings and improve their practice" (Peterson, McCarthey, & Elmore, 1996, p. 148). Furthermore, teacher learners do not see themselves in isolation, but in relationship with other teachers, seeking out colleagues within and beyond their buildings to study and plan curriculum. They talk informally in the halls and more formally in grade-level and school-wide meetings to share ideas. Their relationship is *real*, rather than "contrived collegiality, where collaboration is mandated, imposed, and regulated by managerial decree" (Hargreaves, 1997a, p. 1305). Instead of closing their doors to do their own thing, teacher learners open their minds to new possibilities, substantiating Schmoker's (1996) claim that teachers will "perform more effectively—even exponentially—if they collaborate" (p. 7).

Still other researchers focus on students, believing that teachers who work together work best when they are moving towards the education of children. Louis, Marks, and Kruse (1996) argued: "Although taking responsibility for student learning may be thought of as an obligation inherent to the profession of teaching, until lately the notion has received little research attention." They indicated positive results when teachers take "collective responsibility for student learning" (p. 764). Yet, a focus on student learning is dependent on teacher learning. If teachers aren't learners, how will they communicate a love of learning? If they are not reform advocates, how will they convince students to take new assessments seriously? Lieberman and Miller (1990) argued:

> Neither an exclusive focus on students nor an exclusive focus on teachers leads to comprehensive change in the schools. The two must go hand-in-hand, and keeping both goals alive and well has emerged as a crucial element in successful school restructuring. School-based management and new decision-making structures are not ends in themselves; they are means to achieving more effective environments for learning and teaching. Changes in instructional practices do not take hold in schools that infantilize teachers and push them into patterns of defensiveness and conservatism. Schools that attend to one side of the student/teacher equation without acknowledging the other are schools in which change is more often illusory than real, more often espoused than practiced. (p. 761)

Part of the reason why the *structures* of schooling will not bring about *restructuring*, much less *reculturing* schools is that so much hinges on the relationships within the institution (Fullan, 1993; Hargreaves, 1995). Rather than feeling "infantilized" and pushed into "patterns of defensiveness," reforms should create opportunities for all to engage in collaborative work.

"Cultures of collaboration among teachers" are particularly important, for they "seem to produce greater willingness to take risks, to learn from mistakes, and to share successful strategies with colleagues that lead to teachers having positive senses of their own efficacy, beliefs that their children can learn, and improved outcomes in that learning as a result" (Hargreaves, 1997a, p. 1306). Yet, teachers' relationships exist in a larger web of connection and are dependent on the principal's leadership, the district's support, and children's and parent's willingness to take on the challenge of reform efforts. Thus human capital, the knowledge and willingness to learn on the part of individuals, is inextricably linked to social capital, the relationships of trust and willingness to risk among school networks. And in the face of "ambitious reform" Spillane and Thompson (1997) argued "human and social capital are interdependent: They develop in tandem" (p. 196).

METHODS

In our research, we examined two questions that focus on the interdependent nature of human and social capital: (a) What are the effects of recent Kentucky assessment reform on school structures, professional relationships, classroom practices, and teachers' and students' understandings of assessment? and (b) What factors explain the patterns of success within and across exemplary sites? Here, we discuss our site selection and then describe methods of data collection and analysis.

Site Selection

Hatch (1998) suggested that "Stories about successful and sustained school improvement are rare, but the tales of unrealized expectations and failure in reform efforts are legion" (p. 4). Although we did not read this quote until long after we designed the study, we have heeded a similar call since our work began. Rather than join the "legion" of scholars writing woeful tales, we looked for places where the stories of human and social interactions were more successful. This does not mean that our sites were perfect. Yet, we purposefully sought out exemplary schools—with the word *exemplary* defined by Kentucky educators as places where "good things were happening" within the reform movement.

When talking with these educators, we cautioned that we were not searching for what we called "no wonder" schools—schools with populations from high socioeconomic communities or magnet schools for the gifted. We didn't want our selections to invite comments like, "Well *no wonder* they can do it. Look at their population and resources. That teacher won the educator of the year award. No wonder!" Instead, we wanted schools with diverse populations of children, and where we would have to look deeper than surface explanations for *why* good things were happening.

We selected our schools through an exemplary sampling procedure (Heath & McLaughlin, 1993). In the fall of 1996, we began with advice from Kentucky Department of Education (KDE) administrators and then turned to Regional Service Center directors, cluster leaders (lead teachers in curriculum), and principals, looking for names of schools that repeatedly came up as successful sites. Once we had a list of possibilities, team members made site visits to observe and informally interview teachers and their principals about their schools. We then narrowed the numbers to our final six selections— three elementary schools and three middle schools, with one each in urban, suburban, and rural areas of Kentucky. In this article, we focus on our urban and rural sites.

Two of our sites were in rural areas in Eastern Kentucky, and the figures for free and reduced lunch—80% at Bluejay Elementary and 70% at Eagleview Middle—reflect the high poverty in the area.[5] At Bluejay, the community unemployment rate was 80%, and the school district was the largest county employer. Our urban sites—Eastend Elementary and Mt. Vernon Middle—were more economically diverse with a quarter of their children on free/reduced lunch. They were also more racially and ethnically diverse, while the rural sites were nearly 100% European American.

Data Collection

After site selection, we made three two-day visits to each site—in the spring of 1997, in the following fall, and in the spring of 1998. During each visit we observed accountability grade writing and mathematics teachers, and we conducted formal interviews with teachers and principals about their programs and their views of the Kentucky reform. We collected artifacts of practice—from sketches of bulletin boards to classroom diagrams, from teachers' lesson plans to students' daily work. The teachers helped us to select four to six children in each class as target students, and in our spring visits we used photocopies of the children's writing and mathematics portfolios to interview them on how they were learning these content areas in light of the state's reform.

Data Analysis

Following data collection, we fully fleshed out our observational field-notes and then condensed them into cover sheets that followed specific categories derived from our research questions and modified to reflect patterns that emerged from the data. We transcribed all audio-taped interviews and coded them using the NUD*IST computer program. The codes highlighted practices that were connected to as well as more distanced from the Kentucky reform. Many points in the interviews were double- and triple-coded. For example, a principal's comment on the school's vision might have centered on the leadership of the teachers. Or a teacher's remark on professional development offered by KDE might reflect his/her attitudes towards KIRIS testing or beliefs about pedagogy.

Once we coded the data, we ran NUD*IST reports of coding categories and used these reports to develop "cases" of our schools. Each of the co-authors was responsible for an individual case. In our results, words in quotations indicate direct speech from our participants. Words in brackets are our own and serve to add clarification. Quotes are marked by a letter to signal the participant's role (P=Principal, T=Teacher, S=Student, & A=Administrator from the district, region, or state), the year of the quote, and a final letter to signal the data collection cycle (F=Fall and S=Spring). An interview or observation of a teacher taken in the fall of 1997 would be marked T97F.

In building our cases, we tried to find a representative theme for each school, signified by a hypothetical "school motto," as well as describe the principal's role (see Table 10.1). For example, the Bluejay staff talked about their elementary school as a "university." They focused on constant learning through formal professional development and through their own curiosity. The principal, Ms. Chief, characterized herself as a "teacher helper" who worked to "help teachers to keep growing so that they can keep helping kids."

At Eagleview, the steadfast theme was "Pride and Respect." The administrators, teachers, and students all used this phrase, and some characterized it as the "two watchwords" of the school. Mr. Push, the principal in the second year of our study, closed the announcements every morning with the following phrase: "Have a great day at the best middle school in Kentucky!" He saw himself as a coach who made decisions based on what he saw in his team of teachers. Indeed, he was a former baseball coach and often used sports metaphors in characterizing his role.

Table 10.1. Descriptors of Four Exemplary School Sites

Setting	*School Name*	*SES*	*School Motto*	*Principal's Role*
Rural Kentucky	Bluejay Elementary	• high poverty in a "rural, remote area" • 80% qualify for free and reduced lunch	"Here at Bluejay University ... we really take advantage of any professional development that's offered."	Ms. Chief as a "teacher helper" who "can help teachers to keep growing so that they can keep helping kids."
	Eagleview Middle School	• high poverty to middle class • 70% qualify for free and reduced lunch	"Pride & Respect" "Have a great day at the best middle school in Kentucky!"	Mr. Push as Coach: "You make a decision based on what you see out there."
Urban Kentucky	Eastend Elementary	• "federal housing to half million dollar homes" • 30% qualify for free and reduced lunch	"TEAM!" "It's that team approach, that we're in this together..."	Ms. Conner as "part of the team" willing to "set the tone from the very first day that we will do what's best for children."
	Mt. Vernon Middle School	• "while 60% are upper-middle SES" 24% qualify for free and reduced lunch	"If we are going to be a Fortune 500 Company, you don't wait. You jump on it."	Mr. George as CEO: "I'm an instructional leader," "a facilitator," a "protector," and a "salesman."

Turning to our urban sites, Eastend Elementary's consistent theme was TEAM!—but not in the sense of sports. Instead, the focus was on collaboration, and the principal, Ms. Conner, saw herself as "part of the team," yet also willing to "set the tone from the very first day that we will do what's best for children." Our middle school, Mt. Vernon, characterized itself as a "Fortune 500 Company." They took pride in their district and state leadership, and Mr. George, the principal, was the CEO. Indeed, he was a Jack-of-all-trades who used a number of terms for his role: "instructional leader," "facilitator," "protector" of his teachers, and a "salesman" for the reform. He had been in the military in the past, and found himself "frustrated" at times with the slow pace of change, but he was willing to wear any number of hats to make sure his school was out in front.

Once the individual cases were written, our team once again looked over the data to develop an understanding of the consistent themes across sites, and write our interpretive commentary. Although rare in research reports, an integral part of this article is the use of Appalachian literature to open each section of results. While only two of our sites were located in Appalachia, we feel that the essence of this writing extends far beyond the hollows. Moreover, we wanted to capture the very human and social nature of the sites we visited and people we met, for as Brunner (1994) explained "academic texts define problems and state solutions while literature works to illuminate possibilities" (p. 7). Thus, Appalachian literature will help us deliver the details of people and places in a conscious attempt to highlight the consistent features across our sites.

RESULTS

> Most people have little experience with transforming big ideas into workable practices without losing the essence of the ideas. Working through such complicated issues as establishing democracy in the workplace, developing colleagueship, and expanding responsibilities for teachers and students is complex. And there are no road maps. (Lieberman & Miller, 1990, p. 764)

Moving an idea as big as KERA into workable practice has not be easy for our schools, and none has a distinct road map for the miles they've traveled. Still, there were five common markers— features of their human and social topography that stood in relief and may serve as signposts for others: (a) a strong sense of history and heritage; (b) cooperative rather than singular leadership; (c) reflective alignment with the Kentucky reform; (d) the talent of teachers to teach *to* and *beyond* the test (demonstrated in this article by their focus on writing); and (e) an emphasis that all curricular, instructional, and assessment decisions will be based on their school children. Indeed, the first four features are enfolded in the overarching school motto for all four sites: "It's all for the kids."

History and Heritage

> The owners of these dogs ... have probably lived in Appalachia all of their lives.... The owners of these dogs grew up more used to trees than sky and inside them had this feeling of mystery about the rest of the world they couldn't see because mountains came up so close to them and blocked their view like a person standing in a doorway. They weren't sure about going beyond these mountains, going until the land becomes flat or ocean, and so they stayed.... Those who do go off, who find some way to become doctors or teachers, nearly always come back to the part of Appalachia where they grew up. (Rylant, 1991, pp. 1-5)

To introduce the feature of history and heritage, we felt it essential to begin with this passage for it symbolizes the attachment some Kentuckians feel for the land of their birth. To understand the human and social capital of our individual schools, it is critical to comprehend their attachment to context, especially those in our rural sites. At Bluejay and Eagleview, the administrators and teachers were from the area, often raised in the eastern Kentucky counties where they now taught.

One of our target writing teachers, Ms. Jazz, went to grade school at Bluejay as a child, and her mother was an elementary school teacher there. When Ms. Jazz first began to teach at Bluejay, she taught in her mother's old classroom, though now she taught "in the room right above it." Families of teachers were common in the school, and the principal made it a practice to hire people from the local county. As Ms. Chief explained: "It's a family unit, not just in this building but in the community also because everyone knows everyone. And we're all different families who know each other. And our families have been here for years and years and years" (P97S).

Although Ms. Chief had been born in the county, she had left at the age of ten and not returned until her twenties, and part of her motivation for returning was because the county was "the most close knit place I've seen as far as family ties." She spent eight years as a Bluejay teacher before becoming their administrator, and though she had undergone the rigorous process of becoming a Distinguished Educator, she chose to forego the opportunities it afforded to stay at home.

One of the central reasons Ms. Chief and her staff chose to stay was their commitment to the children of the county. They were proud of their students' accomplishments, especially in light of the stereotypes that have so pervasively portrayed their area of the country. Ms. Jazz explained:

> A lot of people ... find out you're from eastern Kentucky and they ask.... Sometimes they ask some really hurtful [questions] of students. "Do you have bathrooms?" It's stereotyping. And I feel that especially for our students, that's why we put our best foot forward because I don't want them to feel like sometimes I've been made to feel—lesser because you come from eastern Kentucky. And I guess that's why I put my whole self into it. I want them to know as much as they can when they leave me. (T97S)

Being a county insider was also true of many faculty at our eastern Kentucky middle school. As the principal told us, "A lot of the teachers are Eagleview County graduates." Yet, Eagleview Middle was only three years old. In the first year of our study, Mr. Push was assistant principal and the principal, Mr. Driver, was a fellow baseball coach and close friend who explained how the school began: "We asked for teachers around the county who wanted to come...[and] I went out and interviewed... and the only ones that I wanted to come in here got to come. That makes for a very hard working group of people that want to work together" (P97S). Mr. Push so wanted the job of assistant principal that he left an elementary principalship to assist Mr. Driver. Interpreting the board's decision to allow this shift as a sign that they "want[ed] to see us succeed," the response of both administrators was enthusiastic: "Mr. Driver and I have always worked together with ... sports and other things. We were sort of tickled to death with it!" (P97S).

Although the teachers were hand picked, the students were not, yet the emphasis on hard work was also stressed by the students we interviewed. For example, one student told us that the reason they worked so hard was because "We have great pride in this school and respect, and we want to do everything we can to help it. This is our county and we have to present it well." Since we were speaking with a 7th grade boy who could certainly have had other issues on his mind, we pressed him to explain why it was so important to him to have pride in and respect for his school. His reply was certain: "Well, it's our home, and we want to just show what a good place it is" (S97S).

For the teachers, pride in home was often the consequence of battling the insidious stereotypes of eastern Kentucky. Many spoke to us with anger about media portrayals which depicted Appalachia in terms of backwoods poverty, coal mining catastrophes, and the cardboard characters of television programs like "The Beverly Hillbillies." As Appalachian author, Cynthia Rylant (1991), explained: "Those who don't live in Appalachia and don't understand it sometimes make the mistake of calling these people 'hillbillies.' It isn't a good word for them. They probably would prefer 'Appalachians.' Like anyone else, they're sensitive about words" (p. 7). Mr. Bass, an Eagleview 7th grade writing teacher, concurred, explaining that there were times when people questioned their high KIRIS scores because they came from eastern Kentucky:

> But once again, we're rural. We're eastern Kentucky, so we must be cheating. And you know and I know we're not, but I'm saying that's the label. You know, we're all barefoot and pregnant out here. We don't know anything.... And I think, boy, in a weird sort of way, I think that's what keeps our fires lit as well. It's like, by George, I'm going to show you that we're from Eagleview County. We're not rich. We're from eastern Kentucky, but we can still compete with you. Community pride! (T97F)

Our urban sites were not as closely linked to their city in terms of *place*, nor did they have to contend with harmful stereotypes to keep their fires lit. Yet, they were dedicated to their *school* communities, and there was very little faculty turnover. The principal of Eastend Elementary had been there for 20 years, and her husband was principal there before her.

Despite this longevity, Ms. Conner had a particular view when it came to hiring: "It's almost my rule of thumb to take people right out of college, fresh new people ... [because] we want to train them. It's more difficult to bring somebody in here who has already developed habits of what they think teaching is and then try to retrain them" (P97S). Thus, Ms. Conner and her faculty developed their own heritage by enculturating new people into the school, a move that reminds us that the development of human capital—a willingness to learn—can be nurtured by the social context. As Peterson and colleagues (1996) suggested, "Successful relations occur among school structure, teaching practice, and student learning in schools where, because of recruitment and socialization, teachers share a common point of view about their purpose and principles of good practice" (p. 149).

The enculturation of new teachers meant commitment and a great deal of work, for Eastend teachers felt responsible not just for their classes of children, but for the whole school: "There's an attitude here that all of the students are my responsibility to teach, not 'Well, those are your kids and these are my kids, and I don't want them here.' ... It's more 'We have 615 children to teach'" (P97S). Still, Ms. Conner admitted that it would be "difficult to stay here and work in this program without total commitment," and over the years a few teachers, who found the team's responsibility too demanding, left. Ms. Conner explained, "I had a teacher one time who said, 'This is a very difficult program to work in. It's very demanding.' And I said, 'Yes, that's true.' And she said, 'Well, it's really too much work for me.' But she said, 'This is where I want my children to go to school.' And I think that says it all." (P97S)

Community members were also drawn to Mt. Vernon Middle, for this was a school with a unique history. Founded in 1834, it was now housed in an impressive brick building modeled in the 1930s after George Washington's home. Its more recent history was equally impressive, for it was one of the top KIRIS scorers in the state. Indeed, while the history of the building was intriguing, what the predominately mainstream population of parents wanted for their children was the heritage of academic success. Still, as its principal and teachers were quick to point out, it had a nonselective enrollment policy, which helped to balance the predominately upper-middle class student population with 24% of its students on free and reduced lunch. As Mr. George, the principal, explained, "I do not choose my population. I am a *public* school."

Mount Vernon's commitment to all students was reflected in their Mission Statement, which was prominently displayed throughout the school—on Mr. George's office door, in the materials visitors received, and in the student planner: "The faculty, staff, students, and community of Mt. Vernon Middle School are committed to academic excellence and the cultivation of individual strengths and talents in a supportive environment where individual differences and respect for the rights of others guide school and community behavior." Mt. Vernon's allegiance to "academic excellence" was also evident in their image as a "Fortune 500 company." Mr. George's talk was full of business references, statistics, and comments about "marketing strategies." He explained, "If we are going to be a Fortune 500 company ... you don't wait. You jump on it.... I'll be making a lot of decisions based on assessment.... That's what assessments should do ... give you feedback on the directions and your programs and then you make adjustments accordingly" (P97F). And Mr. George asked teachers to analyze their KIRIS scores like stock brokers at the ending bell:

> In mathematics, 25% of my 8th grade students were on a distinguished level.... That is considered a world class standard—the highest level, 25%. Those same kids though on the reading test ... zero [distinguished]. So that shows that we weren't doing things right in reading. So my math scores have continued to go up even though some of my other departments have either flatlined or even made slight declines. [It's] sort of like the stock market, up and down. (P97S)

Even though there were ups and downs in student scores, there was little fluctuation in faculty turnover, for Mt. Vernon Middle was a sound investment for a teacher's career. As Mr. George explained, "This is a real desirable area in Kentucky to teach so teachers hang on to their positions."

Over the years, however, there had been more turnover at the administrative levels. The expectations of parents in the community were "extremely high":

> Parents ... really want their children to learn well and expect that we are in the know or in the position that we can compete on a national level.... I am probably the sixth principal here. The five before me have been taken out.... I have weathered it because I have sought to make reforms like this. I actually introduced a lot of the reforms to the parents. (P97S)

Thus, to make history and create a heritage of academic success, Mr. George felt that a critical part of his role as principal was to attend to "what the community expects and take care of the children."

Although each of our case study school's history was unique, they each established a heritage of success through community pride, dedication to students, communication with parents, and hard work. Still, "weathering" the storm of demanding reform necessitates a level of leadership that is both courageous and cooperative. And it is to this aspect that we turn to in the next section.

Cooperative Leadership

In presenting one of the central characters in her Newbery award-winning novel, *Missing May*, Cynthia Rylant (1992) described May in the following way:

> May was the best person I ever knew.... She understood people and she let them be whatever way they needed to be. She had faith in every single person she ever met, and this never failed her, for nobody ever disappointed May. Seems people knew she saw the very best of them, and they'd turn that side to her to give her a better look. (pp. 15-16)

Inspiring people to turn to their better sides is a singular achievement, especially when teachers are pressed to take on new curriculum, instruction, and high-stakes assessment. In this process, principals shoulder what Evans (1993) calls an "exceptional burden" (p. 20), for they need to see the best in their teachers and encourage all to move towards reform without sacrificing who they need to be. In our schools, the principals often accomplished this through cooperative leadership.

In our urban elementary school, Ms. Conner "set the tone" for the teamwork in her building. The school was divided into six complexes—each containing four teachers for a 100 multi-grade students. Decisions were made within complexes as well as through a strong Site-Based Decision Making council. Ms. Conner characterized her teachers as doing an "excellent job of identifying problem areas and then correcting them" (P97F). Ms. Roby, a 4th/5th grade teacher, talked about how the staff met the curricular challenges that the state demanded, "Our SBDM committees look at each new thing as it comes out and decides who's going to deal with that, and we go on" (T97F).

When aspects of curriculum were under state debate, Eastend teachers persisted in executing what they felt were valuable goals. For example, the mathematics portfolios were withdrawn from the accountability index, but the teachers responsible for this aspect of the curriculum continued to ask their students to complete them. When the Kentucky testing system was in flux (see note #2), there was state-wide debate over the goals and number of pieces to be included in the writing portfolios. One ominous, yet erroneous, rumor flooding the state was that the writing portfolios would also be eliminated, but Eastend teachers remained committed. Still, this is surprising when one considers the amount of work these portfolios require. In many schools, the elimination of the mathematics portfolio and the threat against the writing portfolio caused teachers to drop them or at least hold them in abeyance. Yet, Eastend teachers persevered because they felt that these reform-based practices, though complex and time-consuming, made sense for the education of children.

> I think we have people here who really believe in it and support it, and we have a leader who really believes that it's important. I think all of us have seen a difference in our children and their ability to write and the quality of instruction, and so I don't think that [eliminating them] would happen. But I think if you had a school where there wasn't a committed group of teachers, and good leadership among the teachers themselves, you know ... [it would be a different story]." (Ms. Mitchell, Professional Staff Assistant, P98S)

The emphasis on remaining committed to purpose in the face of changing political winds seemed to be a key outcome of Eastend's distributed leadership.

In setting her sights on shared leadership, the principal, Ms. Conner, carefully constructed teaching teams for the six complexes that contained both leaders and what she called "backbone type people ... [whose] personality is such that they can work with about anybody." When a new teacher was added to an existing complex, the entire team took responsibility for bringing her/him into their school culture. Still, the staff was eager to listen to new teachers as well. Ms. Conner suggested that during faculty hiring, they looked for "people who are very intelligent.... It's important that we try to get the cream of the crop, and typically your better educated, more intelligent person is going to have high standards for children." The end result was a team of dedicated teachers who were quick on the uptake of school reform. As Ms. Conner explained: "There is very strong leadership, and the leadership isn't just my leadership. It's coming from staff. So I think change is a little easier here. And I've been told that if it takes five years to make the change happen, Eastend can probably do it in two. And that's true. So true" (P97S).

The capacity to shift quickly came from Ms. Conner's willingness to "roll up her sleeves" and work *with* her staff, and the same was true at our rural elementary. Bluejay teachers pointed to Ms. Chief's fluid ability to model new practices in their classrooms as well as lead the front office. In fact, Ms. Chief summarized her role "as a teacher helper. Anything that I can do instruction wise and to improve student performance, that's my job" (P97S). She encouraged teachers to "Holler at me, send someone after me, and let me come in and see" the "wonderful" events in classrooms.

Ms. Chief's frequent classroom visits could have been seen as intimidating; instead, they were welcome. She was known as a master teacher, but even more renown for sharing her expertise. This set the standard for her teachers, who exchanged ideas without hesitation. When interviewing two 4th grade teachers, Ms. Jazz and Ms. Rebel, we were struck by the quality of their interaction. They took turns pointing out each other's attributes, and were so in sync they finished each other's sentences. Ms.

Rebel explained that a quality of Bluejay teachers was their willingness to ask:

> [They] don't hesitate to ask if they feel like they need some kind of special training or if they feel like they don't understand a concept fully. They don't hesitate to say, "Well I need this to be modeled for me." Sometimes teachers may hesitate to ask, feeling like, "Well, maybe this is something I should already know" or "I don't sound professional if I ask this question." But here, the whole aura at this school is open. They'll ask if they need something. I don't hesitate to ask. If I don't understand how to do something, I don't hesitate one bit to come over here and ask Ms. Jazz for advice on what I should do. (T97F)

One reason the staff could ask for help was the level of *trust* they had established, an element often cited in research: "If staff members are to commit themselves to innovation and risk its anxieties and losses, they must find the new goal both desirable and feasible.... Teachers are most likely to accept change when it is espoused by someone they trust." (Evans, 1993, p. 20). And trust works both ways for "principals are dependent on teachers' support and trust if reform efforts are to endure" (Muncey & McQuillan, 1996, p. 272).

At Bluejay, trust came not only in professional exchanges, but in personal and sometimes humorous give and take. Teachers told us how they liked to "joke" and generally "cut up." And they felt that a new teacher had finally arrived when s/he was willing to participate in some of Bluejay's famous "practical jokes." Ms. Chief summarized the combination of work and play:

> We've always been a very close faculty. We laugh together and we cry together and we feel like we are very close.... We go on a retreat each year...and it's one of the best things we do to get our faculty off to a good start. We ... laugh and we cut up. But during the professional development during the day, we work. And we can get up and go to lunch, and I'll look around and we've got half of them still sitting there or wanting to work through lunch. How lucky can we get? And when the end of the session comes about, they're still working. And then while they're visiting with each other during the evenings, guess what they're talking about? Work. "I want to do this and this and this this year. What did you do? Can I borrow that?" I'm a strong believer in positive school climate. If you don't have that first, you probably won't get other things. (P97S)

Many teachers characterized the faculty as a "family." As the 5th grade teacher, Ms. Fit, explained: "It's amazing because you feel you really do have a family.... And I would not work anywhere else. I think I would probably have to just go to Wal-Mart or somewhere if I had to" (T97F).

In the research, images of "family" in school can be depicted in disparaging ways. Hargreaves (1997a) suggested that "it is more than a little ironic that many principals refer to their ... staffs as 'families'.... There is little ambiguity about who is the parent and who are the children here!" (p. 1308). Yet, Ms. Chief was not seen as maternalistic; instead, she was a professional colleague. As Ms. Jazz described Bluejay's effort in addressing Kentucky's reform: "It has to be a group effort. It can't be just one person in a building.... Everybody needs to get sold on the idea" (T97S).

Still, selling people on ideas and drawing them into complex reform is easier with a trusted leader at the fore. At Eagleview, this was particularly true. Unlike our other principals, Mr. Push did not do model lessons nor lead professional development, but he actively participated in professional opportunities: "My teachers have to know that I'm interested in it. If it's important enough for me to be there, it's important enough for them to be there" (P97F). More important, when Mr. Push rolled up his sleeves, it was highly strategic. He knew his team members' talents and how to position them for success. When he shifted Ms. Crabtree, an 8th grade writing teacher to the 7th grade accountability position, she didn't want to go, but Mr. Push convinced her:

> I brought her in ... and told her I thought it was the best thing for the school. And she felt that she had the expertise. Ms. Crabtree's been involved more with writing process than anybody I've ever been around.... You know you are sitting there with a pitcher. You got a 20-game winner. And you got one that's *going* to be a good pitcher, but they don't have the experience. That 20-game winner is going to go out on the mound. (P97F)

Mr. Push worked through a combination of caring and charisma, and his self-selected pseudonym is symbolic of his willingness to nudge his teachers into the positions he wanted them to play.

Even when his decisions were questioned, his motivation was not. For example, Mr. Bass, also a 7th grade writing teacher, thought they should distribute the portfolio responsibilities among more teachers so no teacher would be responsible for 110 portfolios, an extraordinary weight for any teacher. But Mr. Push opted to leave the 330 portfolios in the hands of his three 7th grade teachers. Mr. Bass was characteristically honest as he imagined the thinking behind this decision:

> You know, "Mr. Bass's doing okay. Ms. Crabtree's doing okay. Ms. Getmore's done this for years. Just let them keep doing it." If that's the case, I don't appreciate that. But you know, once again, it goes back to the bottom line, and the bottom line is whatever this school needs to do to be the best, that's what we're going to do. (T97F)

Meeting "the bottom line" meant extensive planning, and at Eagleview each grade-level team met daily. Mr. Push felt this time was "key" because his teachers liked to make "a lot of their own decisions. They don't like for me to tell them everything to do. They're professionals" (P97S).

Indeed, far from an unprofessional chat session, each team met to plan, discuss teaching strategies, and brainstorm how to meet the needs of individual students. In our observations, we saw one team's lead teacher take notes, often stopping to summarize the discussion and reiterate which teacher had volunteered for what. Discussions of students were marked with respect. The team's Title I teacher (who worked *in* the classrooms) contributed ideas, and the family resource counselor came in on occasion to provide background on students. Thus, the daily meetings were a time where ideas were shared and decisions were made. As Mr. Bass explained, "I'm of the opinion that some of the greatest teachers in the state are in this county, and they're doing a lot of neat things. I think our system allows us to share those ideas with each other" (T97F).

The teachers were also of the opinion that they had some of the greatest students in the state, and they wanted their students to share in the responsibilities of making Eagleview "the best middle school in Kentucky." As a result, Mr. Push was out in the halls, talking and joking with students or giving them serious advice on a recent project, and his knowledge of students was extensive. He knew about their home lives and dilemmas. When a student had holes in his shoes, Mr. Push made sure he got a new pair. When a student needed her glasses fixed, he noticed and made the trip to a local optometrist for a donation. If he saw a student walking home, he gave him a lift. Indeed, he had visited many of the children's homes, and had close-up knowledge of the poverty in the area, but poverty was not his overriding focus. He saw the *students*, not just the *statistics*:

> We have a very [economically] diverse population, but if you look at our free and reduced lunch, we're about 70% overall.... That tells a lot about the incomes of the students, but I think you have to realize that *that is not what makes it*. I talked to you the other day about how we've got four kids who are going to be getting full scholarships to the University of Kentucky as 8th graders and they are kids [that] have never had anybody in their family be involved in college. Those are the things I think really make a difference for me. Motivate those kids. That's how we're going to change society. (P97S)

His emphasis on changing society came with a strong academic focus. He knew where students stood because each quarter he personally reviewed the 650 report cards and then stopped students in the halls with comments: "The kids like for you to tell them that they did a good job or they need to work to get this grade up. They really like to know that you know and that you get after them when they're not doing right. At least somebody cares enough that they're getting after them." Caring also included meeting with students to discuss future plans: "My biggest strength is bringing kids into my office one-on-one and talking to them. You ask them, 'What do you want to be?' And at least you want them to think, 'Someday I want to do something'" (P98S).

Knowing what they wanted to be was more common for the urban students in Mt. Vernon Middle. In an atmosphere of high parental expectations, the faculty were under even more pressure to do well. Perhaps this pressure drove Mr. George's focus on percentages, marketing strategies, and what it took to be the "CEO of a Fortune 500 company." Thus, in the sense of "cooperative leadership," Mt. Vernon was unique, for the shared vision of the school was often Mr. George's vision. He set the goals and designed ways to achieve them. For example, at KIRIS testing time, he brought in motivational speakers like Tubby Smith, a University of Kentucky coach, or invited the UK cheerleaders to give a pep rally for the kids. Mr. George carefully selected candidates to lead his staff's professional development (PD), and when he couldn't find what he wanted, he did it himself, running a school-wide PD workshop for an hour every week. He packed these sessions with critical topics such as using the four-column method for KIRIS open response questions.

Mr. George's teachers appreciated his leadership style, for he was open to their ideas as well as complaints. Mr. Perry, an 8th grade teacher, explained, "Mr. George's the kind of person [who] gives open invitations to the faculty. 'If you want to come in, shut the door and tell me what you don't like. You can walk in that office, rant, rave, curse, carry on. You know. But let's get it out in the open.'... So everything you've heard me say, Mr. George has already heard" (T97S). Mr. George's willingness to listen is born out in research for, "It is an axiom of organizational change that the larger the innovation, the greater the need for communication.... Authentic leaders are strongly biased toward clear communication. Many are eloquent, but all convey their goals through their very consistency. And they are eager, respectful listeners" (Evans, 1993, p. 22).

Mr. George could also be quite vocal about his faculty. He did not shy away from criticizing teachers who avoided staff development, and his highest compliments went to teachers eager to continue their learning. He described the teachers we worked with, in just those terms:

> Ms. Dawson is outstanding. I don't think you'll find a better language arts teacher in the country.... She is really knowledgeable about teaching and learning. Shows a lot of initiative ... spends a lot of extra time in the academic area. Mr. Perry is very bright, very personable. He goes to all of the meetings.... He likes to be in the know at the state level, and he'll take the initiative to be on state committees. [His] being a regional coordinator has

> helped us a great deal.... So those two teachers are outstanding.... They continue their education on their own. They find ways to improve their learning. (P97S)

Although Mr. George felt that these two teachers stood out, he also felt that his entire faculty was motivated to do well:

> Teachers that are burnt out are teachers that see that what they're trying to do is not being accomplished, and I don't have a burn out here. I have teachers that are in control of a program.... That makes them feel good that they really have input and that they own the school too. I think that brings about a lot of motivation. (P98S)

Motivation might have been difficult considering the school's history with KIRIS. Although Mt. Vernon was one of the state's highest-scoring schools, in our first year there they were "in decline" because their scores had not risen sufficiently. This is a state-wide irony for high-scoring schools, for if your scores are already high, how do you maintain the rate of gain every year?[6] For Mt. Vernon teachers, the realization that their hard work was being criticized instead of acclaimed was daunting. Mr. George described what they went through when their scores first "flat-lined." Initially, the teachers blamed KIRIS, and then they moved into "denial." Ultimately, they accepted responsibility. Mr. George explained, "And that is a long way to come. When a teacher can say, "Okay. Okay. These children did not learn. I had some responsibility in that" (P97S).

Still, taking responsibility is more likely when teachers are given the opportunity to exercise their professional expertise. As McDonnell (1994) suggested, " ... the application of professional knowledge to individual clients' needs requires judgment, so it cannot be reduced to rules or prescriptions for practice" (p. 410). Mr. George, too, felt that there were no easy answers:

> Let's say you have 70% of your kids that are doing well, but you're not reaching 30%. How do you bring those 30% in as well? Your school isn't doing well if it's excluding 30% of your kids. Now, how do you bring them up? A lot of schools have approached it, "Well, the teachers will work harder." But the teachers are really working about as hard as they can work, and they're not going to be able to all of a sudden double their workload.... So, you have to replace what they've traditionally been doing to help them work smarter. (P98S)

For Mr. George and our other principals, working smarter meant giving teachers opportunities to reflect on where their professional judgment about teaching and learning aligned with that of the state reform, and where they still needed to grow, an issue that we turn to in the next section.

Reflective Alignment with Kentucky Reform

> The men and women and children who live in Appalachia have no sourness about them and though they are shy toward outsiders, they will wave to you if you drive by in your car whether they know your face or not.... Most of them are thinkers, because these mountains inspire that. (Rylant, 1991, p. 21)

Another feature of our exemplary schools was their reflective alignment with the reform. Although each school's faculty had thought long and hard about their dilemmas with different aspects, for the most part they believed in the reform. Part of this belief system stemmed from the fact that some of the reform-based changes were things they were already doing. Ms. Chief said that Bluejay was the "first school in this part of the state to have an ungraded primary" (P97S), while Eastend's ungraded program had been in effect for over 30 years. Both Bluejay and Eastend had inclusion programs for their special needs children long before the state recommended it.

More important, however, was a willingness to change in reform-based ways. For example, "Bluejay University" was a place for "reflective thinkers," and the teachers worked to model their thinking processes for their children. Of all the students we interviewed, the Bluejay children asked us the most questions about our questions. They'd stop us mid protocol and ask for clarification, and at the end of their answers they would look at us quite seriously and ask, "Did I answer all the parts of your question? Is there anything else you want to know?" Their teachers felt that the children's questions came from their recent training in a strategy called the "four column method" which helped children analyze KIRIS open response questions in any content area and highlighted the importance of answering all parts of the question. When we commented on the children's thoughtfulness, Ms. Jazz responded: "I hope so! ... Actually it's problem solving. Everything we do—writing, math, science—everything we do involves problem solving. (T97F)

One of the biggest problems to solve was how to address such a complex reform, for traditional methods were now superseded by conceptual approaches. Children still learned basic skills in mathematics, but they were now learning to come up with more than one potential answer as well as to justify the answer they chose. Children still learned grammar in writing, but they were now mastering multiple genres and learning to express their ideas for different audiences and purposes. And for children to learn to do these things, their teachers had to be willing to keep learning about the latest reform-based methods. Ms. Chief described two hypothetical teachers:

> Teacher A goes out and learns all she can, and she keeps learning and she keeps growing and she uses the knowledge and puts it to use with her students and her classroom. But Teacher B teaches in the same mode, the same way, year after year after year. And you've got Teacher A continuously changing and adding on and growing and growing. And both those classrooms are going to be two completely different environments in my opinion. And classroom Teacher A, like all the teachers here at Bluejay Elementary, that's where I would want my child to be. (P97S)

The willingness to grow and change was also reflected in the leadership roles faculty took both inside and outside of school. They didn't just attend professional development seminars, they led them. At Bluejay, Ms. Chief was both a Distinguished Educator and the writing coordinator for her region, training clusters of 4th grade writing teachers from 11 counties. At Eagleview, Ms. Crabtree was involved in writing reform at almost every level and Mr. Taylor was similarly involved in mathematics and also qualified as a Distinguished Educator.

Our urban faculties took on leadership roles as well. At Mt. Vernon, Mr. Perry was regional coordinator in mathematics. At Eastend, Ms. Nicholl was a mathematics cluster leader, while Ms. Roby was both the regional coordinator in mathematics and a cluster leader in writing. Their leadership roles were critical in aligning their school goals with the state goals, for they were in the position to influence the direction of the reform itself as well as access important information faster than the average teacher. As Ms. Roby explained, "A lot of the training travels down quite an avenue before it gets to the individual classroom teacher, so our concern has been to jump in there and get as high up on that as we can to get the information first and help our building" (T97S).

The state's emphasis on assessment aligned particularly well with Eastend Elementary's philosophy. While some schools in the state were startled by the new emphasis on assessment, many of Eastend's decisions were evaluation-based. Each summer they took on a new content area and looked carefully at how their curriculum could be enhanced, as well as how it could be aligned with KIRIS assessment. As Ms. Conner, the principal, explained: "We've been very strong into assessment and that has driven our entire program.... After we've decided what it is children need to learn, then that determines what we're going to teach. So we've done a lot of work on how to assess students and what instruments to use" (P97S). Still, the alignment which our exemplary schools share with the reform does not mean that they followed the state's suggestions lockstep. Ms. Conner added, "We've taken [from KERA and KIRIS] what we believe works with our philosophy, and we've incorporated it. Then the things that we felt were in conflict or weren't exactly right, we've adjusted, or maybe totally dropped them, and made it work for us."

Adjusting things that weren't exactly right was a characteristic of Eagleview Middle as well. For example, Eagleview writing teachers initially found the KDE writing workshops to be enlightening, but now that they'd been teaching reform-based writing for a few years, they wanted to do more professional development in-house. Indeed, because they had worked so extensively together on their writing instruction, they sometimes found state workshops to be "old news." Mr. Bass expressed concerns about a KDE writing workshop: "They were doing a good job with what they gave us. The only problem was it was information that had been around for a while" (T97F). As a result, he and his colleagues came up with their own plan for six hours of PD, using the time collaboratively to develop notebooks of ideas on each of the three kinds of state-assessed writing.

In addition to designing their own PD, the teachers at Eagleview were willing to criticize what they saw as negative patterns in the state assessment. For example, Mr. Taylor questioned an unintended consequence of the state's emphasis on multiple representations, an emphasis common in reform-based mathematics. He explained that when the state first started with portfolios they gave better scores to students who included numerous representations for their solutions. In his view, many teachers had consequently taken the practice to the extreme. As a result, students included useless representations of problems simply for the sake of writing more for the scorer:

> I think you want to see multiple representations, but as a justification for getting their answer. And it has not been used for that. Because [the state] says you can get a good score if you have multiple representations, teachers taught their students, "Include three ways to show [your solution]" regardless of whether it's beneficial or not. So, in the portfolio pieces kids learned multiple representation, but for the wrong reasons. (T97F)

Mr. Taylor felt that providing more than one solution should not be "a step" in receiving a good score. Instead, students should be taught the appropriate uses for multiple representations, such as showing a solution with an example and then moving into the more abstract general solution for the problem. Indeed, he felt that one of the difficulties with the mathematics portfolio was that in many teachers' classrooms there was more of an emphasis on *writing* than on *mathematics*.

In addition to creating their own materials and criticizing pedagogical choices, the Eagleview faculty was committed to distributing the weight of the state assessments, which demonstrates that reflective alignment with reform was not simply the responsibility of accountability grade teachers. Although Mr. Push was unwilling to shift the 7th grade writing portfolio away from teachers he saw as most able to handle the task, he was instrumental in creating an atmosphere of shared responsibility. This was exemplified in his "executive decision" to create "core days"—days in which the entire Eagleview staff shifted their teaching schedules to work for extended periods of time on core subjects. Teachers in non-accountability grades moved to accountability classrooms and worked with students while teaming with the accountability teacher. Even teachers that taught elective courses shifted to accountability subjects on these specially-designated days.

Mr. Taylor explained that on core days, he determined where his students needed the most help and set the schedule. On a core day we observed, students were working on mathematical open response questions, and three additional teachers came to work with his students. In addition to core days, faculty participated in scoring the completed writing portfolios. Mr. Bass explained, "We'll have 20 some teachers who will be trained officially to score [writing] portfolios ... which at scoring time takes a big load off" (T97F).

This kind of collaborative work implies reflection on how to meet KIRIS requirements. It also reiterates McDonnell's (1994) view that new assessments inspire deliberation. Open spaces for talk was a feature of all of our schools, whether through teacher-to-teacher conversations at Bluejay, computer-network curriculum discussions at Eastend, or shared planning time at Eagleview. And these conversations often emerged from trust, for as Spillane and Thompson (1997) found, "trust created an environment in which local educators were comfortable discussing their understandings of and reservations about new instructional approaches, conversations that were essential for reconstructive learning" (p. 195).

Mt. Vernon Middle was especially strategic in its emphasis on reconstructive learning through conversation. In keeping with the Fortune 500 Company theme, Mr. George looked closely at the school's KIRIS scores each year and sought advice from experts about what content still needed work and how they could improve. He then made those areas the focus of staff conversations:

> What the administration has to do is provide a lot of conversation in the area. You do that by talking, and you talk about *instructional* areas, not the ball game tomorrow or buildings and grounds. You focus on what it is you want to improve. If our big push is in writing, then at every opportunity you talk about writing, and you talk about it all day. When the teachers see [it's] important to you, then it will become important to them. (P97F)

Mr. George's call for more talk about writing was not a suggestion that his teachers simply "teach to the test." Instead, he was proposing a long-term conversation about how children learn to express themselves in writing as well as learn to revise their writing to communicate in more effective ways.

These kinds of conversations were true of all four schools. In fact, in thinking about how our schools reflectively changed their instruction to meet the reform, there is perhaps no better case than how they taught writing—an area that we will explore in the next section.

Teaching to and Beyond the Test in Writing

In an essay entitled "Writing in the Smokehouse," Appalachian writer Lisa Koger (1998) talks about the differences between the "basics" of learning to write and learning to write from the heart:

> I think it's hard for me to talk about writing simply because the more I write, the more difficult and inexplicable writing is. Which is not to say that, through reading and spending an unhealthy amount of time on university campuses, I haven't acquired a certain familiarity with the elements of fiction (character, plot, point of view) and gained a passable understanding of how those elements work together in a short story or novel. Any diligent dog can be taught such tricks.... So why write about writing at all? I am only one voice, one opinion, but I'd like to think that by agreeing to write this essay, I'm not only sharing a part of my life but taking a stand on issues that are important to me. (p. 156)

Much has been made of the phrase "teaching to the test," and in writing that would mean just what this quote diminishes—"a certain familiarity with the elements of fiction" which only leads to a "passable understanding." But our Kentucky teachers went well beyond teaching for "diligent dogs" and into substantive reflection of how *children* learn to share their lives and take important stands. Although we could talk about accomplishments in other subjects—such as mathematics, the other content area we studied—for the purposes of this piece we will concentrate on a subject that Kentucky considers one of its strengths: writing. Indeed, the teaching of writing provides us with clear examples of how exemplary teachers reflect on the reform and teach *to* as well as *beyond* the test.

Still, before we proceed to our individual sites, it is necessary to take a step back and think about Kentucky's writing reform in general. In a time where most states are utilizing one-time-only, on demand prompts to test children's writing skills, the Kentucky reform places emphasis on helping children grow as writers in more substantive ways. Indeed, KIRIS testing, which also includes on demand prompts and open response items, is most courageous in its portfolio requirement. Each child in an accountability grade must prepare a portfolio of original writing which includes: (a) a table of contents; (b) personal expressive writing (personal narratives); (c) literary writing (stories, poems); (d) transactive writing ("real world" writing in letters, editorials); and (e) a letter to the reviewer where the student analyzes his or her growth as a writer.

Portfolio preparation takes an entire year, and it requires instruction in the writing process, in the particular features of multiple genres, and in creating multiple opportunities for peer- and teacher-conferencing as well as self-evaluation. Thus, a student's final portfolio represents hours, days, and months of writing, revision, conferencing, reading, and writing some more. Prior to the Kentucky reform in writing, teachers in our schools did not help children prepare portfolios, and they taught writing more as a grammatical skill than as an opportunity for self-expression. But the portfolio stipulations and the subsequent professional development they received to learn about these requirements, encouraged them rethink their instruction. As Mr. Bass explained, "Because of KERA, I changed my style of teaching to a more workshop-oriented approach" (T98S).

But what did this approach look like in our exemplary writing teachers' classrooms? In our eastern Kentucky sites, the emphasis on *voice* was strong. At Eagleview, Mr. Bass learned to share his own experience as well as his own writing with his students, and he urged them to connect their reading and writing to their own lives. In one lesson we observed, he explored types of personal narrative. He reviewed the features of this genre and then used poetry to help his students understand how writing is often inspired by personal experience. All four of the poems he shared were carefully chosen to show how character can be revealed through a description of hands and fingers. He began with a poem about baby fingers ("How beautiful new fingers are, And how complete."). He then read a poem about the appearance of people's hands when they have different careers, and then one about "old people's fingers." He confided that he had attempted to write his own poem on the topic: "A few years ago I came across these poems, and I tried to write a poem called 'Teacher's Fingers.' But I didn't like it. I still don't like it, and I'm probably going to have to go back and revise it again" (T97S).

Mr. Bass's disclosure reveals his emphasis on *writing*, an emphasis that research suggests is common with exemplary teachers of writing who discuss their own writing efforts, stress the need for revision, and emphasize connections between literature and writing (McIver & Wolf, 1999; Wolf & Davinroy, 1998). In addition, as he read the fourth poem he urged the students to "Pay attention to the imagery and the descriptive writing." This final poem was a lesson in itself, for it was written by a teacher at the Eagleview County High School—a woman who had taught Mr. Bass when he was in high school and who would eventually teach many members of his seventh grade class. In introducing the poem, Mr. Bass said: "This one's my favorite, and I hope that all of you have the opportunity to have this teacher—Ms. Roberts. She helped me get started, and she helped me in college. Now I've taught with her and done workshops with her." The poem was entitled "My Own Middle Aged Fingers" and one verse read:

Cramped, yet working, though scarred and rough
Tinged with pink and white from chalk
Identifying mistakes, corrections by the millions
The right, always in love with the pencil
My instrument of individuality. (T97S)

Ms. Robert's poem was longer than the first three poems, and while reading Mr. Bass stopped often to ask questions. After this verse, he asked "How do we know that she is a teacher?" His students volunteered the phrase "pink and white from chalk." Mr. Bass' use of this poem, combined with his comments on his own poetry writing, points to the availability of real writers in the community. Although the poem was not a published piece, Mr. Bass used it to show his students that writing was not an alien endeavor that only came from professional writers in some far away place. Instead, writing was a vibrant part of community life.

At the end of the lengthy discussion of all four poems, Mr. Bass made the assignment: "I want you to look back on your 7th grade year. I want you to think about an incident during this year that made you realize that you were growing up." Following the pattern established in the poetry he shared, the students could choose from an incident in their lives that demonstrated their relationship with an infant, a career-minded grown up, or an older person, or they could simply write about an experience from the current year. Though Mr. Bass offered much assignment choice, all four suggestions focused on the topic of change, and the required genre was a personal narrative.

This long vignette of Mr. Bass and his writing class exemplifies the kind of writing instruction we saw in all our teachers. They were concerned with the test and worked hard to prepare their students for its requirements, but in their effort to meet the state standards, they did not neglect the absolute *art* of teaching writing. Like Ms. Roberts' poetic explanation, they too were "in love with the pencil," but they used it less to make "corrections by the millions," than to demonstrate their own fascination with writing. Although writing a personal narrative was a KIRIS portfolio requirement, the teachers taught the genre not as one more hoop to jump through, but as a unique opportunity for written expression. Our teachers' emphasis on content is similarly accentuated in the research literature. In studying those who take "responsibility for instructional reform," Spillane and Thompson (1997) found that "commitment typically involved helping *students* experience and learn *a particular subject* in more exciting ways" (p. 191).

Across our exemplary sites, the writing teachers' engagement with their content played out in a number of ways. At Bluejay, for example, the teachers talked often about how to improve their practice. The two 4th grade teachers we worked with, Ms. Jazz and Ms. Rebel, said they held almost daily conversations on their practice: "We talk and we share back and forth. Maybe that's it—just sharing and *doing*. 'Cause if you don't do it, you won't ever get it" (T97F).

In addition, their attitude towards *doing* writing—taking risks with a variety of lesson formats and studying the features of particular genres—went well beyond their own conversations, for they looked to outside experts for help. During one visit, we observed the region's writing coordinator conduct demonstration lessons in their classes. Ms. Chief had arranged this day of PD based on the expressed needs of her teachers, and she encouraged non-accountability grade teachers to observe these lessons as well. One of coordinator's lessons was on the features of personal narrative, with an emphasis on the need for authors to demonstrate "feeling" as well as the "lessons learned." The demonstration was a lively one, for the coordinator was an experienced teacher, and the children eagerly participated in discussing the genre's characteristics. When the lesson was over, Ms. Rebel directed the children to write their commentary on the day's events, and one child wrote: "I think personal narratives are great because you have to put in action and feelings."

While the children concentrated on "feelings," Ms. Jazz was more intrigued by the idea of closing the narrative with a "focus on the effect of the event" and the "lessons learned." She had been teaching personal narrative "for years and writing them as well" and had never heard of this concept, though after rumination she could see that closing the genre with comments on the significance of the story was often the case. The writing coordinator, whose job was to enhance teachers' understandings of reform-based writing instruction, said she believed that for "a personal narrative *to be* a personal narrative it had to focus on the *effect*." Ms. Jazz thought for a while and then said, "Maybe what your lesson did was give me words to put on top of something I've already been doing. I've really learned something here. Thank you!" Later in the day, Ms. Jazz was still considering the concept and told us, "That's just like what I was saying last night. You can't really say that you've internalized a concept until you have the words for it" (T97F).

Finding words for the art of writing was integral to the instruction at Eastend Elementary as well. In a writers' workshop lesson we observed in a 4th/5th grade combination class, the teachers asked their children to look over their portfolio contents and choose a personal narrative to rework. Ms. Nicholl suggested that they "fire up" their piece to demonstrate "how they've grown as a writer" (T97S). She asked what things they would expect to see in fine writing, and some children suggested "foreshadowing," while others offered that they wanted to "catch the reader's attention." Ms. Nicholl explained that the "things you're bringing up are things that change and add to the work. They make a piece *way up there*." Ms. Roby commented that "capitalization and punctuation won't make work more exciting." Her remark shows understanding that revision involves the reworking of *content*, while editing focuses on convention and should come later in the writing process. The children added: "help the reader follow the story," "good details," "know your purpose," and "correct grammar." The order of their ideas with "correct grammar" last confirms their understanding that editing does not enhance the story, but makes it more readable. Though there was an emphasis on grammar and spelling in the Daily Oral Language exercises and the English textbook work the students did, it didn't hamper their ability to distinguish between this and what would make an engaging story.

After the children had chosen the pieces they wished to rework, the teachers helped prepare them for peer conferencing. They reminded the children that the peer reviewer should listen to the story twice before commenting. However, in modeling this, Ms. Nicholl suggested that they show a "non example first," to demonstrate how it *shouldn't* be done. Ms. Roby began reading her story but before she finished the first sentence, Ms. Nicholl interrupted to ask where she was going. Ms. Roby pretended mock surprise at the abrupt interruption, and then both teachers used this negative example to reiterate the importance of listening to the piece twice before making comments. Ms. Nicholl explained that in response to a personal narrative the children should first "listen to figure out what they're talking about. As I'm listening, I'm looking for feelings and to be entertained."

Ms. Roby read her story twice, and then opened up the class discussion. One child suggested that the story should "have more feelings," and both teachers broke into song: "Feelings, oh, oh, feelings." Many children giggled, and a child sitting next to us said, "They're always doing stuff like that" (T97S). However, the *stuff* that these teachers did went beyond incorporating humor. They used high-level, technical vocabulary, they encouraged their children to think about revision before editing, they modeled a negative example to demonstrate the need for careful listening, and they brought their children's ideas into the discussion. In short, they positioned their children to think like writers. While preparing their children for the completion of their KIRIS portfolios and encouraging them to make each piece the best it could be, their focus was less on the *test* than on the *talk* that surrounds what good writers typically do to improve their work. Still, the KIRIS test, especially its portfolio requirement, guided them towards this vision of reform-based writing. When we asked Ms. Roby how she had changed her writing instruction to match the KIRIS portfolio, she replied: "We've formatted our teaching style around it. And we've gone through years of training as it's gone along.... So we've worked really hard on that because we believe in it" (T97S). She also valued the KIRIS emphasis on "high standards" and how children learned at a very early age to "communicate their thoughts and ideas," rather than simply "fill in the blank."

Communication was a central part of the writing work at Mt. Vernon Middle as well. Ms. Dawson also asked her 7th graders to reflect on how to improve their portfolio pieces. The students were preparing to write the state-required "letter to the reviewer" in which they analyze their writing for the adult who will score their work. As Ms. Dawson explained, the "purpose of the letter is to talk about the pieces you chose, your growth, and how you've developed in your writing" (T97S). In helping them prepare for their letters, she asked:

Ms. Dawson:	What influenced your writing this year? What helped you grow?
Student #1:	All the reading that we've done ... .
Ms. Dawson:	Do you think the reading is reflected in your writing?
Student #2:	Yeah. And the fact that we have lots of writing—that we do portfolios.
Ms. Dawson:	Is there anything we did on a regular basis that helped?
Student #3:	Sometimes the author would use really rich language.
Ms. Dawson:	So looking at the authors and the way they write?
Chorus:	Yes!

In drafting their reviewer letters, the students revealed their willingness to ponder their pieces. One student said he discovered that one story in his portfolio was "so confusing, [he] practically had to do a whole new story." Another described her genre preferences: "I have trouble with personal narratives, but I like short stories and poems because I like to make things up." Still another commented on his penchant for writing "purpose pieces." When we asked him to elaborate he replied, "When I grow up, I want to be a lawyer so I want to be persuasive and write purpose pieces—like an article or an editorial. So it might improve what level of lawyer I'll be" (S97S).

Research (e.g., Graves, 1994) tells us that reflecting on writing improves the level of writing—whether that writing has pragmatic purposes (like ambitions to become a lawyer) or creative purposes (like "making things up" in a story). The students we met in our exemplary sites were well aware of the pressures of KIRIS as they developed their portfolios and learned how to respond to open response items and on demand prompts. The older students in particular said that they wanted to get "high scores" and measured their progress with the KIRIS vocabulary that permeated the curriculum. For example, a girl in Ms. Dawson's class reflected on the grades she'd received on her portfolio stories over the year: " On my first one I got like a 'proficient,' but on the last one I did, Ms. Dawson gave me a 'distinguished' so that really is a big jump" (S97S).

Still, the students' comments on scores were superceded by insights on their craft as writers. When we asked how they thought teachers and peers would characterize them as writers, they responded with enthusiasm. They compared their current writing with their writing from earlier grades, and they discussed their ability to add detail and "grab the reader's attention." Yet, their enthusiasm did not prevent them from being self critical, for as they looked over their portfolio with us they pointed out places where they could improve, choose a better vocabulary word, or add a transition to help their reader along. In short, they felt valued as writers. And it is to these feelings of value that we turn to in our last section of results.

"It's All For The Kids!"

> The children love all the seasons. They go down by the creek or into the woods or up the dirt roads with their good dogs and they feel more important than anything else in these Appalachian mountains. (Rylant, 1991, p. 19)

Feeling important in the world is a place where teachers and principals want all their children to be, but achieving this depends on capable adults dedicated to making sound decisions for children in their schools. Throughout our results, we have emphasized the ways in which our exemplary sites placed the value of students first. Still, we feel the need to add a brief section to highlight the fifth and ultimately most important feature—the education of *all* students. In fact, if we had to decide on a banner motto that could stretch across our four sites it would be: "It's all for the kids!"

Prior to KERA, especially the flush of money for books, supplies, and professional development that Kentucky offered with their reform (Borko, Elliott, & Uchiyama, 1999), times were tight for schools, particularly for those in eastern Kentucky. As Ms. Chief explained,

> You could have heard an echo in any of the classrooms because of the small amount of materials as opposed to now. [Today] every classroom's got mate-

> rials. They've got learning resources. Our library's well stocked, and each year we keep building. And the technology throughout the building—computers! It's just unbelievable opposed to what it would have looked like if you had walked in here eight years ago. So, it's been a big help to children and that's what's important. (P98S)

While the focus on children was strong at Bluejay, the job was harder in pre-reform years. As a writing coordinator told us as we were selecting sites, "exemplary" would be "different for every region," but we had to know that in eastern Kentucky we would be "dealing with the mountains and mountain people. Traditionally we've been low on the totem pole." With so few resources, he felt that many schools concentrated on the "15% of the kids that are going to college, and left the other 85% by the wayside. But [with KERA] you can no longer ignore these kids" (A96F).[7]

Even in schools where the percentage of children headed for college was larger, the onset of KERA shifted the emphasis from teaching the privileged few to teaching all. This critical reform-based concept was one that all four of our exemplary schools embraced. For example, the CEO/ Principal of Mt. Vernon told us how much he believed that all students can succeed. In fact, he saw it as his and his teachers' responsibility to help all students learn. He contrasted the bell-shaped curve—which he saw as "garbage"—to the metaphor of a surgeon:

> Whenever you tell me that 25% of your kids are going to fail, that is the most awful thing I've ever heard.... You cannot call yourself a good educator and lose 25%. If you go to your surgeon and he says 25% of his patients died, you don't want to go back.... I expect you to use the same intensity as that show on TV, *ER*. When they get a patient in that *ER* room, they don't care how much money they have. They don't care what ethnic background they have. They blitz them. And they use every strategy. They consult with each other. They do every possible thing to save that patient, and that is your job here as teachers. If you lose one of them, ...then part of you goes with it. (P97S)

Mr. George's attitude about the centrality of children was repeated again and again in our interviews. At Eastend, every decision was based on how it would impact children's education, and decisions were often made by teams of teachers rather than individuals. Ms. Conner explained:

> I think there's a very positive atmosphere of wanting to do what's best for children, and therefore I think my people go to great lengths to do that. We're so team oriented, everybody is involved in that here. I think it's difficult to stay here and work in this program without that total commitment. And I probably, in fairness, need to say that there's a lot of peer pressure to

> do what's best for children. When you're on a team and if you have one person on that team who is not making good decisions in terms of what's best for children, the other team members will pick right up on it and will do what it takes to get that problem solved.... You know, everybody's got to do their job and pull their own weight in order for the team to be successful. (P97S)

In Ms. Conner's explanation, teamwork was characterized as both effective and demanding. Decisions about children were not simply the purview of individual teachers; instead, there was "peer pressure to do what's best for children." And when decisions did not line up with Eastend's focus on children, other teachers would step in to "do what it takes to get that problem solved."

Still, doing what it takes often took on a personal dimension. This was especially true at Eastend for as Ms. Conner told us faculty members routinely "elected to have their children and in some cases, relatives, attend Eastend." She and her husband had their own four children attend the school, even though they did not live in the district. She explained:

> Many of us see this school and the staff as contributing factors for the success of our own children. We understand, first hand, the importance of a true commitment to doing what is best for each child in order to ensure a successful school experience for every child. We are also willing to work hard to build a successful program because we are building for own families. That type of ownership for the success of the program cannot be fabricated.

At Eastend, the teachers' ownership for all children's success permeated their philosophy of teaching. As Ms. Nicholl said of the classroom that she and Ms. Roby shared, "I would have loved to have been in this classroom." Ms. Roby concurred, "I would have too. I always want to make a situation that the 4th grade child that's still in me would enjoy coming to every day" (T98S).

The personal dimension of teaching was true at Eagleview Middle as well. Mr. Driver (who was principal when our study began) exhorted his teachers with the same yearly advice:

> I tell our teachers and I say it every year. I say, "When you teach, you teach just like it's your child. Your own child sitting on that front row every class period." And I said, "Now that's how you should teach. Don't cheat any kid. You know you want your child to have the best education they can possibly have, so you teach just like he's sitting on the front row every time you teach a class." (P97S)

The Bluejay staff used similar images to imply how they should think about their school's children—not as distant and unrelated, but as their own, as kinfolk, who deserved every opportunity.

Whether born and bred in the county where they taught, or city folks who liked where they worked and stayed, our principals and teachers seemed uniformly inspired to do the hard work they did because of their children. And whether the principals described themselves as a "teacher helper," "a team player," or a "coach," their help and the plays they called were all for the kids. Even our self-described CEO viewed the business angle of the bell curve as "garbage," and though he cited numbers, his statistics were all about heart.

DISCUSSION

In one of our interviews with Mr. Bass at Eagleview, we got to talking about what it was like to teach within the Kentucky reform. We mentioned the "Kentucky-ism" with which we began this article—"That dog won't hunt"—and how an administrator at KDE had used it to demonstrate that in these times of reform, schools could no longer make excuses for not meeting the needs of all students. Mr. Bass had not heard the expression, but he told us that Kentucky-isms about dogs were legion. Indeed, he felt that an appropriate expression for the demands of KERA and KIRIS on schools and teachers would be, "If you can't run with the big dogs, stay on the porch" (T98S).

He continued, "Now that's true. You know, I feel like I'm very fortunate in that I came through a system that allowed me several opportunities to become very familiar with the intricacies of portfolio development." The opportunities Mr. Bass experienced were social ones—fellow teachers willing to share their ideas and administrators willing to support PD so he could learn to "run with the big dogs." These social events enabled him to expand his own human capacity to take on the new reform, though the costs in terms of work and commitment were admittedly high. Certainly, even at exemplary schools like Eagleview, the pressure was on accountability grade teachers to help students score well on the state's assessments.[8] In our research we had seen and heard about some of these pressures firsthand, and we wondered what motivated schools and teachers to keep going, to keep trying to raise their scores, to always try to make things better for kids. Mr. Bass replied:

> You know, one of my favorite authors, Lewis Grizzard [1986], had a book called *Elvis is Dead and I Don't Feel So Good Myself*—a collection of brief essays, vignettes, and stories. Basically the point he was making was "Unless you're the lead dog, the view never changes." And I think that's so accurate. It means if you're always chasing it from the back, you're always looking right at somebody's rear end. But if you're in front, you can see what's coming. And I think as a school—I think we realized what was coming. (T97F)

Still, realizing what was coming and having the wherewithal to act on it could be two completely different things, but Mr. Bass felt motivated by the "opportunities" he'd had to learn about the new reform in supportive ways. As Hargreaves (1997a) explained, "while there are characteristics of the occupation as a whole that shape the life, work, and culture of teaching ... *where* you are a teacher and *how* the work of teaching is organized in that place will significantly influence the kind of teacher you will become" (p. 1306, emphasis in the original).

Over the past decade, the *where* and *how* of Kentucky teachers has drawn much attention, yet the picture painted by policy makers and researchers has often been bleak (e.g., Jones & Whitford, 1997). This is particularly true because Kentucky represents a place where multiple reform efforts have converged into "one comprehensive set of mandates, ... Kentucky's Educational Reform Act" (Knapp, Bamburg, Ferguson, & Hill, 1998, p. 408). This kind of convergence calls for:

> careful case-study research [that] can capture in some detail how professionals attend to (or ignore) reforms, interpret the meaning of reform activity, engage in reform-related work, and adopt (or reject) reform ideas as part of their practice. As part of this research, investigators must look systematically at the ways in which the different workplace conditions shape and are shaped by the impact of multiple reform initiatives. Such descriptions of contextual change and response to converging reforms have yet to be constructed. Lacking such descriptions, reformers are proceeding on the blind faith that their collective efforts can feasibly and usefully be incorporated into professional practice. (p. 415)

Thus, this article represents at least a part of our team's response to calls for case-study research, particularly our agreement with Knapp and his colleagues' emphasis on the need for *detailed* cases—for it is in the details that social and human capital are revealed. Furthermore, our selection of sites represents a particular view. Rather than focus on how schools attempted to meet the demands of complex reform and failed, we set out to find successful schools.

It should be obvious that how our four schools successfully met the challenge of KERA was unique to each site. Still, there were critical commonalties—their regard for history and heritage, the efficacy of their cooperative leadership, their careful reflection on the reform itself which allowed them to teach to and well beyond the KIRIS test (as exemplified by writing), and, most important, their dedication to students. Yet, these commonalties exist because of *relationships*—connections to place and people—that are held together and supported by *trust* and *talk*.

The role of relationships in our four sites cannot be over emphasized. Indeed, our exemplary school descriptions suggest that willingness to meet the needs of a new reform are often based on human relationships among principals, teachers, and students. These relationships in turn influence the desire to go out into the community to get what's needed to propel learning forward. Our schools characterized themselves as "Fortune 500 companies," and "universities" where ongoing learning was key. But the business side of things was less critical than the emphasis on "family." As Hargreaves (1997b) explained "Openness, informality, care, attentiveness, lateral working relationships, reciprocal collaboration, candid and vibrant dialogue, and a willingness to face uncertainty together are the basic ingredients of effective school-community collaboration, not merely the emotional icing that adorns it" (p. 22). Fullan (1997) agreed, "Along with moving to site-based management, rethinking staff development, assessment systems, and the like, the best way to deal with change may be 'to improve relationships'" (p. 226).

In our four sites, close relationships existed because the participants shared a vision of curriculum and a commitment to children. And the social links they established with each other—both *personal* and *professional*—inspired individual teachers and principals to keep on learning, to challenge themselves to keep growing. As Spillane and Thompson (1997) suggested:

> [places] that are rich in human capital (particularly the leaders' knowledge, skills, and dispositions) and social capital (vital connections to trustworthy sources of knowledge ... and norms of collegiality and trust ...) will get still richer in the human capital that ultimately matters most—the knowledge, skills, and dispositions that teachers need to teach challenging subject matter effectively to a broad array of students. (p. 199)

Still, what creates and confirms human and social capital is *trust* and *talk*. Part of the trust in our schools was built by leaders whose longevity in their buildings was critical. Research tells us that when this is not the case, the results can be quite different for "Macmillan (1996) found that where it is the policy to rotate principals through different schools, enduring staff cultures often successfully resist the change efforts of leaders who are merely passing through" (cited in Hargreaves, 1997a, p. 1309). However, trust is not just built over time, but through a long term commitment to a singular vision. Evans (1993), for example, highlighted "the primacy of *authenticity* in leadership" and explained: "Authentic leaders link what they think, what they seek, and what they do.... Principals whose personal values and aspirations for their schools are consistent, coherent, and reflected in daily behavior are credible and inspire trust—they are leaders worth following into the uncertainties of change" (p. 21, emphasis in the original).

Leaders worth following are also leaders who listen—they leave their doors and minds open to the comments, complaints, and convictions of their faculty. They work to distribute the leadership rather than guard it for themselves. As Louis, Marks, and Kruse (1996) suggested, "providing scheduled time for collaborative planning and giving teachers the responsibility to make key decisions about school policy make strong contributions to professional community" (p. 785). Still, setting aside the time and assigning responsibilities could backfire if principals did not place a strong emphasis on *talk*—substantive talk—for how teachers speak with one another and with their students can make a critical difference in the success of a reform. In the creation of human and social capital, talk is key—a stand which is born out again and again in the research literature. For example, Lieberman and Miller (1990) advocated "discussion about approaches to teaching and learning" (p. 763), Hargreaves (1997b) called it "candid and vibrant dialogue" (p. 22), and Spillane (1999) termed it "rich deliberations" (p. 170). McDonnell (1994) also stressed "deliberation" and cited Lord Lindsay who wrote about the "potency of discussion. A good discussion can draw out wisdom which is attainable in no other way" (p. 415).

To be sure, all principals, teachers, and students talk, but our participants maintained a discussion that focused on the wisdom of practice. In a quote that bears repeating from Mr. George, "What the administration has to do is provide a lot of conversation in the area. You do that by talking, and you talk about *instructional* areas, not the ball game tomorrow or buildings and grounds. You focus in on what it is that you want to improve" (P97F). And what our participants wanted to improve was the quality of their curriculum, instruction, and assessment. They talked to, with, and about each other, and their tones were consistently tinged with "pride and respect." When they disagreed, they were open in their commentary, but their individual views were often sublimated to the larger good. As Mr. Bass told us when he disagreed with Mr. Push's unwillingness to distribute writing portfolio responsibilities among more teachers: "But once again, it goes back to the bottom line, and the bottom line is whatever this school needs to do to be the best, that's what we're going to do" (T97F).

Still, there is another bottom line that we need to address before we close this piece. Mr. Bass characterized Eagleview Middle as doing "whatever [it] needs to do to be the best," and our other schools—Bluejay, Eastend, and Mt. Vernon—were similarly inspired. Yet, policy makers as well as practitioners might question whether the schools' *inspiration* and *inclination towards change* was the result of the Kentucky reform (KERA) and its accountability demands (KIRIS), or whether they would have gotten where they were on their own. In other words, is what we've described in these four schools "caused" by the reform? And the answer, as is true of many complex questions, is both "yes" and "no."

Let's begin with "no." Long before the onset of KERA, these schools already had a history and heritage of shared experiences. With the exception of Eagleview (which was only three years old at the beginning of our study), all of our schools had time on their side. The principals had been there for years, and they as well as their faculties had links to the community that were well established. And even though Eagleview was relatively new, faculty members were long-time county insiders who had made a conscious choice to move to a reform-based site. In addition to longevity, the principals shared a vision of distributed leadership. When KERA mandated site-based decision making, the principals were already sharing decisions with faculty whom they described as "professionals" who were "intelligent," "outstanding" and "the cream of the crop."

Certainly, the human capital among faculty was notable; the teachers with whom we worked were leaders in their schools, and when the reform appeared they took on increasing leadership in their districts as well as in the state as cluster leaders, writing and mathematics regional coordinators, and even Distinguished Educators. As Ms. Roby explained, they wanted to "jump in there and get as high up on that [leadership ladder] as we can, to get the information first and help our building." The social capital was equally in place—for they had already established trusting links to communicate with one another, through both work and play. These social links had allowed them to create innovative change within their institutions that predated KERA—such as the ungraded primary and inclusion programs at both Bluejay and Eastend, and the accelerated mathematics program at Mt. Vernon. But the answer to the question of whether KERA/KIRIS caused change in these four sites is also "yes," and the reasons are

But the answer to the question of whether KERA/KIRIS *caused* these schools to change is also "yes," and the reasons are tied to financial as well as social capital. In this article, we have only touched on the huge shift in school finances that KERA brought about, but change in support for professional development "increased dramatically, from $1.1 million in 1990-91 to $11.6 million in 1994-95" (Boston, 1996, p. 12). The resources Kentucky provided were clearly consequential for all our sites. For example, at several schools they provided summer stipends for teachers to work on curriculum alignment. The importance of financial considerations was particularly true in eastern Kentucky, however. As Ms. Chief poignantly pointed out, "You could have heard an echo in any of the classrooms because of the small amount of materials as opposed to now."

Even more important, the *financial* capital expended helped to extend the schools' *social* capital. Teachers told us that, prior to the reform, they talked often about curriculum, but the discussions they had at district, regional, and state reform meetings helped them enter into deeper and wider conversations—deeper because they talked about more substantive curriculum and wider because they were able to talk with teachers and curricular leaders from across the state. The conversations over writing are again illustrative. When we asked an eastern Kentucky writing coordinator how KERA had changed writing instruction, he replied: "I'm in writing and people ask me, 'Is it better?' And I say, 'Well, I don't know. We didn't have writing before.' I'm not kidding! We just taught grammar! I think the writing's just opened worlds for kids" (A96F).

Opening worlds for children meant introducing them to process writing and showing them that the purpose of writing is to make meaning. Grammar and spelling conventions are a means to an end, not the end point itself, and in constructing meaning, clear and creative communication always holds sway. In addition, such meaning-making can be altered and shaped for a variety of audiences and purposes and can take on a number of different forms. Yet, these essential understandings would be lost, or at least much diminished, if all our teachers had to do was prepare students for a once-a-year, on demand prompt. Though this was a part of the state's assessment, the larger component was helping their students compose several original and genre-varied portfolio pieces. Indeed, the KIRIS writing portfolio—one of the most courageous pieces of assessment we've seen at the national level—made these understandings come alive.

The lessons we shared from our writing teachers help to illustrate this point. Mr. Bass discussed personal narrative and poetry to show that writing was not only personal expression, but a vital part of community life. Ms. Roby and Ms. Nicholl encouraged their children to revise their writing to make it "way up there," as well as to listen well to their peers' writing in order to offer the best criticism. Ms. Dawson's children learned to reflect on their writing, not only for their "letter to the reviewer" but to enhance their own critical self reflection. And Ms. Jazz, who had been teaching personal narratives for years, learned a completely new concept about the importance of "lessons learned" in closing this particular genre. In reflecting on the lessons she had learned from the day of professional development with the regional writing coordinator, Ms. Jazz said: "You can't really say that you've internalized a concept until you have the words for it."

Giving words to teachers and children so they could internalize critical concepts was the driving force in the Kentucky reform. While it is true that our schools were poised to listen well to the new vocabulary and enact the reform-based practices the words defined, they took these words and practices to heart through substantive discussion that occurred formally on core days and in weekly professional development sessions as well as more informally in daily team meetings and hall conversations. These extended deliberations strengthened the positive and trusting relationships that had already existed among participants, as they rolled up their sleeves to do the work of the reform. When we asked Ms. Chief what motivated her and her "Bluejay University" teachers to do the best they could do she replied:

> Because this is our home. These are all our kids. We love this school. We have a school spirit here that cannot be equal to any other, anywhere else. I'm sure.... We're not perfect... But we try all the time, each and every day to keep growing and keep learning. And in the face of any type of obstacle, we've always stuck together. We've laughed together. We've cried together. But the bottom line is we love these kids, we love this school, and there is NOTHING we won't do to make it a success. (P98S)

The nothing they, as well as their colleagues in our other exemplary sites, wouldn't do included extensive and collaborative planning, shared leadership and vision, and dedication to high-level curriculum, instruction, and assessment to help their students—*all their students*—be the best that they could be. In a deceptively simple statement in her book about Appalachia, Rylant (1991) commented: "The owners of these good dogs work pretty hard" (p. 3). Yes. And the participants in our study worked hard as well. But what they worked the hardest on were the relationships that connected them, the trust that sustained them, and the talk that supported them and propelled them forward, both personally and professionally, and, above all, for their children.

AUTHOR'S NOTE

This chapter first appeared in 2001, in the *American Education Research Journal, 37*(2), 349-393, and is reprinted by permission of the author and AERJ.

NOTES

1. Shelby Wolf, Hilda Borko, Rebekah Elliott, and Monette McIver serve as team members for a Center for Research on Evaluation, Standards, and Student Testing (CRESST) study entitled "The Effects of Standards-Based Assessment on Schools and Classrooms." The team spent two years studying reform efforts of exemplary schools in Kentucky and is now collecting comparable data in the state of Washington. In addition, the Colorado team works with Rand partners, Brian M. Stetcher and Sheila Barron, who

conduct statewide surveys on the impact of the Kentucky and Washington reforms on curriculum and instruction in writing and mathematics in accountability grades. The work reported herein was supported under the Educational Research and Development Centers Program, PR/Award Number R305B60002, as administered by the Office of Educational Research and Improvement, U.S. Department of Education. The findings and opinions expressed in this report do not reflect the positions or policies of the National Institute on Student Achievement, Curriculum, and Assessment, the Office of Educational Research and Improvement, or the U.S. Department of Education.

2. The authors would like to express our heartfelt gratitude to the exemplary teachers and principals we worked with in Kentucky. Although their real names are submerged in pseudonyms, we hope their lively voices resound through this guise of writing to bring their classroom and school life off the page and into the minds of our readers.

3. Responding to concerns raised by educators, parents, and testing experts, the 1998 General Assembly passed House Bill 53, which effectively dismantled KIRIS and replaced it with the Commonwealth Accountability Testing System (CATS). However, during the years of our study (1996-1998), KIRIS was the accountability system in place.

4. Kelley (1998) described the distinguished educator as "an exceptional educator from the state of Kentucky, hired and trained by the state to provide technical assistance to schools to help them meet accountability goals. Distinguished educators are on leave from their regular teaching or administrative assignments and are appointed for 1 year" (p. 307).

5. The school site names as well as the names of all of the principals and teachers are pseudonyms selected by the participants themselves. In addition, all participants have read this article and approved its content as accurate representations of their sites.

6. Jones and Whitford (1997) explained Kentucky's demand for continual improvement: "Setting the formula for establishing school threshold scores—the score each school must meet or exceed every two years to be rewarded and avoid sanctions—was an especially thorny problem. Based on the premise that 'all students can learn at high levels,' state education leaders decided that, in 20 years, schools must register a score of at least 'proficient,' defined numerically as 100 out of 140 possible points. By that time, the argument went, all students would have experienced a KERA-based school system from beginning to end. This reasoning then led to the creation of the following method for determining a school's threshold score. Since there are 10 two-year cycles in a 20-year span, in each cycle schools must gain one-tenth of the difference between their first baseline score and the target of 100. Thus, if a school originally scored 30 in 1992, its baseline would be 30, and its target for 1994 would be 37 (i.e., 10% of the remaining 70 points to get to 100). Each school is expected to reach or exceed its target during each two-year cycle. To say that teachers and school administrators feel that this is an arbitrary expectation is an enormous understatement. The assumption of a constant rate of growth, cycle after cycle, toward total 'proficiency' in 20 years has not been well received, to say the least" (p. 279). This is particularly true for schools who began with a high threshold score.

7. The writing coordinator's view of his region's position was confirmed in Kelley's (1998) research: "In rural eastern Kentucky, principals and teachers in some schools indicated that the design of the program enabled them to compete for the first time ever on a level playing field with some of the best schools in Kentucky. The additional resources KERA provided and the focus of the program on student improvement ... enabled these schools to be motivated to work toward an achievable goal" (p. 315).
8. This comment is born out in the research of Kelley and Protsik (1997) who studied six award-winning Kentucky schools: "In five of the six schools we visited, teachers and principals expressed how the burden of the assessment fell to the assessment grade-level teachers." As one of the researchers' informants explained, "we try to share the responsibility of the assessment, but when those test scores come in, teachers say 'How did the fourth-grade teachers do?'" (p. 498).

REFERENCES

Adams, J. E., & White, W. E. (1997). The equity consequence of school finance reform in Kentucky. *Educational Evaluation and Policy Analysis, 19* (2), 165-184.

Ball, D. L., & Cohen, D. K. (1995, April). *What does the educational system bring to learning a new pedagogy of reading or mathematics?* Paper presented at the annual meeting of the American Educational Research Association, San Francisco, CA.

Borko, H., & Elliott, R. (1999). Hands-on pedagogy versus hands-off accountability: Tensions between competing commitments for exemplary math teachers in Kentucky. *Phi Delta Kappan, 80* (5), 394-400.

Borko, H., Elliott, R., & Uchiyama, K. (1999). *Professional development: A key to Kentucky's reform effort.* (CSE Tech. Rep. No. 512) Los Angeles: University of California, Center for Research on Evaluation, Standards, and Student Testing (CRESST).

Boston, B. (1995). *From dilemma to opportunity: A report on education reform 5 years after the Kentucky Education Reform Act of 1990*. Lexington, KY: The Partnership for Kentucky School Reform.

Boston, B. (1996). *From dilemma to opportunity: A report on education reform 5 years after the Kentucky Education Reform Act of 1990, Volume II*. Lexington, KY: The Partnership for Kentucky School Reform.

Brunner, D. D. (1994). *Inquiry and reflection: Framing narrative practice in education.* Albany: State University of New York Press.

Coleman, J. (1988). Social capital in the creation of human capital. *American Journal of Sociology, 94*, S95-S120.

Evans, R. (1993, September). The human face of reform. *Educational Leadership*, 19-23.

Foster, J. D. (1991). The role of accountability in Kentucky's Education Reform Act of 1990. *Educational Leadership, 48* (5), 34-36.

Fullan, M. (1993). *Change forces*. New York: Falmer Press.

Fullan, M. (1997). Emotion and hope: Constructive concepts for complex times. In A. Hargreaves (Ed.), *Rethinking educational change with heart and mind* (pp.

216-233). Alexandria, VA: Association for Supervision and Curriculum Development.

Grizzard, L. (1986) *Elvis is dead and I don't feel so good myself.* New York: Warner.

Graves, D. (1994). *A fresh look at writing*. Portsmouth, NH: Heinemann.

Hargreaves, A. (1995). Renewal in the age of paradox. *Educational Leadership, 52,* 14-19.

Hargreaves, A. (1997a). Cultures of teaching and educational change. In B. J. Biddle, T. L. Good, & I. F. Goodson (Eds.), *International handbook of teachers and teaching, Volume II* (pp. 1297-1319). Dordrecht, The Netherlands: Kluwer.

Hargreaves, A. (1997b). Rethinking educational change: Going deeper and wider in the quest for success. In A. Hargreaves (Ed.), *Rethinking educational change with heart and mind* (pp. 1-26). Alexandria, VA: Association for Supervision and Curriculum Development.

Hatch, T. (1998). The differences in theory that matter in the practice of school improvement. *American Educational Research Journal, 35,* 3-31.

Heath, S. B., & McLaughlin, M. W. (1993). *Identity and inner-city youth: Beyond ethnicity and gender.* New York: Teachers College Press.

Jones, K., & Whitford, B. L. (1997, December). Kentucky's conflicting reform principles: High-stakes school accountability and student performance assessment. *Phi Delta Kappan*, pp. 276-281.

Kelley, C. (1998). The Kentucky school-based performance award program: School-level effects. *Educational Policy, 12* (3), 305-324.

Kelley, C., & Protsik, J. (1997). Risk and reward: Perspectives on the implementation of Kentucky's school-based performance award program. *Educational Administration Quarterly, 33,* 474-505.

Knapp, M. S., Bamburg, J. D., Ferguson, M. C., & Hill, P. T. (1998). Converging reforms and the working lives of frontline professionals in schools. *Educational Policy, 12* (4), 397-418.

Koger, L. (1998). Writing in the smokehouse. In J. Dyer (Ed.), *Bloodroot: Reflections on place by Appalachian women writers,* (pp. 154-166). Lexington, KY: The University Press of Kentucky.

Lieberman, A., & Miller, L. (1990). Restructuring schools: What matters and what works. *Phi Delta Kappan, 71* (10), 759-764.

Louis, K. S., Marks, H. M., & Kruse, S. (1996). Teachers' professional community in restructuring schools. *American Educational Research Journal, 33,* 757-798.

McDonnell, L. M. (1994). Assessment policy as persuasion and regulation. *American Journal of Education, 102,* 394-420.

McIver, M. C., & Wolf, S. A. (1999). The power of the conference is the power of suggestion. *Language Arts,* 77 (1), 54-61.

Muncey, D. E., & McQuillan, P. J. (1996). *Reform and resistance in schools and classrooms.* New Haven, CT: Yale University Press.

Peterson, P. L., McCarthey, S. J., & Elmore, R. F. (1996). Learning from school restructuring. *American Journal of Education, 33,* 119-153.

Rylant, C. (1991). *Appalachia: The voices of sleeping birds,* illustrated by B. Moser. San Diego, CA: Harcourt Brace Jovanovich.

Rylant, C. (1992). *Missing May.* New York: Orchard Books.

Sarason, S. B. (1993). *The case for change: Rethinking the preparation of educators*. San Francisco, CA: Jossey-Bass.

Schmoker, M. (1996). *Results: The key to continuous school improvement*. Alexandria, VA: Association for Supervision and Curriculum Development.

Simpson, J. F. (1991). Journal of the reform year. *The Executive Educator, 13* (12), 29-31.

Spillane, J. P. (1999). External reform initiatives and teachers' efforts to reconstruct their practice: The mediating role of teachers' zones of enactment. *Journal of Curriculum Studies, 31* (2), 143-175.

Spillane, J. P., & Thompson, C. L. (1997). Reconstructing conceptions of local capacity: The local education agency's capacity for ambitious instructional reform. *Educational Evaluation and Policy Analysis, 19*, 185-203.

Stecher, B. M., Barron, S., Kaganoff, T., & Goodwin, J. (1998). *The effects of standards-based assessment on classroom practices: Results of the 1996-97 RAND survey of Kentucky teachers of mathematics and writing*. (CSE Tech. Rep. 482). Los Angeles: University of California, CRESST.

White, K. A. (1999, May 5). High-poverty schools score big on Ky. assessment. *Education Week*, pp. 18, 20.

Wolf, S. A., & Davinroy, K. A. H. (1998). "The clay that makes the pot": The loss of language in writing assessment. *Written Communication, 15* (4), 419-464.

Wolf, S. A., & McIver, M. (1999). When process becomes policy: The paradox of Kentucky state reform for exemplary teachers of writing. *Phi Delta Kappan, 80* (5), 401-406.

CHAPTER 11

REFORMING SCHOOLS BY REFORMING RELATIONSHIPS

The Bryan Leadership Development Initiative

Kathleen Ponder, Jennifer Martineau, Karen Dyer, and Shera Johnson

ABSTRACT

This case report describes the Bryan Leadership Development Initiative (BLDI), a five-year program designed to develop and enhance the capacity of school leadership teams (principals, teachers, parents, staff) to make effective, collaborative instructional and program decisions that responded to a mix of outcomes, including state and national accountability measures, child development, personal and professional leadership development of teachers and others, and public communication. The BLDI was a joint venture of the Center for Creative Leadership, consistently ranked by *Fortune* and *Businessweek* as one of the leading executive leadership training organizations in the world, the school district, and the local Joseph M. Bryan Foundation, the major funder for the initiative. Twenty-one school leadership teams and the Superintendent's Executive Cabinet participated in the initiative, which featured CCL's trademark leadership development philosophy with its focus on intrapersonal and interpersonal development, the

Deep Change: Cases and Commentary on Reform in High Stakes States, 201–228

feedback-intensive assessment-challenge-support learning framework, and heavily experiential learning activities. The BLDI encountered numerous barriers (e.g., large-scale movement of principals and a change in superintendents). But the lessons in relational leadership—the time and effort required to change relationships and establish trust and openness, the importance of positional leaders, the value of conversation and climate—offer important markers on the route to sustainable reform.

INTRODUCTION

You could hear a pin drop in the Executive Cabinet meeting. The superintendent's sharp and cutting remarks to Bob Clark, his Associate Superintendent, caused gasps and embarrassment. This wasn't the first time the superintendent had exploded publicly and chastised someone. In fact, many of the Central Office executives and principals in the district lived in fear that they would be next. Bob grabbed in his pocket for his ulcer medicine and thought to himself, "I hate this guy and I hate coming to work. How much longer do I have to put up with this?"

Having a smart school leader isn't enough. At a gut level, we know that how a leader treats people matters—and relationships with the leader matter. Research confirms this (McCauley, Moxley, & Van Velsor, 2003). While the neocortal part of the human brain busily laps up information and applies rational principles to understanding and deciding what to do, the limbic brain relies upon emotionality to sense the innermost states and motives of others (Lewis, Amini, & Lannon, 2000). Invisible but powerful relational bonds influence whether we follow or resist our leaders, whether we support and defend them—or quietly sabotage their plans. Emotional states leap from one to another. They are wordlessly communicated, but deeply understood. If a leader proposes an ingenious idea, those around don't spontaneously develop the same concept. Like a magnet, our emotional rather than cognitive connection with others either pulls us toward the ideas or repels us from them. Strong relationships allow ideas to propagate and spread.

Positive emotional processes of leadership are important, and many studies recount the benefits (Rozin & Royzman, 2001; Gardham & Brown, 2001). Leaders who provided continuous, small emotional "uplifts" (a kind word, praise, humor) were consistently the most effective (Peeters, 2002). Conversely, a single negative leader behavior (i.e., public humiliation, lack of communication, a betrayal of trust) evokes from the person on the receiving end intense and long-remembered feelings and reactions that can interfere with performance (Larsen & Diener, 1992; Dasborough, 2003). Leaders who led problem solving by providing conceptual frames for the task but provided no time to let members get to know and trust the leader and each other increased understanding of the task—but impaired their ability to do it! Leaders who shape their affective behavior to promote harmonious relationships motivate employees to be productive and satisfied with their work.[1]

A study comparing scores of leaders on a 360 assessment of leadership skills and perspectives (Benchmarks©) to measurements of emotional intelligence indicated that higher levels of emotional intelligence are associated with better performance in ten areas of leadership (Ruderman, Hannum, Leslie, & Steed, 2001). They also found that successful change management connects to high levels of emotional intelligence, and that the careers of leaders with low levels of E.Q. (emotional intelligence) were much more likely to "derail" (be fired or not promoted), with "Problems with Interpersonal Relationships" being a key factor. These findings counter popular images of tough, take charge leaders—the Donald Trumps and John Waynes—who mow over their subordinates freely and frequently. In fact, Jim Collins found that organizations that could *not* sustain high performance over a period of 15 years had leaders who personally led the organization through "sheer force." In contrast, the leaders of great organizations that sustained high performance conducted "autopsies" of business disasters without blame, were *not* personally ambitious, and built community. Here is a description of one remarkable leader.

> this was a man who spent nearly all his waking hours with people who loved him, who loved what they were doing, and who loved one another. (Collins, 2001, p. 61)

Clearly, there is more to organizational success than just having the right ideas, strategies, and structures.

For at least 25 years, researchers observing the interactions of adults and children in school environments have talked around the significance of relationships. School improvement and higher student achievement have been linked to the state of school climate (how things "feel" in a school), to a leader's valuing of faculty and staff, and to the affective behaviors of teachers (Dellar, 1998; Fullan, 2001; Hess, 1999; Kerman, 2000; Leithwood & Menzies, 1998; Rice et al., 2001; Vandenberghe, 1995).

Yet the majority of school reforms have focused almost exclusively on altering the *structures* of schooling, the knowledge, skills, and accountability systems for students and teachers. Site-based management, another structural reform of school governance mandating a shift in decision-making authority from central administration to individual schools, gained wide popularity in the 1990s. Unfortunately, only some sites adopting this governance practice demonstrated clear changes in student achievement. Reasons given for this failure are numerous. Some studies pointed to the incongruence between the call for school autonomy and the imposition of state and federal mandates. However, most studies cited a lack of preparation for collaborative work—an inability to form relationships strong enough to pull them through the daunting challenge of meeting the needs of all children (Beck & Murphy, 1998; Brown, 2001; Dempster, 2000; Elmore, 1995, 1993; Fullan, 2001; Hannaway, 1996; Helfin & Helfin, 1995; Hunter, 1999; Leithwood & Menzies, 1998; Marks & Louis, 1997; Shen, 2001; Pae, 2000; Tanner & Stone, 1998; Tyak, 1993; Wohlstetter et al., 1997).

Interestingly, a few schools *were* successful, and they shared something in common. They spoke of a "professional and family-like learning community" that took collective responsibility for *every* child's achievement (Beck & Murphy, 1998). They talked of educators creating cultures of trust, support, risk-taking, honest communication, and honest reflection. They found time for teachers to collaborate and build relationships. In these successful schools the affective side of school life played a critical role. Like a magic elixir, positive relationships breathed life and energy into the site-based management governance structures, creating empowered and energized communities, able to elicit the best thinking from all members.

Studies of successful school leaders tell the same story. School leaders who have made a difference demonstrate positive affect. They show a capacity for sharing leadership, rely less on titles and more on personal power, trust, and respect, and pay attention to the human and symbolic dimensions of their work (Barth, 1990; Bolman & Deal, 1991; Dyer & Carothers, 2000; Hall & Hord, 2001; Holmes, 1990; Howard, Howell, & Brainard, 1987; Sergiovanni & Moore, 1989). They also intentionally build caring communities of learners with less formal school cultures and higher morale. When implementing change, they are aware of the feelings of faculty and pay attention to teachers' perceptions of them. But, school reforms have gone forward with little attention to feelings and relationships, pushing change with data, concepts, and mandates.

A RELATION-CENTERED REFORM

> Relationships have taken on the status of weather—everyone talks about them but who knows what to do? (Thomas Lewis)

North Carolina, like other states, mandated that its school districts adopt site-based management (SBM) in the mid-1990s. The North Carolina conception of site-based management was to produce "a shared process in which parents, teachers, the principal, and other school staff are all involved in making many of the decisions for the local school."

When the Piedmont County, N.C. Schools began implementing this mandate, two community agencies, the Bryan Foundation and the Center for Creative Leadership (CCL), were asked to assist. The president of the Bryan Foundation knew that Piedmont County's educators needed assistance in learning how to adopt SBM, and he pledged $5 million to provide them with leadership development. Right in his "back yard" sat the Center for Creative Leadership, an internationally recognized nonprofit organization devoted to developing leaders, and he asked them for help. CCL agreed, and matched the Bryan Foundation's $5 million contribution with its own in-kind contributions. Then the Bryan Foundation went further. Each participating school received $10,000 to be spent on whatever their site-based team thought would enhance their success. The school district then provided $100,000 to fund associated research and evaluation activities (Martineau, 1998).

With such generous funding, a long-term process for development was conceived: five years of CCL's leadership development process for 21 school leadership teams—each with 15 members, 74 school principals, and the superintendent and his 12 member Executive Cabinet. The initiative, named the Bryan Leadership Development Initiative (BLDI), held a kick-off banquet in spring, 1997. While the school district continued its work to enhance the knowledge base of teachers regarding research-based teaching and learning practices, CCL would build the leadership capacity of school leaders—teachers, parents, principals, the superintendent, the school board—to implement site-based decision making (Holmes-Ponder, 1997).

A group of former educators and a research scientist with children in the local school district headed the initiative for CCL. Together, they seized an opportunity to add a missing piece to this school reform. Unlike historic reform efforts, this one would consciously address the emotional and relational capacity of the people involved as a means of strengthening leadership capacity and allowing effective teaching and learning processes to take hold. Strengthening important non-cognitive abilities—self-awareness, social awareness, self-management, and social skills—emotional intelligence—would be the focus of the Bryan Leadership Development Initiative (Goleman, 2000).

CCL's definition of leadership development—"the expansion of the capacity to enact the basic leadership tasks needed for collective work: setting direction, facing adaptive challenges, creating alignment, and maintaining commitment" made sense to these school leaders (McCauley, Moxley, & Van Velsor, 2003). But it was the *how*—the process of development that puzzled them at first. The superintendent, his Cabinet, and most of the school community expected some version of the many graduate courses they had taken. Most expected to read the latest books on leadership, hold lively discussions about how they could apply the content, and engage in lecture and intellectual dialogue in a classroom setting.

But instead of studying cognitive concepts *about* leadership, power and influence, CCL asked them to explore how they actually *used* their *personal* power. While they expected to approach leadership development by accumulating knowledge *about* sharing power and leading, CCL's development process sought to foster a deeper experiential awareness about *their* selves and how they either strengthened or diminished the communal bonds that move people. Developing knowledge about leadership took a back seat. Instead, they would observe their behaviors and interactions to see and feel *their* impact on their important work.

THE BEGINNING—CONSTRUCTING THE CURRICULUM

CCL's team began curriculum development by asking Piedmont County school administrators to attend an intensive needs assessment session called a "Leadership Summit." CCL faculty asked the principals to share their pressing leadership issues, to assess the leadership needs of their school's leadership team, to share the obstacles blocking effective team functioning, and to define what a successful program would look like to them. The superintendent and his executive team went through the same process. Not surprisingly, most of their answers related to affective matters, not cognitive concerns.

Not a word about needing more knowledge—no comment about unprepared faculty and staff, although many school administrators worried about logistics. How many school-based personnel could attend programs together (no more than five at a time from one building)? How would substitute teachers be paid (schools looked to the district to pay for additional substitutes)? How would schools and teachers be selected to participate (a blind lottery was held to pick schools and a streamlined application process used to choose teachers)?

A second phase of needs assessment began once the 21 participating schools were chosen. All 315 members of the 21 school leadership teams selected were asked to share their vision of an effective school, changes they thought were needed and the obstacles preventing the vision from being realized. Again, a familiar refrain: *affective, relational concerns dominated*. The list, in order, included: need for teamwork, a positive school

Table 11.1. Responses to Needs Assessment Questions: Sample Responses

Leadership Team's Needs:
- Being willing to take ownership,
- Practice no fault thinking - understand each others' perspective Build more trust,
- Be a team player, plan for the entire school rather than grade level or individual needs.
- Adapt to change - take more risks & become accepting of new ideas

Barriers to Developing Leadership Teams:
- How can I keep morale high and still focus on test scores?
- Working hard but still being part of what the STATE labeled as a low achieving school.
- Paperwork overshadowing leadership responsibilities;
- The district's constant badgering is reducing teachers and principals to frustration and apathy.
- They're unwilling to take on any more responsibility;
- Teachers are competitive
- What everyone brings from the past as well as their personalities—they're jealous to the point of not wanting to share;

Challenges to Effective Principal Leadership
- I'm not here to build a resume for the superintendent but I sometimes think we do things to make him and the system look good when our time should be focused on helping students attain success.
- It seems everyone has an agenda. I can't keep everyone happy.
- I need to be able to be more candid with my parents and staff and not go away worrying about what the person thinks of me.
- Lack of support from personnel in making changes.
- Central office is constantly implementing new programs without support or interpretation.

Challenges Faced by Schools:
- Very difficult to meet the needs of fragile children.
- Low SES kids and a transient population.
- How do you get teachers to believe that all children can learn?
- Creating a supportive climate among staff.
- The biggest challenge is motivating a standard teacher to move to a higher level of performance.

climate, competent leadership, more of a focus on the well-being of students, honoring of diversity, more resources (i.e., classroom space, special services, technology, staff development) and more parental involvement.

In July 1997 CCL convened a committee of experienced CCL faculty and research scientists, two school district Assistant Superintendents, and 12 experts on special topics related to leadership to help with the design. The BLDI leadership development curriculum, like all other CCL programs, would be grounded in CCL's core beliefs about leadership development and the curriculum committee adopted the following guidelines regarding the instructional process of the BLDI:

1. It would reflect CCL's philosophy of leadership development, with its focus on intrapersonal and interpersonal leader efficacy.
2. The program would use CCL's signature feedback-intensive "*assessment-challenge-support*" constructivist learning framework.
3. *Experiential activities*, including case study work, simulations, role-plays and reflective dialogues, would comprise the majority of program learning activities, with didactic instruction playing a minor role (Holmes-Ponder, 1997).

To further focus the curriculum, "framing questions" focused work at the individual, team, and organizational level and formed the evaluation framework. The evaluation protocols included intense and ongoing formative and summative processes to enable real-time alteration of less effective processes and the gathering of interview and observational data to discover developmental themes.

As the initial curriculum committee began designing the initiative's component parts, they knew that engaging the affective and emotional processes and experiences of the teachers, principals and school leadership teams would offer them a "stretch." They would be engaged in a process that would ask them to see school leadership as a socially constructed process, engaging emotions as well as reasoning capabilities. Assessment instruments, experiential activities and simulations would be used to sharpen self-awareness and create an arena for the exercise of "emotional intelligence." Coming to a CCL leadership class meant that teachers and principals, the superintendent and his cabinet would have to bring their "whole self" to the process.

After four months of curriculum development, a five-year framework of target learnings and annual objectives for each of nine (9) content strands emerged. The BLDI would focus successively on developing relational leadership capacity in the individual, the school leadership team, the school as a whole, the school within the district, and the school within the community. The multi-level delivery venue included:

- Programmatic developmental experiences. School teams and Executive Cabinet cohorts would engage in customized programs at the CCL Headquarters facility. These custom programs included key elements in learning about self and relational leadership as well as deep understandings about working in cross-functional teams. The superintendent would spend a week in a Leadership at the Peak experience at CCL's Colorado Springs facility at the foot of Pikes' Peak, where self-learning and relational leadership are "ramped up" to accommodate the needs of the executives from around the world who meet the minimal entry requirements of a $250,000 annual base salary or managing a corporate budget of more than $5 M.

- Job-based developmental experiences. School-based coaches ("Transition Guides") were assigned to the principals and school-based leadership teams to provide observation and feedback functions as the School Leadership Teams began the tough tasks of implementing relational leadership skills (e.g., understanding the perceptions and actions of team members based on their Meyers-Briggs types and FIRO-B tendencies toward factors of control, wanting to be liked (or not), and wanting to be included (or not). Coaches also worked with the superintendent and executive cabinet to integrate classroom insights and learnings and increase the potency of lessons from job experiences.

YEAR ONE, PHASE ONE—HIGH ANXIETY AND EARLY WINS

> OK, I'll ask you. What are they going to do to us at CCL? I'm a little afraid of what these assessments might show. I've never gotten feedback from people I work with about how I'm doing and I'm not sure I want to show myself to everyone! You're our coach—can you give us a hint at what we're in for?

Phase One, designed to heighten each person's awareness of how they see and interact with others and how they are seen by them, lasted the whole 1997-98 school year and consisted of two on-site programs and multiple visits with Transition Guides for each school team. After the Transition Guides completed their first visit to each school, an unexpected finding emerged: everyone was afraid to come to CCL! It was the assessment portion of the BLDI—taking the extensive "long form" Myers-Briggs Type Indicator assessments, taking the FIRO-B to help assess their capacity for working in groups and teams, having peers and principals complete a Benchmarks 360 degree feedback instrument, and having the results interpreted in a private "feedback" session with a trained psychologist or counselor—that scared them most. For this reason, their first session was altered to include only descriptive data about themselves. Feedback from their peers and the 360 assessment feedback reporting how others perceived their leadership would wait until Session 2. Anxiety levels were so high that a three-day "Getting to know each other and the BLDI" session was held. Teachers and principals walked around the CCL campus, saw the one-way mirrors used to observe participants and most important, met the CCL faculty who would work with them.

The meeting turned on discussion of the rule regarding strict confidentiality of individual data. CCL faculty told the teachers, principals, and central office staff that this rule was so crucial to our work that we agreed to accept physical torture rather than reveal data to anyone other than the participant! That helped a lot. Teachers had been afraid that their principal would see their data. Principals were afraid their superintendent would see their scores. A sigh of relief swept through the room as they realized that they had total control over who saw their data.

During this same period, the superintendent expressed his doubts about the focus of the CCL work. His preference was to use the funds to share research-based practices with teachers. He was not convinced of the value of working on relational leadership. This caused some angst for building principals, who feared retribution for participating. CCL faculty and principals held long, confidential conversations about their fears and how, collectively, they could be afforded some protection. The CCL President and faculty met with the superintendent and listened to his concerns. Eventually, the superintendent grudgingly supported the initiative, and CCL faculty wondered about the impact of lukewarm support from the top.

Session One

As trust of the CCL faculty grew, the initial fear of assessments faded and previously unseen team dynamics and the shape of their own personal characteristics emerged and intrigued team members:

> I attended in a very nonthreatening environment.
>
> I was very unsure about what to expect from this, but wow! I learned so much about myself and others!

The environment of CCL also had a curious affect. CCL's main campus consists of a collection of contemporary stone buildings on manicured grounds at the edge of a lake. The serene and beautiful retreat setting, developed as a research and training facility for an international clientele of corporate executives, is in stark contrast to most public schools, including the ones where the BLDI participants worked. On the first Monday, many participants were astounded at the gourmet quality and generous portions of food in the CCL cafeteria, the comfortable seats, the artwork and other features of the attractive environment, and the professional treatment accorded them. They ate meals surrounded by business executives from all over the world. By Wednesday, CCL faculty noted a general change in how teachers and principals held themselves—they seemed prouder of who they were and what they did:

> The facilities are marvelous.... I felt so important and safe here. I realized that my voice counts.

At the conclusion of Session 1, the curriculum committee met to review the composite group profiles of descriptive assessment data for all participating to get a sense of group characteristics. The Myers Briggs Personality Type Indicator (MBTI), the Change Style Indicator (CSI), the Fundamental Interpersonal Relations Orientations and Behavior indicator (FIRO-B), the Rokeach Values Instrument, the Organizational Stress Inventory, and the Life Styles Inventory were reviewed.[2]

Some interesting patterns with potential for relationship tension emerged:

- The school leadership teams' "hardwired" *MBTI* personality preference for "S" (sensing) and the Executive Cabinets preference for "N" (Intuition), were in conflict. The Executive Cabinet, with a propensity for big-picture thinking, may have been continually frustrated because principals and teachers did not share their preference for strategic conversations. Teachers and principals may be frustrated when administration does not give them detailed guidance regarding expectations and implementation of school reforms.
- Given the school leadership teams' hardwired *CSI* preference for a *Conserver* change style (preferring incremental, slow change to expansive, rapid change), they may be most comfortable with refining current educational practices rather than dealing with large scale reform and restructuring. Conserver school teams might also see their superintendent and cabinet as making too many changes without thinking through implementation. Conversely, the superintendent and cabinet, showing a clear preference for the *Originator* perspective (preferring change that is rapid and expansive) may grow exasperated with principals and teachers who take too long to get on board with new initiatives.
- Group *FIRO-B* profiles (showing strength of three interpersonal needs for *Inclusion, Control,* and openness or *Affection*) revealed differences. The teams' *Inclusion* scores indicated that they may have difficulty shifting out of the isolated environment of the classroom or school and into a more participatory, interactive role with their colleagues and community. When principals' scores are disaggregated, a clear difference exists between expressed and wanted *Inclusion* scores. Their high expressed scores may be indicative of job responsibilities that force them to be more social and engage in more social functions than they really want to, which can send confusing messages to their school community. While they may be initi-

ating and attending school social events (i.e., the school carnival, fund-raising suppers) because they "have to" as the principal, they may prefer solitary or family-only activities and isolate themselves from faculty and parents. They may also prefer to associate with a few "chosen" faculty rather than socialize with many, and this could lead to an appearance of favoritism. The school leadership teams *"Control"* scores (both wanting to control others and willingness to accept control from others) indicate a strong need for self-sufficiency and independence and reluctance to both lead *and* be led. Generally, their stance is "don't control me, and I won't control you." They prefer leadership that holds them accountable for outcomes but lets them decide how to do the work. They like leaders who ask for their input and offer options in how to move forward. In contrast, *Control* scores for the Executive Cabinet reflect a strong desire to take charge. When they see a need for leadership, they readily jump in and push for their ideas to be adopted. They have some difficulty including others in decision making. Their high need to be in control is in tension with the needs of principals and teachers for self-sufficiency and independence. Both groups needed coaching to understand how their styles affect their work.

The pattern of moderate Openness/*Affection* scores (wanting to receive warmth and openness from others and wanting to express warmth and openness to others) of school teams, principals, and administrators fell within the "golden middle," indicating a moderate need for expressions of warmth and personal valuing. This indicated that, overall, this group of educators has an easy time forming meaningful connections with students and colleagues, but can also interrupt that connection to make hard calls when needed. School teams and the Executive Cabinet each contain a few individuals with either a very low or very high need to express openness and warmth. A challenge would be honoring the person who prefers team members to be close friends (high Openness/Affection scores) and the person with a preference for keeping personal matters private.

Transition Guides used these data with school and district teams to explore team dynamics and reasons for misunderstandings and relational leadership breakdowns.

Session Two

Although participants nicknamed this session "leadership boot camp," because they were challenged to examine themselves and their perceptions closely, participants seemed less apprehensive. The work was demanding—psychologically strenuous simulations (one focused on decision making, the other addressing diversity issues), open dialogues with each other about feelings and being presented with "360" data and finding out what their boss, their peers, and the support staff really think of their skills, knowledge, and attitudes.

On Day 4, each participant sat alone with a trained feedback specialist (a practicing psychologist or counselor) for an hour and a half to integrate their assessment data and begin developing action plans for changing their attitudes and behaviors to improve relationships and gain leadership potential to get the work results they wanted:

> I'm becoming comfortable leading activities; I also am practicing being quiet and listening.
>
> I have rights as a group member to be heard.
>
> By realizing what people's comfort zone is, you can try to see where they are coming from.
>
> Gagging ('Going Against the Grain') has never been a strong point but now I see it's OK.

The Executive Cabinet also went through a modified "boot camp." It began with a group activity in which they were asked to express their thoughts anonymously about the current state of their school system and the working relationship of Executive Cabinet members using group computer software. Because their identity was protected, a free flow of genuine perceptions and thoughts ensued which helped the group get ready to more deeply reflect on the state of relationships among Cabinet members. The Cabinet also got an opportunity to work on pressing school district issues. During the first year, the superintendent attended an intensive, feedback-rich, five-day "Leadership at the Peak" CCL program with other C.E.O.s, Generals and Admirals. He received extensive assessment feedback on how his personal characteristics and leadership style impacted the organization's success.

Session evaluations showed that school leadership team members rated the instructional modules of Session 1 and 2 a 4.5 or 5 on a 5-point scale and rated the faculty and feedback coaches' work from 4.7-4.9. Stories were told of school leadership teams sharing with others what they'd learned:

> It amazed each of us that we felt comfortable enough, trusting enough, to sit down and actually throw some things out, go out on that limb and feel like we weren't the only one on the limb. So it built trust within ourselves and within that team.

The Executive Cabinet reported feeling more comfortable sharing how they feel with each other and the superintendent reported that the Cabinet had already improved the way they schedule and work with each other. He admitted that the focus on both personal and work issues had been extremely helpful. A most remarkable finding at the end of the BLDI's first year was the finding that the rate of BLDI school leadership team membership turnover was only 4%, a low level the superintendent proclaimed "amazing." Many principals and teachers reported that they had experienced "life-changing insights" during the programs.

The Curriculum Committee met to review composite group reports for Session 2 assessments—the *Denison Organizational Survey*, the *KEYS Survey of Creativity and Innovation*, and the Skillscope 360 Assessment.[3] A summary report, coalescing all BLDI participant Skillscope data, showed the groups' perceived leadership and managerial strengths and their developmental needs. The assessment results had clear implications for future BLDI development plans (Table 11.2).

School team group reports suggested that friendly, congenial relationships were maintained at the expense of having authentic conversations about points of conflict. Reports also suggested that principals were "pushing" school reforms without investing in relationship fuel, as was the executive cabinet. Summary reports for both school leadership teams and principals show that they underestimate their strengths. Overall, they rated themselves lower than others did. However, the Executive Cabinet members rated themselves higher than others did. Both groups needed assistance in aligning their self-perceptions with how others see them.

When asked to identify key insights and learnings, several themes were heard. They found learning about self and interpersonal relationships invaluable:

> All the personal feedback was very beneficial.
>
> The opportunity to talk with my team ... about how we need to address leadership issues and how that would affect the output and morale of the school was valuable.
>
> I realized that much of the anger I had about problem students stemmed not so much from their disrupting problematic behavior but from my inability to relate and a lack of time and resources to offer what they needed.

They were surprised that the program focused on their personal needs and how to deal with stress effectively:

> The OSI gave me a really good idea of what stresses me the most and what I need to do to make some things easier for me.

Table 11.2. Strengths and Developmental Needs of BLDI Members

SCHOOL TEAM MEMBERS:

Strengths:

- Strong in seeking information, observing others;
- Good relationships with others;
- Relating to different kinds of people, listening, collaborating;
- Having integrity and being trustworthy;
- Conveying a clear sense of purpose.

Developmental Needs:

- Effective at managing conflict and confronting others;
- Sometimes abrasive;
- Not able to make a point effectively;
- Not decisive;
- Not creators of change;
- Not team-builders;
- Not accepting criticism well;
- Not managing time well;
- Spreading themselves too thin.

PRINCIPALS:

Strengths:

- Strong in being goal-directed, persistent;
- Driven to achieve objectives;
- Capable and cool in high pressure situations.

Developmental Needs:

- Conflict management;
- Building of relationships.

EXECUTIVE CABINET:

Strengths:

- Seeking information;
- Observing people and events;
- Having integrity and trustworthiness.

Developmental Needs:

- Effective in managing conflict;
- Being competent with other people's feelings;
- Recognizing others work;
- Being tolerant of the idiosyncrasies of others;
- Building relationships;
- Weighing consequences of their actions;
- Being readily available to others;
- Giving subordinates appropriately structured and challenging assignments.

> My awareness to take care of my own needs will have a greater impact on others and my performance than I thought.

They reported that they felt trusting of their teammates and understood the unique contributions all members could contribute:

> Knowing each other allows us to work through problems more effectively.
>
> The session allowed me time to get to know other staff members in a different way and learn things about them that I'd not been aware of.
>
> I've worked with my team for 4 years and 10 years on other teams—but I've shared more this week than ever in the past.
>
> The trust and respect between members that came about because of the sharing was awesome.

And they talked of increasing confidence in their leadership abilities and commitment to improve:

> Everyone at different times and during different experiences can be a leader!'
>
> Each individual has important contributions for leadership.
>
> I'll lessen my responsibilities by doing a better job of delegating authority and turning over responsibilities.
>
> I'm going to become a force to gather and produce group interaction in a positive atmosphere and create experiences for others to utilize what I've learned here at CCL.
>
> I'm going to develop empathy and compassion as elements of decision making.
>
> I'm going to pick my battles and cope with the pessimism of my peers.

Progress reports from CCL BLDI faculty, Transition Guides and feedback specialists revealed individual school patterns of growth, and the next year's curriculum offering was tailored to each school's readiness. But one overarching issue stood out. Serious issues of trust existed throughout the district and interfered with school and district performance.

YEAR TWO: A ROCKY ROAD

Before the BLDI began, CCL faculty and program leaders insisted, based on the heavy evidence of the three to five-year window required for successful educational change (e.g., Fullan, 2001) that members of the school leadership teams commit to staying with the team for a minimum of three years (Fullan, 2001). Further, they sought the superintendent's commitment to leave the principals and their teams in place for the same three-year minimum. But during the second year, despite promises to keep the teams together, the superintendent transferred nine out of the 21 principals to schools not participating in the BLDI. One principal left the district to join a statewide reform team. New and fragile school team cohesion suffered. Anxiety about shrinking school leadership teams ran rampant. The teams had learned how to work collaboratively, how to trust and give feedback to each other. Would these new ways of behaving crumble? And how do they introduce new members to their team?

Another problem surfaced. A second school leadership team was formed in conjunction with a reading program initiated by the central administration. There was confusion about which team led the school. The realization also grew that central administration was still struggling to let teams decide how to run their school. So the focus of Year 2 became how to help teams professionally and effectively assert themselves and "manage upward."

As anticipated, during Year Two the anger and mistrust that simmered underground began to surface. CCL faculty members received calls at home from principals, telling them about their mistrust and fear of central administration. Some feared for their jobs. The superintendent became agitated as he felt he was losing control of his principals. He had abruptly disbanded the principal's association. And a struggle over the use of the $10,000 allocated by the Bryan Foundation to each of the schools erupted. Central office administration wanted it to be used to pay for teacher substitutes, and school leadership teams had other plans.

Monthly, a confidential principals-only meeting at CCL was put into effect, a forum that gave principals a chance to voice their concerns. CCL facilitators intended to use the meetings to challenge the principals to get in touch with the fears preventing them from having candid conversations with the central administration and work to remind them of their personal power and responsibility. The superintendent balked at not having district personnel present—he didn't understand the need for a confidential forum for principals. Relationships between CCL faculty and the superintendent were strained—a developmental period of "storming" began. Under protestations of CCL faculty who explained that candidness and growth only would come from having a safe environment in which to discuss issues, the superintendent insisted that someone from his office be present whenever principals assembled. As it turned out, executive cabinet member attendees stayed for a brief time to answer questions, and then left.

Adversity sometimes strengthens. And this was the case for many involved in Year 2 activities. Individuals on the school leadership teams stepped up and brokered conflict and volunteered to conduct sessions for new members on what they'd learned during BLDI programs:

> We're bringing important issues to the forefront concerning school needs.
>
> I'm not intimidated by people. I'm stepping forward and taking charge instead of always being a follower.
>
> I'm getting over my fear of speaking up, fear of what other people will think, fear of differing with someone else's point of view, and my avoidance of confrontation.

But for others, the tenuous support of central administration for continuing the BLDI, a program designed to empower teachers and principals, took its toll. The CCL team also realized the monumental obstacles they faced in creating a long-term program of development for educators.

YEAR THREE: TRANSFERS, MOVEMENT, AND CHANGE

Early in Year 3 the superintendent resigned to take a position in another state. For most of the year, the school board searched for a new superintendent while a longtime associate superintendent, trusted and loved by many in the community, was appointed interim superintendent. In the latter part of the year, the board decided not to appoint her as superintendent and, instead, brought in an 'outsider'. Shortly after his arrival, principals and teachers moved like pieces on a chessboard. The BLDI teams lost 44 members. One team lost nine of its fifteen members. New principals—nine of whom were first-timers—were appointed to 17 schools. Central administration positions were shuffled, and by the end of the year, only seven of the original Executive Cabinet remained. Ten new people, all from outside the district, were appointed to executive cabinet roles (assistant superintendents) and most BLDI schools had new central administration supervisors.

Then, another change—adoption by the superintendent and school board of a new accountability policy for principals. Because the changes were made without any involvement of the principals or other school level personnel, BLDI teams lost belief in the "site-based management" ideal. External changes—more stringent accountability metrics and public announcements of school ratings—pushed on the educators as well.

The shifts of people and policies brought significant change—new people, new priorities and new leadership styles. School leadership teams and their principals faced heightened levels of ambiguity and uncertainty within the district at the same time they continued to deal with an increasing number of poor, fragile students and families. Many of the emerging positive changes in relationships slowly slipped away. Again, much time was spent convincing the new superintendent that building solid leadership relationships was worth it.

YEAR FOUR: RELATIONAL REGULATORS

In Year 4, fractured school teams looked to each other and to CCL facilitators for support. While the BLDI curriculum called for enhancing their ability to lead their fellow faculty in developing, communicating, and acting on a team vision for their school, time was necessary for listening and processing feelings:

> you're always hoping for success but there's times where some failure or fall back occurs and you need support to keep your confidence going.

Four hundred forty-two leadership team members from 21 schools attended four two-day programs at CCL and received multiple individual visits from their Transition Guide.

A Year 4 goal, encouraging responsibility for the whole school community rather than just a classroom or school, was met with skepticism and discouragement. "Managing upward" sounded like a good idea, but experience was telling them that their input wasn't valued:

> I've seen a person in leadership who has not been inclusive really and I've grappled with why that person has viewed things that way ... this person acts as an island and tries to insulate what they're doing ... and I've seen a definite impact that it's had throughout the organization.

> You don't come in and change everything right away, even though you may see things that you'd like to change. You have to understand the people who were here before and where they're coming from, the whole situation and then work from there.

And they felt burned out by too many demands to change, to assume more work, and by an avalanche of communications:

> And there's information coming down email after email ... this will happen, this will happen, and this will happen—all teachers have to do this, all students will do this, and it's just too much information for all of the teachers to know right now!

> They totally ignore all of the pressures and amount of work that a classroom teacher has.

Principals felt a pull between meeting superintendent demands and attending the BLDI. Many felt that the superintendent didn't see the value of leadership development—he just wanted his new mandates met. Year 4 was spent supporting, refocusing, reflecting, and helping educators deal with overwhelming reporting responsibilities.

In Year 4, a significant shift in curriculum took place. The new superintendent demanded more involvement of the principals' supervisors in designing CCL programs, and he wanted more time to be spent by the school leadership teams addressing "real problems of the schools." Working on leadership capacity from a relational perspective seemed "soft" and he wanted the district educators to work on "hard" issues. The new executive cabinet associate superintendents influenced how time would be spent and on what topics. Slowly, school problem analysis shifted back to focus more heavily on the content of reforms. The relational process of leading implementation of reforms, a process of buy-in relying upon the quality of the connections and relationships among district educators, moved quietly to the background.

The Executive Cabinet did not take part in team-based formal training activities at CCL. Instead, members who hadn't attended a five-day CCL Leadership Development Program (new staff and others who had not participated) signed up. They also participated in a two-day CCL program, "Coaching for Results." This program was co-designed by the school district and CCL to enable those who supervise schools to coach principals more effectively and included a good amount of didactic teaching of models.

During this year, the principals-only meeting occurred over lunch at CCL. As the year wore on, fewer principals attended. Those routinely attending took the opportunity to share confidential impressions of what was happening in the district and how they all might 'survive'.

CCL faculty used previously learned relational leadership skills to help school teams attack one problem at a time.

Helping new school leadership team members "catch up" was another key challenge for Year 4. Topics for the sessions were individualized for each school. All focused on implementing and evaluating school level change.

YEAR FIVE: HIGH PERFORMANCE ISLANDS AND AN INITIATIVE IN SEARCH OF SCALE

During Year 5, the principals decided on a new format for their meeting. Due to time pressures, principals requested that their principal-only meetings happen only four times this year, rather than monthly, but they lengthened it to four hours. Both CCL faculty and principals chose topics.

Each of the principals also had an opportunity to receive another 360 assessment of their leadership skills and another one-on-one session with a feedback coach to delve deeply into the implications of their scores. Of 21 principals, 19 participated.

As the year came to a close, the Bryan Foundation continued to support the growth of leadership capacity throughout the district, even offering funding to support additional activities. At the end of Year 5, CCL faculty gathered to review the pitfalls and promises of the BLDI. Two of the 21 BLDI schools had received national awards for excellence during the time of the Initiative, and each attributed substantial credit for their success to the Bryan Leadership Development Initiative and the relational leadership skills they had learned at CCL. One elementary school won the Governor's Entrepreneurial Excellence in Education Award. The school had gone from a poor performing school to being a "school of distinction." A videotape telling the story of this school's dramatic, three-year turnaround told the story of the custodian, who went from seeing himself as a steward of floors and desks to a steward of children. The principal talked of her deliberate strategy to "shut up" and help others find answers. School team teachers told of overcoming a fear of authority figures and confidently stepping forward and presenting a research-based argument convincing the central office to let them "do what they knew was best for kids." The principal at the other school began listening to teachers more, enthusiastically inspiring them by getting artists to paint murals on the walls and by writing grants to get more funding support for the school. Together, the principal and teachers started working feverishly to find ways to involve parents—renting buses to bring parents without transportation to the school and providing babysitters.

There were other school level successes as well: less teacher turnover, a problem in a time of teacher shortages; increased collaboration between school team members and the principal and a strengthening of bonds among all members of the school community, and more whole-school, rather than classroom commitment—all faculty and staff cared about all kids.

But the envisioned district reform did not happen on the scale originally hoped and intended. Yet many important lessons remained.

LESSONS LEARNED

Relational Leadership–A Walk in the Shadows

Lurking in the shadow of the cold, objective words of state law, district edict, and principal policy are the people who must implement them—

people with needs for relatedness, affiliation, loyalty, and nurturance (Hofer, 1995, Ornish, 1998). As the superintendent or principal presents plans, accountability systems, or school schedules, feelings silently color what is heard. In the silent recesses of minds all around the room, distracting little questions interrupt concentration: "Do I trust him/her?" "Does he or she know how this impacts me?" "Will she/he support me when the going gets tough?" "Can I handle this?" Yet most school administrators (and other executives) spew directives as if all their listeners were like the emotionless Mr. Spock from Star Trek. In this district, it was no different. Directives cascaded downward, leaders distanced themselves from faculty and staff:

> There just isn't time for that relational leadership—we're under the gun from the state to get test scores up. We lose money if we don't perform. If principals and teachers can't perform, they'll be removed and we'll find others that can.

Yet the schools managing to raise student achievement *did* pay attention to relationships. They worked at understanding each other, supporting each other—and finding ways to build positive relationships with parents. Elegant cognitive frameworks and refined rational arguments alone *don't* excite people to action. It's the *person* occupying the positional leader role, not his/her order or credo, not his spatial location in the room or dress, not exquisitely chosen words that create personal, change agent potency. A Pied Piper leader at any level feels the emotional pull of minds in the school community audience and responds with genuine care and interest, with empathy, and support. She or he wraps rational arguments of the need for school reform with relational language designed to build partnerships and arouse passion and commitment. Their emotional, relational leadership approach emanating from the brain's limbic system allows their rational, analytic neocortex to present ideas and mandates in a way that evokes passion and commitment far beyond that evoked by an idea or mandate alone.

The neural architecture of the human brain places *relationships* at the crux of our lives. It is the feeling, limbic portion of the brain that senses whether the *proposer* of an idea is friend or foe and gives or denies permission to the analytical neocortex to process and act on a rational notion. Out of the shadows and authentically communicated, a leader's feelings open the door to mutual understanding and interpersonal motivation. The emotional medium *is* the message. Yet leaders vary in their awareness of emotional imperatives. And when feelings fail to connect, when followers are hurting and alienated from their leader, they turn to the emotional content of other relationships—colleagues, family, friends—to help them understand, to guide them in thought. With emotional ties broken, the leader walks alone, left only to scream angrily, "Do it or else!" (Lewis et al., 2000).

Changing Relationships—What it Takes

Five years is a long time to fund and run a school reform initiative. But deeply ingrained ways of feeling, thinking, and behaving aren't erased over night. New ways of feeling, thinking, and behavior need long-term support to move from fumbling first attempts to more elegant, easily remembered ways of doing and being. Relationship changes live on time. Reframing another's emotional rhythms and needs require multiple encounters with the new behavior before they become believable. Changing a teacher's approach to working with children, her principal, the central office administrators—or parents—calls for patience.

And it calls for a leader with high levels of personal energy. Businesses provide onsite fitness equipment or reduced-fee health club memberships to their employees, and many are preaching the value of fitness in the workplace. Most school districts don't. Yet the connection between high performance and fitness is strong. Close relationships also instill a resilience to counteract the degenerative influence of stress (McDowell-Larsen, 2002; Colon, Callies, Polpkin, & McGlave, 1991).

Positional Leaders Matter

Although leadership ebbs and flows between and among all people in school communities, the person "at the top" exerts a special and powerful influence over everyone. What the positional leader values and whom they see as worthwhile (or not) washes over everyone.

The person in charge—superintendent, principal or teacher leader—brings to the task hardwired ways of relating to others. Leaders who come to the task chock full of ideas and knowledge of successful teaching and learning practices can provoke minimal success. But leaders who come armed with those ideas and knowledge *and* relationship talent inspire greatness. Throughout the BLDI, we observed principals who worked hard on themselves. They kept an ear close to the schoolyard for emotional clues while they scoured the literature for the best educational tools they could find. They paid attention to their school's emotional climate and searched for signs of burnout. They kept morale high among their faculty and also kept central office happy. They led with exceptionally well developed relationship talent.

But many more didn't get there. Fear of humiliation and punishment from the superintendent or principal for not meeting state mandates, exhaustion from trying to meet a plethora of often conflicting demands from central office, principal, parents, and students shut them down. They approached others guardedly and with outright suspicion, thinking they were playing a perpetual game of "gotcha!" Educators, like other professionals, are faced with an extremely complex and ambiguous environment. Having leaders who can act as a buffer, who foster a spirit of "we're in this together," and who show care for everyone in the school community give teachers a fighting chance to meet the needs of their students. School leaders who hope to get exceptional results must get their own emotional house in order. And school boards and school councils looking for top notch leaders would do well to assess the E.Q. as well as I.Q of their candidates.

Leadership Development: Silent Forces

An organization's culture and its climate are written about as if "it" were a tough taskmaster, a living being that sprang up mysteriously from ... somewhere. And developmental practices are often labeled fundamental, embedded internal organizational forces determining how "things are done around here" (Bolman & Deal, 1991; Hofstede, 1997). Like mischievous ghosts, these forces hover in the background and invisibly push and pull upon the people and the actions they take. They help determine beliefs about leadership development, the way learning should be shared, whether structures and strategies are flexible and responsive or rigid, and they influence whether systems do or don't support leadership development.

Yet organizations and their climates and cultures are not alive. They are concepts, without conscience, emotional life, and grand thoughts. *People* create and sustain them, build their systems of accountability, information, development, and learning. *People* give life and style to the organization's strategies, structures, and problem solving. And it is *people* who determine how human and material resources are handled.

Prevailing organizational forces reveal a lot about the people, present and past. The school district bears the beauty and the scars of *people*—those currently leading and participating as well as imprints left by past leaders and followers. The "CCL Way" met the "Piedmont County Schools' Way." Two organizational forces, two cultures, met and the resultant product was a sometimes-volatile, sometimes-productive mixture.

The organizational forces affecting leadership development in the school district shifted as superintendents came and went. Two of the three district superintendents heading up the district during the life of the BLDI were strong, directive leaders. Both frequently exerted control and dominance by yelling and telling. At one BLDI celebratory banquet, the superintendent at-the-time ordered the CCL president, the head of the funding organization, and the CCL faculty into a small room and harshly castigated an action they'd taken.

Over time, actions such as this one formed an unspoken, unwritten organizational rule that governed all school interactions. The rule got into the bloodstream of the school community: *Leadership development and school improvement require control over others. Change has to be forced.*

Creating a healthy school climate, a culture that breeds success, means having leaders who are, themselves, healthy—able to inspire healthy relationships supportive of faculty, staff, and student success. Change forces focused on raising test scores affected the BLDI's success. Two superintendents believed that their wills and the power of centralized authority were the way to succeed. But the greatest stories of achievement and sustainability among the BLDI schools were stories of relational leadership and community-building. Those seeds of promise in this school district echo the stories of success in the education, nonprofit, and corporate worlds. Reforming organizations means reforming relationships.

NOTES

1. Berry and Broadbent (1984—reference not found in original); Weiss and Cropanzano (1996); Peeters (2002); Rozin and Royzman (2001); Fisher (2000—reference not found in original).
2. The instruments used are the *Myers-Briggs Type Indicator* (Isabel Briggs Myers and Katharine C. Briggs), the FIRO-B, an instrument that explores relationship preferences in areas of inclusion, control, and closeness or affection, and the *California Psychological Inventory 434*. all instruments are available from CPP, http://www.cpp-db.com/products.
3. An additional instrument used was the *Change Style Indicator*, Christopher Musselwhite, Developer, Discovery Learning, Inc.

REFERENCES

Barth, R.S. (1990). *Improving schools from within.* San Francisco: Jossey-Bass.

Beck, L.G., & Murphy, J. (1998). Site-based management and school success: Untangling the variables. *School Effectiveness and School Improvement*. *9*(4), 358-385.

Bolman, L., & Deal, T. (1991). *Reframing organizations: Artistry, choice, leadership*. San Francisco: Jossey-Bass.

Brown, F. (2001, April) Site-based management: Is it still central to the school reform movement? *School Business Affairs*, Association of School Business Officials International web-based article, http://asbointl.org/WhatsNew/School BusinessAffairs/index.asp?bid=50

Collins, J. (2001). *From good to great*. New York: Harper-Collins.

Colon, A., Callies, A., Polpkin, M., & McGlave, P. (1991). Depressed mood and other variables related to bone marrow transplantation and survival in acute leukemia. *Psychosomatics, 32*, 420-425.

Dasborough, M.T. (2003). *Cognitive asymmetry in employee affective reactions to leadership behaviors*. Unpublished paper submitted for the Kenneth E. Clark Student Research Award, Center for Creative Leadership.

Dellar, G.B. (1998). School climate, school improvement and site-based management. *Learning Environments Research, 1*(3), 353-367.

Dempster, D. (2000). Guilty or not: The impact and effects of site-based management on schools. *Journal of Educational Administration, 38*(1), 47-63.

Dyer, K., & Carothers, J. (2000). *The intuitive principal*. Thousand Oaks, CA: Corwin Press.

Elmore, R.F. (1995). Structural reform in educational practice. *Educational Researcher, 24*, 23-26.

Elmore, R.F. (1993). School decentralization: Who gains? Who loses? In J. Hanaway & M. Carnoy (Eds.), *Decentralization and school improvement: Can we fulfill the promise?* (pp. 33-54). San Francisco: Jossey Bass.

Fullan, M. (2001). *The new meaning of educational change*. New York, Teachers College Press.

Gardham, K., & Brown, R. (2001). Two forms of intergroup discrimination with positive and negative outcomes: Explaining the positive-negative asymmetry effect. *British Journal of Social Psychology, 40*(1), 23-34.

Goleman, D. (2000). *Emotional intelligence*. New York: Bantam Books.

Hall, G, & Hord, S. (2001). *Implementing change: Promises, pitfalls, and potholes*. Boston: Allen and Bacon.

Hannaway, J. (1996). Management decentralization and performance-based incentives: Theoretical consideration for schools. In E. Hanusek & D. Jorgensen (Eds.), *Improving America's schools: The role of incentives* (pp. 97-109). Washington, DC: National Research Council.

Heflin, O.L., & Heflin, J.F. (1995). *Redefining leadership roles for site-based management systems*. Paper presented at the Annual Meeting of the Mid-South Eductional Research Association, Biloxi.

Hess, G.A. (1999). Expectations, opportunity, capacity, and will: The four essential components of Chicago school reform. *Educational Policy, 13*(4), 494-517.

Hofer, M.A. (1995). Hidden regulators: Implications for a new understanding of attachment, separation, and loss. In S. Goldberg, R. Muir, & J. Kerr (Eds.), *Attachment theory: Social, Developmental, Clinical perspectives*. Hillsdale, NJ: Analytic Press.

Hofstede, G. (1997). *Cultures and organizations: Software of the mind*. New York: McGraw-Hill.

Holmes, K.M. (1990). *The concept of vision in American school reform*. Unpublished doctoral dissertation, University of North Texas.

Holmes-Ponder, K. (1997). *Strengthening school leadership: A leadership development program for Guilford County school leaders*. Unpublished proposal to the Joseph F. Bryan Foundation, Greensboro, NC, Center for Creative Leadership.

Howard, E., Howell, B., & Brainard, E. (1987). *Handbook for conducting school climate improvement projects*. Bloomington, IN: Phi Delta Kappa Educational Foundation.

Hunter, M.A. (1999). All eyes forward: Public engagement and educational reform in Kentucky. *Journal of Law and Education, 28*(4), 485-516.

Kerman, S. (2000). *Teacher expectations and student achievement*. Los Angeles: Los Angeles County Board of Education.

Larsen, R.J., & Diener, E.E. (1992). Promises and problems with the circumplex model of emotion. In M.S. Clark (Ed.), *Review of personality and social psychology: Emotion and social behavior* (Vol. 114, pp. 25-29). Newbury Park, CA: Sage.

Leithwood, K., & Menzies, T. (1998). A review of research concerning the implementation of site-based management. *School Effectiveness and School Improvement, 9*(3), 233-285.

Lewis, T., Amini, F., & Lannon, R. (2000). *The general theory of love*. New York: Vintage Books.

Marks, H.M., & Louis, K.S. (1997). Does teacher empowerment affect the classroom? The implications of teacher empowerment for instructional practice and student academic performance. *Educational Evaluation and Policy Analysis, 19*(3), 245-275.

Martineau, J. (1998). *BLDI year one formative evaluation report*. Unpublished evaluation report. Greensboro, NC: Center for Creative Leadership.

McCauley, C., Moxley, R., & Van Velsor, E. (2003). *Handbook of leadership development*. San Francisco: Jossey-Bass.

McDowell-Larsen, S. (2002, May-June). Stress takes a toll on leaders. *Leadership in Action, 22*(2).

Ornish, D. (1998). *Love and survival: The scientific basis for the healing power of intimacy*. New York: Harper Collins.

Pae, H. (2000, April). *School reform: Effects of site-based management reform practices on restructuring schools to facilitate inclusion*. Paper presented at the Annual Meeting of the American Educational Research Association, New Orleans, (ED 451 612).

Peeters, G. (2002). From good and bad to can and must: subjective necessity of acts associated with positively and negatively valued stimuli. *European Journal of Social Psychology, 32*, 125-136.

Rice, R., Delagardelle, M., Buckton, M., Jons, C., Lueders, W., Vens, M.J., Joyce, B., Wolf, J., & Weathersby, J. (2001). *The Lighthouse inquiry: School board/superintendent team behaviors in school districts with extreme differences in student achievement*. Paper presented at the American Education Research Association Annual Meeting.

Rozin, P., & Royzman, E.B. (2001). Negativity bias, negativity dominance, and contagion. *Personality and Social Psychology Review, 5*(4), 296-320.

Ruderman, R., Hannum, K., Leslie, J.B., & Steed, J. (2001). *Leadership skills and emotional intelligence*. Greensboro, NC: Center for Creative Leadership.

Sergiovanni, T., & Moore, J. H. (1989). *Schooling for tomorrow: Directing reforms to issues that count*. Needham, MA: Allen & Bacon.

Shen, J. (2001, Spring). Teacher and principal empowerment: National, longitudinal, and comparative perspectives. *Educational Horizons*, 124-129.

Tanner, C.K., & Stone, C.D. (1998, March 1). School improvement policy: Have administrative functions of principals changed in schools where site-based management is practiced? *Education Policy Analysis Archives*, *6*(6), (http// epaa.asu.edu/epaa/v6n6.html)

Tyack, D. (1993). School governance in the United States: Historical puzzles and anomalies. In J. Hannoray & M. Carney (Eds.), *Decentralization and school improvement*. San Francisco: Jossey-Bass.

Vandenberghe, R. (1995). Creative management of a school: A matter of visions and daily interventions. *Journal of Educational Administration, 2*, 31-51.

Weiss, H.M., & Cropanzano, R. (1996). Affective events theory: A theoretical discussion of the structure, causes, and consequences of affective experience at work. In B.M. Staw & L. Cummings (Eds.), *Research in organizational behavior* (Vol. 19, pp. 1-74). Greenwich, CT: JAI Press.

Wohlstetter, P., Van Kirk, A.N., Robertson, P.J., & Mohrman, S.A. (1997). *Organizing for successful school-based management*. Alexandria, VA: Association for Supervision and Curriculum Development.

CHAPTER 12

RURAL SCHOOL IMPROVEMENT NETWORKS

Creating possibilities for Significance in the 21st Century

Vernon Farrington, Mark L'Esperance, and Steve Mazingo

ABSTRACT

This chapter provides a case report of one small rural district's transformation of itself from a traditional, district-centered management approach to a collaborative school renewal effort through the use of school improvement networks. The networks were formed using three central principles: (1) building meaningful dialogical relationships to reach common meaning and purpose around the work (Burbules); (2) moral leadership and the sharing of power and authority (Sergiovanni); and (3) understanding the process and characteristics of change (Fullan et al.). The case describes the "Genesis" model, in which data are infused as a principal tool in directing reform, rather than as a "driver" for changes in policy and practice seeking immediate—and usually short-term—increases in test performance.

Deep Change: Cases and Commentary on Reform in High Stakes States, 229–254

INTRODUCTION

> The reputation of a thousand years may be determined by the conduct of one hour. (Japanese Proverb—Watkins, 2001)

Schools are facing the most difficult and complex changes in the history of American education. The ongoing challenges of new technology and seismic shifts in the global economy cause many to wonder if schools are capable of making the "leap" into Information Age demands. With the window for action reduced to "real time" for business and political leaders, school leaders feel pressure to produce significant results immediately. Quite literally, the Japanese proverb rings true, with society's collective legacy being determined by the decisions and actions of the current hour.

As educators seek solutions to the chaotic demands of the "Accountability Age," success stories are emerging that inspire hope for the future. Currently, North Carolina is experiencing one of the most radical transformations in state history. With the loss of thousands of jobs in textiles, furniture manufacturing, and tobacco, the state has been faced with many difficult economic challenges. The dilemma has forged a network of educational, business and political leaders with a vision that includes a high quality education for all students.

The purpose of this chapter is to provide a case report of how one small rural school district has been able to take on the current challenges by transforming itself from a traditional, district-centered leadership approach into a collaborative school renewal initiative by developing and utilizing school improvement networks. The major premise of this chapter is that the single most important component in describing the process of successful school reform is defining the role of leadership. In doing so, an integrated theoretical framework centered on three aspects of leadership will be examined. The first aspect is that leadership creates an opportunity in which stakeholders can build meaningful dialogical relationships in order to reach common meaning and purpose as outlined in the work of Burbules. The second aspect of the framework is Sergiovanni's notion of moral leadership. Sergiovanni has described how authority and power can be negotiated and shared in legitimate and moral ways. The third aspect relates to the extent that the leaders understand the process and characteristics of change as outlined by Fullan, Collins, and Goleman, Boyatzis, and McKee. This understanding includes the process of creating a climate for sustainable organizational change and the ongoing need for reassessment and refinement (Burbules, 1993; Collins, 2001; Fullan, 2001; Goleman, Boyatzis, & McKee, 2002; L'Esperance, Strahan, Farrington, & Anderson, 2003; Sergiovanni, 1990, 1992, 1996;).[1]

THE SETTING: EASTERN NORTH CAROLINA

Driving through the acres of snow-white cotton fields or the waving leaves of tobacco in early autumn, the first reaction is to appreciate the manifest beauty of creation displayed throughout eastern North Carolina. This rustic setting belies the harsh economic realities that face many area residents who struggle to make ends meet and provide needed services for their families. While a number of residents live in comfortable surroundings, a more complete tour of the area would include many rundown mobile homes or three-room shacks where school-age children live, desperately in need of an education more tailored for the future than the past.

With a long-standing agrarian economy, farming is central to the lives and identities of most eastern North Carolina residents. More recently, there has been a large influx of Hispanic immigrants. Originally, workers migrated seasonally to work on the farms and then return to their families in their homeland. Now, many have permanently relocated their families to Greene County, thus increasing the complexity of the educational needs for the school system.

With the economy almost totally dependent on agriculture, the region has been affected adversely by two major factors. First, increasing hardships for farmers in two of the region's major revenue sources ... tobacco and hog farming ... have resulted from litigation and growing health awareness Second, and even more devastating, was the destruction left in the wake of Hurricane Floyd in 1999. Widely recognized as one of the worst natural disasters in U.S. history, the aftermath left an already struggling region with scores of its residents homeless and without future job prospects. With "normal" poverty exceeding state averages, the flood left the region with very limited resources after redirecting all available funds to disaster relief efforts. In addition to the financial expense, the cost in human pain and suffering was immense and will continue for years to come (L'Esperance, 2003).

The problems of eastern North Carolina are reflected in the findings of a study conducted by the advocacy group Save the Children (2002) entitled *America's Forgotten Children: Child Poverty in Rural America*. Specifically, the findings state,

- Education provided for poor rural children is often inadequate and substandard. There is a greater shortage of rural teachers, and less money is spent in rural schools than urban ones.

- Child and youth development opportunities are limited—there are fewer after school, recreational, childcare or early childhood development education centers.
- Rural children do not receive adequate health care; in fact rural children are 50% more likely not to have health insurance than urban children, and 68% of all federally designated "health professional shortage areas" are in rural America.
- Poor rural communities lack basic services that people in urban areas take for granted, from safe drinking water, adequate plumbing and sewer connections to telephones and public transportation. The lack of transportation is a severe problem, limiting parents' access to employment and in many cases children's access to health care.

Breaking the cycle of poverty and achieving self-sufficiency is difficult in poor rural America, where wages do not lift families out of poverty, and jobs are less likely to offer benefits (Save the Children, 2002, p. 12).

The Case: Greene County Schools

Sitting near the geographic center of eastern North Carolina is the small town of Snow Hill. It is picturesque, and the center of activity in Greene County. In addition to the central geographic location, the school system also sits near the center of an ongoing school reform initiative that has produced a number of promising results for the county's future.

A casual review of the data from Greene County might cause one to have little hope for significant school improvement. The county ranks as one of the ten poorest counties in the state with an average family income of $19,043. With 25% of the total population living below the poverty level and 70% of its students qualifying for free or reduced lunch, the entire county is searching for answers in the midst of an economic recession. The Greene County School district comprises one primary school, one elementary school, one middle school and one high school. For the 2002-2003 school year, there were 762 students in the primary and elementary school, 763 in the middle school and 835 in the high school. Fifty-four percent of the students are male. Thirty-six percent of the students are white, 51% are black, and thirteen percent are Hispanic. Only 2% of the student population is enrolled in Advanced College Prep Courses.

THE GENESIS MODEL—AN EDUCATION RENEWAL NETWORK

The concept of generating a renewal effort specifically "tailored" for an individual school or district has been the focus of the Project Genesis research for over a decade. The Genesis Model synthesizes instructional theory and literature with local expertise and feedback to form a list of "best practices." Thus, "genesis" speaks to the unique variables that exist in each school setting and the "origin" of a focused effort for renewal. The focus of this network is to work with stakeholders in order to build common purpose and commitment in achieving goals (Lieberman & Grolnick, 1999).

In the early years of the Genesis model each school or particular group of teachers were focused on identifying ways in which opportunities for individual and collective teacher growth could occur (Lieberman & Wood, 2003). As the information and accountability age took center stage in state and national educational policy, it became apparent that the foundational precept of Genesis, teacher growth, had to be expanded to meet the needs of a broader base of stakeholders in individual schools and entire districts. Thus, Genesis took on the task of assisting entire educational communities in the process of developing strategic plans to meet the unique individual and collective goals of each setting. Two hallmarks of this model are its flexibility and its ability to adapt to the local needs of schools and districts.

When describing successful networks, Lieberman and Wood (2003) state, "these loose, borderless, flexible organizations can move quickly, inventing new structures and activities as necessary, to respond to the changing needs and concerns of their members." In addition, the Genesis Model redefines the traditional paradigm of funding by moving away from the primary emphasis on the need for grant or foundation funding, thus addressing the barrier issues outlined by Lieberman and Grolnick (1999). Each school or district which participates in the Genesis initiative provides its own financial resources. This form of funding allows for greater local control of activities, a greater commitment by the educational stakeholders to participate (i.e., "Since we are paying for it—we need to have this as a major priority and focus"), and allows the Genesis team discretion in matching professional expertise with the specific needs of the project. This is a customized approach which often eliminates the bureaucratic paradigm of previous assistance models.

The need for networking and partnering for meaningful change at both the local and central level is well documented. According to Darling-Hammond (1997):

> just as widespread school change cannot occur solely by policy mandate, neither can it occur by school invention alone, without supports from the policy system. If school level reforms continue only by waiver and exception, they will surely evaporate in a very short time, long before good schooling spreads to the communities where it is currently most notable by its absence. And if policies do not address questions of educational goals, systemwide capacity, and equity, the outcomes of bottom-up efforts will be inadequate to the needs of a democratic society. Neither a heavy-handed view of top-down reform nor a romantic vision of bottom-up change is plausible. Both local invention and supportive leadership are needed, along with new horizontal efforts that support cross-school consultation and learning. (pp. 210-211)

With the need for collaborative structures, Genesis serves as a "creative hub" which connects a variety of research and resource networks. This approach creates relational partnerships which can open avenues of communication while generating new and fresh approaches to system reform.

The Greene County Process

To create the Greene County initiative, the Genesis Team combined with district/university stakeholders to form a project team. The team began to collect data from a variety of sources to get a baseline "snapshot" of the district's status. While "No Child Left Behind" and other accountability models also stress the utilization of data, the Genesis approach recognized a critical distinction in the use of data related to its function as a tool versus an outcome. While many organizations are quick to label themselves as *data-driven,* the Genesis approach stressed that data alone do not give an organization the moral imperative needed to create the urgency to begin and sustain district and school reforms.

As a result, data-driven approaches may contribute to the "dehumanization" of the educational setting with students being viewed more as objects than as young people with individual gifts and needs. Conversely, the Genesis approach to reform is data-directed with data fully infusing the environment as another tool and indicator for action. To give the reform sustainability and meaning, the Genesis initiative always stresses that schools are to be "purpose-driven" with the emphasis always on student development and well-being (L'Esperance et al., 2003). This moral purpose has long been the primary reason for answering the "call" to the profession and will continue to be a key for sustainability in the future.

Understanding Significance

In addition to understanding the contextual roles of the moral purpose to drive the district and data to direct the strategies and interventions, a framework for significance was established (L'Esperance et al., 2003). The framework applies the following four broad categories to schools:

> *Schools of Surrender*: These schools long ago succumbed to the overwhelming odds of low expectations and the lack of a dynamic, shared vision for a better tomorrow. An ethos of failure permeates their environment with an easily apparent lack of financial, spiritual, and curricular support. Their infrastructures are crumbling and the mission is vague and distant from the daily lives of students ... Devastated by years of low academic achievement, lack of leadership, and high teacher turnover ... with neither affective nor cognitive strategies in place, (there is) no vision, no passion, no plan, and thus no hope for students. These schools have given up.
>
> *Schools of Survival*: These school function only at a survival level ... The leadership teams may desire school renewal but do not have a plan for energizing (the process) ... (There are) many schools of survival. Participants spend most of their energy reacting to challenges that arise. There is little visionary leadership ... These "survival specialists" wish they had a plan for taking their school to the next level, but lacking one, they are likely to settle for having completed another year with the ship afloat near the water line of proficiency (requirements) ... Sadly, a comparison with schools of surrender bring solace, which may hinder their chances of ever doing more than simply surviving.
>
> *Schools of Success*: These schools have been judged to be successful by most stakeholders. High student attendance, low teacher turnover, considerable parent involvement, and stereotypically low poverty levels have combined to produce a reputation of high student achievement and positive school climate ... Ironically, their success often presents barriers to further school improvement ... Because of their legacy of success, they do not continually review ... school theory or engage in strategic planning for academic improvement. As a result, they engage in yearly maintenance checks instead of participating in ongoing school renewal. Considered flagships of their districts, these schools are content to patch holes instead of considering significant design changes. "If it ain't broke, don't fix it" is an appropriate theme for schools of success. These schools are in danger of remaining in a maintenance mode. *Any* school not in ongoing renewal fails to offer the very best for its students and community.
>
> *Schools of Significance*: Schools of significance may evolve from any of the three models previously mentioned. They (are being transformed) and empowered by the collective vision of entire school communities.

> Their cultures are rich with indicators of broad and deep renewal with data to support (the efforts) ... Schools of significance are in a constant mode of reflection ... (They) are *data-directed not data-driven* ... (and are becoming) student-centered communities that promote academic achievement for all children (L'Esperance et al., 2003, pp. 3-5).

In addition to the Significant School indicators, the Project Team synthesized several theoretical frameworks to build the foundation for next steps. Fullan (1990) noted that effective school reform consists of four essentials: (1) Shared Purpose; (2) Norms of Collegiality; (3) Norms of Continuous Improvement; and (4) Supportive Organizational Structures (p. 17). This framework called for establishing common purpose that will be the driving force for school improvement in the district. This is a moral underpinning that supports every initiative, plan, program, and funding request. It is clearly the focus of the district and transcends all personal and political agendas. In Greene County, this focus is on educating *every* child for the 21st century. After agreeing on purpose, the remaining three norms were defined as:

1. *Collegiality:* Processes for interacting with one another. This included sharing information and expertise to accomplish a goal.
2. *Continuous Improvement:* This included the establishment of both general and specific goals. It also included the establishment of informal, ongoing assessments.
3. *Supportive Structures:* These include providing the necessary resources such as time for collaboration, money, space, materials, and administrative support to foster the district/school goals.

With a baseline established for terminology, the team began by checking the "data pulse" of Greene County Schools.

Data That Define the Core Principles and Ideals of the School Community

In the spring of 2002, the Project Genesis Project Team conducted a system wide analysis of the Greene County School district. The project team consisted of fifteen individuals who had expertise in several areas related to content, leadership and school renewal. The needs assessment was based on the nine goals adopted by the Green County Board of Education in December of 2001. The team collected data in all program areas utilizing the "5 P's" (program, people, policies, processes, and places) framework developed by Purkey and Strahan (1995). A focus was given to district-wide programs and initiatives along with school-based school improvement plans and program areas. Data included surveys, state documents, district documents, school documents, individual interviews, observations, focus groups, and a comparative analysis of school districts across North Carolina that had similar demographics to Greene County.

The initial findings of the needs assessment revealed that the Greene County Public School district had a clear district vision that is committed to every child being given the knowledge and skills to reach individual potential. Furthermore, the initial findings indicated that there was a strong core of dedicated professional educators in each of the four schools and district office. Each school had a number of successful programs that appeared to be on the verge of significance as defined in the significance framework.

More important, the needs assessment revealed three major areas of growth. First, the project team found, "pockets of survival," teachers or programs that had little or no direction and were constantly reacting to situations. The teachers in these programs complained of the lack of resources and the cognitive levels of students in their classrooms. A major finding was that these program areas lacked a clear communication process to solicit and disseminate information. The second major finding was that the district lacked consistency and continuity in several content areas and programs across and within each school. Over the course of the last four years the district office had begun to experience initial success in this area. It was clear from the data collected by the project team that communication remained the number one concern. The third critical finding of the assessment was that each school had difficulty in developing a framework to monitor and evaluate individual school improvement plan strategies. The findings of the need assessment were presented to the Superintendent, school administrative teams, faculty members at each school and a public Greene County Board of Education meeting. Additionally, Superintendent Steve Mazingo shared the findings with groups of parents.

Promoting Dialogue Related to the Change Process: Combining Theory and Practice

Based on the need to reach each classroom and every stakeholder with the renewal initiative, the team established *dialogue* as the energizing catalyst for change. With the reality that teachers spend the majority of their time in teaching and paperwork, they can find their job to be quite isolated from their colleagues. As a result, dialogue can be powerful from the perspective of improving instruction. According to McGreal (1998), "the more teachers talk about teaching, the better they get at it" (p. 4).

In addition to the discussion of practice, dialogue enhances a school culture by nurturing the creation of new ideas and strategies for raising achievement. Dialogue can create an atmosphere of openness that is essential for school improvement efforts. Burbules (1993) stated, "A successful dialogue involves a willing partnership and cooperation in the face of likely disagreements, confusions, failures, and misunderstandings" (p. 19). Burbules also suggested that a true dialogical relationship over time produces the mutual characteristics of concern, trust, respect/appreciation, affection, and hope within the participants. These relationships build communication avenues that are essential for understanding meaningful and sustainable change.

To better understand these considerations, there was a need to build a *"dialogical infrastructure"* within the district which enhanced both personal and networking relationships. L'Esperance et al. (2003) point out the role of dialogue in the school improvement process. After some beginning discussions that set the stage, "The next step in the process is to immerse the setting in the dialogue" (p. 15). They go on to explain the difference in discussion and dialogue, pointing out that dialogue occurs in a forum where people consider each other's ideas.

> As stakeholders engage in dialogue, relationships are formed and strengthened. Trust is created as people seek to understand and be understood. Emerging from the dialogue is an energy that will fuel ongoing renewal in the School of Significance. The dialogue will refine the process and generate new ideas to redirect and improve renewal efforts. From this point, dialogue becomes critical in all efforts that follow. It is essential to have appropriate settings and conduits to foster and encourage ongoing dialogue. (p. 16)

The team's next step was to create and foster *conduits of communication* throughout the district. Without the capacity to include the stakeholders in this broad and deep initiative, the likelihood of success was diminished. According to Van Tassel-Baska, Hall, and Bailey (1996):

> One lesson ... is that changing a school's philosophy and/or mission is only one step toward systemic change. Having a coherent mission, even under the guidance of a visionary leader, does not complete the school reform process. The level of change necessary needs to trickle into each classroom. This will not happen until curriculum and instruction are reformed in the same manner that structural organization has been reformed. (p. 111)

Fullan and Stiegelbauer (2001) noted the need to deal with understanding both the objective and subjective meaning of change for individuals within the organization. With an emphasis that relied heavily on feedback and input, the next steps involved hearing about the stakeholders' vision for the district. "What should happen in Greene County Schools?" was the question asked to the various leadership teams. This was the next step in the formation of a theoretical framework that combined best practices in the literature regarding dialogical relationships, moral leadership, and the change process. Utilizing the "Hedgehog Concept" outlined by Collins as a focal point for dialogue, the stakeholders created their own "Hedgehog Concept" and determined that all work in the district would relate to the following:

A. *Being best in the world in consistency and continuity of programs*: Because of their small size, the Greene County Schools will excel in creating organizational structures and institutional practices that foster ongoing collaborative development. These will be driven by the values of excellence, fairness, inclusion, and harmony.
B. *Passionate about creating a positive learning environment*: The school district will create teaching and learning environments characterized by dialogical relationships that promote social, emotional, and cognitive health among all stakeholders.
C. *Economic engine as the quality of teaching balanced with standards:* The school district will provide the resources and processes for teachers and students to engage in collaborative activity and dialogue that develop intellect, literacy, and complex thinking across a culturally relevant curriculum (Collins, 2001).

Building Dialogical Networks Through Working Committees: Linking the Vision and Needs of the School Community

When Mazingo entered into the five-year project with the Genesis Network, one of the priorities addressed was the creation of organizational structures that would facilitate district-wide school renewal. The "guiding principles" included:

A. Establishing structures to promote shared decision-making and collaborative leadership.
B. Establishing a process for collaborative development of school improvement plans.
C. Establishing ongoing processes for monitoring, evaluation and revision of the school plans.

D. Promotion of effective, two-way communication between students, parents, community and school.
E. Development of an effective staff development plan that aligns with the goals outlined in the school improvement plan.

The working committees formed as part of the dialogical network are a synthesis of nation wide reform efforts and adaptations from the Bloomington, Indiana Harmony Education Center's reform movement (Comer, Haynes, Joyner, & Ben-Avie, 1996; McQuillan & Muncey, 1994). The committee structure is composed of a school leadership team and five additional school renewal committees. The leadership team is responsible for the oversight of the larger school vision, and it functions as both a steering and finance committee. It is primarily responsible for laying the groundwork for the school renewal plan and it consists of teachers from each grade level and academic area. In addition, administration, non-certified staff, and parents are represented on the team. If possible, university representation may also be helpful for planning and consultative assistance.

The five working renewal committees are:

Staff Development and Curriculum Committee
This committee is responsible for developing a schedule for staff development that focuses on the curricular, instructional, and assessment components of education. In addition, the committee arranges workshops for the school community that relate to the other areas of the school culture.

Public Relations Committee
This committee is responsible for working with the surrounding community to evoke a positive image of the middle school. This may involve the media, businesses, and community organizations.

Family/Student Support Committee
This committee is responsible for creating ways to increase parental involvement at the middle School. In addition, this committee will develop strategies that will assist parents of at-risk and special needs students.

Student Empowerment Committee
This committee is responsible for developing and implementing strategies that incorporate the developmental and social concerns of the students into the school community. Students serve on this committee.

Social Climate Committee
This may be the most important committee. This committee is responsible for developing activities that celebrate the accomplishments of

the school community. Examples include: staff picnics, school and community functions, "relaxation days," etc.

The five renewal committees are made up of various combinations of teachers, staff, parents and students. The facilitator of each committee is also a member of the Leadership Team. Teachers are given a list of the committees to choose from and are asked to rank their top three choices. The principal assigns parents and other staff to their committee of choice based on numbers.

Develop a Strategic Plan Based on a 3-5 Year Implementation Period

With the formal dialogical network established, the district began to develop a strategic plan for the next 3-5 school years. In December 2002, the Greene County Schools had already adopted a list of goals for the ensuing five years. According to Superintendent Steve Mazingo, his reading of Jim Collins' book, *Good to Great,* caused him to consider how his school needed to move ahead:

> According to Collins, we must "confront the brutal facts" before we can plan to improve ... (this) had major implications and applications for me as a leader. The reading of *Good to Great* came at a time when our school system had set nine long-range goals. We did this without having a clue how we would reach those goals.... Shortly after adopting the goals we entered into an agreement with Dr. Mark L'Esperance, Director of the Rural Education Center at East Carolina University, and a team of experts he assembled to help us achieve our goals. His first suggestion was ... to do a thorough assessment (confront the brutal facts). I was more than a little apprehensive about this process ... I now understand that Collins is absolutely correct. You must have a culture in your organization where confronting the brutal facts is a natural and normal part of what you do. (Field Notes, 2003; Collins, 2001).

The early goals established by Greene County prior to their reform initiative included the following:

1. Ninety percent of students will be at grade level in reading and math by the end of second grade.
2. Ninety percent of students will be at or above grade level in reading and math as determined by state mandated tests in grades 3-8.
3. Sixty percent or more of high school seniors will take the SAT and the school average will be at or above the state average.
4. Eighty-five percent of seniors will graduate from high school having completed the appropriate course of study required for college

entrance. At least 80% will enter either a 2 or 4-year institution of higher learning or enter the military.

5. There will be less than 2% difference in the average scores in the number of students that score above all grade level in all grades and all subjects tested when (assessed) by gender and/or ethnic origin.
6. Ninety percent of the students that enter ninth grade will meet the requirements of their course of study in at least 5 years.
7. Seventy-five percent of newly-hired teachers who remain in education will work in Greene County Schools for at least five years.
8. All students will (attend school) in permanent, well-maintained classrooms that are configured for optimal learning.
9. All graduating seniors will possess the necessary social and emotional tools needed to secure a job and become a productive citizen. These tools include but are not limited to the ability to work in groups, possession of character traits necessary for success in our American culture, and the knowledge and skills needed to participate in our democratic form of government.[1]

KEY PROJECTS: COLLABORATION IN ACTION

As the initiative evolved, it became more action-oriented as each school began to focus on small steps toward the district goals. Kouzes and Posner (1987) addressed action planning by stating:

> Problems that are conceived of too broadly overwhelm people, because they defeat our capacity to even think about what might be done, let alone begin doing something about them.... The most effective change processes are incremental—they break down big problems into small, doable steps and get a person to say *yes* numerous times, not just once.... The scientific community has always understood that major advances in medicine ... are likely to be the results of hundreds of researchers conducting studies all over the world, involving experiments generally focused on pieces of the problem. Major breakthroughs are the results of countless contributions that begin to add up to a solution. (p. 218)

Each step began by dealing with a small "piece" of the reform jigsaw.

Develop School Improvement Plans related to district goals. Each school developed strategic School Improvement plans based on the findings of the needs assessment and additional related data for each committee. The plans provided an accountability process for each committee that was focused on the monitoring and evaluation of each strategy. Additionally the project team developed a matrix of more than fifty indicators and two hundred sub indicators related to the district's achievement goals. The district office reviewed each strategy and allocated the necessary resources for implementation.

Reorganization of Administrative Teams. Each of the four schools analyzed and developed a plan that most effectively utilized the principal and assistant principals. The specific roles and responsibilities of each administrator were clarified to ensure that program development became consistent within and between schools. One key change to the administrative teams was the addition of a Guidance Coordinator, a Literacy Facilitator, a Technologist, and a Special Educator. This ensured that all projects were being discussed, monitored, and integrated into each school.

Leadership Team/Communication Web staff development. Each leadership team had specific staff development on creating the process of maximizing communication. Additionally, each leadership team has been provided ongoing training in leadership skills.

Implement individual or district wide projects. Throughout the course of the spring and summer, Genesis project team members collaboratively planned with Greene County personnel to implement several district wide and site-based projects.

Implement School Improvement Plan strategies. The team worked with faculty to ensure that a plan of action that considers timelines, persons responsible, resources needed and evaluation measures were in place at the beginning of the 2002-2003 school year.

Reorganization of the middle school. The needs assessment revealed that Greene County Middle School has stopped using the basic organizational structures of the middle school concept. A complete "overhaul" of the middle school will take place. Interdisciplinary teams, Academic Advisory, scheduling, clubs, intramurals etc. will be added.

The development and implementation of at risk programs at key transitional periods. (pre-k, 3rd, 6th and 9th grades).

The implementation of a school wide discipline and classroom management plan. Reduce and lower the number of discipline referrals by creating a dialogical learning environment (L'Esperance et al., 2003).

Develop /Implement literacy project (Pre-K-12): Network expansion and support.

With the development of a comprehensive literacy project, the reform efforts again sought the resources of an expanding educational network. When appropriate, both external and internal networks were utilized to integrate both human and material resources to accomplish the district goals. This resulted in an introduction of a Literature Circle Framework as an impetus for moving toward more participatory teaching and learning with a focus upon critical analysis of text. The plan shifts the philosophy from an extrinsic reward system (Accelerated Reader) to a more diagnostic and intrinsic form of reading that includes literature circles, independent reading and portfolio assessment. The plan also includes expanding the network to include:

- Dollywood Foundation—GCPS partners with the Dollywood Foundation to provide every child in Greene County ages 0-5 a free hardcover book once a month. Additionally, the district is working with the local Literacy Council to teach skills to parents to read with young children.
- Los Puentes—A Dual Language Immersion Program that addresses the growing Hispanic population needs by teaching subjects in Spanish and English for ESL and traditional English learners.

Comprehensive Counseling Plan. The district developed and implemented a preK-12 plan that incorporates three major strands that include crisis intervention, proactive psychological wellness, and a major emphasis on career planning that includes a federal grant call GEAR UP (Gaining Early Awareness and Readiness for College). As a result of Greene County's efforts in this area, the North Carolina Department of Public Instruction adopted this initiative as a state model.

Develop and Implement pre-K -12 comprehensive Special Education Plan. This plan included developing a clear vision for inclusion of *all* students in the county's mission and goals. This vision needed to be developed and accepted by the Board of Education, county and school administrators, school faculty and staff, families and students, and the public. This was a critical, immediate activity of the district's Project Significance efforts. It also included revising the district's plans to specifically include *all* EC programs as integral, embedded components rather than categorical components. The ultimate goal is to forge a stronger formal and informal link between EC and Curriculum and Instruction. This linkage is critical if all faculty are to be more comfortable supporting students with diverse learning styles and skills *within* the North Carolina Standard Course of Study (the state's mandated curriculum).

Developing a Communication Web to Strengthen the Renewal Process: A Strong Internal Network

As we have worked in many schools, we have discovered one of the ironies of our profession that we believe is the basic reason for the lack of community. Communicators don't communicate. Though schools are staffed by professionals who are hired to be effective communicators, effective communication between staff members is rare. When we survey faculty in a school regarding their awareness of mandates, decisions, innovations, or guidelines, or effective practices employed by others in their own work setting, few seem to be aware of what is happening. Very little interaction seems to take place that is intended to capitalize on the tremendous effort and skills across a school staff. It seems to be assumed that everyone knows what should be done or what could be done. Faculty and administrators are "left out of the loop" because no information loop seems to exist. The assumption that everyone knows what to do or what could be done is reflected in the lack of a structure to ensure the flow of information to all staff members and critical players in a school. We concluded that this had to be addressed.

We proposed the development of a "communication web" in each school and throughout the district to create a true sense of community. Our contention was that an information network that was deliberately designed and implemented to ensure that all teachers and support staff members were fully involved in the school decision-making process would benefit everyone. The intent of a communication web is to enhance the flow of ideas and recommendations from the school leadership to the teachers and from the teachers to the school leaders. This type of system would benefit everyone. It would enhance the relevance of staff development through teacher input into decisions and improve the effectiveness of leaders because school decisions would be much more enlightened.

A priority to assure that dialogue guides every aspect of the school renewal process begins by the leadership team creating a "communication web." Communication webs have two purposes:

- Establish ongoing two-way communication involving all faculty to keep the entire staff informed and to solicit input on all matters related to the middle school renewal process.
- Establish ongoing two-way communication to provide information and solicit input from the school community (parents, students, and community) on various school renewal and related activities.

Initial Indicators of Significance

After the first year of implementation (2002-03), the initial indicators were suggesting very significant trending toward school goals. For example:

- Proficiency levels increased significantly at the elementary, middle and high school levels. (Elementary 75% to 83.2%; Middle 72.4% to 78.7%; High 62% to 67%)
- Average SAT scores increased by 31 points.
- Discipline referrals decreased at the elementary, middle and high school levels with the middle school decreasing more than 60%.

In addition to the above data, the district has noted an increase in SAT scores among minority students combined with a decrease in the dropout rate among all students at the high school level. In addition, early data suggested that the new implementation of technology into the daily instructional process for the first semester had not caused an immediate "implementation dip" often experienced in the initial stages of such programs.

While these trends were positive, the team realized that much work remained to be done. The accountability structure put into place by NCLB for Annual Yearly Progress (AYP) is causing every school district to search for new and effective methods for reaching *every* child. In 2002-03, Greene County met 76.5% of AYP goals for high school; 89.7% for middle school; and 93.1% for elementary school. With this challenge in place, the district moved into the future with plans to embed additional support for teachers and leaders within each school.

YEAR TWO: NEW PROJECTS ... NEXT STEPS

With the completion of a very busy year of significant progress, the district continued to move forward in the second year with bold steps. According to Collins (2001):

> There is nothing wrong with pursuing a vision for greatness. After all, good-to-great companies also set out to create greatness. But, unlike the comparison companies, the good-to-great companies continually refined the *path* to greatness with the brutal facts of reality. (p. 71)

Having internalized Collins' assertions regarding his own personal responsibility to lead his school district, Superintendent Mazingo refined his organization's path with brutal facts pertaining to leadership and technology. According to Mazingo:

> I have not been very aggressive in developing leaders inside the organization. One of the problems in Greene County Schools is that most of the senior leadership will soon retire. We have not adequately prepared for an inevitable transition in leadership including the transition in the superintendency. As a result of ... (my reading about Collins' Level 5 leadership) ... I am spending more time and effort developing leadership inside the organization. (Field Notes)

As a result of this need, the Genesis team met with Mazingo to develop and implement a component that was designed to build leadership capacity at various levels within the school district.

Building Leadership Capacity Through a Customized Coaching Model

The team quickly realized the need to build and develop leadership at every level of the organization. The team sought effective ways to combine traditional instructional leadership theory with a more global approach. The district selected one book to utilize as a primary source of moving an organization to the next level. *Good to Great*, the national best-seller by Jim Collins (2001), researched corporate success over an extended period of time to determine the attributes held by companies that break through to a level of greatness.

The book was ordered for a variety of stakeholders to begin understanding basic concepts of greatness such as:

> **Leadership:** Compared to high-profile leaders with personalities who make big headlines and become celebrities, the good-to-great leaders seem to have come from Mars. Self-effacing, quiet, reserved, even shy—these leaders are a paradoxical blend of personal humility and professional will. They are more like Lincoln and Socrates than Patton or Caesar.
>
> **First Who ... Then What:** We expected that good-to-great leaders would begin by setting a new vision and strategy. We found instead that they *first* got the right people on the bus, the wrong people off the bus, and the right people in the right seat—and *then* they figured out where to drive it.
>
> **The Culture of Discipline:** All companies have a culture, some companies have discipline, but few companies have a *culture of discipline*.

> Great leaders know that when they have disciplined people, they do not need hierarchy; when you have disciplined action, you do not need excessive controls.
>
> **The Fly Wheel and the Doom Loop ...** no matter how dramatic the end result of good-to-great transformations never happen in one fell swoop. There was no single defining action, no grand program, no one killer innovation, no solitary lucky break, and no miracle moment. Rather, the process resembled relentlessly pushing a giant heavy fly-wheel in one direction, turn upon turn, building momentum until a point of breakthrough, and beyond (Collins, 2001, pp. 12-14).

With a common language developed between the team and a cross-section of school leaders, the process began with dialogue and vision casting. Understanding the need to build leadership capacity at every level, the district made a commitment to leadership development for teachers, school-based principals and assistant principals, and district office supervisors. With an underpinning of school renewal theory, the quest for greatness began as the team sought the input and direction of stakeholders.

One phenomenon of the Information Age is rediscovering the value of human potential in moving an organization to "the next level." According to Hughes, Ginnett, and Curphy:

> Most people are familiar with the idea of a personal fitness trainer, a person who helps design a fitness program tailored to a specific individual's needs and goals. Coaching programs provide a similar kind of service for executives in leadership positions. Coaching programs are quite individualized by their very nature (and include) ... a one-on-one relationship between the manager and the coach ... which lasts from six months to more than a year. The process usually begins with (extensive feedback sessions) ... The coach and manager meet regularly (roughly monthly) to debrief the results of the feedback instruments and work on building skills and practicing target behaviors ... Other valuable outcomes of coaching programs include clarification of manager's values, identification of discrepancies between their espoused values and their actual behaviors, and strategies to better align their behaviors with their values.... A coaching program can be quite expensive, and it is reasonable to ask, are they worth it? (Smith, 1993). The answer seems to be yes, at least sometimes (Hughes, Ginnett, & Curphey, 1996, p. 236).

The Genesis Team developed a multi-year plan to build leadership capacity at four basic levels of school leadership. These areas included: superintendent, principal, assistant principal and teacher leadership. The model would include a variety of group and individual sessions which provided learning opportunities with ongoing personal and professional feedback. The "coaching staff" comprises experts that thoroughly understand leadership at various levels of public schooling. The sessions were developed within the budget parameters of the initiative and are designed to be ongoing throughout the initiative.

ITECH: THE FUTURE IS NOW IN GREENE COUNTY

The second project in year two was also the result of the Superintendent's vision for moving his small, rural district boldly into the 21st century. According to Mazingo:

> I knew that computers and the Internet had tremendous potential to aide our ... vision of being the model district for rural education.... We already had a lot of technology in place but I knew it had little impact on our students' success. We had a state-of-the-art wide area network and high speed Internet in every classroom but little had changed about the way teachers taught and little had changed about the way students learned. So far our investment was yielding zero results. (Field Notes)

According to Collins, technology was not a panacea that solved all problems but was a valuable tool for accelerating change (Collins, 2001). Expanding their networks to include Apple Computers, the iTech project (Information Age technology-enhanced learning for every child) was born. Greene County has partnered with Apple Computer to provide the resources to meet the needs of the technology age. Specifically, the objectives for this project are that the district will:

1. provide a lap top computer for every middle grades and high school student;
2. develop a framework that effectively integrates technology with the No Child Left Behind legislation;
3. create a model to recruit and retain teachers in rural settings;
4. raise student achievement in all academic areas;
5. close the black/white achievement gap;
6. develop a framework to integrate community and school economic resources.

REFLECTIONS ON THE DISTRICT RENEWAL PROCESS: THE MORAL LEADERSHIP OF THE SUPERINTENDENT

Seen through the perspective of moral leadership, the superintendent of Greene County Schools moved away from the traditional style of centralized leadership. Mazingo created a site-based decision model founded upon moral leadership. Mazingo clearly communicated his value system to the other stake holders involved in the renewal process. He set aside his own self interests to attend to the intrinsic and extrinsic motivators of others to carry out his vision. By allowing decentralization to occur, Mazingo placed his value system in the open for all to see, thus becoming a moral leader. He displayed courage by turning over the responsibility of decision making to the school community even though he would still be held solely accountable if the renewal process failed (Bundy, 1995; Evans, 1995; Sergiovanni, 1992).

Mazingo exhibited Sergiovanni's (1992) three sources of authority for leadership. In relation to psychological authority, Mazingo utilized his motivational and human relation skills in a number of different ways. He had several small "town hall" meetings with various constituents. He spent a considerable amount of time with individual members of the Board of Education in order that they would understand precisely how change would occur in the district. These meetings included individual and group updates conducted by the superintendent, members of his staff or project team members. By implementing the Genesis committee structure at every school, the superintendent created an environment in which staff members have an outlet to voice their concerns and be part of the decision making process. In turn, the teachers responded by accepting this responsibility in an appropriate fashion and committing themselves to the process. Secondly, Mazingo gained the professional authority from his staff because his teachers came to view him as a person who has a great deal of professional knowledge and personal experience in education. Finally, Mazingo has been able to articulate his vision, values, ideas, and ideals to his staff.

The decentralization process at Greene county Schools created what Sergiovanni (1992) calls "substitutes" for leadership. The renewal process has produced in the minds of the staff and other stake holders a vision of Greene county Schools as the model rural school district in the nation. The majority of individuals involved in the renewal process believe that they share a common vision for educating the children and are committed to work together to embody these values. The small number of individuals who initially avoided participating in this process were given the opportunity and venue to discuss their concerns if they so chose. At the same time, the majority of administrators, teachers and staff committed themselves to the professional ideal of working toward this vision. This is evident in the development and implementation of the detailed School Improvement Plan at each of the four schools. In addition, there is a growing sense among the staff that the renewal process has allowed teachers to gain new meaning and intrinsic rewards for their actions at both the organizational and embedded levels. Staff members are still concerned that the relentless onslaught of mandates is an impediment to full commitment. However, staff members feel connected to one another to a greater degree than in the past and this sense of collegiality is perceived as a professional virtue.

REFLECTIONS ON THE DISTRICT RENEWAL PROCESS: THE MEANING AND IMPLICATIONS OF CHANGE

When reflecting on the change process in Greene County, the catalyst has been the combination of networks that have coalesced around strong and visionary leadership. According to Fullan (2002), "Effective school leaders are key to large-scale, sustainable education reform" (p. 16). He also noted:

> Moral purpose is social responsibility to others and to the environment. School leaders with moral purpose seek to make a difference in the lives of students. They are concerned about closing the gap between high-performing and lower-performing schools and raising the achievement of—and closing the gap between—high-performing and lower-performing students ... (the leader) works to develop other advance reform after he or she departs. In short, (the leader) displays explicit, deep, comprehensive moral purpose. (p. 17)

Superintendent Mazingo displayed such moral purpose in his leadership role as superintendent in Greene County.

Serving such a small district allows more direct involvement in the change process at each school than in larger, metropolitan areas. In his reflections on the process, Mazingo noted:

> Our best-in-the-world Circle consists of consistency and continuity of programs.... With one school at each level and the physical proximity of the schools, we can create a seamless environment for students that cannot be found anywhere else. Our economic engine is driven by quality of teaching balanced with standards. We must constantly talk about the quality of what happens in a classroom and focus on a quality experience for all children.... We know we could not serve as a model for a large, urban district. We may not be able to share much of what we accomplish with wealthy suburban districts. What we can do is to be the best at providing children in a rural district with a quality, relevant education ... our vision is to simply be the best rural school district in the nation. (Field Notes)

With Mazingo's compelling vision and the Genesis initiative embedding in the culture of the district, the next steps deal with reaching an invisible wall that is often found in reform efforts. This marks the boundaries of the initial efforts and can be called the "end of the beginning." Many districts reach this after some time of working harder and longer. With some initial gains due to "sweat equity," the district wonders how it can experience a "breakthrough" into a higher level of proficiency on the road called "Annual Yearly Progress."

In Spring 2004, Mazingo and the Genesis team have begun exploring "portals" through this boundary (L'Esperance, 2004). These portals are created by identification of barriers and tension points within the organization. These can be programmatic, procedural, or relational. A portal is created when the barrier or tension point is identified, an action plan developed and the barrier removed or redefined. A series of these small breakthroughs will provide momentum that takes the organization through additional change and reform.

In many respects, Greene County has much in common with many schools in rural America today. It is small, isolated, and lacking an abundance of state and local school funding. Instead of focusing on what it lacks, Greene County Schools have chosen to focus on its most abundant resource, the ability to change.

As Greene County quietly goes about its business of educating its children for the 21st century, the network continues to expand. A reporter from the state capital recently visited the district to hear more about this small, rural district's efforts. He began his article:

> Greene County is an unlikely setting for the cutting edge, unless it's attached to a tractor. Hogs far outnumber computers in the Eastern North Carolina county of farm fields and livestock barns. Fewer than half the families own a computer; fewer still are connected to the Internet. But inside the county's only middle and sole high school, the technology revolution is in full swing like no other district in the state. (Silberman, 2004)

Several days after the article, the newspaper's editorial page noted that "students are receiving practical experience with the most important tool of the modem workplace. That's power all Tar Heel youngsters must have."[2]

While rural isolation may have hampered some school districts in the past, the new potential of rural schools to network may provide some needed answers in an age of many questions. The stakeholders in Greene County have promised the future to its children. Utilizing the power of both internal and external networking capabilities, Green County becoming a prototype for 21st century rural education.

NOTES

1. Superintendent's Report, Greene County Board of Education, December 2002; Author's note: These goals were established by the Board of Education prior to implementation of the Genesis initiative. As a result of the renewal efforts and the accountability standards from both the federal and state levels, some of these goals appeared to be quickly outdated. Some related thoughts regarding this issue are addressed later in this chapter.
2. Letter to the Editor. *Raleigh News & Observer*, April 2, 2004.

REFERENCES

Bundy, E. (1995). Fredericks Middle School and the dynamics of school reform. In A. Lieberman (Ed.), *The work of restructuring schools: Building from the ground up*. New York: Teachers College Press.

Burbules, N.C. (1993). *Dialogue in teaching: Theory and practice*. New York: Teachers College Press.

Collins, J. (2001). *Good to great*. New York: Harper Collins Publishers.

Comer, J., Haynes, M., Joyner, E., & Ben-Avie, M. (Eds.). (1996). *Rallying the whole village: The comer process for reforming education*. New York: Teachers College Press.

Darling-Hammond, L. (1997). *The right to learn: A Blueprint for creating schools that work*. San Francisco: Jossey-Bass.

Evans, D.L. (1995, January). Some reflections on doing the principalship. *NASSP Bulletin*, 4-15.

Fullan, M. (2002a). The change leader. *Educational Leadership, 59*(8).

Fullan, M. (2002b). Moral purpose writ large. *The School Administrator, 59*(8).

Fullan, M. (2001). *Leading in a culture of change*. San Francisco: Jossey-Bass.

Fullan, M. (1990). Staff development, innovation, and institutional development. In B. Joyce (Ed.), *Changing school culture through staff development*. Alexandria, VA: ASCD.

Fullan, M., & Steigelbauer, S. (2001). *The new meaning of educational change* (3rd ed.). New York: Teachers College Press.

Goleman, D., Boyatzis, R., & McKee, A. (2002). *Primal leadership: Realizing the power of emotional intelligence*. Boston: Harvard Business School Press.

Hughes, R., Ginnett, R., & Curphey, G. (1996). *Leadership: Enhancing the lessons of experience*. Boston: Irwin McGraw-Hill.

Kouzes, J., & Posner, B. (1987). *The leadership challenge: How to get extraordinary things done in organizations*. San Francisco: Jossey-Bass.

L'Esperance, M., Strahan, D., Farrington, V., & Anderson, P.J. (2003). *Raising achievement: Project Genesis, a significant school model*. Westerville, OH: National Middle School Association.

Lieberman, A., & Grolnick, M. (1999). Networks and reform in American education. In L. Darling-Hammond & G. Sykes (Eds.), *Teaching as the learning profession* (pp. 292-312). San Francisco: Jossey-Bass.

Lieberman, A., & Wood, D.R. (2003). *Inside the national writing project: Connecting network learning and classroom teaching*. New York: Teachers College Press.

McGreal, T. (1998). Evaluation for enhancing instruction: Linking teacher evaluation and staff development. In S.J. Stanley & W.J. Popham (Eds.), *Teacher evaluation: Six prescriptions for success*. Alexandria, VA: ASCD.

McQuillan, P.J., & Muncey, D.E. (1994). Change takes time: A look at the growth and development of the coalition of essential schools. *Journal of Curriculum Studies, 26*(93), 265-279.

Purkey, W., & Strahan, D. (1995). School transformation through invitational education. *Research in Schools, 3*(2), 1-6.

Save the Children. (2002). *America's forgotten children: Child poverty in rural America*. Westport, CT: Author.

Sergiovanni, T. (1990). *Value-added leadership: How to get extraordinary performance in school*. New York: Harcourt Brace Jovanovich.

Sergiovanni, T. (1992). *Moral leadership*. San Francisco: Jossey-Bass.

Sergiovanni, T. (1996). *Leadership in the schoolhouse*. San Francisco: Jossey-Bass.

Silberman, T. (2004, March 29). Classrooms get upgrades. *Raleigh News & Observer.*

Van Tassel-Baska, J., Hall, K., & Bailey, J. (1996). Case studies of promising change in schools. *Research in Middle Level Education Quarterly, 19*(2).

CHAPTER 13

SUCCESSFUL MIGRANT STUDENTS

The Case of Mathematics

Pedro Reyes and Carol Fletcher

ABSTRACT

The purpose of this project was to examine successful migrant mathematics programs and identify specific pedagogical and instructional strategies that could then be implemented in other less successful schools. Our findings suggest that the organizational culture of a school affects overall student achievement and, thus, migrant student achievement as well. Though this was not a theme we expected to encounter, it was prevalent at each school we visited. Consequently, organizational culture, though less tangible than specific instructional techniques, emerged as the most relevant component of the successful migrant education programs investigated.

The findings from teacher interviews suggested that their success with migrant students had less to do with specific programs than with the overall organizational culture of the school. The importance of organizational culture to a school's success is documented in the school effectiveness lit-

Deep Change: Cases and Commentary on Reform in High Stakes States, 255–283

erature. Organizational culture is concerned with the overall attitudes, beliefs, values, and behavioral norms that motivate actions and commitment to the organization's mission. Four common practices and school components emerged throughout the teacher interviews: (1) a workplace culture focused on instructional improvement, (2) a culture of respect for all students, (3) student-centered instruction, and (4) a spiraling curriculum which emphasized constant review. Taken together, these components suggest an encompassing attitude and culture in each of the examined schools that has contributed to their success with all students in general and, thus, with migrant students specifically.

LITERATURE REVIEW

To date, there is no available research specifically concerned with effective methods for teaching mathematics to migrant students. Thus, the literature reviewed for grounding this study came from a variety of related themes such as migrant education, minority education, mathematics education for minorities, effective school literature, and education reform literature. High mobility, low expectations, lack of self-esteem, poverty, limited English proficiency and interrupted school attendance are factors that interfere with migrant students' educational experiences. Hence, teachers and principals must devise ways to maximize learning while migrant students are in the classroom. Migrant and minority education research suggests that there are certain strategies that can lead to success in teaching these particular student populations.

Instructional Practice. The importance of culturally relevant teaching in educating migrant students was a prevalent theme throughout the literature. Culturally relevant (Ladson-Billings, 1995) or culturally congruent (King-Stoops, 1980) instruction is an approach that has been found effective in teaching migrant and non-majority students. This strategy incorporates aspects of the child's culture into the school curriculum by including lessons that relate specifically to the migratory lifestyle. The use of pictures or other cultural referents that the students are familiar with are also appropriate. This type of instruction reinforces and validates identity and culture. As the migrant student realizes that he has significant contributions to make to the class, he is more likely to be drawn into the classroom setting and become a more active participant in the educational process.

Leon (1996) also has discussed the importance of culturally responsive teaching specifically as it applies to language. A natural transition to English is more beneficial to minority students. According to Leon, this transition can be accomplished more effectively by "teaching migrant students to read and write in English while encouraging them to maintain their native tongue." Cummins (1993) has suggested that this form of cultural and linguistic incorporation empowers minority students. This validation of the native language further enhances self-esteem and leads to positive feelings of self-worth. As with other culturally congruent strategies, this method also helps in bridging the gap between the diverse cultures of the migrant students' home life and the classroom environment.

To further enhance self-esteem, Kindler (1995) and Leon (1996) have recommended that teachers incorporate extracurricular activities (such as clubs and athletics) and educational field trips (such as trips to museums, theaters, science fairs, and universities) into the usual curriculum. Extracurricular activities establish closer relationships between students and can help students develop their self-confidence. Field trips allow teachers to combine various different disciplines into an exciting educational experience that can be shared by all students. Teachers can design and incorporate reading and writing lessons to go along with the field trips. Listening and speaking skills are also reinforced. Furthermore, this exposure to different settings and people helps to develop social skills.

According to *The Handbook of Effective Migrant Education Practices* (U.S. Department of Education, 1990), providing extra instructional time for migrant students is an effective way to maximize learning. Supplemental services should aim to compensate for the loss in school attendance due to migrant mobility. "These services should be designed to strengthen the students' academic skills and to build their self-confidence in an academic setting" (U.S. Department of Education, 1990). Examples of supplemental services are more personalized instruction throughout the class day, specific methods targeted toward the migrant population such as in-class, replacement or pullout models, or extended-day programs such as after-school tutoring, weekend or evening classes, and summer programs. These supplemental activities can increase a student's level of comfort in a school environment.

Cooperative and collaborative learning are effective strategies in teaching minority and migrant students. Cooperative learning is less competitive and less intimidating and more closely resembles the home learning environment of the migrant student. King-Stoops (1980) indicated that teachers should make an effort to encourage migrant students to share their experiences with the class. Migrant students travel throughout the country and have a wealth of knowledge that can be used as an instructional tool and can reinforce or introduce lessons. For example, teachers can develop lessons that allow migrant students to share their knowledge of geography, their travel experiences, and their ability to overcome hardships (Menchaca & Ruiz-Escalante, 1995). This allows migrant students to interact successfully with their classmates and exposes other students to the migratory lifestyle.

Through cooperative learning, migrant students are likely to feel encouraged by the support of their fellow classmates. Migrant students will take an active part in the educational process as they share their own knowledge and learn from their peers. Students become responsible for one another's learning. Furthermore, Garcia (1991) noted that it was "during student-student interactions that most higher-order cognitive and linguistic discourse was observed." "Students asked each other hard questions and challenged each other's answers more readily than they did in interactions with the teacher" (Garcia, 1991).

This cooperative learning and sharing of knowledge are a natural occurrence in the home environment of Mexican American children. Mexican American households draw upon "funds of knowledge" to educate their children (Moll, Amanti, Neff, & Gonzalez, (1992). Children learn easily from their relatives whom they trust and who know them as complete individuals, as opposed to the school setting where teachers confine students to learning a prescribed set of data, and the students' previously stored knowledge and skills are kept separate (Reyes, Scribner, & Wagstaff, 1996). Teachers should capitalize on the wealth of knowledge that these students bring to the classroom. This knowledge is broad and diverse and includes information about farming, animal management, construction, business, and finance (Moll et al., 1992).

A component of cooperative and collaborative learning is parental and community involvement in the educational process. Increased parental and community involvement is particularly helpful for minority students who often feel a conflict between their community and their academic obligations. A wealth of information can be brought to the classroom by parents who might be asked to come and speak to the class regarding their job, a hobby, or some other topic with which they are familiar. The minority student begins to see that their own community has a great deal of knowledge to offer, and that it is not necessary to make a complete break with their community in order to succeed (Ladson-Billings, 1995).

Cummins (1993) and Secada (1992) have discussed the role of institutional practices in educating minority students. Because most minority students are often automatically labeled "at risk" they are confined to a curricular track that leads to "learned helplessness." The students are given tasks that are designed to teach only the basics. There is an emphasis on rote memorization, and there is no development of metacognitive learning. The students become passive learners. Hence, lessons should be written to encourage independent learning and higher-order thinking skills. Teachers should "instruct students to employ alternative strategies once they have recognized and determined a breakdown in comprehension" (Menchaca & Ruiz-Escalante, 1995). The focus of instruction should shift from rote memorization and the learning of basic skills to the analysis of purpose and meaning (Moll, 1988).

Highly committed teachers who view themselves as innovators and who have high expectations of their students are also relevant components of effective minority and migrant classrooms (Garcia, 1995). Research has suggested that teachers who feel they have a sense of autonomy over their curriculum have more success in teaching minority students. These teachers are able to incorporate various techniques into their regular classroom practices in order to enhance learning for targeted student populations. These teachers consider themselves artists and feel responsible for providing their students with a challenging level of instruction that can lead to their academic success. They are committed to their students and respond to their needs. Ladson-Billings (1995) noted that successful teachers "demanded, reinforced, and produced academic excellence in their students."

The literature shows that appropriate diversity of instruction is an effective strategy for teaching minority students (Moll, 1988; Morse, 1997; Ladson-Billings, 1990). Thus, teachers must be allowed some degree of autonomy. This is made possible by principals who encourage innovation and allow teachers flexibility in their classroom practices. Though state-mandated guidelines are necessary, supportive principals are also necessary in order to allow teachers enough freedom to respond and adapt to their students' needs. Diverse activities "appeal to all modes of learning (art, music, verbal, logic, physical)" (Morse, 1997). These are "fun" activities that encourage greater student participation and higher-order thinking. Examples of ways to diversify instruction are regular writing in journals, dramatizing books, and incorporating contemporary music into lessons.

One of the difficulties in mathematics education is that students do not see a connection between math and their everyday lives. There is a greater emphasis on drill and practice than on mathematical reasoning. Teachers must make mathematics an engaging subject that holds relevance to their students' lives. Teachers need to begin to allow students the opportunity to question mathematical procedures and thus become more active in the learning process, thereby acquiring problem solving and reasoning skills (Loewenberg-Ball, 1991; Cardelle-Elawar, 1992).

Cardelle-Elawar (1992) discussed the effectiveness of metacognitive learning and individualized feedback in teaching mathematics to bilingual students. Using metacognitive approaches, the standard classroom is transformed into an arena where discussion and inquisitiveness is encouraged. There is open communication between the students and the teachers regarding what they are learning and why and how they are learning.

The teacher provides individualized feedback via written comments or oral communication. Thus, through the students' discussion and personal communication, the teacher begins to connect with each student and learns how each student thinks, learns and solves problems. This information is then used to adapt teaching patterns to accommodate students' needs. This method is similar to cognitively guided instruction (CGI), which has been recommended for regular, special education, and bilingual students.

> Teachers select math problems that relate to the everyday life of the student with whom they are familiar. During instruction, teachers listen to and build upon students' responses, prompt students to use or apply their knowledge when solving problems, challenge students to test their conclusions, and encourage students to investigate new concepts and strategies. (Reyes, Scribner, & Wagstaff, 1996)

Ethnomathematics, culturally relevant math, and multicultural math are also suggested as effective methods for teaching minority and migrant students (Reyes, 1998; Martinez & Ortiz de Montellano, 1988; Strutchens, 1995). Culturally relevant approaches allow students to develop a sense of pride in the contributions that their ancestors made to mathematics and provide a familiar cultural base from which to learn. An example of a culturally relevant math lesson for Mexican American students is the study of Mayan mathematics and the Mayan calendar. These methods further reinforce cultural values and self-esteem. Moreover, students will begin to see mathematics as having meaning in their present and future lives. Ethnomathematics also seeks to make a connection between students' lives and mathematics instruction. Teachers can build on the mathematical knowledge that the student brings with them from their home environment. Nunes (1992) suggested that teachers use natural language and familiar cultural contexts to help students begin to view mathematical concepts as problem-solving tools.

Multicultural mathematics incorporates the following five strategies into the mathematics classroom. *Content integration* incorporates different cultural contributions to the field of mathematics into the classroom. *Knowledge construction* is concerned with how different cultural groups view and practice mathematics. *Prejudice reduction* encourages positive attitudes toward different cultural groups through the use of mathematics to study social and cultural issues. A *mutual respect* between teachers and students is a vital component in equitable pedagogy in which teachers help students make connections with their cultural identities. Lastly, an *empowering school culture and social structure* is of vital importance to the success of minority students in mathematics. Components of the school structure that should be examined are "grouping practices, social climate, assessment practices, participation in extracurricular activities and staff expectations and responses to diversity" (Strutchens, 1995).

Secada (1992) found a relationship between bilingualism and mathematics achievement. Limited English proficiency (LEP) students encounter language barriers in learning mathematical concepts. Since numerals are not universal in all languages and cultures, concepts could be misinterpreted. Furthermore, language barriers can lead to difficulty in understanding the particular vocabulary, semantics, and syntax of the mathematics classroom. Thus, to increase the effectiveness of mathematics instruction to LEP students, teachers could incorporate the following into their classroom practices: opportunities for bilingual peer tutoring; close monitoring and individualized feedback; use of limited, simple instruction techniques; use of multicultural referents in the lessons; and exposure to "manipulative, concrete, sensory and hands-on activities" to support discussion (Mather & Chiodo, 1994).

Another effective approach for teaching mathematics to minority students is personalization of instructional context. In a study of 123 seventh-grade Hispanic boys and girls, Lopez and Sullivan (1992) found that personalization of instruction led to higher math scores than for students who received non-personalized treatment. Personalization is effective because it leads to improved memory through increased association. The problem is made more concrete "by placing it in a context that is familiar to the child rather than in the more abstract unfamiliar setting of non-personalized problems" (Lopez & Sullivan, 1992). For example, substituting a particular student's name into a word problem makes math become more concrete, eases cognitive demands, and makes the problem easier to solve.

School Culture. A healthy and successful school culture should be based on bargaining, collaborating, and participatory decision making on a collegial basis. Under such conditions educators feel supported and validated and are more likely to take an active part in ensuring the success of their school. This positive atmosphere is then transferred to the classroom through instructional practices and curricular strategies, and all students are the direct beneficiaries. This, then, affects the overall climate of the school as students begin to feel more confident in the learning process and in themselves.

Changing schools is not solely a matter of inserting ingredients. That is similar to treating the symptoms of a disease. Instead, the problem should be considered on a more holistic level. What is necessary is the modification of school organizational structures and the transformation of peoples' ideas and behaviors. This type of culture modification has been successful in some schools. The common strategies that characterize these successful schools are "the promotion of collaborative planning, a collegial workplace, and a school atmosphere conducive to experimentation and evaluation" (Purkey & Smith, 1983).

Linda Darling-Hammond (1997) discussed the importance of building a professional culture within schools. Citing a report issued by the National Commission on Teaching and America's Future, Darling-Hammond noted that "teacher expertise is the single most important determinant of student achievement." Teachers come to the classroom equipped with various levels of preparation, which accounts for most of the differentials in achievement between White and minority students. Thus, a greater emphasis should be placed on teacher education programs, training, licensing, and recruitment practices. A professional culture between the principal and the teacher is important so that teachers will be provided with opportunities to improve their own strategies and knowledge. For example, teacher training should shift in focus from traditional passive learning methods to modern active learning methods that will become essential for students and educators in the 21st century.

Darling-Hammond also discussed the effectiveness of creating learning organizations within schools. "Learning organizations provide ways for everyone in the school, regardless of role, to form teams of adults who work with and help one another in structures that enable them to share responsibility for student learning " (Darling-Hammond, 1997). Activities such as study groups, peer coaching, and research-into-practice teams should be a regular part of the school climate. Through these activities, "teachers' day to day work becomes a form of high-quality professional development." Thus, teachers maintain a professional atmosphere that fosters continual personal and professional growth and development.

A vital component of these learning organizations is collegiality, the ability to connect on a professional level with other school staff. This allows for the dissemination of knowledge and ideas throughout the school and leads to a momentum of continuous improvement. Teachers feel comfortable sharing their strengths and weaknesses and seeking advice from their administrators and from each other. Teachers are likely to feel empowered by this network of support. Thus, learning organizations support "action orientation" (Mitchell, 1995). That is, due to this network of support, teachers are more likely to take risks in experimenting with different learning strategies that are responsive to their students' needs.

The appropriateness of the school culture concept is rooted in corporate ideas of organizational theory (Purkey & Smith, 1983). The notion of organizational culture is complex and multifaceted. Owens (1991) captured the myriad components that play a part in forming organizational culture with the following definition: the norms that inform people what is acceptable and what is not, the dominant values that the organization cherishes above others, the basic assumptions and beliefs that are shared by members of the organization, the "rules" of the game that must be observed if one is to get along and be accepted as a member, the philosophy that guides the organization in dealing with its employees and clients. Deal and Kennedy (1982) synthesized these factors into layman's terms by focusing on three major components: An organization's culture consists of what its members believe is true, what they value as important, and how they get things done.

Most recent studies related to organizational culture in educational systems found their roots in business management literature. In the 1980s, American businesses began to embrace the notion that economic success was more than just a function of processes and products but was inextricably tied to an effective organizational culture. Peters and Waterman (1982) found in a study of 62 successful businesses that the values and culture of these organizations were more influential than formalized management structures and control systems. The organizational culture and the tacit values, beliefs, and behavioral norms that it embodied motivated and sustained individual employees' commitment to the organization's mission. Kanter's (1983) research comparing highly successful with less successful companies supported this notion and extended it by contrasting particular characteristics of interaction between the two types of organizations. She stated that successful companies were most likely to have integrative organizations that viewed issues and problem-solving holistically. The less successful companies tended to reflect what Kanter called segmented organizations, consisting of employees with little knowledge of the organization's overall structure and how they fit into the big picture. As a result, the employees of these companies felt a commitment only to the small portion of the organization in which they were involved.

METHODS

In determining the four "successful" school districts for selection in this study, we turned to the Migrant Education Office of the Texas Education Agency (TEA), which provided data on school districts praised for doing an exceptional job with migrant students. The Migrant/TEA selection criteria commended migrant-impacted school districts that had attained at least an 80% migrant graduation rate, at least an 80% migrant promotion rate, and at least a 94% migrant school attendance rate. These rates were obtained from the Public Education Information Management System (PEIMS) database.[1]

We were also interested in interviewing key administrators and parental involvement personnel on individual campuses within these school districts. The selection criteria we used to identify these schools also came from the Migrant Office at TEA.

> *Exceptional*: Campuses must have 10 or more migrant students tested in all areas of the TAAS (math, reading, and writing) and have at least 80% of test-taking migrant students passing all areas of said test.
> *Excelling*: Campuses must have 10 or more migrant students tested in all areas of the TAAS and have at least 70% of test-taking migrant students passing all areas of said test.

The data from the Migrant Education Office at TEA identified "exceptional" and "excelling" schools and school districts for this study. Finally, the TEA Migrant Education Office worked closely with the research team to help select schools for the final sample. A total of six highly successful school districts were selected for this study (four school districts in Texas, one in Illinois, and one in Montana). We interviewed key personnel at both the district and building levels. These individuals included district- and building-level administrators, community liaisons, migrant recruiters, program administrators, teachers, and other school paraprofessionals.

We conducted interviews over a 5-month period, relying on a semistructured interview protocol to gather information from informants. This method allowed us to obtain a level of consistency across school districts while exploring new concepts, ideas, or issues raised during interviews. While most interviews were scheduled in advance, at times impromptu "interviews" were conducted. This flexibility in method was particularly useful—especially in moments when formal methods were inappropriate. Most interviews ranged from 60-90 minutes in length. All interviews were audio-recorded and transcribed with the consent of the informants. We also gathered data through field notes and observation, as well as relevant documents given to the study by respective schools and districts. All data were coded individually by respective research teams and analyzed according to themes that emerged across respective interviews. Trustworthiness was obtained through inter-rater reliability and a dialogue process that identified prevalent themes across research cases.

FINDINGS

Though the teachers we spoke with represented almost every grade level and three different school districts in the Rio Grande Valley, the issues they stressed were surprisingly similar. Four major themes emerged in our conversations with teachers asked to describe their math programs and how they worked with migrant students: (1) a workplace culture focused on instructional improvement, (2) respect for all students, (3) student-centered instruction, and (4) a spiraling curriculum that emphasized constant review.

Workplace Culture Focused on Instructional Improvement

A culture in which teachers work together as professionals to articulate, implement, and continuously reflect on the goals they have for student achievement was clearly evident in most of the schools we visited. This workplace culture includes four basic components:

1. *extensive collaboration and communication* among teachers;
2. a pervading sense of *collegiality*;
3. a *shared vision* with a clearly articulated set of objectives, scope and sequence for reaching that vision; and
4. continuous *reflection* regarding specific curriculum and pedagogical techniques appropriate for achieving targeted objectives.

The teachers in this study frequently cited examples of how they communicated and collaborated with their colleagues both formally and informally. This regular communication and collaboration resulted in an atmosphere of collegiality among teachers. Teachers at every school noted that their math departments met regularly to discuss student scores on the state standardized test, the Texas Assessment of Academic Skills (TAAS), and to plan instruction based on areas they identified as needing improvement. Schools could then plan a scope and sequence, or timeline, to insure that all teachers were focusing on these problem areas.

Teacher: What we did was early in the year, the seventh grade teachers, at least, we got together, and we developed our timeline: what we wanted to teach. And we went over some of the past material that we have, and we said, well, this is not something that we should cover. We decided how many days, you know, we set up the timeline. Of course, we took TAAS into consideration, we also took future education, what are they going to need for Algebra, what are they going to need for Geometry, into consideration. And we kind of combined both, the essential elements for each, and said, OK, we've covered all that.

Now, what else do we want to cover? (Edcouch junior high)

In Weslaco ISD they have collaborated on a common scope and sequence for each course, and they administer a district-wide six-weeks exam in both elementary and middle school for each math course. An elementary teacher from Weslaco ISD summed up the entire process succinctly:

Teacher: And so teachers, together with administration and everybody, got together and everybody met at their school, then they met at the district and they said, "How do we want to set this up? How do we want to organize it?" And they've taken their ... TAAS objectives ... and we sequenced them, we put them in order. And some of them we repeat because those that are, that children find difficult to do we've repeated those so there's constant reinforcement. And what we've done is we've set so many objectives up per six weeks. At the end of the six weeks we test those particular objectives to make sure they have mastered them.... The district test is given to every student at the same time on the same day and then those scores are taken to the district and then we get a computer feedback on which objectives were missed, individually and as a class. So we're always able to constantly reinforce what was not mastered or what any individual needs to work on more. Then the second six weeks we are tested, we go through the same thing.... Plus, that test includes the first six weeks. So we're constantly, constantly reassuring that they keep practicing the ones that they've mastered. (Weslaco elementary)

Other formal communication included math meetings that were built into the workday. At these meetings, teachers reflected on their instructional objectives and shared ideas regarding successful or unsuccessful instructional techniques.

Teacher: We meet more than once a week. We have what we call cluster. The fourth grade is divided into clusters also. And then we have grade-level meetings also, and we have TAAS level meetings. Throughout the week, one time during our conference period we meet as a cluster. (Edcouch Elementary)

At the high-school level in Edcouch school district, the last period of the day Monday through Wednesday is the tutorial program, called PASS. On Thursdays there is no PASS and the teachers have department meetings where they talk about "what's working and what's not—what ideas do you have?"

The collegial atmosphere was truly reflected in teachers' willingness to present their ideas and successes in front of their peers.

> **Teacher:** What we are doing now is we are training ourselves. Teachers are training teachers. And so when we meet, we discuss, you know, well, we had to cover this concept today. This week in math I experienced some difficulty in teaching, let's say, rounding. How is it that you're doing it? And did your students accept it? Did they respond to it in a positive way? ... So what we do is we develop in-services based on that. And we try to be very open-minded, friendly. And if you're going to go in there and present, nobody's going to attack you. You're going to be helping us out.... But I guess we started out by saying, "Hey, let's see, you're doing such a good job, and look at your kids, how well they're succeeding. Can you help me out?' and "Sure!" This is the kind of atmosphere that we now have. Everybody supports each other, and they share with each other. We look forward to meetings. (Edcouch Elementary)

Some teachers reported discussing instructional techniques with their colleagues on a daily basis before school. Others observed their peers in the classroom if they were struggling with teaching a certain concept in order to get new ideas on how to present that concept to their own students.

> **Teacher:** I think we have kind of like an open door policy here. There may be, if it's at that moment, I'll ask, I'll say to someone else, "Can you step into my room for just a minute," you know, someone right next to me, "I'm not sure how to explain this." And they'll come in and do that with me. I know I have two teachers that are more into the math area than I am, and I will double check. And I like for my children to see that because I believe in peer teaching and collaborating, and I expect for them to do the same thing in class. (Edcouch elementary)

All of these forms of communication and collaboration resulted in a shared vision across most of these schools regarding the goals and specific instructional objectives of their mathematics programs. That is not to say that teachers taught a uniform curriculum. None of the teachers we spoke with discussed using anyone particular textbook or curriculum. Each teacher indicated that instruction was based on an eclectic mix of resources, often including textbooks, district curriculum guides, things the teacher learned in professional development workshops, and self-generated materials. While consistent instructional objectives helped to provide focus to a school's mathematics instruction, it did not appear to limit a teacher's own sense of professional autonomy. This shared vision allowed teachers to concentrate their energies more on *how* they were teaching rather than on choosing *what* they were teaching.

Teacher: Our curriculum is pretty well defined in what we're going to teach but how we go about teaching it, that's very much a personal thing. We get very little direction on that. But as far as *what* we're going to teach, we do have a set curriculum for that. We have a lot of freedom in how we go about teaching. (Weslaco middle school)

Teacher: We try to get together as a department so we can have our curriculum such that the teachers can pretty much stay together. If they are teaching Geometry, for example, that they are like, in the same section, pretty much the same materials. They don't necessarily have to stick with exactly the same handouts or same pages or whatever, but as long as they are within range. (Edcouch high school)

Continuous reflection was the necessary ingredient that made this dynamic process involving communication, collegiality, and shared vision function effectively. Teachers often cited how they evaluated themselves in a number of ways.

Teacher: And if I taught something, and I had a big portion of the class not pick it up, then I know I need to go back and totally use a different modality, or it could have just been the way I explained it. I would say when that happens then I did something wrong. Right away, I reflect, I did something wrong here, it's not the kid, it's me. (Edcouch elementary)

In addition to their daily, personal reflections after a lesson, these teachers consistently spoke of reflecting on their practices in terms of the school or district's instructional objectives.

Teacher: We have our conference period and then our Staff Development. And that's exactly what we do, we share Reading, Math, whatever it is that we're lacking, and we do discuss what our weak areas are, and then we research material that we get, and then we share it. That way we try to cover every gap. (Weslaco elementary)

Respect for All Students

A second theme that emerged from this study was that each of the schools we visited had a school culture that reflected a great deal of respect for the students who attended it. This pervasive culture of respect for students, both migrant and non-migrant alike, is composed of five basic components:

1. the belief that *all students can learn*,
2. the belief in the students' ability to perform which results in *high expectations*,
3. a *respect for the culture of migrancy*,
4. the *use of the culture of migrancy to teach*, and
5. *teachers that really care*.

Time after time teachers expressed the opinion that their migrant students were just as capable as their non-migrant students of achieving academic success.

Teacher: I have my kids there and I don't think of them, "O.K., you're migrant, you're this, you're bilingual." I don't. To me, it's just my classroom. I teach them, I do whatever I can for them. If they need one to one, I give it to them. If they have to stay after school, we'll keep them after school and in our PASS program. I would be lying if I told you anything else. They're just like a regular student in my classroom. (Edcouch elementary)

The fact that they often enrolled late or had to leave early was merely a logistical roadblock to be overcome by both teacher and student when the time came. Other than that, no special pedagogical techniques or curricula were deemed necessary for migrant students in particular.

Teacher: They pretty much follow the same curriculum, and I think that's important because the curriculum we have set up at this school, it really targets a lot of the objectives that are for the TAAS, and even the PSAT. And I don't know that we would even want to consider, this is my opinion, consider giving them a separate curriculum. We know what we have in place is working, and we can only build from that. (Mission high school)

Often this sense of respect for migrant students appeared to stem from the fact that many of the teachers we spoke with were themselves migrants or grew up in this area struggling with the same types of issues these students face today. Thus, the teachers were familiar with and had a respect for the culture of migrancy.

Interviewer: If you had to give me your insight into why you think this district seems to be very successful with migrant students, what would you say?

Teacher: I guess because we've been there. The teachers. I would honestly say, because I've been there, I'm able to relate to my students. We have a lot of students that come from broken homes and with single parents and you know, we usually give our life story to them. Like I always tell them, "Look kids, I lost my mom when I was five, my dad when I was twelve. My ninety-three-year-old grandma took care of me. And you can be successful."(Edcouch junior high).

Teacher: Once we identify the students, we are very sensitive to the fact that they need to make up their work. I think that's the main word is being very sensitive to their system. My wife was a migrant, and I know how it is because I've worked in the fields myself, and I know how hard it is to come in and have to ... parents are dictating the time, you know, you don't have a choice. You have to go away with them at a certain time. So personally, I make sure that I am sensitive to ... I tell them to cover certain sections of things that we've already covered or that we are going to cover later on, depending on the time of the year. And try to be not over-demanding, but at the same time, expect them to do their part. (Edcouch high school)

Several teachers also attributed some of the success their schools had with migrant students to the level of respect between students and teachers. Undoubtedly, this respect was facilitated by teachers' sincere efforts to help their students succeed. The teachers demonstrated that they really cared about their students.

> **Teacher:** We have a very large migrant population, this is just me guessing here, back to Sammy, the student that wanted to play basketball, he always came with failing, failing, failing, grades—horrible grades. And I'm like, Sammy, you're a smart kid, why are you failing up there, but you're doing the work and you can do it here? And he said, "Well, they don't care about us up there and the grades don't count so I mainly work when I come here." And so I think a lot of them feel like this is their home and they're not going to really, they don't really fit in there. The teachers know they're leaving, and maybe they don't spend the time with them that they need to. This is all my opinion, and so they come here, and I'm going to give them that extra time because I want them to get caught up. I want them to know that yes, they do belong. (Weslaco middle school)

The teachers' respect for their students was further demonstrated through the use of the migrant culture to reinforce their lessons.

> **Teacher:** And as ... I bring a lot of my background to the class, and the kids really enjoy that. You know, as a migrant, myself, I understand the roads going up and down, and yeah, we bring it up from Social Studies. When you're going up north, you know, and they'll say, "Yeah, you know, when I went up north, I went through this ... " and so there's a lot of input from them in relating their stories from their past or events that happened to them, and we bring it in for scaling, when we're weighing things. You know, they'll remember when they're cutting things and weighing them, sacking them. And that kind of sense. And I, since I usually make my word problems, I'll relate them to that, you know. (Weslaco elementary)
>
> **Teacher 1:** And we draw from, you know, we ask them, like if we're going over something, let's say a reading story. We ask them, you know, have you ever seen this ... and they've experienced so much more. They've seen so much more than other kids, you know?

Teacher 2: Yeah, "In Michigan we did this ... " or "in Florida we did this ... in Tennessee." See, and what I do when I have that, I actually teach them to the map. Say we're studying North Americans. "He came from Colorado," and we'll actually trace his travels to the north, so I bring it all in. I don't know how others might do it, but I feel like that's authentic. It's real life. (Edcouch elementary)

Student-Centered Instruction

The workplace culture notions of collegiality, respect for students, and reflection geared toward problem solving and continuous improvement are found not only at the school level but are represented in the classrooms as well. None of the schools in this study used a unique curriculum or instructional techniques for migrant students. However, there was a great deal of consistency throughout the schools researchers visited with regard to the most common style of instruction. The term *student-centered instruction* encompasses a number of pedagogical techniques. In this context, the four elements teachers most often discussed when asked to describe their teaching were:

1. an *emphasis on choosing relevant content to teach skills and concepts*;
2. *teaching problem solving as a life skill*, especially in the elementary schools;
3. *student collaboration* in the learning process; and
4. *providing support systems* for their students.

Problem solving using relevant real world examples were mentioned a number of times as a specific goal of a school's math program.

Interviewer: What is the goal of fourth-grade mathematics instruction?

Teacher: Problem solving. One of our district goals, which applies to any subject, would be we want to develop long life problem solvers so that they can go out there to the real world and be successful, cooperative citizens. We're trying to give them also a lot of real life experiences. (Edcouch elementary)

Teacher: I want my kids to be able to go to the store and know whether or not they are getting ripped off. I want them to be able to balance their checkbook and fill out their taxes and basic problem solving—know how to figure out how much wallpaper to buy. There's so many real life situations where they need math and to get them to understand, and that's my hardest job right now is to get them to understand that, yes, they will use this after TAAS! (Weslaco middle school)

Several teachers described how they specifically related problem-solving situations to their own lives or to students' lives.

Teacher: I give them a lot of examples, there's real life examples that we've actually, that I have actually gone through. There's a lot of polygons when, you know, you're trying to build a house. And I tell them, I use my mom's house as an example. You know, you're supposed to have, well, my mom's house in this case was supposed to have a square, a rectangular base, foundation, and it turned out to be a trapezoid, which means that one of the walls was a little bit off to the side. And I tell them how that affected putting on the tile, on the floor, putting on the sheet rock, everything else, you know, all the way up to the roof. (Edcouch high school)

The effect of peer tutoring and student collaboration as an instructional technique was discussed frequently in school effectiveness literature (King-Stoops, 1980; Garcia, 1991). One teacher even stated that she felt this was one of the primary reasons her students were so successful last year.

Teacher: I would attribute that as one of the successes last year, as far as doing well on the TAAS. I would say that was our big one. If I have to give credit to anybody, it would have to be to the kids tutoring the kids. (Edcouch junior high)

Teacher: A lot of peer tutoring where they help each other out. And it's weird, you might explain it five times, and then another student explains it to him, and they pick it up. (Weslaco elementary)

Observations of several classrooms and a sampling of student-produced materials also supported the notion that students are taking an active role in their own learning and feel quite comfortable helping each other out in constructive ways. This sense of student empowerment and collaboration is remarkably similar to the cultural values emphasized earlier in teacher's workplace interactions.

Another facet of student-centered instruction is an emphasis on support systems for students. While teachers maintain consistently high expectations of their students, they also provide them with the support necessary to succeed. This support comes from the teachers themselves as well as through highly structured institutional programs. It is important to note that most of these support mechanisms were designed to assist all students who need extra help, not just migrant students. While teachers put a great deal of faith in the ability of their students, they also made it clear that they were personally available to help students at any time if they were struggling, again demonstrating their dedication and level of caring for their students.

Interviewer: So when you think about what it is that appears to make your school district so uniquely successful with these migrant students, can you identify any characteristics that you think might contribute to that?

Teacher: I think that it's because they feel that we treat them special because we take the time to get to know them, to conference with them and ask them "What are your needs?" And we also tell them, never be embarrassed to admit that you need help. PASS is not only for students that don't know … PASS is for students that want to learn. Even if you just want to get your work out of the way, we welcome you. And the classroom, it's not just myself but all of the other teachers, during PE, they are welcomed to stay if they need help on something. You can work with a partner, with a friend, if that friend's going to be helping you learn something. You're welcomed to come after lunch. We don't mind giving up our lunch period, or half of it. After school, many of us stay until closing time, 6:00 p.m. Some of these parents make two or three trips to see, "Is he ready?" If not, if he needs to work, that's fine, I'll come back. So, I think that all of the teachers go out of their way to help the students succeed. (Edcouch elementary)

In addition to assistance from individual teachers, a number of formal support systems were available to the general student population, and migrant students were expected to take advantage of these support systems when they found it necessary. According to a Mission High School teacher, the Crossroads Program "is intended for juniors and seniors that have gone through a course and perhaps not mastered it. So they are there, a daily program, trying to retrieve the credit." The program also offers an evening tutorial program and bus transportation directly afterward to a student's home in order to encourage students to attend. The Extended Day program at the Weslaco elementary school we visited also offers bus transportation home.

The middle school in Weslaco holds a Saturday school every other week from 8:00 a.m. to noon to help students who are struggling or who have enrolled late and need to catch up on their work. The concept was originally intended to serve migrant students only but was unsuccessful at attracting a significant number. Now it is open to all students who are struggling, and those who attend all six Saturdays are rewarded with a trip to the theme park Fiesta Texas in San Antonio.

Though most teachers don't appear to use technology in their individual classrooms, many of them did mention that their schools had computer lab facilities where students could use self-paced software to brush up on skills and to prepare for the TAAS. A unique new program at Mission High School designed specifically for migrant students allows them to check out laptop computers for use at home while they attempt to catch up on missed work or to get ahead before leaving in order to take an end of course exam.

Spiraling Curriculum that Emphasizes Constant Review

Another common thread that links each of these schools emerged when teachers were asked to describe their curriculum or a typical lesson in their math class. Apparently due to the pressure these districts feel to perform well on TAAS objectives, constant review has been incorporated as a normal function of most courses. This is especially evident in courses offered below tenth grade since the exit-level TAAS is given at the tenth-grade level. This process of constant review (a) is *an integral part of the scope and sequence for most math courses*, (b) requires *making connections between concepts*, and (c) maintains *high expectations from top to bottom*.

Interviewer: Can you describe any practices which you incorporate into your math class that specifically help migrant students succeed?

Teacher: Well, going back and reviewing, going back and reviewing, going back and reviewing. It helps all of them. (Weslaco middle school)

Teacher: The pacing guide works very ... repetition, you know, we cover the same objective maybe four or five times during the year. And it's always constantly reviewed, it's not "Well, we covered it in first six weeks, we're not going to cover it again." You know, and since we're reviewing, like a student that comes in the middle of the year, it's not going to be, well, we covered place value the first six weeks, we're not going to cover it again, or you have to wait. We cover it on a daily basis. And the foundation is covered every single day in our daily review and that would help the migrant student that comes in and misses that first six weeks of the extensive teaching on place value. (Weslaco elementary)

Teacher: On Tuesdays, Thursdays, and Fridays when they first come into the room, they're going to take a quiz. The quiz might be over something we did yesterday or it might be something we did the first six weeks that I want to be sure they haven't forgotten. Kind of a spiraling kind of thing. (Weslaco middle school)

The pedagogical techniques these teachers use reflect a classroom culture that values the contributions and inherent abilities of the students. The collegiality evident in the teachers' workplace environment is clearly reflected in the collaboration teachers encourage between their students. A sense of "we're all in this together" seems to permeate both the way teachers interact to improve themselves professionally, and the way they conduct classroom instruction.

Similarly, learning to use mathematics is presented as a lifelong skill, not a series of disconnected concepts from the pages of a textbook. By incorporating similar values and norms in both the school-level organizational culture and in their classroom cultures, these schools have produced a synergistic effect in which the successes in one arena encourage greater collegiality, risk taking, attention to reflection, and problem solving in the other arena. In addition, the fact that these cultural values and norms are reflected in both the way teachers interact with each other and the way that they run their classrooms lends credence to the notion that culture plays a significant role in the overall effectiveness of these schools.

Finally, our discussions with teachers illuminated the pervasiveness of this culture of high expectations from top to bottom. It was clear that principals and administrators held high expectations of their teachers combined with support systems for reaching these expectations, just as teachers did for their students. One teacher summed up their school's success in the following way:

Teacher: But I think the teachers, along with the supporting staff and administration, working together, to me, that's your success right there. It's not just the textbooks. It's not just the worksheets and the material that you provide the teachers. It's the teachers themselves, and the staff that help the child along the way, and your supporting administration. It all works together. (Weslaco elementary)

Teacher: I think that we have very high expectations, period. And it comes from our instructional leaders. If you don't have it in your instructional leaders, then you're going to tend to not put it out. So, if their expectations are high, so will ours. And sometimes you feel like, well, it's a burden, or I feel really stressed. But if you pick up your expectations here, you know, the child, instead of being way down here, is going to pick up ... (Edcouch elementary)

Administrators' high expectations of their teachers have become even more formalized at an Edcouch elementary school. At this school, the principal requires every teacher to develop a professional portfolio.

Teacher: I found a lot of professional growth in having done that portfolio. I knew where I was weak and where I needed to work, and it made me more aware of what I needed to work on. Personally, I came back and did that in my classroom, and I'm so glad that she's requiring everybody to have one.

Interviewer: So it was really a good opportunity for reflection, not just a way of somebody evaluating you.

Teacher: It's not just that, it's not just an evaluation. It's actually, in the evaluation itself you're evaluating yourself, you're saying, "Gee, I need to go back and go to some more in-services. I need to pick up something else," or "I want to get up there and present, I don't want to be just showing up and be a participant." (Edcouch elementary)

DISCUSSION

The schools and districts included in this study stand out due to the high degree of success they have had with migrant students. The themes described previously indicate that there are many similarities between these schools that contribute to this success. Beyond these patterns of similarities, there are at least two other lessons for significant reform to be learned from this research.

- Organizational culture appears to exert more influence on the success these schools have with migrant students than specific curricula or pedagogical techniques.

Although this study began with an explicit focus on curriculum and pedagogy, teachers repeatedly turned conversations toward issues such as what they believed about students, the collegiality they valued, and the specific actions they took to reflect on and to solve problems individually and as a team. It soon became clear that, though teachers may not have used the specific term *organizational culture*, they believed that their success was more a reflection of their shared vision than of any particular type of curriculum or teaching style. This research, therefore, supports the growing notion that organizational culture is as equally powerful in defining successful schools and districts as it has been in describing successful businesses (McLaughlin, 1993; Owens, 1991; Purkey & Smith, 1983).

McLaughlin observed that teachers' responses to their students in contemporary classrooms generally fell into one of three patterns:

1. maintaining traditional standards,
2. lowering expectations for coverage and achievement, or
3. adapting practices and pedagogy.

Clearly, the teachers in these schools that are successful with migrant students have chosen the third option. Through critical examination of their own curriculum and pedagogy, these teachers are able to constantly modify their content and approach in order to meet the needs of their students. As one teacher stated,

> We don't fit a program, we just teach the kids. We don't fit the kid into the program, we'll take several programs and extract whatever we are going to be using to help that child accomplish or succeed with the objective.

This study supports McLaughlin's contention that workplace factors mediate the type of response teachers make to challenging student populations. The success these schools have with migrant students appears to extend beyond the fact that they employ extremely talented and dedicated professionals. In order to sustain that talent and dedication, these schools have developed cultures that explicitly promote reflection, feedback, and problem solving. These behavioral norms are ingrained in the organizational culture of the schools themselves and have become integrated into the shared vision the teachers hold regarding their responsibilities as professional educators.

These schools and districts have been able to create the organizational capacity (Mitchell, 1995) to realize their vision of excellence. By clearly defining their instructional objectives, creating a productive work environment in which teachers have the capacity and support to make professional decisions, and focusing on continual improvement, the schools cited here have, wittingly or unwittingly, adopted the tenets of performance management (Mitchell, 1995) advocated by reformers in business and public education. The learning organizations that they have developed are reflected not only in the context of the teachers' workplace but in the classroom cultures as well.

- State standardized testing in the form of the TAAS has provided an impetus for these districts to focus their priorities.

Calls for increased accountability on the part of public schools are widespread. Taxpayers and legislators want to be assured that the dollars they are investing in public education are paying off in greater student achievement. In many states, standardized tests are used as a tool for measuring student achievement. Since 1993, the state of Texas has administered the Texas Assessment of Academic Skills (TAAS) in mathematics to all children in grades three through eight. Students taking Algebra are also required to pass an Algebra end-of-course exam in order to receive credit. In addition, all Texas students must pass an exit-level test that includes mathematics in order to receive a diploma. This exit-level test is first administered in the tenth grade. TAAS results in mathematics are combined with those on the reading and writing portions of the tests to determine an overall rating for schools of Exemplary, Recognized, Acceptable, or Low Performing. These ratings are made public and are used by the state to determine which schools will receive monetary rewards for excellent or greatly improved performance and which schools could possibly have their accreditation removed for consistently low performance. As a result, the TAAS has become a very high-stakes test to which most school districts give a great deal of attention.

As with most standardized tests, however, controversies abound as to the appropriateness of placing so much emphasis on testing. Advocates point to the utility of the TAAS for determining whether schools are adequately preparing students for graduation. Detractors complain that high-stakes testing encourages schools to "teach to the test" rather than provide students with a challenging, broad-based curriculum. Though it was not the purpose of this study to debate the pros and cons of the

TAAS, one thing did become clear in discussions with teachers. The existence of the TAAS has caused district employees at all levels to reexamine their mathematics programs. As a result, these schools and districts have invested resources into improving their mathematics programs not just in piecemeal fashion, but with a cohesive plan including clearly defined objectives and areas of emphasis at each grade level. School boards and administrators have apparently supported teachers with the time, resources, personnel, and school-level support systems necessary to reach these objectives. It is impossible to determine whether these same improvements would have been made without the existence of the TAAS. However, the fact that some of these schools performed quite poorly on TAAS when it was first administered appears to indicate that standardized testing and the accountability associated with it has been a driving force for improvement rather than a hindrance. One teacher from the middle school in Weslaco hit on this point specifically during an interview:

> **Teacher:** We were not successful on the TAAS until last year. We had very low scores, very few passing until last year. Last year we really improved, and I think it's largely because we aligned our curriculum to the TAAS, and we're not teaching to the test, but if you don't teach the material that you're going to be tested on, you don't have a chance.... We'd better make sure we teach those things in addition to anything else and in addition to any way that we want to teach them.

An additional criticism of TAAS testing is that schools, especially at the elementary level, place too much emphasis on the areas of reading, writing, and math (because they are part of the accountability system) at the expense of subjects such as science and social studies. While this may be true for some schools, the elementary schools in this study prove that student exposure to science and social studies need not be sacrificed in order to insure success on the TAAS. Neither of the elementary schools visited chose to eliminate or even to reduce the time they spent on science or social studies in order to drill for TAAS. In fact, the hallways of one of the schools were wallpapered with evidence of recent student projects related to astronomy.

In short, the TAAS has served as a catalyst for fundamental changes in the mathematics programs of these districts. While it is impossible to conclude that the success these districts are having with migrant students could not have been achieved without the TAAS and its associated accountability, evidence indicates that the changes made as a result of

TAAS testing have been beneficial for all students, migrant and non-migrant alike.

IMPLICATIONS

The implications of this research clearly point to the need for an increased focus among policy makers, stakeholders, and funding agencies on the ways in which organizational culture can be more effectively employed to create and sustain successful schools. This study identifies the characteristics of schools with effective organizational cultures that have led to successful students. This study indicates that a culture conducive to high expectations (for both students and teachers) and continuous improvement starts at the top with principals and administrators and cannot be sustained by classroom practices alone. This study is merely a snapshot, however, and does not describe the process by which these cultures have arisen in various schools and districts. Further research is needed in this area.

Other implications apply specifically to the education of migrant students. Given that factors associated with workplace culture exerted a greater influence on the success of the migrant students in these schools than curricula or teaching techniques, it appears that resources may be better spent toward modifying and improving the professional workplace culture of a school or district than toward purchasing or designing curricular materials specifically for migrant students. A previous review of the literature related to mathematics curricula and programs designed specifically for migrant students and funded primarily by state and federal migrant education programs indicated that, in many instances, these programs failed to address the unique characteristics of migrant students adequately enough to justify their funding by migrant education organizations. In addition, the glaring lack of research indicating that particular curricular projects are more effective with migrant students than those used with the general population supports the contention that resources and funding in migrant education can be most effectively utilized by examining ways to improve the overall culture of schools of which migrant students are a part.

Last, the success these schools and districts are having with migrant students, not only on the TAAS but on graduation rates and college attendance as well, indicates that standardized testing and accountability are playing a legitimate role in the improvements seen thus far. Though accountability based on standardized testing has some justifiable drawbacks, this study indicates that it can also serve as a catalyst for change and improvement. For migrant students who have traditionally been marginalized or ignored by the educational system, this is a welcome transformation.

NOTE

1. See the TEA Web site, www.tea.state.tx.us

REFERENCES

Cardelle-Elawar, M. (1992). Promoting self-regulation in mathematics problem solving through individualized feedback to bilingual students. *The Bilingual Review, 17* (1), 36-42.

Cummins, J. (1993). Empowering minority students: A framework for intervention. In L. Weis & M. Fine (Eds.), *Beyond silenced voices: Class, race, and gender in United States schools*. New York: State University of New York.

Darling-Hammond, L. (1997). Principals and teachers must devise new structures and strategies to meet the challenges of education in the 21st century. *Principal*, 5-11.

Deal, T.W., & Kennedy, A.A. (1982). *Corporate cultures: This rites and rituals of corporate life*. Reading, MA: Addison-Wesley.

Garcia, E.E. (1991). *The education of linguistically and culturally diverse students: Effective instructional practices*. Santa Cruz, CA: National Center for Research on Cultural Diversity and Second Language Learning.

Kanter, R.M. (1983). *The change masters: Innovation and entrepreneurship in the American corporation*. New York: Simon & Schuster.

Kindler, A.L. (1995). Education of migrant children in the United States. *Directions in Language & Education, 1*(8), 1-12.

King-Stoops, J.B. (1980). *Migrant education: Teaching the wandering ones*. Bloomington, IN: Phi Delta Kappa Educational Foundation.

Ladson-Billings, G. (1995). Toward a theory of culturally relevant pedagogy. *American Educational Research Journal, 32*(3), 465-491.

Ladson-Billings, G. (1990). Culturally relevant teaching. *The College Board Review, 155*, 20-25.

Leon, E.R. (1996). *Challenges and solutions for educating migrant students*. Lansing, MI: ERIC Document Service No. ED 393 615.

Loewenberg-Ball, D. (1991). Teaching mathematics for understanding: What do teachers need to know about subject matter? In M.M. Kennedy (Ed.), *Teaching academic subjects to diverse learners* (pp. 63-83). New York: Teachers College Press.

Lopez, C.I., & Sullivan, H.J. (1992). Effect of personalization of instructional context on the achievement and attitudes of Hispanic students. *Educational Technology Research and Development, 40* (4), 5-13.

Mather, J.R.C., & Chiodo, J.J. (1994). A mathematical problem: How do we teach mathematics to LEP elementary students? *The Journal of Educational Issues of Language Minority Students, 13*, 1-12.

Martinez, D.I., & Ortiz de Montellano, B.R. (1988). *Improving the science and mathematics achievement of Mexican American students through culturally relevant science*.

Las Cruces, NM: Clearinghouse on Rural Education and Small Schools, *ERIC Digest*, ERIC Document Service No. ED 296 819.

McLaughlin, M.W. (1993). What matters most in teachers' workplace context? In J.W. Little & M. McLaughlin (Eds.), *Teachers' work: Individuals, colleagues, and contexts* (pp. 79-103). New York: Publisher.

Menchaca, V.D., & Ruiz-Escalante, J.A. (1995). *Instructional strategies for migrant students*. Charleston, WV: Clearinghouse on Rural Education and Small Schools, ERIC Digest, ERIC Document Service No. ED 388 491.

Mitchell, S.M. (1995). Performance management in education. In S.B. Bacharach & B. Mundell (Eds.), *Images of schools, structures and roles in organizational behavior* (pp. 201-238). Thousand Oaks, CA: Corwin Press.

Moll, L.C. (1988). Some key issues in teaching Latino students. *Language Arts, 65* (5), 465-473.

Moll, L.C., Amanti, C., Neff, D., & Gonzalez, N. (1992). Funds of knowledge for teaching: Using a qualitative approach to connect homes and classrooms. *Theory into Practice, 31*(2), 132–141.

Morse, S.C. (1997). Unschooled migrant youth: Characteristics and strategies to serve them. Charleston, WV: Clearinghouse on Rural Education and Small Schools, *ERIC Digest*, ERIC Document Service No. ED 405 158.

Nunes, T. (1992). Ethnomathematics and everyday cognition. In D.A. Grouws (Ed.), *Handbook of research on mathematics teaching and learning* (pp. 557-574). New York: Macmillan.

Owens, R.G. (1991). *Organizational behavior in education*. Needham Heights, MA: Allyn & Bacon.

Peters, T.J., & Waterman, Jr., R.H. (1982). *In search of excellence: Lessons from America's best run companies*. New York: Harper & Row.

Purkey, S.C., & Smith, M.S. (1983). Effective schools: A review. *The Elementary School Journal, 83*, 427-452.

Reyes, P. (1988). Learning in mathematics for linguistically diverse students: Challenges for Hispanic students in Texas borderlands schools. In *Effective border school research and development initiative*. A Partnership between The University of Texas-Austin, Region 1 Service Center and School Districts, and University of Texas-Pan American.

Reyes, P., Scribner, J.D., & Wagstaff, L. (1996). *Migrant education policy and practices*. Austin: A Partnership between The University of Texas at Austin and The Texas Educational Agency.

Secada, W.G. (1992). Race, ethnicity, social class, language and achievement in mathematics. In D.A. Grouws (Ed.), *Handbook of research on mathematics teaching and learning* (pp. 623-660). New York: Macmillan.

Strutchens, M. (1995). *Multicultural mathematics: A more inclusive mathematics*. Columbus, OH: Clearinghouse for Science, Mathematics, and Environmental Education, *ERIC Digest*, ERIC Document Service No. ED 380 295.

U.S. Department of Education. (1990). *Handbook of effective migrant education practices, Vol 1: Findings*. Arlington, VA: Development Associates.

CHAPTER 14

BEATING THE ODDS

Teaching Middle and High School Students to Read and Write Well

Judith A. Langer

ABSTRACT

This study investigated the characteristics of instruction that accompany student achievement in reading, writing, and English. It focused on English language arts programs in schools that have been trying to increase student performance, comparing those whose students perform higher than demographically comparable schools with schools whose scores are more typical. The study took place in four states and included 25 schools, 44 teachers, and 88 classes studied over a 2-year period each. Although the sample was diverse, including urban and suburban sites, schools with poor and diverse student bodies predominated. Analyses specified six features that permeated the environments and provided marked distinctions between higher and more typically performing schools. Although some of these features were present to varying degrees in the English programs in the more typical schools, they were all present all of the time in the higher performing schools, forming a consistently supportive environment for student learning.

Deep Change: Cases and Commentary on Reform in High Stakes States, 285–333

This is a report of a 5-year study focusing on characteristics of educational practice that accompany student achievement in reading, writing, and English. English classrooms have long been considered places where "high literacy" (Bereiter & Scardamalia, 1987) is learned, where students gain not merely the basic literacy skills to get by, but also the content knowledge, ways of structuring ideas, and ways of communicating with others that are considered the "marks" of an educated person (Graff, 1987). To distinguish this kind of literacy from the more popular notion of literacy as a set of "basic" reading and writing skills, in this work I define the term high literacy in an everyday sense to refer to the literacy gained from a well-developed middle and high school English curriculum. Although basic reading and writing skills are included in this definition of high literacy, also included are the ability to use language, content, and reasoning in ways that are appropriate for particular situations and disciplines. Students learn to "read" the social meanings, the rules, and structures, and the linguistic and cognitive routines to make things work in the real world of English language use, and that knowledge becomes available as options when students confront new situations. This notion of high literacy refers to understanding how reading, writing, language, content, and social appropriateness work together, and using this knowledge in effective ways. It is reflected in students' ability to engage in thoughtful reading, writing, and discussion about content in the classroom, to put their knowledge and skills to use in new situations, and to perform well on reading and writing assessments including high-stakes testing.

THEORETICAL FRAMEWORK

This work is anchored in a sociocognitive perspective (especially Bakhtin, 1981; Vygotsky, 1987; see Langer, 1986, 1995). From this perspective, learning is seen to be influenced by the values, experiences, and actions that exist within the larger environment. Students' and teachers' voices and experiences, learned within the primary and secondary communities to which they belong (see Gee, 1996), make a contribution to what gets learned and how it is learned. It is largely from these diverse contexts that notions of what counts as appropriate knowledge and effective communication gain their meaning. Bakhtin (1981), in his conceptualization of dialogic thinking and the multivocal nature of language and thought, offers us a way to think about high literacy and its development. Rather than seeing it as composed of independent skills or proficiencies that are called upon at needed moments, he offers us a vision in which the educated individual calls upon a multilayered history of experiences with language and content, cutting across many contexts—assuming that multiple and sometimes competing voices (or ways of interpreting) add richness and depth to emerging ideas. For example, he argues that the discourse of a nation includes an awareness of the special experiences and rhetorics of many subgroups; we recognize and respond differently, he says, to the characteristic prose of doctors, lawyers, or clergy, ways of communication and interpretation that stand in dialogue with one another rather than being reconciled into a single "common" discourse. Such diverse voices also occur both within and across classrooms and subject areas (Applebee, 1996), as students bring the voices of their out-of-school experiences as well as the conversations within their particular academic courses to bear on the topic at hand. Students are enculturated to understand and use these voices (or perspectives) across the grades; their growing proficiency is shaped by the interactions that are fostered in the classrooms in which they participate. It is largely from these diverse contexts that notions of what counts as appropriate knowledge and effective communication gain their meaning. From this perspective, in a learning environment, students and teachers call upon the voices they have already acquired and are given opportunities to gain new voices. They also have opportunities to hone their ability to sift through these multiple sources in understanding purposes and audiences, creating effective ideas and arguments, and entering forms of discourse that help them move forward.

Vygotsky's sociocultural framework (1987) offers a way to conceptualize teacher and student learning as occurring within an environment in which both can participate in thoughtful examination and discourse about language and content because it is an integral part of the social way the educational environment operates and gets work done. The related views of situative theorists (e.g., Brown, Collins, & Daguid, 1989; Greeno, 1997; Greeno & the Middle School Through Applications Group, 1998; Lave & Wenger, 1991) posit that the way in which people learn particular knowledge and skills is reliant on the environment in which the learning takes place; environment is a fundamental part of what gets learned, how it is interpreted, and how it is used. Beginning from this theoretical frame, the present project sought to examine the deeply contextualized nature of both teaching and learning (Dyson, 1993; Myers, 1996; Turner, 1993) in more and less successful middle and high school English classrooms.

RELATED RESEARCH

Although there is a long tradition of research examining specific features of writing and literature instruction (cf. Hillocks, 1986; Purves & Beach, 1972), there have been few previous attempts to study the characteristics of more- and less-effective English programs as a whole at the secondary level. One of the earliest was Squire and Applebee's (1968) examination of 158 programs in the 1960s. Although Squire and Applebee had intended to contrast "award winning" with "recommended" programs, they found few differences between their two samples. Their report is useful for its description of best practice, as well as common problems, in the programs they studied. Overall, these programs were marked by the professionalism of the teachers, the availability of resources for instruction, an emphasis on the teaching of literature, and a general lack of attention to the needs of lower-track students.

In a later study that focused on literature instruction, Applebee (1993) surveyed three groups of unusually successful English programs (programs that consistently produced winners in the national Achievement Awards in Writing competition, programs designated as Centers of Excellence by the National Council of Teachers of English, and programs nominated as excellent by administrators and university colleagues) and contrasted them with random samples of private and public English programs. As in the earlier Squire and Applebee study, teachers in the more successful programs tended to be more highly professionalized, to have more adequate resources available, and to enjoy more community support for their efforts. They were also more likely to be influenced by recent reform movements in the teaching of English, emphasizing process-oriented writing instruction, active involvement of students in discussion, and reader-response approaches to literature. Such differences were differences in degree rather than in kind from programs in the random samples of schools, and in general reflect the advantages that flow from better funding rather than from different approaches to curriculum and instruction. Although the 25 years between the Squire and Applebee (1968) and Applebee (1993) studies led to many differences in specific aspects of curriculum and instruction in English, there is no way to link any of these differences to student achievement.

At the elementary level, a number of studies have examined curriculum and instruction in classrooms where students have made unusual progress in reading and writing achievement, in contrast with classrooms where achievement is more typical. Wharton-McDonald, Pressley, and Hampston (1998), for example, studied 9 first-grade teachers in New York State who differed in their effectiveness in promoting literacy. In the most effective classrooms, there was a high level of engagement in challenging literacy activities, a web of interconnections among tasks (so that writing, for example, was often related to what was being read), and skills were taught explicitly but in connection with real reading and writing activities. In a related study, Pressley et al. (1998) studied 30 first grade classrooms in five states, contrasting typical teachers with outstanding teachers in the same school. The most effective teachers were again characterized by high academic engagement in challenging literacy tasks, explicit teaching of skills, interconnections among activities, and careful matching of tasks and instruction to student competence levels.

Taylor, Pearson, Clark, and Walpole (1999) investigated school and classroom factors related to primary grade reading achievement in a sample of 14 schools identified as most, moderately, or least effective on several measures of reading achievement. At the school level, important factors included parental support, systematic assessment of student progress, good communication among staff within the building, and a collaborative model for the delivery of reading instruction. At the classroom level, significant factors included more use of small group instruction, more time for independent reading, high levels of engagement in higher level literacy tasks, the use of scaffolding to link skill instruction to real reading tasks, and strong links between school and home.

However, no studies have focused on the features of instruction that differentiate English achievement in higher versus lower performing middle and high school programs. In the present study, I have examined the educational experiences of both teachers and students, as teachers gain professional knowledge and students achieve higher literacy (as evidenced in reading and writing high stakes test scores) than their peers in other contexts. In an earlier article (Langer, 2000), I reported on how teachers' professional lives support student achievement. Building from that work, the present article describes features of English instruction that support student achievement, and the kinds of attention given to helping students gain both knowledge and skills in English. My project team and I have been studying these features in order to better understand the various components that make a difference in helping students become more highly literate.

As background, there are six issues at the center of current educational debate in English and literacy, and that were in turn reflected in differences that emerged (through a process of constant comparison that continued throughout the study) among the classrooms we studied.

APPROACHES TO SKILLS INSTRUCTION

Throughout at least the 20th century, there has been an ongoing debate about the manner in which instruction is delivered, with some scholars positing the effectiveness of skill and concept learning through experience-based instruction (e.g., Dewey, 1938) and others stressing mastery of concepts and skills through decontextualized practice (e.g., Bloom, 1971). This has led to a pedagogical side-taking that continues in English and literacy today. For example, Hirsch (1996) calls for students to remember culturally potent facts, and genre theorists (see Cope & Kalantzis, 1993) call for teaching students the rules of organization underlying written forms, while Goodman and Wilde (1992) and Graves (1983) call for teaching skills and knowledge within the context of authentic literacy activities. Yet, studies of reading and writing instructional practice throughout the century (see Langer & Allington, 1992) indicate that teachers tend to blur distinctions, using what may appear to theorists as a fusion of theoretically dissimilar approaches.

APPROACHES TO TEST PREPARATION

In recent years there has been a widespread call for systemic reform of schools and school systems (e.g., Brown & Campione, 1996; Smith & O'Day, 1991). One part of systemic reform requires that there be alignment between curriculum and assessment. In times such as these, with a widespread focus on achievement scores, how this is done becomes a critical issue. On the one hand, some educators focus primarily on practicing sample test items and helping students become "test wise"; they teach such test-taking skills as ways to select a best answer or how to best respond to a writing task from a reading item. Others advocate teaching the needed literacy abilities throughout the year, as part of the regular grade-level curriculum. In both cases test results are the focus; however, in the first case, improvement in test scores is the primary goal, whereas the second focuses on raising both test scores and student learning by improving the curriculum.

CONNECTING LEARNINGS

The education literature on learning and instruction is replete with evidence that student learning and recall are more likely to be enhanced when connections can be made to prior knowledge gained from both in- and out-of-school experiences than when the content of instruction is treated as if it is entirely new (see for example, Bransford, Brown, & Cocking, 1999; Brown & Campione, 1996). Well-developed knowledge is also linked around important concepts and its relevance to other concepts is well understood. Although many curriculum guides as well as scope and sequence charts have attempted to depict links among specific learnings within and across the grades, too often the connections have been implicit at best, and often in the mind of the teacher or curriculum developer rather than shared with the students (see Applebee, 1996).

ENABLING STRATEGIES

During the last 25 or more years, a sizable group of research literature has emphasized the contribution of students' strategic awareness to learning and performance and the importance of teaching students strategies for carrying out reading, writing, and thinking tasks (e.g., Hillocks, 1995; Paris, Wasik, & Turner, 1991; Pressley et al., 1994). This work highlights the importance for students to learn not only content, but also intentional ways of thinking and doing. In response, instructional approaches have been developed to help students become aware not only of the content, but also of the particular tasks. Although the fields of science and mathematics have always seemed to be natural environments for teaching strategic approaches that enhance student performance (e.g., the scientific method, steps to mathematical solutions), teaching strategies and helping students to be strategic in the ways in which they approach a task (e.g., process approaches to writing, reflective literacy, or reciprocal teaching) are newer to the English language arts.

CONCEPTIONS OF LEARNING

What counts as knowing has become a much-used phrase in the educational literature. It is often used as a way to make distinctions among educators who focus on facts and concepts and those who focus on students' abilities to think about and use new knowledge. At one time a student's ability to give definitions, select right answers, and fill deleted information into sentences and charts was considered evidence of learning. But at least two bodies of research changed that: one focused on disciplinary initiation, where the goal became to help students learn to better approximate expert thinking in particular fields, such as thinking like an historian (e.g., Bazerman, 1981); and the other, on critical thinking, where the focus was on higher levels of cognitive manipulation of the material (e.g., Langer & Applebee, 1987; Schallert, 1976). More recently, the issue has turned to engagement (Guthrie & Alverman, 1999). Here concern goes beyond time on task to student involvement with the material. Although all three bodies of work have had an affect on literacy pedagogy, the most recent National Assessment of Educational Progress (NAEP) (1998) reports that fewer than 7% of students in Grades 4, 8, and 12 perform at the "advanced" level, which is the highest of four possible achievement levels in reading. This level represents students' grade-appropriate ability to deal analytically with challenging subject matter and to apply this knowledge to real world situations.

CLASSROOM ORGANIZATION

In recent years, a variety of approaches to classroom organization have been proposed to provide students with more opportunities to learn through substantive interaction with one another as well as with the teacher. These approaches include collaborative (Barnes, 1976) and cooperative groups (Slavin, 1983), literature clubs (Raphael & McMahon, 1994), peer writing groups (Graves, 1983), and envisionment-building classrooms (Langer, 1995). These and other similar approaches have been developed in response to both theory and research from a sociocognitive orientation that sees interactive working groups around shared problems to be supportive environments for learning. Bakhtin's (1981) notion of heteroglossia (see also Nystrand & Gamoran, 1997) suggests that all learning is dialogic, reliant on and gaining meaning from the many past and present relevant voices. In dialogic groups students bring their personal, cultural, and academic knowledge to the interaction as they play the multiple roles of learners, teachers, and inquirers, and in thus doing have an opportunity to consider the issue at hand from multiple perspectives. Students can interact as both problem-generators and problem-solvers. New ideas can be entertained and new ways of thinking modeled as more and less expert knowers of the content and those more and less familiar with the task share expertise, provide feedback, and learn from each other, Such contexts emphasize shared cognition, in which the varied contributions of the participants allow the group to achieve more than individuals could on their own. However, several studies have indicated that such groupings are not pervasive in American schools (NAEP, 1998; Applebee, 1993; Nystrand, Gamoran, & Heck, 1992).

These six issues provided a set of lenses through which to understand differences in instructional practices in higher and lower performing schools.

THE STUDY

The Excellence in English project examined educational practices in middle and high schools that have been trying to increase students' learning and performance in English language arts. The study focused on the workings of schools, teachers, and classrooms that strive to increase student performance and, despite obstacles and difficulties of serving the poor, beat the odds on standardized tests in reading and writing; that is, gain higher literacy, beyond comparable schools. My research team and I wanted to understand why—to identify features of instruction that make a difference in student learning and to contrast those schools where test scores are higher with demographically comparable schools in which they are not. We asked the following research question: How are the following enacted in school English programs where, when the schools are otherwise comparable, students score higher on high-stakes reading and writing tests than where they do not: approaches to skill instruction, approaches to testing, approaches to connecting learnings, approaches for enabling strategies, conceptions of learning, and classroom organization?

METHOD

This study took place over a 5-year period, permitting observations and interviews as well as identification and testing of patterns to take place over time. The 5-year period also allowed us to complete data gathering in successive cohorts in four states. Each teacher and school was studied for 2 years, permitting extensive study of how patterns in curriculum and instruction played themselves out in schools and classes across time. The project as a whole focused on both the professional and classroom activities that contribute to the English instruction the students experienced. Results from the study of the professional lives of the teachers have been reported in Langer (2000); the present report focuses on analyses of instructional activities.

PROJECT SITES AND PARTICIPANTS

To identify potential sites, recommendations were solicited from university and school communities in four states: Florida, New York, California, and Texas. The states were chosen to include diversity in student populations, educational problems, and approaches to improvement. The schools were nominated by at least three independent sources as places where professionals were working in interesting ways to improve student performance and test scores in English. Test data reported on each state education department's web site were checked to identify (a) those schools that were scoring higher than schools with similar student bodies, and (b) those schools that were scoring more typically (more like demographically similar schools). In each case, we examined literacy-related test data that carried high stakes for the students, the school, and the district; the relevant data varied from pass rates on Florida Writes! to performance on the Stanford 9 test. Schools whose performance on the high-stakes literacy tests was markedly above that for schools serving demographically similar populations were designated "beating the odds" schools. Schools whose performance did not deviate from that of schools serving demographically similar populations were designated "typically performing" schools. Referencing scores against those from schools serving demographically similar student populations controlled for the overall tendency for "high-performing" schools to be wealthy and suburban (cf. NAEP, 1994). It also means that typically performing schools serving more affluent populations can have higher raw scores than beating the odds schools serving high proportions of children in poverty.

Because we were particularly interested in identifying features of excellence in urban schools, we wished to more heavily sample schools and districts serving poor and culturally diverse students. However, because we also wanted to identify features that marked excellent programs across demographic areas, several suburban and urban fringe schools were also identified. We visited the most promising programs based on a combination of recommendations and test scores, and from these made a final selection based on the teachers' and administrators' willingness to work with us over a 2-year period as well as the school's ability to contribute to the overall diversity in student populations, problems, and locations in our sample. In the end, 25 schools, 44 teachers, and 88 classes were selected to participate in the study, with a focus on 1 class for each of the teachers in each of 2 consecutive years. Fourteen of the 25 participating schools are places where students were beating the odds, performing better on state administered high-stakes reading and writing tests than schools rated as demographically comparable by statewide criteria. The other 11 schools are also all places that came highly recommended, with administrators and teachers who were trying hard to improve student performance, but the school literacy scores were more typical of other schools with similar demographics.

Types of schools. Selecting schools from Florida. New York, California, and Texas led to great variety in programs and student populations. The Florida sample included schools from the Miami-Dade County area, representing a very diverse student population. The Dade County School District has long been involved in cutting-edge efforts to improve education in English, including in part: Pacesetter (sponsored by the College Board), the Zelda Glazer/Dade County Writing Project, the education of all teachers in the education of non-native English speaking students, the creation of interdisciplinary teams, and the early development of school-based management.

The New York sample encompassed a large geographic area, with populations ranging from rural to suburban, and middle class to urban poor. It included a number of districts in New York City and the Hudson Valley region that have earned reputations for student-centered and response-based English education, an emphasis on writing and reading across the curriculum, implementation of Goals 2000, and an interdisciplinary approach to math, science, and real-world studies through the English language arts. Two programs we studied (at King Middle School and International High School) focus on high academic competence for English Language Learners.

The California sample included schools from the Los Angeles area, a region with a very diverse student population, which has long been a bellwether for educational innovation and change in English language arts designed to benefit all students. Most recently, in an effort to raise student performance on statewide assessments, a new curriculum, an end to social promotion, a requirement for schools to adopt one of several reform programs, school accountability for student achievement (with schools placed on probation for failure to increase scores), and extra funds for tutoring efforts were put into place.

The Texas schools were in a large urban city district. Both the state and district have been involved in major efforts to improve student performance in literacy achievement including an end to social promotion and a stringent school accountability program to monitor achievement. The district put into place several measures to support improved achievement in literacy, and the state high-stakes tests were being revised at the time of our study. Summary information about the schools is presented in Table 14.1.

As can be seen in Table 14.1, schools with poor and diverse student populations predominate in the study. In terms of representation, the schools range from a 92% African American student body and no White students in one school, to 86% Hispanic and 2% White students in another, to 97% White students in another, with the other schools populated by students of greater ethnic and racial diversity. The schools also differ in the amount of student poverty, with school records indicating from 86% of the student body to 5% of the student body eligible for free or reduced lunch. We worked closely with 1 or 2 teachers at each school (one class each, each year), as well as other teachers and administrators with whom they coplanned, cotaught, or were otherwise engaged (including teams, departments, and other working groups) in the planning and review as well as implementation of instruction. Although we studied each teacher's entire class, 6 students from each class, representing the range of performance in that class as judged by the teacher, acted as key informants, collecting all their work and meeting with us to discuss that work, their classroom activities, and what they were learning.

Teachers Within Schools. The study design allowed us to examine the English teachers within the context of their teams, departments, and districts. Over the years in which we worked in the schools, we came to understand the extent to which the teachers were affected by the larger context in terms of professional growth or malaise, or were achieving

Table 14.1. School Demographics

School	*Student Membership*	*% Free or Reduced Lunch*	*Selected Features*
Florida			
Reuben Dario Middle School[a, b]	83% Hispanic 12% African American 4% White	80%	Team and decision making councils; reading and language arts across areas
Highland Oaks Middle School[a, b]	47% White 23% African American 27% Hispanic	34%	Interdisciplinary teams; academic wheels; collaborative partnerships
Palm Middle School	60% African American 39% Hispanic 1% White	85%	Media Arts Magnet; tracking; interdisciplinary teams
Hendricks High School	56% Hispanic 43% African American	47%	International Business and Finance Magnet; Jr. ROTC; dropout prevention
Miami Edison High School[b]	92% African American 8% Hispanic	38%	New academies; teams; writing and English in subject areas
Wm. H. Turner Technical Arts High School[a, b]	63% African American 33% Hispanic 4% White	45%	Dual academic and work related academies; workplace experience; Coalition of Essential Schools
New York			
Henry O. Hudson Middle School[a]	92% White 4% African American	5%	Interdisciplinary teams; active departments
Stockton Middle School	62% White 23% African American 14% Hispanic 1% Asian	76%	Interdisciplinary teams; departments

School	Student Membership	% Free or Reduced Lunch	Selected Features
Abraham S. King Middle School[a]	33% Hispanic 21% African American 43% White	40%	Interdisciplinary teams; active departments; dual language program
Crestwood Middle School	66% White 25% African American 5% Asian 4% Hispanic	62%	Interdisciplinary teams; departments
International High School[a, b]	48 Countries 37 Languages	84%	Academic teams; internships; portfolios; exhibitions
New Westford High School	68% White 22% African American 6% Hispanic 4% Asian	36%	Departments; grade level teams; arts focus
Tawasentha High School	97% White	12%	Curriculum teams; facilitators
California			
Rita Dove Middle School	58% Hispanic 41% African American	72%	Literacy coaching; Health/Science Career Magnet; district wide reform initiative
Charles Drew Middle School[a]	55% Hispanic 32% White 8% African American 4% Asian	57%	Literacy coaching; Strategic Reading Program; district wide reform initiative
James A. Foshay Learning Center,[a] Foshay Middle School[a,b] Foshay High School[a, b]	69% Hispanic 31% African American	86%	USC precollege enrichment; New American School; Urban Learning Center; academies; district wide reform initiative
Rutherford B. Hayes High School	86% Hispanic 7% Asian 3% Filipino 2% White 2% African American	74%	Humanitas program; teams; Math/ Science Magnet; service learning

Table continues on next page

Table 14.1. Continued

School	*Student Membership*	*% Free or Reduced Lunch*	*Selected Features*
Springfield High School[a]	63% Hispanic 15% White 10% African American 9% Asian	26%	Foreign Language/International Studies Magnet; UCLA; Career Ed; Bilingual Business/Finance Academy; district wide reform initiative
Texas			
Parklane Middle School[a]	47% Hispanic 38% White 13% African American 3% Asian	46%	Active English dept.; reading and language arts (double dose)
Ruby Middle School	83% African American 15% Hispanic 2% White	67%	English dept.; reading and language arts (double dose); language arts consortium with Lincoln High School
John H. Kirby Middle School[a]	42% White 34% Hispanic 17% African American 7% Asian	32%	Annenberg Beacon Charter School; Vanguard Magnet; Pre-Int'l Baccalaureate program; school-based center for teacher development; special program for low-motivated students; reading and language arts double dose for sixth grade; interdisciplinary teams
Lincoln High School[a]	78% African American 18% Hispanic 2% White 1% Asian	41%	Active English dept.; Aviation Sciences Magnet: Navy ROTC; Language Arts Consortium with Ruby Middle School

School	*Student Membership*	*% Free or Reduced Lunch*	*Selected Features*
Lyndon B. Johnson High School[a]	53% Hispanic 23% White 21% African American 2% Asian	37%	Research & Technology Magnet; Int'l Baccalaureate Program; ROTC; departments; grade teams
Sam Rayburn High School	87% Hispanic 7% African American 5% White 1% Asian	58%	Computer technology magnet; Annenberg Challenge Reform Initiative; extensive vocational program; ROTC; double English in grades 9 and 10; departments

Notes: Each school's racial/ethnic composition is described using the terminology supplied by the school and/or district. ROTC = Reserve Officers Training Corps: USC = University of Southern California: UCLA = University of California-Los Angeles.
[a]Denotes schools whose scores on state assessments were above those of demographically comparable schools.
[b]Denotes participants preference to use real names. In such cases, the actual names of schools, project teachers, and their colleagues are used For the schools not marked with a superscript b, pseudonyms are used throughout this paper.
[c]We studied both the middle and high school programs at Foshay Learning Center.

unusually good results in spite of the context in which they worked. This led us, eventually, to recognize three broad but distinct patterns within our sample of teachers; (a) exemplary teachers whose work was sustained, perhaps even created, by the supportive district and/or school context; (b) exemplary teachers in more typical schools who achieved their success due to professional contexts unrelated to the school and/or district (often through participation in professional organizations such as local affiliates of the National Council of Teachers of English, the International Reading Association, and writing projects, and collaboration with local colleges and universities); and (c) teachers who were more typical, who did not beat the odds, who were dedicated to their students, but working within a system of traditions and expectations that did not lift them beyond the accomplishments of other comparable schools.

In the first category above (beating the odds teachers within beating the odds schools) we found that these unusual teachers were not unusual within the contexts in which they worked; that is, their school and/or district (often both) encouraged all teachers, not just those in our study, to achieve comparable professional goals, and our observations of department meetings and interviews with supervisors and administrators suggested that the instructional approaches of the teachers in our study were widely accepted and carried out in their schools. In working with the second category of teachers (beating the odds in more typical schools) we found that they did not work in contexts that provided students and teachers with consistent and strong curriculum and instructional approaches and development. Thus, while their students may have scored higher than those in other classes in the school, there was no consistent and strong support that sustained student achievement beyond their individual classrooms. We found the third category of teachers (typical teachers in typical schools) in departments and schools that did not support their individual growth and that lacked collective consensus about the most effective approaches to educating their particular student body. Table 14.2 provides a quick summary of the schools and teachers in the study.

DESIGN

This study involved a nested multicase design with each English program as a case, and the class including the teachers and student informants as cases within. This design permitted shifting lenses among the three contexts (program, teacher, and students) as ideas for instructional change and delivery were considered, discussed, and enacted. Field researchers worked with each program, following the teachers' professional as well as classroom activities and interactions, including their interactions with central office staff, to develop an understanding of their roles in instruction. The field researchers each studied one or more programs for 2 years; hence we were able to study the instructional concerns, plans, and enactments over time, with two sets of students. (Case study reports for some of the schools are available at http://cela.albany.edu.) The sample involved 2 years each with 44 teachers working in 25 schools, and included some 2640 students and 528 student informants.

None of the schools we studied were dysfunctional, and none of the teachers were considered to be other than good. Fourteen of the 25 schools were performing better than schools serving demographically similar populations, based on scores on high-stakes tests, and the teachers in the other schools in which we worked were recommended by district administrators as good, although the overall performance of their schools was more typical. Thus, this is a study of English instruction within both higher performing and more typically performing schools.

Table 14.2. Project Schools and Key Teachers

School	*Teacher*	*Category*
Florida		
Reuben Dario Middle School[a]	Karis MacDonnell	1
	Gail Slatko	1
Highland Oaks Middle School[a]	Rita Gold	1
	Susan Gropper	1
Palm Middle School	Nessa Jones	3
Hendricks High School	Elba Rosales	2
	Carol McGuiness	3
Miami Edison High School[a]	Shawn DeNight	2
	Kathy Humphrey	2
Wm. H. Turner Technical Arts High School[a]	Chris Kirchner	1
	Janas Masztal	1
New York		
Henry O. Hudson Middle School	Cathy Starr	1
	Gloria Rosso	1
Stockton Middle School	Helen Ross	3
Abraham S. King Middle School	Pedro Mendez	1
	Donald Silvers	1
Crestwood Middle School	Monica Matthews	3
International High School[a]	Marsha Slater	1
	Aaron Listhaus	1
New Westford High School	Elaine Dinardi	3
	Jack Foley	3
Tawasentha High School	Margaret Weiss	2
	Nicole Scott	3
California		
Rita Dove Middle School	Jonathan Luther	3
	Evangeline Turner	2
Charles Drew Middle School	Alicia Alliston	1
	Tawanda Richardson	1
James A. Foshay Learning Center Middle School[a, b]	Kathryn McFadden-Midby	1
James A. Foshay Learning Center High School[a, b]	Myra LeBendig	1
Rutherford B. Hayes High School	Ron Soja	3
Springfield High School	Celeste Rotondi	1
	Suzanna Matton	1

(Table continues)

Table 14.2. Continued

School	*Teacher*	*Category*
Texas		
Parklane Middle School	Rachel Kahn	1
	Amy Julien	1
Ruby Middle School	Shaney Young	3
	Erica Walker	3
John H. Kirby Middle School	Cynthia Spencer-Bell	1
	Matt Caldwell	1
Lincoln High School	Viola Collins	1
	Vanessa Justice	1
Lyndon B. Johnson High School	Thelma Moore	1
	Nora Shepherd	1
Sam Rayburn High School	Carol Lussier	2
	Jo Beth Chapin	3

1 = Beating the odds teacher in beating the odds school.
2 = Beating the odds teacher in typically performing school.
3 = Typical teacher in typically performing school.
[a]Denotes participants' preference to use real names. In such cases, the actual names of schools, project teachers, and their colleagues are used. For the schools not marked with a superscript a, pseudonyms are used throughout this paper.
[b]We studied both the middle and high school programs at Foshay Learning Center.

PROCEDURES

Each field researcher spent approximately 5 weeks per year at each site, including a week at the beginning of each year to interview district personnel as well as teachers and students about their goals, plans, and perceptions; to make initial observations of the classes we would be studying; and to plan for the year ahead. This was followed by 2 weeks of additional visits per semester to observe classes, to conduct informal interviews with participating teachers and students, and to shadow the teachers in their professional encounters (i.e., team, department, building, district, and other relevant meetings).

In addition to the on-site visits, we set up e-mail accounts or spoke by phone or in person in order to maintain weekly contact with the teachers and students, during which time we discussed ongoing classroom activities, including examples of student work provided from the student informants (student informants maintained portfolios and their work was collected and mailed to us weekly), reflections on those lessons, as well as future plans.

DATA

Parallel sets of qualitative data were gathered at each of the sites. Data consisted of field notes of all meetings, observed classes, and conversations; e-mail messages; artifacts from school and professional experiences; tape recordings and transcripts of all interviews and observed class sessions; and in-process case reports developed by the field researchers. Table 14.3 summarizes the major types of data collected.

Three types of collaborations contributed to the development of the database within and across cases: full project team, collaborative dyads, and case study sessions.

Full-project team. In addition to meetings with the teacher participants in each state, the teachers and research team interacted in ongoing e-mail discussions about the approaches, activities, and progress in the participating classes and the teacher's experiences in helping students improve their literacy performance.

Collaborative dyad. Each teacher and field researcher communicated via e-mail approximately once a week to develop, discuss, and reflect on the teacher's professional interactions as well as class sessions and student performance.

Case study sessions. The field researchers and I met weekly for case study sessions. During these meetings, the field researchers presented inprocess case study reports about the professional networks and instructional activities and offerings at their sites. These sessions offered opportunities for case-related patterns to be discussed, tested, and refined, and for cross-case patterns to be noted for further recursive testing and analysis.

Coding. Coding for this project was used to organize and index the various types of data in ways that permitted us to locate the participants' focus on key areas of concern. For example, where possible, all data were initially coded for the type of community the participants were focusing on or referring to: professional, classroom, or social, as well as for their focus on instruction, curriculum, and assessment. More targeted codes for particular types of knowledge, skills, and processes were also coded. This scheme served as an indexing system that allowed us to later retrieve and more carefully analyze data from one categorical subsection of the data pool, compare it with another, and generate data-driven subcategories for later analysis.

ANALYSES

Data were analyzed by a system of constant comparison, where patterns were identified and tested both within and across cases. For this study, we

Table 14.3. Data Gathered at Each Site

I.	Interviews
	Teacher: entry and exit
	Preparation and experience
	Recent coursework and workshops
	Professional memberships and activities
	Instructional goals
	Pedagogical beliefs and teaching concerns
	Topics of instruction
	Content
	Approaches
	Materials
	Activities
	Patterns of discourse
	Chair/principal/district supervisor
	School/district reform efforts
	School/district goals
	School/district initiatives
	School/district content
	School/district consultants
	School/district committees
II.	Observations
	Baseline (before commitment to the study)
	Entry: 1 week at beginning of school year
	Ongoing: 2 weeks each semester, for 4 semesters
	Topics of instruction
	Content
	Approaches
	Materials
	Activities
	Patterns of discourse
	Student engagement and performance
III.	Ongoing contact
	Weekly, telephone or e-mail
	Assignments, content, instruction, concerns, plans
IV.	Student informants
	Formal and informal discussions of curriculum, instruction, and student work
	Portfolios of all work for English
V.	Shadowing (professional lives study, in press)
	Professional meetings
	Curriculum development and other working groups
VI.	Documents
	State, district, and school documents, including textbooks and other instructional materials: what is available, what is used, and how

returned to each coded instance as well as the full data set to qualitatively analyze the conditions under which each existed: this in turn led us to identify the features that differentiated the approaches of the three groups of teachers. Thus, the various data sets were keyed to the individual teacher and classroom, providing multiple views of each instructional context, permitting both in-depth case studies and cross-case perspectives to be developed. In each case, we triangulated the data, drawing on various aspects of the classroom communities for evidence. As key issues began to emerge in the qualitative cross-case analyses, they were checked against the entire sample. Thus overall ratings of how each teacher dealt with the six features of instruction discussed in the present report are based on the full range of data gathered for each teacher over a 2-year period, including interviews, observations, ongoing conversations (e-mail or telephone), and student reports. Specific categorizations of each teacher's practices were made by the field researcher responsible for data collection at each site, after lengthy discussions with the project team.

Although the findings are limited to the 44 teachers we have studied, the study required the field researchers to shadow and gather data about the teachers, their colleagues, and their school's English language arts programs as the teachers interacted with others at team, departmental and other meetings, and workshops, and as they planned and sometimes cotaught with their colleagues. The field researchers also interviewed the teachers and administrators with whom the participating teachers interacted in order to understand the larger professional and instructional context of each. Thus, although the focus was on one or two teachers in each school, we were able to gain more first-hand "living" knowledge of each school's English program, including the curricular and instructional emphases of the school and district.

In previous studies of effective literature instruction (Langer, 1995), we found that successful instruction was characterized by its adherence to certain underlying principles rather than by any uniformity from teacher to teacher in specific activities or pedagogical routines. The present study thus assumed that currently popular approaches to English and literacy instruction (e.g., process writing instruction, response-based literature instruction, attention to grammar and mechanics) would be realized in multiple ways by different teachers and students. The notion is related to Sternberg and Horvath's (1995) argument that expert teaching should be viewed in terms of a prototype that allows for considerable variation in the profiles of individual experts, except that our "prototypes" are construed as features within the instructional environment rather than the psychological characteristics (insight, efficiency) that Sternberg and Horvath propose. Thus, the analyses and findings of this study do not focus on the surface content and form of instruction, but rather the underlying principles, beliefs, and approaches that are enacted in different ways in the context of each individual classroom.

RESULTS

I will begin with a brief overview of the results from the cross-case analyses of English instruction in higher and more typically performing schools, and then deal in detail with the six central instructional issues that capture the major differences between these groups.

Although each of the higher performing schools had its own distinctive emphasis, all were marked by active and engaged students and teachers in academically rich classrooms. Furthermore, they were marked by the professionalism, knowledge, and dedication of the teachers and by collaborative participation of the students in quality, "minds-on" activities. Students were well behaved and remarkably on task almost all the time. Each school managed to create an effective learning environment in which students had opportunities to think with, about, and through English, both as a vehicle for getting things done and as an object of study in its own right. The students in these schools were learning a great deal about high literacy, including the functions and uses of language. The students were learning how language works in context and how to use it to advantage for specific purposes. They were learning grammar, spelling, vocabulary, and organizational structure—sometimes in context but also with carefully planned activities that focused directly on the structure and use of language. We observed a great deal of writing, reading, and oral language as students explored their understanding, prepared presentations, and polished final products. Students in the high-performing schools were beating the odds, as evidenced by higher test scores than in comparable schools.

Both qualitative and quantitative analyses indicate that certain noteworthy features related to the six issues (approaches to skill instruction, approaches to test preparation, approaches to connecting learnings, approaches to enabling strategies, conceptions of learning, and classroom organization) affected the students' experiences with English; these features permeated the environments and provided marked distinctions between higher and more typically performing schools. In each of the six sections below, I present and discuss these results, relating each to one of the educational issues. Table 14.4 provides a preliminary overview of the six issues along with the ways they differed across instructional contexts.

Approaches to Skill Instruction

Analyses of the approaches to skill instruction in the classrooms in this study identified three distinct approaches that I call separated, simulated, and integrated. Separated instruction is what most educators would con-

Table 14.4 Issues and Concern and Overview of Findings

Issue	*Beating the Odds Schools and Teachers*	*Typical Schools and Teachers*
Approaches to skills instruction	Systematic use of separated, simulated, and integrated skills instruction	Instruction dominated by one approach (which varies among schools and teachers)
Test preparation	Integrated into ongoing goals, curriculum, and regular lessons	Allocated to test prep: separate from ongoing goals, curriculum, and instruction
Connecting learnings	Overt connections made among knowledge, skills, and ideas across lessons, classes and grades, and across in-school and out-of-school applications	Knowledge and skills within lessons, units, and curricula typically treated as discrete entities; connections left implicit even when they do occur
Enabling strategies	Overt teaching of strategies for planning, organizing, completing, and reflecting on content and activities	Teaching of content or skills without overt attention to strategies for thinking and doing
Conceptions of learning	When learning goal is met, teacher moves students beyond it to deeper understanding and generativity of ideas	When learning goal is met, teacher moves on to unrelated activity with different goals/content
Classroom organization	Students work together to develop depth and complexity of understanding in interaction with others	Students work alone, in groups, or with the teacher to get the work done, but do not engage in rich discussion of ideas

sider to be direct instruction of isolated skills and knowledge. Often this takes place separately from the context of a larger activity, primarily as introduction, practice, or review. It can be recognized when the teacher tells students particular rules, conventions, or facts, or when instructional material focuses on listings of vocabulary, spelling, or rules. Sometimes this instruction is used as a way to "cover" the curriculum; other times as a way to help students understand and remember underlying conventions and to learn ways in which they are applied. Teachers use the separated activity as a way to highlight a particular skill, item, or rule. It is presented in a lesson that is generally not connected to what is occurring before or after it in class.

In comparison, simulated instruction involves the actual application of those concepts and rules within a targeted unit of reading, writing, or oral language. These are often exercises prepared by the teacher or found in teaching materials, where the students are expected to read or write short units of text with the primary purpose of practicing the skill or concept of focus. Often students are asked to find examples of that skill or concept in use in their literature and writing books, as well as in out-of-school activities. They sometimes practice it within the confines of small and limited tasks. I call it simulated because the tasks themselves are specially developed for the purpose of practice.

Integrated instruction takes place when students are expected to use their skills and knowledge within the embedded context of a large and purposeful activity, such as writing a letter, report, poem, or play for a particular goal (not merely to practice the skill) or planning, researching, writing, and editing a class newspaper. Here, the focus is on completing a project or activity well, with primary focus on the effectiveness of the work in light of its purpose. This is the time when the skill or knowledge is put to real use as a contributing factor in the success of the work. This becomes a time when the teacher might remind the students of a rule they learned during separated or simulated activities and how it might be useful in the completion of the activity at hand. If extra help is needed, it is provided by other students or the teacher.

Each of the teachers was rated in terms of how they typically went about introducing new language or literacy skills. The results are summarized in Table 14.5. As the table indicates, the more successful teachers were more likely to make systematic use of separated, simulated, and integrated skills instruction; two thirds or more of the more successful teachers in both beating the odds and typical schools used all three approaches. In comparison, only 17% of the more typical teachers in typically performing schools made systematic use of all three approaches; their instruction was much more likely to be dominated by a single approach. Although 50% of the typical teachers used separated instruction as their dominant approach, none of the more successful teachers did so.

Although English teachers in the higher performing schools tended to use all three types of skills instruction, there was great variety in the specific activities they chose to use. For example, in the higher performing schools, the skills and mechanics of English (grammar, usage, vocabulary) were taught within the context of literature and writing instruction, but there was often a great deal of separate and overt targeted instruction and review in the form of exercises and practice. Gail Slatko and Karis MacDonnell at Reuben Dario Middle School, for instance, had students check each others' grammar even when they did not do peer revision. They, like most of the teachers in the high performing schools, also engaged in direct teaching of grammar and usage (e.g., sentence structure, punctua-

Table 14.5. Percent of Teachers Using Particular Approaches to Instruction

	Percent of Teachers		
Dominant Approach	*Beating the Odds Teachers in Beating the Odds Schools (N = 26)*	*Beating the Odds Teachers in Typical Schools (N = 6)*	*Typical Teachers in Typical Schools (N = 12)*
Approaches to skills instruction			
Separated		50%	
Simulated		17%	
Integrated	72%	33%	17%
All three	73%	67%	17%
Approaches to test preparation			
Integrated	85%	83%	
Separated		75%	
Both	15%	17%	87%
None			17%
Connecting learnings			
Within lessons			17%
Across lessons	12%		
In and out of school			25%
All three connections	88%		100%
No connections			58%
Enabling strategies			
Overly taught	100%	100%	17%
Left implicit			83%
Conceptions of learning			
Focus on immediate goal			100%
Focus on deeper understanding	100%	100%	
Classroom organization			
Shared cognition	96%	100%	8%
Individual thinking	4%		92%

tion), and used these lessons as models for their students to rely on when responding to each others' as well as their own work.

At Springfield High School, Celeste Rotondi and Suzanna Matton, both teachers who embedded skills and mechanics in long-range activities, always exposed their students to separated and simulated as well as integrated experiences and continually monitored their students' acquisition of new skills, as well as noting where special help was needed. To help her students learn language and comprehension skills, Celeste selected difficult vocabulary words out of context and showed her students how those words could be used in class. She often did this as a simulated activity, in the context of the book they were reading, or to incorporate it into their writing practice. Using both separated and simulated lessons, she also helped her students learn to justify their answers, summarize information, and make connections. However, these new learnings were continually expected to be applied during integrated activities, such as literature circles.

Suzanna also used literature circles as activities that call for students' use of the skills and knowledge they were learning. For example, in one instance her students were divided into literature discussion groups and assigned the following roles that changed each week: discussion director, literary illuminary, vocabulary enricher, summarizer, and connector. Each student took responsibility for enriching the group discussion from the vantage point of the assigned role. Because these groups continued throughout the year, each student had many opportunities to practice the skills in context, and to see them modeled by the other students. When Suzanna saw that extra help was needed, she either helped the individual or offered a separated or simulated activity to several students or the entire class, depending on need.

In comparison, one teacher at Hayes High School, a more typical school, responded to the call for greater emphasis on grammar by raiding the book room for a classroom set of Warriner's English Grammar and Composition. She said,

> Well, this is how I do it (holding up the book). I work hard and have no time to read professional journals. I teach 5 periods and mark papers. I know I have to teach grammar. My students didn't get it before, so I have to teach it. So I use this (Warriner's) because it lays out the lessons, and my students can also use it as a reference.

Her skills lessons, through Warriner's, were primarily out of context, separate from the rest of her teaching.

Like the Hayes teacher, Carol McGuiness at Hendricks tended to maintain her "old ways" of teaching vocabulary, using a vocabulary workbook in which students did periodic assignments in parsing words to get at Latin and Greek roots. Although she saw this as giving them a tool for encountering new words, a tool to learn how to learn, it was primarily a separated activity and we saw no evidence that she had students use these root word skills elsewhere.

Thus, although teachers in higher performing schools used a number of well-orchestrated instructional approaches to provide instruction and practice of targeted skills and knowledge in ways that suffused the students' English experiences, more typical schools' approaches to skills development seem to be more restricted and separated from the ongoing activities of the English classroom.

APPROACHES TO TEST PREPARATION

Our analyses of approaches to test preparation found two qualitatively different approaches used by the teachers in this study. One approach treated test preparation as a separated activity, involving test practice and test-taking hints. The second approach integrated test preparation with the regular curriculum by carefully analyzing test demands and reformulating curriculum as necessary to be sure that students would, over time, develop the knowledge and skills necessary for accomplished performance.

Almost all the teachers we studied used both integrated and separated approaches to test preparation some of the time, but there were marked differences in the approaches that received dominant emphasis. Table 14.5 summarizes the relevant results. As the table indicates, more than 80% of the more successful teachers in both kinds of schools integrated the skills and knowledge that were to be tested into the ongoing curriculum as their dominant approach to test preparation; the others used integrated and separated approaches equally. In comparison, 75% of the more typical teachers used a separated approach to test preparation, primarily teaching test preparation skills and knowledge apart from the ongoing curriculum. The more typical teachers who did not teach test preparation at all were not teaching students who were scheduled to take a high-stakes test that year.

Teachers in the higher performing schools used the tests as an opportunity to revise and reformulate their literacy curriculum. The primary approach to test preparation involved relevant teachers and administrators in a careful deconstruction and analysis of the test items themselves, which led to a deeper understanding of the literacy skills, strategies, and knowledge needed for students to achieve higher levels of literacy performance. This was followed by a review and revision of both the curriculum and instructional guidelines to ensure that the identified skills and knowledge were incorporated into the ongoing English program the students would experience. Before a test, the format was generally practiced to ensure students' familiarity with it. However, not much teaching time was devoted to this. It was the infusion of the needed skills and knowledge into the curriculum that seems to have made a difference. Students were also taught to become more reflective about their own reading and writing performance, sometimes using rubrics throughout the school year in order to help them gain insight into their better or less well developed reading and writing performance in response to particular tasks.

Again, however, the specific ways that schools and districts orchestrated the process of understanding and responding to the demands of high-stakes tests varied with their individual situations. Some of this variation will be illustrated in the examples that follow.

At Foshay. Kate McFadden-Midby and Myra LeBendig strove to understand the test demands of Stanford 9 and help their students make connections between their ongoing curriculum and academic and real-life situations, including testing. To accomplish this, Kate collaborated with a group of teachers to design a series of lessons that would incorporate the skills tested by the Stanford 9 into their literature curriculum. They identified certain areas in which their students did least well (e.g., vocabulary, spelling, and reading comprehension) and planned lessons that would integrate their use in meaningful ways into the students' everyday experiences. They developed a series of eight lessons as models to be used with a variety of literature. These lessons served as ways for the teachers to create other opportunities to address areas of concern within the regular curriculum.

In higher performing schools, district-level coordinators often created working groups of teachers, and together, the coordinators and teachers collaboratively studied the demands of the high-stakes tests their students were taking and used their test item analyses to rethink the curriculum, what to teach, and when to teach it. For example, when the Florida Writes! test was instituted, the Dade County English language arts central office staff and some teachers met to study and understand the exam and the kinds of demands it made on students. Together, they developed an instructional strategy (grade by grade) that would create yearlong experiences in the different types of writing, including the kinds of organization, elaboration, and polishing that were required. This coordination began some years before our study, and the instructional changes that led to greater coherence were very evident in the classrooms we studied. All classes were replete with rich and demanding writing experiences, including direct instruction and help at all stages. In many classes, the teachers spent the first 5 or 10 minutes of each period on an exercise assigned on the board for the students to begin alone or with others as they entered. Sometimes this involved doing analogies or writing their own, or reading a passage and developing multiple-choice questions for others to answer (after studying how the questions were constructed). The student work was always discussed in class and connected to how it might be useful not only on a test, but for their own writing or reading. Connections were made to this activity later in the day, week, or year.

In some schools, teachers selectively used materials and created activities because they knew that their students needed to practice skills and knowledge that would be tapped by the test. For example, Suzanna Matton at Springfield High was constantly aware of enriching her students' vocabulary. She selected words she thought they would need to know, gave them practice, and followed with quizzes every 6 weeks. She also had her students do a great deal of analytic writing throughout the year, helping them become aware of strategic ways to write a well-developed analytic paper in response to the material they read as well as in response to writing prompts. For example, she helped her students trace how a conflict developed and was worked through in a story, and how allusion was used and to what affect, and then had them write about it, providing evidence. The students also learned to judge their own and others' writing and gained ability in a variety of writing modes.

Test preparation looked very different in the more typically performing schools. Rather than an opportunity to improve their literacy curriculum, teachers in these schools treated the tests as an additional hurdle, separated from their literacy curriculum. Here, the primary mode of test preparation offered practice on old editions of the test, teacher-made tests, and practice materials, and, sometimes, commercial materials using similar formats and questions to the test-at-hand. In such cases, if test preparation occurred at all, there was a test-taking practice 1 or 2 weeks (or more) before the exam, or the preparation was sporadic and unconnected across longer periods of time. At Palm Middle School, for example, the Improvement Plan called for 15 test-taking practice assignments to be given to the students across the curriculum during the course of the year, but these assignments, if done at all, were most often inserted into the curriculum as additions rather than integrated. How to take a test, rather than how to gain and use the skills and knowledge tested, seemed to be the focus.

Some teachers in typically performing schools seemed to blame the students, or the test, but not themselves. At Hayes, although the principal is a highly motivating personality and told the faculty, "We can do it," there was an underlying belief among the faculty with whom we interacted that the students were not capable of scoring well on the exam. They did not believe they could make a difference. For example, Ron Soja said, "They don't know anything. It's like they never did anything." Ron did not seem to feel personally accountable for ensuring his students possessed the underlying knowledge and skills to do well. He said, "The Stanford test is not a good test to see whether they are achieving in school or not, because up until this year it hasn't meant anything. Half the kids, they think it's a big joke."

Beginning 2 years hence, students in this district would need to achieve a certain percentile score (not yet determined) on the Stanford 9 test to be eligible for high school graduation. Ron rationalized that the students scored badly on the test because they did not take it seriously (did not understand its implications), rather than focusing on his efforts to prepare them for it.

Practice activities are often developed by states and districts or commercial material developers, but are not meant to be the sole activity schools use to help students do well. To prepare for the New York State English Regents Exam, which all students must pass to graduate, New Westford High School, a more typically performing school, sent 2 teachers to a state education department meeting designed to brief them on grading procedures. They, in turn, transmitted what they had learned to their colleagues. The English language arts district supervisor bought sets of guide booklets for Regents practice, and Elaine Dinardi bought yet another for additional practice. The books present Regents Exam-like activities for the students to practice. The department faculty also made up grade-level take-home finals that followed the Regents format. Elaine interspersed these practice activities around her usual curriculum until some time in April, when she began to stress Regents practice in her class. This practice became the major class activity, in effect became the curriculum, for the entire quarter, in preparation for the June exam. Over this time, the practice focused on the kinds of essays the test would require: writing for information, compare and contrast, and critical lens (relating a quote to a work that was read), presented in the form required by the test. It should be noted that this was the first year that the English Regents Exam was mandated for all students. In prior years, the school's percentage of students passing (based on average grade enrollment) was at or below 50%. Consequently, district educators were very apprehensive about the Regents. Like those at Hayes, teachers in New Westford did not believe the average student had the capability to perform well on the test.

Administrators of other typically performing schools sometimes purchased professional services or programs that were not integrated into the ongoing program. For example, at Hendricks, an outside consultant was hired to give test-taking strategy workshops to 10th grade students to help improve their scores. The prepackaged materials exhibited little understanding of the specific test or the needs of the students.

Overall, higher performing schools seemed to focus on students' overall literacy learning, using the tests to be certain the skills and knowledge that are tested are related to and being learned within the framework of improved language arts instruction. They regarded tests as one of many literacy activities students needed to learn to do well, and believed that the underlying skills and knowledge required to do well on tests were related to the underlying skills and knowledge needed to do well in coursework, thus needing to be encompassed within the ongoing curriculum. In contrast, the more typical schools viewed test performance as a separate goal, apart from the regular curriculum. Therefore, they saw test preparation as requiring a focus on the tests themselves, with raising test scores, rather than improving students' literacy learning, as the primary goal.

APPROACHES TO CONNECTING LEARNINGS

Our analyses of instruction in the participating classrooms found that the teachers overtly pointed out connections among three different kinds of student learnings: connections among concepts and experiences within lessons; connections across lessons, classes, and even grades; and connections between in-school and out-of-school knowledge and experiences. Results are summarized in Table 14.5. As the table indicates, at least 88% of the more successful teachers in both types of schools tended to make all three types of connections with approximately equal focus. In comparison, the more typical teachers tended to make no connections at all, and when they did, they tended to be "real world" connections between school and home. None of the more typical teachers emphasized all three types of connections.

In the higher performing schools, the teachers worked consciously to weave a web of connections. Thus, at Springfield High School, Suzanna Rotundi planned her lessons with consideration to the ways in which they connected with each other, with test demands, and with the students' growing knowledge. For example, when discussing her goals for the reading of Invisible Man by Ralph Ellison, she said,

> My primary goal is to provide them with what I consider a challenging piece of literature that will give them an excellent resource for the AP exam. It fits in well with the works we have studied in that it explores the inner consciousness and makes use of a recurring image/symbol that has been the key to several other literary works ... that of blindness. It allows them to explore the way a symbol can convey meaning in several literary works. Personally, I feel that Ellison's is a monumental literary work. The ramifications in terms of social psychology with the concept of invisibility applies to so many different life experiences. I try to open the students' appreciation of how this work relates to their own world and it introduces them to the question of identity and how the daily interactions are crucial to identity formation.

Thus, her lessons connected texts, tests, and life.

Even in hectic times when the teachers felt the burden of many demands on their instructional time, those in the higher performing schools and the excellent ones in the more typical schools still tried to weave even unexpected intrusions into more integrated experiences for their students. For example, when his long-range plans were disrupted, Shawn DeKnight, an excellent teacher in a lower performing school, did what he called "curricular improvising." He said, "If it's possible to bend the disruption so it fits in some way with my instructional plans, then I feel I have triumphed." When a grade-wide project was a field trip to a senior citizens center, his theme was "An Inter-Generational Forum: Senior Citizens and Teens Discuss What it Means to be Liberal or Conservative." He had planned to teach his students to write character analyses, based on their class readings. He decided to use the visit to the senior citizens home as a starter; interviewing the seniors "would force my students to interact with the seniors," he said. But what to do with the interviews? He asked them to write a character sketch. He explained,

> The writing follows a similar format to a persuasive essay, something my kids worked on a couple of months ago. It will also be a nice segue into the character analysis in the sense that both types of writing establish a thesis that a person has a certain character trait, then goes on to provide specific evidence to support the thesis. For the character sketch, the evidence that a person was liberal or conservative or moderate would come from the interviews. With the character analysis, which we will begin in a couple of weeks when we finish Romeo and Juliet, the evidence comes from things the character has said or done in the play.

Shawn made connections such as these throughout each day, week, and year, pointing them out to his students so they could recognize ways in which their skills and knowledge were productively used in a range of situations.

Springfield High School, a higher performing school that was preparing for accreditation, was in the process of revising its mission and approaches to education. Self-study led the reachers to develop a more integrated approach to learning, fostering connections both within school and between school and community. One part of the mission statement focuses on students as effective communicators. Faculty members were collaboratively working on teams to ensure that the skills needed for effective communication would be taught and reinforced across the grades and across the curriculum. This process was followed for the other components of the school's mission as well, and these were coordinated with the statewide standards. The teachers were aware of making these connections. For example, Celeste Rotondi said,

> Standards, as much as they're a kind of pain in the butt when we have these meetings and align the standards and all that stuff, it has helped me.... My curriculum is strong. But once I started really looking at the standards I realized I didn't have a lot of oral writing activities, and so it kind of helped me to conceptualize that a little better and forced me to incorporate that.

It never occurred to Celeste to simply add a few oral activities to her lesson plans. Instead, she rethought ways in which reading, writing, and oral language could be interrelated across the curriculum and across the year in ways that would stengthen her students' oral as well as written communication abilities.

In addition to connectedness of goals, skills, and experiences across the day and year (connections Celeste would plan and make overt to her students when appropriate), she also wanted to ensure that her students could learn to make connections across the literature they were reading as well as connections from literature to life. She wanted her students to learn to read the text and the world. To do this, Celeste organized her literature instruction around thematic units, for example pairing *The Glass Menagerie* and *A Raisin in the Sun* to permit her students to focus on family relationships and ways families deal with the situations they face. For such units, she typically created study guides that provided scaffolding for her students and made overt to both her students and herself the particular connections that were at focus. Comparisons across the pieces helped her students compare and critique aspects of structure, language, and style while they also focused on thematic elements across the pieces and connected (e.g., compared and critiqued) them based on related situations in the world today.

As contrast, in the more typical schools, even when the lessons were integrated within a unit, there was little interweaving across lessons; there were few overt connections made among the content, knowledge (literary or otherwise), and skills that were being taught. Class lessons were often treated as separate wholes—with a particular focus introduced, practiced, discussed, and then put aside. For example, at Hayes High School, Ron Soja said that in his yearlong plans, he moved the students from more subjective to more objective writing tasks. However, we saw no indication he shared this distinction with his students or helped them make other connections among the kinds of writing he assigned.

At Stockton Middle School, Helen Ross asked questions that encouraged her students to make connections, but because discussions were carefully controlled, the connections the students would make were predetermined. For example when they read *The Diary of Anne Frank* in play form, taking turns reading parts, she asked, "These are real people your age. How would you react in that situation?" "What would you do?" Although these seem open ended, she was actually leading in a particular direction, toward the diary. She steered the discussion with questions and comments until a student came forth with the idea she sought. Then she said, "Her diary. That's how she escapes," marking the conclusion of that day's discussion.

This same pattern of questioning can also be seen in Carol McGuiness' class, at Hendricks High School, as she opened the discussion after reading a chapter of *Anpao: An American Indian Odyssey.*

> **T:** In the Judeo-Christian tradition, do we have animals that converse with God?
> **S1:** No.
> **T:** Only one, and which one is that?
> **S2:** The snake.
> **T:** The snake. Representative of—?
> **SSS:** Satan.
> **T:** Right. Satan. In this case the animals are benevolent. They are not evil. How is humanity according to this legend?

Rather than encouraging her students to make their own connections, or showing them how, Carol guided them to guess the connection she has made. Following this very short pseudo-discussion, Carol had the students sequence 24 events that she had taken from the first chapters of the text. This sequencing activity was disconnected from the discussion that had preceded it and was followed by another disconnected activity the next day, when she planned to have them act out a scene from the text.

The lack of connectedness in the classrooms of Helen and Carol was also reflected in the larger curriculum across the grades; their departments did not foster connectedness. For example, in Helen's district, department chairs in the middle and high schools were eliminated a few years ago in favor of a K-12 English Language Arts Coordinator for the district's schools. He had been trying to foster curriculum coherence and continuity through cross-grade dialogue and within-grade curriculum coordination; however, because of his many responsibilities, he had difficulty accomplishing all his goals. As he told us, "Too many buildings, too many kids, too many teachers. I just can't do what I want anywhere. So I do what I can. You have to keep your sights limited to what you can do."

Although the central office in Carol's district was making monumental efforts to make the language arts program more cohesive, her department chair at Hendricks made little effort to follow through with his teachers. He said that although he gets good ideas and materials from the central office, he just puts the packages in the teachers' mailboxes instead of meeting, discussing, planning, and collaboratively developing ways to incorporate the ideas into the curriculum.

In the more typical schools, when educators gain information from professional encounters, or adopt predeveloped programs or commercial materials, they seem not to use them in the full and integrated ways in which they were intended. Connie McGee, an English Language Arts

Supervisor for the Miami/Dade County Schools, calls it the "Key Lime Pie syndrome." She said that even though a set of activities has been planned, demonstrated, and explained within a particular rationale and sequence, with features that build on each other, some teachers choose only the parts that appeal to them. Connie says, "I show them how to make the whole pie, but they make just the meringue or just the filling and wonder why it doesn't taste like key lime pie." The resulting failure of the activities is then blamed on the poor "recipe" or the poor students rather than lack of a coordinated whole.

APPROACHES TO ENABLING STRATEGIES

Our analyses of classroom instruction also found considerable differences in the ways teachers went about teaching students strategies to engage in reading and writing activities and to reflect on and monitor their performance. In some of the classrooms, students were overtly taught strategies for thinking and doing; in others, the focus was on new content or skills, without overtly teaching the overarching strategies for planning, organizing, completing, or reflecting on the content or activity. Table 14.5 summarizes the relevant data. As the table indicates, there were distinct differences in ways the more successful and the more typical teachers approached the teaching of strategies. All of the more successful teachers overtly taught their students strategies for organizing their thoughts and completing tasks, whereas only 17% of the more typical teachers did so. The other 83% of the more typical teachers left such strategies implicit. Examples of the variety of ways in which teachers went about teaching (or not teaching) such strategies follow.

In the higher performing schools, the teachers often segmented new or difficult tasks, providing their students with guides for ways to accomplish them. However, the help they offered was not merely procedural; rather it was designed so that the students would understand how to do well. Sometimes the teachers provided models and lists, and sometimes evaluation rubrics. Strategies for how to do the task as well as how to think about the task were discussed and modeled, and reminder sheets were developed for student use. These strategies provided the students with ways to work through the tasks themselves, helping them to understand and meet the task demands. For instance, at Hudson Middle School, Cathy Starr taught her students strategies to use to reflect on their progress as they moved through an activity. After a research activity, the students were to rate themselves on their research and writing using rubrics they had developed:

1. Where do you think you fall for the research [grade yourself]? Did you spend the time trying to find the information? Did you keep going until you had learned enough to write your report?
2. Whether this is a short and informal or longer and more formal piece, you should spend time thinking about the writing. Did you plan what you were going to say? Did you think about it? Did you review it and revise it before putting it in the back?
3. Did you edit? Did you check the spelling and punctuation?

Most of the teachers in the higher performing schools shared and discussed with students rubrics for evaluating performance; they also incorporated them into their ongoing instructional activities as a way to help their students develop an understanding of the components that contribute to a higher score (more complete, more elaborated, more highly organized response). Use of the rubrics also helped students develop reflection and repair strategies relevant to their reading, writing, and oral presentation activities.

Kate McFadden-Midby at Foshay also provided her students with strategies for completing a task well if she thought it was going to be new or challenging. For example, when her students were learning to do character analyses and to understand differing perspectives, she asked them to begin by developing a critical thinking question and then to choose two characters from the book (or books) they had read, in order to compare the characters' viewpoints on that question. The critical thinking questions needed to be ones that anyone could discuss even if they had not read the book (e.g., one student asked. "Why are people so cruel when it comes to revenge?"). Before they met in groups, she provided this outline: (a) share your critical thinking question with your group; (b) tell your group partners why you chose that particular question and what situation in the book made you think about it; and (c) tell which two characters you have chosen to discuss that question in a mini-play. The students engaged in deep and substantive discussion about their classmates' questions, because Kate's strategy list had helped them gain clarity on the goals and process of the task. Discussions were followed, the next day, by a prewriting activity in preparation for writing a description of the characters they chose. Kate instructed them on how to develop a T-chart on which one character's name is placed at the top of one column of the T and the other character at the other side. She told them to list characteristics: what their characters were like, experiences they had, opinions, etc. She provided them with strategies to identify characteristics and then ways to compare them across the two characters.

This was followed by group sharing, where the students presented their characters. Here, Kate scaffolded the students' thinking by asking questions about the characters: What kind of person was the mother? What are some adjectives that might describe her? How do you think those things could influence how she feels? Over time, when the students had been helped, through a variety of supportive strategies, to develop deeper understandings of their characters, they were then helped to write a mini-play depicting those same characters involved in the issue raised by their critical thinking question. Although this was a highly complex activity, the students were provided with supportive strategies along the way, gaining insight not merely into the characters themselves, but into ways they could understand characters and differing perspectives when reading and writing on their own.

In the more typical schools, instruction focused on the content or the skill, but not necessarily on providing students with procedural or meta-cognitive strategies. For example, in the sequencing activity in Carol McGuiness's 10th grade class at Hendricks mentioned earlier, two of the three groups of students were having some difficulty putting the 24 events in sequence. Rather than eliciting any strategies that might be useful, Carol simply told them, "OK. Divide your slips into thirds. OK? This is research. Start with the beginning, the middle, and the end and put the strips into three different piles. Get this done and you'll have a method." But her guidance did not help the students understand the concept of sequencing any better, nor what it meant to create temporal order from story. Only one group of students seemed to understand what she meant and completed the task. So although Carol wanted her students to practice the skill of sequencing, she provided them with little guidance for doing so, either with her help or on their own.

The English chair at one of the more typically performing schools, speaking about his teachers in general said, "Incorporating strategies is difficult for most of us because it's hard for us to pull ourselves out of our comfort range. You know, unless we're prepared to teach the strategy, we're inclined to do something the old way."

CONCEPTIONS OF LEARNING

When we examined how the teachers in the present study conceived of successful learning, two quite different views emerged. For some of the teachers, learning was seen as successful and complete once students exhibited an initial understanding of the focal skill or concept. For other teachers, such immediate understandings were simply the beginning of the learning process, which continued with related activities to move students toward deeper understandings and generativity of ideas.

Results for the three groups of teachers are summarized in Table 14.5. Unusually successful and more typical teachers' approaches to student learning were decidedly different. As the table indicates, all of the more successful teachers took a generative approach to student learning, going beyond students' acquisition of the skills or knowledge to engage them in deeper understandings. In comparison, all of the more typical teachers tended to move on to other goals and activities once they had evidence that the target skills or knowledge had been learned. Examples drawn from more successful and more typical classrooms follow.

Alicia Alliston at Drew Middle School never stopped her literature lessons when she was confident her students had understood the book and developed their own defensible interpretations. Once arriving at this level of expertise, she provided an array of activities that provoked her students to think and learn more. For example when her students were reading and writing about *The Midwife's Apprentice* by Karen Cushman, they also discussed the history, life, and art of the Renaissance. They did research into the life and social patterns of the period and ended with a Renaissance Faire. Celeste Rotondi, at Springfield High School, had her students work in literature circles where they discussed both the commonalities and differences in the books they read. Literature circle time was her students' opportunity to go beyond the texts they were reading, as more mature discussants and critics. One literature circle involved students in reading the following teacher-selected books: *The Great Gatsby*; *Bless Me, Ultima*; *Slaughterhouse Five*; and *Always Running*. At the end of the cycle of discussions the students wrote and performed songs about the books and their deeper meanings and created CD cases with fictional song titles, covers, and artists. The class also read *Night* by Elie Weisel. To prepare for it, Alicia had her students look at photos from concentration camps and write down words and phrases that were relevant. These were used to create poems. While reading *Night*, the class visited the Museum of Tolerance, completed an assignment while they were there, and wrote letters from three points of view (seven to choose from), all involved with the Holocaust in some way. Thus, the reading of *Night* became not merely an understanding and critique of the work itself (though this was done), but rather an integrated opportunity to contemplate historical, ethical, political, and personal issues raised by the reading.

Gloria Rosso at Hudson Middle School wanted to teach her students research skills using the World Wide Web, hard copy material, and interviews as sources of information. To do this, she engaged her students in a generative activity that would extend their learning of content as well as of the research process. She began with what she called a mini-unit on the students' surnames—what they meant and their histories—leading to essay writing, the development of coats of arms, and class presentations.

In addition to teaching students to access data on genealogies on the Web, she also taught them to develop good questions for interviews with family members, and how to read materials and take notes and citations. They were invited to explore the use of symbols, as used in coats of arms, as a background to devising their own. While Gloria helped with the research skills, the students discussed what they were learning and ways in which the histories of their names provided a living trail of history. This led into her next and more extensive research unit on African Americans, where once again, the students not only did research and wrote papers but interacted around the larger implications of the stories of African American experiences and present day life.

In contrast, in the more typical schools, the learning activity and the thinking about it seemed to stop with the responses sought or the assigned task completed—at a level Vygotsky (1987) calls "pseudo concepts," in which the learning is more a superficial recall of names, definitions, and facts than a deeper and more highly conceptualized learning.

For example, when Jack Foley's class at New Westford High read *To Kill a Mockingbird*, he asked questions about the content and vocabulary. He called on students to provide the answers and when they did, he either added additional comments to their responses or moved on to the next question. Neither the text nor the students' responses were used during the discussion to generate historical, social, or other connections and elaborations.

At Hayes High School, after reading *Romeo and Juliet*, Ron Soja gave his students the following issues and asked them to select the one they most "leaned" toward: Romeo and Juliet are victims of fate. Romeo and Juliet are victims of the society, or Romeo and Juliet are victims of their own passions. The next day they discussed their selections and reasons, then Ron went on to the next topic.

At Hendricks High School, Carol McGuiness ended her lessons when her students provided the answer she was after. Using the example of the sequencing activity again, as soon as the first group finished, Carol asked them to read the strips in sequence. Then the activity was over, even though the other groups were in the midst of struggling with the task. No connection was made either to the chapter as a whole or to the forthcoming chapter, nor to sequencing itself as a sometimes useful skill. Even the fact that the teacher was willing to end the task before all but one group had finished was evidence of the lack of value that was attributed to it as a thought-provoking learning experience. Similarly, when her students studied verb tenses, they were given a homework sheet that was a continuation of what they were doing in class. It was more of the same, rather than a generative activity that built upon the new knowledge.

Thus, in the higher performing schools, students were constantly encouraged to go beyond the basic learning experiences in challenging and enriching ways. In contrast, students in the more typical schools had few opportunities for more creative and critical experiences.

CLASSROOM ORGANIZATION

The final aspect of instructional approaches that differentiated among the teachers in the present study had to do with the extent to which the classrooms were organized to provide students with a variety of opportunities to learn through substantive interaction with one another as well as with the teacher. In some classrooms, English learning and high literacy (the content as well as the skills) were treated as social activity, with depth and complexity of understanding, and proficiency with conventions growing out of the shared cognition that emerges from interaction with present and imagined others. Other classrooms emphasized individual activity and individual thinking, with students tending to work alone or to interact primarily with the teacher. Even when group work occurred in such classrooms, the activity usually involved answering questions rather than engaging in substantive discussion from multiple perspectives.

The relevant data are summarized in Table 14.5. As the table indicates, the dominant classroom interaction patterns in the more successful classrooms differed sharply from those in the more typical classrooms. In the higher performing schools, at least 96% of the teachers helped students engage in the thoughtful dialogue we call shared cognition. Teachers expected their students to not merely work together, but to sharpen their understandings with, against, and from each other. In comparison, teachers in the more typical classes focused on individual thinking. Even when their students worked together, the thinking was parallel as opposed to dialogic. Examples of both approaches follow.

In the classes of the higher performing schools, students not only worked together in physical proximity, but they gained skill in sharing ideas, reacting to each other, testing out ideas and arguments, and contributing to the intellectual tenor of the class. They engaged in the kind of teamwork that is now so highly prized in business and industry, although sometimes suspect in school settings where solitary work is still too often prized.

All the classes at International High School, including Marsha Slater's, work collaboratively. In Marsha's class, from the first days of school and throughout the year, students are taught to work together, discussing issues and reacting to each others' ideas even as they are gaining a common language through which to communicate. (All students at International are recent immigrants.) During one of the first few weeks of school, Marsha introduced a literature research and writing activity that required group work throughout. The students divided into groups and started planning their strategy. We saw a similar pattern in science, where the students were graphing and mapping on computer the results of their group-accomplished experiments. It is part of the educational philosophy of the school that "The most successful educational programs are those that emphasize high expectations coupled with effective support systems, individuals learn best from each other in collaborative groupings." Throughout our study, Marsha's emphasis was on collaborative and active learning. Activity guides helped the students in a group work together toward a common goal, but debriefing sessions and conferences provided a time for each student to discuss not only the group's work but also to describe her or his own areas of accomplishment and need. In all the higher performing schools, such collaborative activities were common. Students worked together to develop the best thinking or best paper (or other product) they collectively could; they helped and learned within the same activity as in life.

In the higher performing schools, even whole class activities, particularly discussion, were used to foster similar cognitive collaborations. At Foshay, although her students sometimes worked in groups, Myra LeBendig often favored whole class discussions. She used discussion as a time for exchanging ideas and stimulating thought. exploration, and explanation. As a whole class, her students were taught to work together, listening to and interacting with one another about the ideas at hand. For example, throughout one whole-class discussion about *The Invisible Man*, her students raised ideas and freely engaged in literary dialogue. One student brought up the issue of how race was treated in the book, and another the symbolism of blindness as ignorance (as portrayed in the book), of not being able to see. One student said he thought Dr. Bledsoe had self-hatred, in response to which a classmate said she didn't think it was self-hatred, but that he [Bledsoe] didn't know where he fit in and didn't know how to connect his two cultural parts. "He hasn't found himself. He's in-between." This generated a discussion that continued for half an hour, with the students in deep discussion about their interpretations of the text and its connection to social issues of identity. Myra explained that she uses such discussions to help students "work through their evolving understandings, ideas, and opinions that will change as they continue reading the book." She explained that early in the year she told her students, "Fight to teach me," meaning she wanted them to disagree with her (and each other) and extend her (and their) thinking with their comments. This is exactly what they did in class discussion.

At the same school, Kate McFadden-Midby's classes often worked in collaborative groups. Group Share was a common activity during which students came up with interesting questions about what they were reading for the group to consider and discuss. When it was group time, the students immediately began interacting in productive ways. They knew what to do and were eager to interact. Kate explained that early in the school year she told students about her expectations, time management, and ways in which their thinking was valued. Her goal was to have her students truly share ideas and stimulate each other's thinking by engaging in real conversations. We have already seen how she orchestrated such activities, in the example of her lessons on character analysis presented in the section on strategy instruction. In that example, the students worked together to sharpen their individual and collective understandings of characters in books they had read, even though they had read different books. In turn, the understandings that emerged from those discussions helped the students to develop rich characters in plays of their own. Throughout, they were absorbed in discussion and thought.

Cathy Starr, at Hudson Middle School, used both whole class and small group activities; they wove into one another and together supported students' developing thinking. For, example, in response to reading assignments, she asked her students to bring three thought-provoking questions to class to stimulate discussion. Students met in groups to discuss these questions and come up with one or two "big" questions for the entire class to discuss. Cathy moved from group to group, modeling questions and comments, and provoking deeper discussion and analysis. After the whole class discussion, Cathy listed on the board items on which the students had agreed as well as issues that still needed to be resolved. In both small groups and whole class discussions, the students needed to interact in thoughtful ways; the social activity was critical to moving their understandings forward and doing well. These discussions were interspersed with assignments the students were to complete in groups. For example, while reading *The Giver*, she gave the following assignment:

> Group Task 1—Government [this is one of a set of four] Form a group of no less than three and no more than five students to complete this task.
>
> Review the chapters we have read. Design a chart that illustrates how the government for this community functions. Include all information you can find about who makes the decisions and who has power in the community. Include the roles of individuals in this structure.

This task required the students not merely to locate information, but to discuss and refine what they meant by government and how it functions in the story, as well as the implicit roles the various characters serve. Some of the teachers in this study called such working groups "mind to mind," stressing the thoughtfulness they expected.

In classes in the more typical schools, such collaborative work rarely took place. For example, Monica Matthews at Crestwood Middle School explained that she has tried to have her students work in groups, but "they're unruly." She had them work together in groups minimally "because they talk off task." Similarly, Elba Rosales at Hendricks High School "saved" group work for the honors and advanced placement classes, claiming that the regular students require more lecture and don't handle group work well. Often the group work that was assigned to what she considers her higher functioning classes required the students to work independently to complete their part of a task, then put the pieces together as final product. For example, after reading *Animal Farm*, each group was to create an Animal Farm Newspaper. However, each group member selected a segment (e.g., obituary, horoscope, cartoon, editorial) and completed it as homework: then the pieces were assembled into a four-page newspaper. While the group effort could be said to reflect what happens at a real news office, the students missed opportunities to work through ideas together for each of the components that was incorporated into the final product.

In other classes, group work often took place, but the students did not "chew ideas" together or challenge each other intellectually. They cooperated in completing the task but did not work conceptualizations through. For example, when Jack Foley's students at New Westford High School worked together doing study guides, they kept the guides in front of them, moving from item to item down the page. As one student called out the answer, the others wrote it onto their worksheets, and together they moved on to the next question.

Thus, there is an essential difference in the way learning activity is carried on in the higher performing and more typical schools, with the higher performing teachers treating students as members of dynamic learning communities that rely on social and cognitive interactions to support learning. In contrast, the more typical teachers in more typical schools tend to treat each learner as an individual, with the assumption that interaction will either diminish the thinking or disrupt the discipline. However, because the schools in this study had similar student bodies, it became evident that the students were more actively engaged in their school work more of the time when English and literacy were treated as social activity.

DISCUSSION

This study focused on students' achievement of high literacy as it is taught in English classes and results in scores on high-stakes assessments of reading and writing. We began the work holding a sociocognitive view of instruction, postulating that learning is influenced by the values, experiences, and actions that exist within the educational environment. From this perspective, it is posited that student performance in reading and writing is influenced by the instructional context the students experience, as well as on the larger educational environment that gives rise to what counts as knowing, what gets taught, and how it gets taught. Because educational environments differ in their goals, procedures for arriving at them, and what gets rewarded as success, this view suggests that differing types of environments will result in different approaches to teaching reading, writing, and English, and different types of learning. This study of higher and more typically achieving schools bore out the theoretical expectations and identified the following distinguishing features of instruction in the higher performing schools: (a) skills and knowledge are taught in multiple types of lessons; (b) tests are deconstructed to inform curriculum and instruction; (c) within curriculum and instruction, connections are made across content and structure to ensure coherence; (d) strategies for thinking and doing are emphasized; (e) generative learning is encouraged; and (f) classrooms are organized to foster collaboration and shared cognition.

These features dominated the higher achieving English and language arts programs. In contrast, some aspects of these features were present in some of the more typical schools some of the time and other features none of the time. It is the "whole cloth" environment, the multilayered contribution of the full set of these features to the teaching and learning interactions, that distinguished the higher achieving programs from the others. These features are obviously related to teachers' visions of what counts as knowing and the goals of instruction that guide the teaching and learning process. They shaped the educational experiences of students and teachers in the high performing schools we studied. All of the teachers with whom we worked were aware of concerns about test scores and students' acquisition of skills. Yet in the most successful schools, there was always a belief in students' abilities to be able and enthusiastic learners; they believed all students can learn and that they, as teachers, could make a difference. They therefore took on the hard job of providing rich and challenging instructional contexts in which important discussions about English, language, literature, and writing in all its forms could take place, while using both the direct instruction and contextualized experiences their students' needed for skills and knowledge development. Weaving a web of integrated and interconnected experiences, they ensured that their students would develop the pervasive as well as internalized learning of knowledge, skills, and strategies to use on their own as more mature and more highly literate individuals at school, as well as at home and in their future work.

These findings cut across high-poverty areas in inner cities as well as middle class suburban communities. They occurred in schools that were scoring higher in English and literacy than other schools serving comparable populations of students. They involved concentrated efforts on the part of teachers to offer extremely well-conceived and well-delivered instruction based on identified goals about what is important to be learned, and on an essential understanding of how the particular knowledge and skills identified as learning goals occur and are used in the carrying out of real literacy activities. From these teachers, we have learned that it is not enough to teach to the test, to add additional tutoring sessions or mandated summer school classes, or to add test prep units or extra workbooks on grammar or literary concepts. Although many forms of additional and targeted help were evident as parts of the effort to improve student achievement in the higher performing schools, these alone were not enough. The overriding contributor to success was the whole-scale attention to students' higher literacy needs and development throughout the curriculum, which shaped what students experienced on a day-to-day basis in their regular classrooms. Such revisioning of both curriculum and instruction requires a careful rethinking of the skills and knowledge that need to be learned, their integration for students' use in broader activities, and continued practice, discussion, and review of them as needed over time. The English and literacy learning goals, at once recognizable and overt, can then permeate a range of direct literacy and literacy-embedded activities. They are at the heart of the kind of English and language arts teaching and learning across the grades I discussed in the introduction to this article, and underlie the development of the higher literacy and deeper knowledge this entails. Thus, the findings provide us with not merely a vision, but also a set of principles and an array of examples to use as guides in revisioning effective instruction.

It is important to emphasize that in the higher performing schools, the six features worked in conjunction with one another to form a supportive web of related learning. It would be erroneous to assume that the adoption of any one feature, however well orchestrated, without the others could make the broad-based impact needed to effect major change in student learning. Rather, it was the suffusion of the school environment with related and important learnings that were highlighted by the teachers and recognized by the students as making a difference. My earlier article (Langer, 2000) dealt with the principle-led creation of professional contexts in schools that beat the odds; this article adds that next critical dimension, principle-led practice. I hope these reports will be helpful to educators in making decisions about effective paths toward the improvement of student achievement.

LIMITATIONS AND NEXT STEPS

Because this was an observational study, it cannot prove causality. It does, however, add to our knowledge of the differences between schools and classrooms whose students are attaining higher than expected levels of literacy achievement, and those who are not, across a very diverse range of schools and student populations. The schools, teachers, and teaching styles in this study differed in many ways, but they reflected a cohesive set of underlying approaches to curriculum and instruction, despite the many variations in how these general approaches were implemented. Although the approaches were quite consistent across the schools that beat the odds, some also were present in some of the lower performing schools, but with lesser consistency or pervasiveness. At least two types of follow-up investigation would be helpful. One would focus at a more micro level on teacher and class differences to specify what differences can be tolerated, and to what degree, before achievement is compromised. The second would be an instructional intervention, attempting to put into place the features of beating the odds schools in more typical, lower performing schools, studying whether these features, when placed in schools that do not already have them, will positively affect student performance, and the kinds of professional and instructional development activities needed for this to occur.

AUTHOR'S NOTE

This chapter first appeared in winter, 2001, in the *American Education Research Journal, 38*(4), 837-880, and is reprinted by permission of the author and AERJ.

ACKNOWLEDGMENTS

This report is based on research supported in part under the Research and Development Centers Program (award number R305A60005) as administered by OERI. However, the contents do not necessarily represent the positions or policies of the Department of Education, OERI, or the Institute on Student Achievement. The research was completed with the hard work of an expert team of field researchers: Paola Bonissone,

Carla Confer, Gladys Cruz, Ester Helmar-Salasoo, Sally Kahr, Tanya Manning, Eija Rougle, Steven Ostrowski, and Anita Stevens. I offer sincere thanks to the many teachers, students, and schools for their cooperation. It was their commitment to increasing English teachers' knowledge about ways to improve student learning and achievement that motivated each of them to participate. I am grateful.

REFERENCES

Applebee, A. N. (1993). *Literature in the secondary school.* Urbana, IL: National Council of Teachers of English.

Applebee, A. N. (1996). *Curriculum as conversation: Transforming traditions of teaching and learning.* Chicago: University of Chicago Press.

Bakhtin, M. M. (1981). *The dialogic imagination.* Austin: University of Texas Press.

Barnes, D. (1976). *Communication and the curriculum.* London: Penguin.

Bazerman, C. (1981). What written knowledge does: Three examples of academic discourse. *Philosophy of the Social Sciences, 11*(3), 361-387.

Bereiter, C., & Scardamalia, M. (1987). An attainable version of high literacy: Approaches to teaching higher order skills in reading and writing. *Curriculum Inquiry, 17*(1), 10-30.

Bloom, B. S. (1971). Mastery learning and its implications for curriculum development. In E. W. Eisner (Ed.), *Confronting curriculum reform.* Boston: Little, Brown.

Bransford, J. D., Brown, A. L., & Cocking, R. R. (Eds.). (1999). *How people learn: Brain, mind, experience, and school.* Washington, DC: National Academy Press.

Brown, A. L., & Campione, J. (1996). Psychological theory and the design of innovative learning environments: On procedures, principles, and systems. In L. Schuable & R. Glazer (Eds.), *Innovations in learning: New environments for learning.* Mahwah, NJ: Erlbaum.

Brown, J. S., Collins, A., & Daguid, P. (1989). Situated cognition and the culture of learning. *Educational Researcher, 18*(1), 32-42.

Cope, B., & Kalantzis, M. (1993). The power of literacy and the literacy of power. In B. Cope & M. Kalantzis (Eds.), *The powers of literacy: A genre approach to writing* (pp. 154-178). Pittsburgh, PA: University of Pittsburgh Press.

Dewey, J. (1938). *Education as experience.* New York: Collier.

Dyson, A. (1993). *Social worlds of children learning to write in an urban primary school.* New York: Teachers College Press.

Gee, J. (1996). *Social linguistics and literacies: Race, writing, and difference.* London: Taylor & Maxwell.

Goodman, Y., & Wilde, S. (1992). *Literacy events in a community of young writers.* New York: Teachers College Press.

Graff, G. (1987). *Professing literature: An institutional history.* Chicago: University of Chicago Press.

Graves, D. (1983). *Writing: Teachers and children at work.* Exeter, NH: Heinemann.

Greeno, J. G. (1997). *On claims that answer the wrong questions. Educational Researcher, 26*(1), 5-17.

Greeno, J. G., & the Middle School Through Applications Project Group. (1998). The situativity of knowing, learning, and research. *American Psychologist, 53*, 5-26.

Guthrie, J. T., & Alverman, D. E. (Eds.). (1999). *Engaged reading.* New York: Teachers College Press.

Hillocks, G., Jr. (1986). *Research on written composition.* Urbana, IL: National Conference on Research in English.

Hillocks, G. W. (1995). *Teaching writing as reflective practice.* New York: Teachers College Press.

Hirsch, E. D. (1996). *The schools we need and why we don't have them.* New York: Doubleday.

Langer, J. A. (1986). A sociocognitive perspective on literacy. In J. Langer (Ed.). *Language, literacy and culture: Issues of society and schooling* (pp. 1-20). Norwood, NJ: Ablex.

Langer, J. A. (1995). *Envisioning literature: Literary understanding and literature instruction.* New York: Teachers College Press.

Langer, J. A. (2000). *Excellence in English in middle and high school: How teachers' professional lives support student achievement.* American Educational Research Journal, 37(2), 397-439.

Langer, J. A. & Allington, R. L. (1992). Curriculum research in writing and reading. In P. W. Jackson (Ed.), *Handbook on research on curriculum* (pp. 687-725). New York: MacMillan.

Langer, J. A., & Applebee, A. N. (1987). *How writing shapes thinking: A study of teaching and learning* (Research Report No. 22). Urbana, IL: National Council of Teachers of English.

Lave, J., & Wenger, E. (1991). *Situated learning: Legitimate peripheral participation.* Cambridge, UK: Cambridge University Press.

Myers, M. (1996). *Changing minds.* Urbana, IL: National Council of Teachers of English.

National Assessment of Educational Progress (1998). *National writing summary data tables for grade 8 teacher data.* Retrieved October 10, 1999, from http://www.nces.ed.gov/nationsreportcard/TABLES/index.shtml.

National Assessment of Educational Progress (1994). *NAEP 1992 Report Card.* Washington, DC: Government Printing Office for the National Center for Education Statistics, U.S. Department of Education.

Nystrand, M., & Gamoran, A. (1997). *Opening dialogue.* New York: Teachers College Press.

Nystrand, M., Gamoran, A., & Heck, M. J. (1992). Using small groups for response to and thinking about literature. *English Journal, 83*, 14-22.

Paris, S. G., Wasik, G. A., & Turner, J. C. (1991). The development of strategic readers. In R. Barr, M. L. Kamil, P. Mosenthal, & P. D. Pearson (Eds.), *Handbook of reading research.* New York: Longman.

Pressley, M., Allington, R., Morrow, L., Baker, K., Nelson, E., Wharton-McDonald, R., Block, C., Tracey, D., Brooks, G., Cronin, J., & Woo, D. (1998). *The nature of effective first-grade reading instruction* (Report No. 11007). Albany, NY: Center on English Learning & Achievement.

Pressley, M., El-Dinary, P. B., Brown, R., Schuder, T. L., Pioli, M., Green, K., & Gaskins, I. (1994). Transactional instruction in reading comprehension strategies. *Reading and Writing Quarterly, 10,* 5-19.

Purves, A., & Beach, R. (1972). *Literature and the reader.* Urbana, IL: National Council of Teachers of English.

Raphael, T. E., & McMahon, S. I. (1994). Book club: An alternative framework for reading instruction. *The Reading Teacher, 48*(2), 102-116.

Schallert, D. L. (1976). Improving memory for prose: The relationship between depth of processing and context. *Journal of Verbal Learning and Verbal Behavior, 15,* 621-632.

Slavin, R. E. (1983). *Cooperative learning.* White Plains, NY: Longman.

Smith, M., & O'Day, J. (1991). Systemic school reform. In S. H. Fuhrman & B. Malem (Eds.), *The politics of curriculum and testing: The 1990 yearbook of the politics of education association.* London: Falmer.

Squire, J. R., & Applebee, R. K. (1968). *High school English instruction today.* New York: Appleton-Century-Crofts.

Sternberg, R. J., & Horvath, J. A. (1995). A prototype view of expert teaching. *Educational Researcher, 24*(6), 9-17.

Taylor, B., Pearson, P.D., Clark, K.F., & Walpole, S. (1999). *Beating the odds in teaching all children to read* (Report No. 2-006). Ann Arbor, MI: Center for the Improvement of Early Reading.

Turner, J. C. (1993). *Situated motivation in literacy instruction.* Reading Research Quarterly, 28(4), 288-290.

Vygotsky, L. S. (1987). Thinking and speech. In R. Rieber & A. Carton (Eds.), *The collected works of L. Vygotsky.* New York: Plenum.

Wharton-McDonald, R., Pressley, M., & Hampston, J. (1998). Literacy instruction in nine first-grade classrooms: Teacher characteristics and student achievement. *Elementary School Journal, 99,* 102-119.

CHAPTER 15

BEYOND ISLANDS OF EXEMPLARY CASES

Michael Fullan

ABSTRACT

This commentary chapter uses examples from the case studies in the first part of the book to discuss the tensions and possibilities embedded in the policy and practice discourse about school reform. In particular, this chapter contrasts the decades-long policy/practice dichotomy between the pressures of mandated high stakes accountability systems such as those in Texas and North Carolina and the culture-changing need to create community and build capacity among the teachers and leaders charged with accomplishing school improvement. Both perspectives are necessary, but there is still too little attention to creating the conditions that will disturb the "social realities" of schools and create local capacity for learning and change. These cases provide lessons and examples of the work it will take to create schools for low income students in which teachers simultaneously work on multiple agendas and develop community commitments that integrate their own social learning with the instructional needs of their students in these schools.

Deep Change: Cases and Commentary on Reform in High Stakes States, 335–345

INTRODUCTION

The five chapters in Part II of *Deep Change* form a rich and detailed exploration of school improvement. This chapter is divided into three sections. I first provide a broad, comprehensive model for understanding school improvement initiatives. Second, I delve into the five chapters of Part II. Third, I return to the model in drawing conclusions and making recommendations for the future.

THE TRI-LEVEL MODEL

After 35 years of studying and promoting implementation we have little to show for it if we use large scale, sustainable reform as the criterion of success. We have of course a long litany of failed implementations. But we also have many pockets of success that not only do not connect but also come and go at a random rate. Recently in *Change Forces with a Vengeance* and *Leadership and Sustainability* (Fullan, 2003, 2005), I have made the case that we need to develop a tri-level orientation to the problem, namely, (i) what has to happen at the school and community level, and (ii) what has to happen at the district level, and (iii) what has to happen at the state or policy level.

At the school level, for example, we have considerable knowledge of what makes individual schools effective. Newmann, Kings, and Young's (2000) findings about school capacity is a case in point. They define school capacity as "the collective power of the full staff to make improvements at the school and classroom level that makes a difference in student achievement." They found five elements of school capacity:

- individual skills, knowledge and dispositions;
- professional learning community;
- program coherence;
- technical resources;
- principal leadership.

In other words, they found that when schools select and develop individual teachers, establish learning relationships among teachers, focus on priorities and coherence of curriculum, mobilize ideas, time and expertise, and are led by principals who foster the previous four components, they get results; that is, they focus on curriculum, instruction, learning and assessment in a way that "raises the bar" and closes the gap in student achievement.

As we will see, the chapters in Part II confirm the Newmann et al findings and extend them, for example into classroom details, and into community linkages. In any case, detailed development of new learning cultures at the school is the foundation of the three levels.

We have also found that you can't get very far if you just focus on individual school development. We need scores of schools moving in new directions, and learning from each other as they go. It is for this reason that many of us have been working on district-wide reform. In these initiatives the goal is to engage the district-level and *all* schools in the district in moving forward, let us say in raising the bar and closing the gap of student achievement.

We have done work in a number of districts, not only to analyze district-wide improvements, but also "to cause it" through capacity-building. For example, in a literacy initiative in York Region just north of Toronto we started with 40 of 135 elementary schools in September 2002. We worked with school teams of three (the principal, the literacy coordinator and the special education resource teacher) and provided seven days of training per year over a three-year cycle focusing on the Newmann et al kind of capacity-building. In September 2003 we were to add 40 more schools, but in fact added a further 65 because of the widespread interest. In September 2004 all York Region schools joined including all high schools in the district.

We have done similar work in other districts in which the goal is to increase the capacity of individual schools through district-wide development. In a recent article, Fullan, Bertani, and Quinn (2004) summarized ten lessons from our work over the past decade. We found that for district-wide reform to be successful the following ten conditions must be met:

1. *A compelling conceptualization*
   (district leadership must have a conceptualization of student learning and equally a clear, driving commitment and focus on capacity-building with respect to how to get there)
2. *Collective moral purpose*
   (moral purpose must go beyond the level of individuals so that it is manifest in how people think of the school and the district as a whole, for example, a commitment to raise the bar and close the gap district wide)
3. *The right bus*
   (this concerns the structures, roles and role relationships that are redefined to focus in concert on teaching and learning)

4. *Capacity-building*
(training and development for those in the roles)
5. *Lateral capacity-building*
(a powerful new strategy whereby schools learn from each other with two positive outcomes; greater access to knowledge, and greater identity beyond one's school)
6. *Ongoing learning*
(a commitment and mechanisms to access data on an ongoing basis for the purpose of solving problems, pushing forward)
7. *Productive conflict*
(a recognition that all change produces conflict, and a commitment to allowing differences of opinion to surface as part of the problem-solving process)
8. *Demanding cultures*
(professional learning community does not mean consensus but raises high mutual expectations for moving forward)
9. *External partners*
(wise and selective use of external partners in order to increase resources and help develop internal capacity)
10. *Focused financial investment*
(through the reallocation of existing money and the acquisition of new resources, districts increase financial investment on teaching and learning).

The work on district-wide reform is greatly expanding in the present, so we can expect many more developments with respect to this crucial mid-level part of the solution, which was largely neglected in the 1985-1995 period, as site-based management became the focus. Our conclusion is that *you can't have strong school-based development on any scale in the absence of a strong local infrastructure in the form of the district.*

The third-level—state policy—is the weakest of the three in the sense that we are talking about self-conscious policy development, strategic actions and resource allocation at the state and federal levels deliberately intended to increase capacity and accountability at the other two (district and school) levels. Many states have focused on accountability; few have combined this with a strong capacity-building commitment.

One exception is England with its National Literacy and Numeracy Strategy (NLNS). Its starting point was 1997 in which just over 60% of its 11-year olds were achieving proficiency in literacy and numeracy. The English government set targets for 2002 of 80% for literacy and 75% for numeracy. They used an ambitious strategy of high challenge (accountability) and high support (capacity building) to get there. High challenge included targets, monitoring, identifying failing schools and districts. High support meant new leadership roles in literacy and numeracy at the school, district and regional/national levels, high quality curriculum materials, training, support of networks, and so on.

Our evaluation of NLNS provided good news and bad news (Earl, Levin, Leithwood, Fullan, & Watson, 2003). The good news was that by 2002 achievement has improved from the low 60 percentiles to 75% for literacy and 73% for numeracy. This is a remarkable achievement in that we are talking about 20,000 schools in an entire country substantially improving in less than five years.

The bad news was that the results leveled off in 2002 and have been flatlined or plateaued since. This is another indicator that we have not yet gone deep enough. New strategies are needed which go deeper into the ownership and problem solving at all levels of the system. We have begun to work on these ideas under the label of "system thinkers in action" in which leaders begin to foster leadership in others through widening leaders' perspectives and experiences, so that they can work with larger parts of the system (Fullan, 2005).

In any case, my point is that there is very little *deliberate* attempt at the state and policy level to formulate policies and actions based on the tri-level model of combining accountability and capacity-building, and until this happens we have little hope for realizing change on any scale.

Let's now take a closer look at the five chapters in Part II.

PART II CHAPTERS

Wolf et al.'s chapter on exemplary school change efforts in four elementary schools (two urban and two rural) in Kentucky is a good example of the "islands of exemplary cases" problem. The schools were selected as "exemplary." The findings of what made them successful are congruent with but go deeper than Newmann et al.'s research reported in the previous section. The context for the school improvement efforts was a high stakes state level policy—the Kentucky Education and Reform Act and its accountability sidekick—the Kentucky Instructional Results Information System (KIRIS). The new resources found five common themes associated with the success of the four schools:

1. a strong sense of history and heritage;
2. cooperative rather than singular leadership;
3. reflective alignment with the Kentucky reform;
4. the talent of teachers to teach to and beyond the test;

5. an emphasis that all decisions will be based on the needs of children.

A brief interpretive comment on each is in order. The first issue, history and heritage, is insufficiently captured in the school effectiveness literature (such as Newmann et al.). It concerns the emotional and purposeful attachment that teachers have to the community and the state—in other words, their commitment to the deeper value of the *context* in which they work. This turned out to be a very large motivator beyond any external requirements.

Cooperative leadership by this or any related name (distributive, executive) is becoming clearer in the literature and is well exemplified in the four cases. Leadership for improvement requires leaders who can motivate others despite (or even because of) the obstacles being faced. It requires leaders who are committed to developing leadership in others. The result is a collective commitment and trust to work together for the good of each other and for the good of the children.

Third, reflective alignment with the Kentucky reform is a key ingredient. This finding means that effective schools in high-stakes states do not have to reactively "fight" imposed curriculum and accountability schemes, nor do they have to passively comply. Active schools are already doing many of the things contained in state requirements. What they do is to proactively take into account new demands so that they can "exploit" new policies and resources. There may be aspects of state policy that are troublesome but by and large they use policy to further their own school's development. Schools have a choice and the greater their capacity the more they can influence their own destiny.

Fourth, and another example of being stimulated rather than limited by state policy, Wolf et al.'s exemplary schools used state tests as instruments of school improvement. They taught "to" the tests but they also used the state scheme as an occasion for going beyond the test into the teaching of writing. They went deeper into the curriculum.

Finally, and somewhat a cumulative affect of the previous four factors these schools focused on "all" kids. These used the children as a reminder and rallying point for doing what was best for all children.

Standing back from the four schools, two conclusions are warranted. One is that high stakes' systems can be helpful *if* the school already has the capacity and the commitment to improve. Second, and troublesome, we don't know how these schools compare to other schools in their district or their state. We do know that they were selected on the basis of their "exemplariness" so they would be in the minority.

More to the point of this chapter is Newmann et al.'s conclusion about external policies and programs. Recall that these researchers did identify schools that have high capacity. They then asked the question, if these schools had high capacity, where did they get it? They hypothesized that capacity could come from district and state policies and programs that fostered capacity building. In answering their own question they found no evidence that individual school capacity was "caused" by what districts and states did to foster it.

Where, then, did capacity come from in these Kentucky schools? My own guess is that it is a matter of serendipity and luck. The right principal and combination of teachers are attracted to each other and gel as a unit, which then feeds on itself to get better. The problem with luck is that by definition it will always be in the minority, and that it will never last beyond the tenure of the group. In the Kentucky case we have exemplary schools that went deep, but we have no confidence that they are not more than episodic islands of excellence.

Ponder et al's chapter does focus on one district—at least on 21 schools of the 114 in the district. Again our hypothesis is that system engagement is essential for larger scale, sustainable reform. This chapter traces the development of high quality leadership training for large teams from each of the 21 schools (a total of 315 individuals). The curriculum strands and modules were developed and put into practice by the Centre for Creative Leadership (CCL), one of the leading executive leadership development agencies in the world. The training spread over several sessions over a two-year cycle, included nine components (such as leading with purpose; acting as change agents, teaming up, handling conflict etc.). All indications are that the experience was enormously beneficial for the 315 "individuals."

On the other hand, if we put on our system hat we would want to know how the training impacted "team action," "school-wide" development, and "district-wide" improvement. It is no criticism of the CCL training to note that most indicators show that organization impact was not great. This was partly because the initial superintendent (there were three superintendents over the period of the training) did not use the CCL project as an instrument of district development. If anything he did the opposite. In year two, as the authors note, "9 of the 21 principals in the participating schools were transferred" (not to mention teachers on the teams). All and all the very leadership qualities we saw evidenced in the Wolf et al. chapter went missing. They did not have a chance to develop at the school level (due to instability at the district level), and district leadership never got its act together to take advantage of the initiative. We have what appears to be a district-wide project, which does not even produce a few exemplary schools (there were no doubt some, but my argument is that it was not because the district caused it).

There are very few studies of rural school and district improvement, so the chapter by Farrington et al is of special interest. This is a study of one rural district consisting of four schools. Much like the characteristics we saw in Newmann et al., the Wolf et al. chapter, and in Fullan, Bertani and Quinn leadership was key to the success of this district's network of developments. Leadership focused on dialogical relationship among stakeholders, moral purpose, and understanding and working with the change process.

In assessing initial potential, Farrington et al identified district vision and a strong sense of dedicated professionals in each of the four schools, but they also found three gaps (i) lack of communication to exchange ideas about programs being implemented, (ii) lack of consistency and continuity in several content areas, and (iii) limited framework and capacity to monitor and evaluate progress.

The superintendent, drawing on a network model established an initiative intended to address the problems through ongoing structures of communication and activities that included: shared decision making; collaborative development of school improvement plans; processes for ongoing monitoring and evaluation; two-way communication with stakeholders; and an aligned staff development plan.

Improvements began after year one (in achievement scores for example), but the superintendent began to focus on longer-term leadership development. This includes developing leaders for the future with a focus on coaching, development and leadership selection. Most important the superintendent has established a collaborative and collective sense of moral purpose, which is fuelled by new initiatives that are carefully monitored. Two lessons stand out: one is that coordinated leadership can transform a system in the relatively short run; the second is that the work is never done. This district is currently exploring new "portals" that will enable it to go beyond their initial success. What we don't see in this case is the role of the third level, the state, nor do we know what will happen beyond the tenure of the existing superintendent. The case is a very good example of continuity to push the boundaries using the kinds of knowledge that are evidenced in the various chapters in this book.

The remaining two chapters in Part II continue to explore high performance schools and classrooms. Reyes and Fletcher examined successful mathematics programs for migrant student populations in four "successful" school districts. The authors expected to find that differences in curriculum and pedagogy would account for high performance. Instead what they discovered was that the "workplace culture" was the key factor. Workplace culture consisted of four components: extensive collaboration and communication; a pervading sense of collegiality; a shared vision; and continuous reflection about teaching techniques and results. They also found that "respect for all students," "student centered instruction," and a "curriculum that was constantly reviewed" were part of the constellation of success.

The authors draw two overall conclusions: (i) "organizational culture appears to exert more influence on the success these schools have with migrant students than specific curricula or pedagogical techniques"; and (ii) "state standardized testing in the form of the Texas Assessment of Academic Skills (TAAS) has provided an impetus for these districts to focus on their priorities" (much as we have seen in the Wolf et al study in Kentucky).

In short, what we get from the Reyes and Fletcher study is confirmation of the vital importance of school and district culture. What we don't get are any data on *how* these cultures developed in the schools and districts in question. And thus we are no further ahead with respect to how to foster it in wider system terms.

Finally, Langer's study is especially valuable because she compares high performing English classrooms with those that are less highly performing in middle and high schools. In the high performing classrooms it is very clear that teachers used much deeper and sophisticated teaching pertaining to (1) skills instruction (2) approaches to test preparation (3) correcting language (4) enabling strategies (5) conceptions of learning and (6) classroom organization.

Schools were selected from four states: Florida, New York, California and Texas as places where "professionals were working in interesting ways to improve student performance and test scores." Interestingly Langer found three patterns:

- exemplary teachers whose work was sustained, perhaps even created by the supportive district and/or school context;
- exemplary teachers in more typical schools who achieved their success due to professional contexts unrelated to the school and/or district;
- teachers who were more typical who did not beat the odds, who were dedicated to their students, but working within a system of traditions and expectations that did not lift them beyond ordinary accomplishments.

What we have here are two confirmatory finds. One consists of specific examples of teachers going deeper to provide integrated, connected learning. For example in test preparation, exemplary teachers "integrated [test preparation] into ongoing goals, curriculum and regular lessons" versus typical teachers who "allocated time to *test* preparation separate from ongoing goals, curriculum and instruction." Another example related to connected learning; for exemplary teachers "overt connections [were] made among knowledge, skills and ideas across lessons, classes and grades, and across in-school and out-of-school applications" versus typical teachers where "knowledge and skills within lessons, units and curriculum [were] typically treated as discrete entities; connections left **implicit** even when they do occur". And so on. Exemplary teachers taught a richer, more coherent and connected program.

The second finding was that school and district context mattered. Some cultures provided a setting that fostered exemplary practices whereas others were neutral at best. The exemplary schools "managed to create an effective learning environment in which students had opportunities to think about, and through English, both as a vehicle for getting things done and as an object of study in its own right. The students in these schools are learning a great deal about high literacy, including the functions and uses of language."

The Langer study is especially valuable because it shows powerful teaching in contrast with typical teaching. Once again it does not address *how* these schools and teachers developed their sophistication.

IMPLICATIONS

The five chapters in Part II provide rich and detailed analysis of exemplary practice over a wide range of settings: urban and rural, migrant populations, different curriculum areas. There are also clear, specific accounts of deep change at work.

All of this makes great contributions to what we need to know, but in a way it still leaves us at the starting gate. We do not know how to foster and develop exemplariness even in specific situations let alone on a large scale.

My own recommendations are to go beyond research (which is what the five chapters represent) into development. Effective development, of course, must have a good research base. But what it does additionally is to form partnerships where the goal is to deliberately produce or "cause" greater exemplary practice. We know also from these chapters that this will not just involve great pedagogy. Time and again the authors discovered that school and district *culture* contained the greatest explanations and power.

Because culture and context are so powerful, future research and development initiatives should explicitly build-in the system parameters. All classroom studies should incorporate the culture of the school. All school studies should include the district as part and parcel of the analysis and action. And all district studies should include state context.

In our own current developmental work we are focusing on producing more "system thinkers in action" (Fullan, 2005). These are practitioner leaders (principals, superintendents, teacher leaders, chief policy makers, politicians) who take into account larger parts of the system as they go about their work. They are explicitly aware that their job is to help foster system thinking in other leaders with whom they work. They are the true transformative leaders because they not only take into account context in their thinking and actions, but they also try to change context for the better.

We need in short, to go beyond "islands of exemplary cases" into archipelagos and land masses of systems and cultures that make high performance **normal**, not exceptional.

REFERENCES

Earl, L., Levin, B., Leithwood, K., Fullan, M., & Watson, N. (2003). *Watching and learning 3: England's national literacy and numeracy strategy.* London: Department for Education and Skills.

Fullan,M. (2005). *Leadership and sustainability: System thinkers in action.* Thousand Oaks, CA: Corwin Press.

Fullan, M. (2003). *Change forces with a vengeance.* London: RoutledgeFalmer.

Fullan, M., Bertani, A., & Quinn, J.A. (2004, April). New lessons for district-wide reform. *Educational Leadership, 61*(7), 42-46.

Newmann, F., King, B., & Youngs, P. (2000). *Professional development that addresses school capacity.* Paper Presented at the annual meeting of the American Educational Research Association.

CHAPTER 16

"SCALING UP" IN TURBULENT TIMES

Small Steps and Big Toward Deep Change

David Strahan and Gerald Ponder

ABSTRACT

This commentary chapter uses examples from the case studies in the first part of the book to discuss the tensions and possibilities embedded in the policy and practice discourse about school reform. In particular, this chapter contrasts the decades-long policy/practice dichotomy between the pressures of mandated high stakes accountability systems such as those in Texas and North Carolina and the culture-changing need to create community and build capacity among the teachers and leaders charged with accomplishing school improvement. Both perspectives are necessary, but there is still too little attention to creating the conditions that will disturb the "social realities" of schools and create local capacity for learning and change. These cases provide lessons and examples of the work it will take to create schools for low income students in which teachers simultaneously work on multiple

Deep Change: Cases and Commentary on Reform in High Stakes States, 347–354

agendas and develop community commitments that integrate their own social learning with the instructional needs of their students in these schools.

"How can you accomplish good change in times of great turbulence and cynicism?" A friend in the corporate world asked us that question recently. She was talking about moving forward in the business sector, where speed, uncertainty, and ambiguity reign, and where, even if you do everything right, the economy might not reward your efforts. Or you might be outsourced, downsized, or right-sized. In any case, you would be out of work, or at least out of that job. Because of this uncertainty, workers may be less willing to commit their loyalty to a company. In such an environment, how can business organizations move their practices toward good change? The same question might be asked of expectations that schools sustain the gains of reforms in turbulent times, while scaling up new ways of learning and teaching to the levels of districts and states.

The studies of school reform that we have presented in this text show how difficult it is for schools to accomplish good change in times of turbulence. In her commentary, Ann Lieberman reminded us that educators are trying to enhance learning and teaching in a time of social changes as dramatic as those of the industrial revolution. She noted that the successes reported in the school cases in the first section resulted from exceptional levels of commitment and energy from teachers and administrators, levels that are difficult to achieve and perhaps even more difficult to sustain (Lieberman, 2005).

As Michael Fullan noted in the preceding chapter, educational research has helped us learn a great deal about successful reform at the school level over the past few years (Fullan, 2005). The chapters in this book have demonstrated that well-crafted case studies can provide fresh insights into these dynamics. With views up close, researchers have learned that there are two principal—and possibly opposing—types of reform: those that produce an apparent quick fix, and those that nurture productive changes in the culture of the school. Using the tools of case study research, the authors of these chapters have helped us understand more about reform as it occurred at the school and project level. Although our understanding of successful reform at the school level grows ever stronger, Fullan argued for dramatic increases in research that examines reform at the district and state levels (Fullan, 2005). In this chapter, we identify patterns from the studies in this book that may help us extend our investigations of "deep change" and engage more educators in meaningful reform in a climate of high stakes accountability.

WHY IS DEEP CHANGE SO PRECIOUS?

In our introductory chapter, we suggested that "deep change" means a focus on *learning* for everyone involved with the work of the school. For students, deep change means that the adults in their school focus on broader ideas of development and learning than those represented in mandated tests. For teachers and administrators, deep change means a continuing search for better practice to reach each student, each parent, each teacher. We noted that "deep change" recognizes the *process* of successful practice, a process with no fixed destination, only a direction toward improvement characterized by a focus on the "dailiness," the everyday work, of learning and teaching.

The cases and commentaries reported in this text have convinced us that deep change is both possible and precious. In schools like Hunter, Central, Callaghan and Main Street, teachers and administrators have achieved moments of significance, times when they have transformed the quality of schooling to make a difference in the lives of students, teachers, and community members. In initiatives like those profiled in the second section of the text, participants have pursued the ideal of significance, collaborating toward improvements in schooling that might transcend technical outcomes. These case reports document not only the journey, but also the fragile nature of these accomplishments.

Pursuing significance is difficult work. As Ann Lieberman cautioned, this work goes against the grain of the prevailing emphasis on technical reforms and mandated changes. In his commentary, Michael Fullan concluded that significant reforms are "islands" of success that may not characterize the mainstream of efforts to improve schooling.

Recent studies have shown just how precious and fragile these gains can be. Fullan described both the successes—and the plateauing and negative effects of lowered morale and energy among teachers and principals—of reform gains in the Numeracy and Literacy initiative in England in the previous chapter (Fullan, 2005). And other reports also have described the "plateau effect"—the leveling and sliding of gains in test score performance—in No Child Left Behind reports, especially from high stakes accountability states.[1]

Indeed, when we step back to consider school reform broadly defined, we cannot help but note the uncertainties inherent in this enterprise. Will "typical" schools learn from the successes of the few? Will isolated pockets of reform grow larger and spread? Will increasing numbers of children and adolescents experience the types of learning that are possible? Will they have access to good teaching? Can we achieve the type of democratic future that Ann Lieberman envisions? Can we go beyond research to development as Michael Fullan proposes?

HOW MIGHT WE ENGAGE MORE EDUCATORS IN DEEP CHANGE?

These questions lead naturally to issues of sustainability and scale. When we examine carefully the pictures that have emerged from the studies in this text, there are a few basic patterns that may help guide our efforts to engage more educators in deep change. One pattern is the powerful potential of data and dialogue to shape school reform. An earlier report of the results of the North Carolina Lighthouse study suggested that the cultures of successful schools grow stronger in an upwardly spiraling fashion (Strahan, 2003). As represented in Figure 16.1, this pattern begins when teachers and administrators work collaboratively to identify priorities for school improvement and initiate conversations about instruction. When they use data to guide their dialogue, they target areas for instructional improvement and coordinate their efforts more precisely. As student engagement grows and achievement improves, teachers develop stronger professional learning communities and the school culture grows even more collaborative. At each step, data-directed conversations about learning and teaching shape the process.

In many ways, these dynamics parallel those identified in the study of astrophysics. When stars form, matter grows dense enough for gravity to create heat and pressure and for those forces to begin the process of fusion. To accomplish deep change, schools need a "critical mass" of involvement. The energy that fuels the upward spiral of reform is the hard work of individual teachers and administrators, parents and community members. Their hard work creates momentum only when it is aligned however. Gravity must balance centrifugal force. One or two teachers might work together to help each other improve their teaching. Their efforts are not likely to transform an entire school until a number of colleagues join them. Results from Hunter, Central, and Callaghan suggest that meaningful change may not require the involvement of each teacher, but it certainly requires enough teachers to create momentum. As the sixth grade teachers at Main Street learned in their efforts to create community, it can be difficult to sustain momentum without the involvement of the rest of the school.

While the schools and projects studied in this text vary considerably, these core dynamics seem very similar. This pattern of reform as a spiraling process guided by data and dialogue suggests to us that teachers and administrators in schools that have not yet experienced deep change might begin by initiating dialogue about learning and teaching using data and student work from their schools. The more that they focus these conversations on instruction and align professional development to support the priorities they identify, the more likely it will be that they can recruit enough "kindred spirits" to achieve critical mass. When this happens,

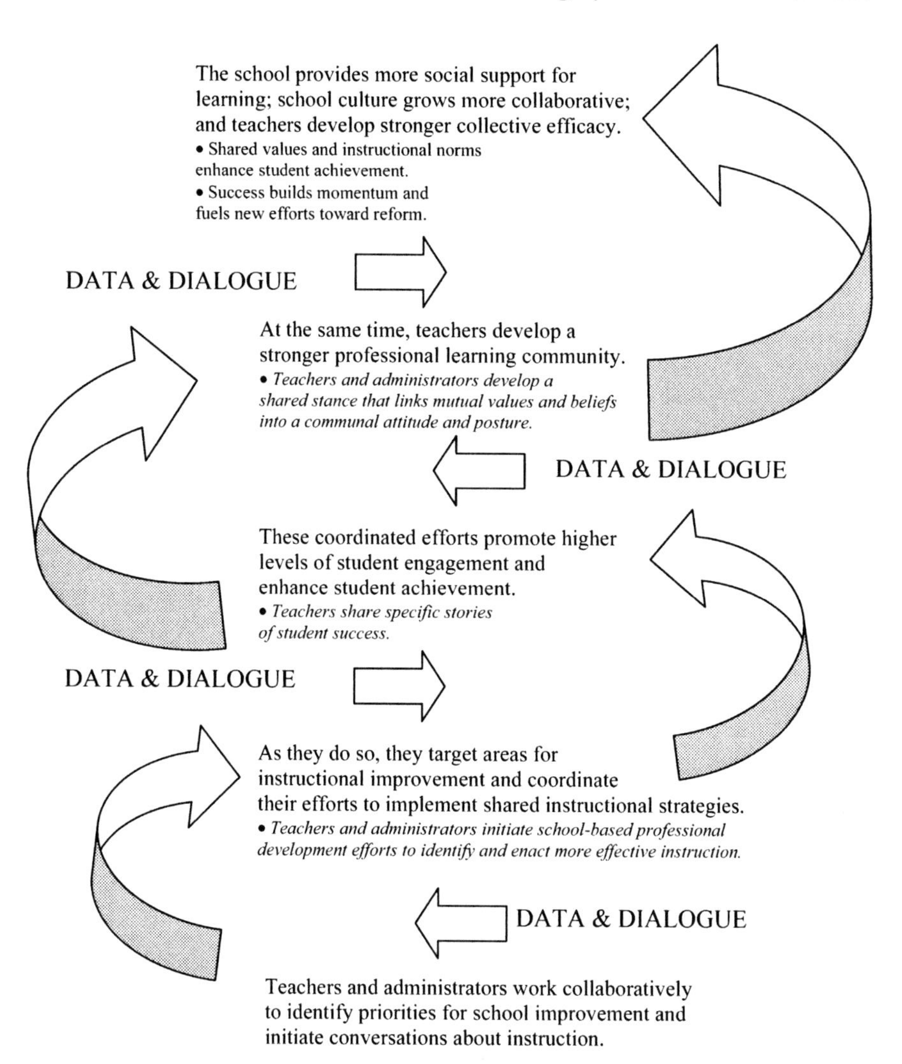

Source: Strahan (2003).

Figure 7.1. A framework for analyzing the dynamics of school reform.

they may begin to experience meaningful reform. Meaningful reform—deep change—is hard work. But there is no alternative.

In the final analysis, issues of sustainability and scale are questions of energy. Deep change requires substantial human energy. Extra hands—helping hands—and minds help. Partnerships can help fuel deep change. Dialogue can lead to community, to common learning, and to higher levels of intentionality. These cases offer that guidance to researchers and policy makers. The work of schooling requires renewable—and expandable—sources of energy.

This insight has a number of implications for enriching and extending professional—and personal—development, for simultaneous broadening through professional development and deepening through professional learning communities and identity development. The ideas involved in Perkins' "collaborative conversations" and the creation of "smart organizations"—that "progressive interactions" move things forward, help groups and organizations become both "process smart" (exchanging information in ways that lead to good decisions, good solutions to problems, and good, far-ranging plans) and "people smart" (feelings of productive cohesiveness, good feelings about working together, and looking forward to doing more together)—generate renewable and expandable sources of positive and productive energy (Perkins, 2003). Data, dialogue, good will, and openness can lead to community, to simultaneous personal, professional, and organizational learning, and to "process smarts" in Perkins' terms (of course, there also are downwardly spiraling examples of teacher discussion groups that have the form, but not the learning function of professional learning communities). And networked school level collaborative conversations might lead to larger communities, "Archipelagos" of effects, to use Fullan's metaphor.

The possible futures of deep change in school reform are many. One is a continuing cycle of initiation, inertia, and collapse from the weight of the complexities of resistance from the existing cultures of schooling and its industrial-age structures and functions, the needs for command and control of charismatic and ego-based leaders (including the imposed need to demonstrate quick success faced by many superintendents), the nonrational, political dimensions of change efforts, and the "Sorcerer's Apprentice" model of initiating and sustaining change in which teacher leaders and other change agents repeatedly start over, reintroducing the same ideas, practices, and developmental possibilities to successive waves of new faces due to high rates of teacher turnover (Little, 2002).

Another is a future in which collaborative conversations, community, and distributed leadership—especially teacher leadership—take hold and become instruments of capacity building, organizational change, and cultural transformation. Building community is essential for sustainability and scalability. Local, self-sustaining networks of teachers and other change agents—principals, community leaders, university faculty, parents, and students—less training and more development, more inquiry, and different models like Japanese lesson study all could produce a far different—and potentially more powerful—conception of professional development. And different organizations from the hierarchical and conserving schools, too often full of regressive conversations, that we now have (Little, 2002).[2]

Yet another altogether is the kind of organizational future imagined in ***Presence*** by Peter Senge and his colleagues (2004). In this book, which moves far beyond Senge's former conceptions of organizational change and improvement based on collaboration and renewal, Senge and his colleagues conceive of non-mechanical, living systems and living organizations, with not only the potential, but also the purpose of creating and recreating themselves. They propose a "U Movement" in which seven core capacities and the activities they enable lead to suspending taken-for-granted realities ("seeing our seeing"), redirecting our perceptions and conceptions in a systemic, wholistic manner ("seeing from the whole"), letting go (of conceptions, preconceptions, control, command, and prediction), and "letting come" the emerging forms of self and institutions waiting to be seen and imagined. At the bottom of the "U" is "presencing"—transforming self and will and creating profound collective change. One of the authors described "presencing" as "waking up together—waking up to who we really are by linking with and acting from our highest future Self" (Senge, 2004, p. 240). Pretty heady stuff. But the power and potential of progressive interactions and collaborative conversations is now proven. And community-building can lead to spirituality (not religiosity) in which mutually responsible and mutually supportive educators serve a common moral purpose—learning for themselves and their students—at least in localized, self-sustaining networks.

The lessons we have learned from these studies suggest that achieving critical mass and generating renewable energy at a district or state level will require social and financial support that we have only begun to envision. Perhaps most importantly, it will require a major shift, a solar event of sorts, in the prevailing emphasis on technical reforms and mandated changes. For school cultures to grow more collaborative, for educators to develop stronger collective efficacy, for students and educators to form meaningful learning communities, we will need to shift away from the uninformed assumption that reform can be accomplished from the outside. Ultimately, the willingness of policy makers to address the human cost of deep change will determine whether the schools who have achieved deep change sustain their gains and whether more schools—other islands of excellence—join them in that accomplishment.

NOTES

1. Bruce Fuller, "Accountability Rises, Scores Fall." *Los Angeles Times*, August 22, 2004. Retrieved as http://wwwlatimes.com/news/printedition/opinion/

la-oe-fuller22aug22,1,2166470.story. Fuller describes the "plateau effect" in California school scores from 2004; he includes Florida, Michigan, and Texas in the list of "plateauing" states. See also the September, 2004 issue of ENEWS (vol. 8, No. 12) from the UCLA-based School Mental Health Project, http://smhp.psych.ucla.edu, for discussions of alternative conceptions of school reform.

2. See also Ann Lieberman's comments for the same conference ("Discussants Reflect: TERC Conference on Sustainability," retrieved at http://sustainability2002.terc.edu/invoke.cfm/page/27/show.

REFERENCES

Fullan, M. (2005). Beyond islands of exemplary change. In G. Ponder & D. Strahan (Eds.), *Deep change: Cases and commentary on reform in high stakes states.* Greenwich, CT: Information Age Publishing.

Lieberman, A. (2005). Shaping mandates for school reform: Practices, problems, possibilities. In G. Ponder & D. Strahan (Eds.), *Deep change: Cases and commentary on reform in high stakes states.* Greenwich, CT: Information Age Publishing.

Little, J.W. (2002). *Discussants reflect: TERC conference on sustainability.* retrieved at http://sustainability2002.terc.edu/invoke.cfm/page/28.

Perkins, D. (2003). *King Arthur's round table: How collaborative conversations create smart organizations.* Hoboken, NJ: John Wiley and Sons.

Senge, P., Scharmer, C.O., Jaworski, J., & Flowers, B.S. (2004). *Presence: Human purpose and the field of the future.* Cambridge, MA: Society for Organizational Learning, Inc.

Strahan, D. (2003, November). Promoting a collaborative professional culture in three elementary schools that have beaten the odds. *Elementary School Journal, 104*(2), 127-146.

ABOUT THE AUTHORS

Hilda Borko is a professor in the School of Education at the University of Colorado at Boulder and past president of the American Educational Research Association. She was coprincipal investigator of this CRESST research project on school-based practices after the Kentucky Education Reform Act. Her research addresses teacher cognition and the process of learning to teach. Her current work explores teachers' learning of reform-based instructional practices, professional development experiences that support such learning, and assessment tools for measuring instructional practices.

Heidi Carlone, is an assistant professor of science education at UNC Greensboro, is interested in studying cultural perspectives on teaching and learning in reform-based environments. Her interest in this project grew out of a desire to understand and enact successful reform through participation in a meaningful Professional Development School partnership.

Cheryl Craig is a professor in the Department of Curriculum and Instruction in the College of Education at the University of Houston. She is currently president of the American Association of Teaching and Curriculum. Her research centers on how context shapes what it is that teachers know, and it is conducted in schools and in collaboration with educators. Her recent book is *Narrative Inquiries of School Reform: Storied Lives, Storied Landscapes, Storied Metaphors.*

Fern Dallas is the director of the Middle Grades and Literacy Programs at Lenoir-Rhyne College in Hickory, NC. Her research interests include K-12 literacy improvement, teacher development, and school improvement using the Professional Development School model.

Gerald Duffy is the William E. Moran Distinguished Professor of Reading and Literacy at the University of North Carolina at Greensboro. Before this recent appointment, he was for 25 years a professor and senior researcher in the Institute for Research on Teaching at Michigan State University. His major research interests are classroom reading instruction and teacher development.

Karen Dyer serves as manager of the education sector at the Center for Creative Leadership, a global nonprofit provider of leadership development to business, education, and non-profit executives.

Rebekah Elliot is an assistant professor in the College of Science at Oregon State University. She was a research assistant on the KERA research project sponsored by CRESST. Her teaching and research interests are in mathematics teacher learning, teacher leadership, and professional development.

Vernon T. Farrington is an assistant professor in educational leadership at East Carolina University. His research interests include leadership development and coaching for school administrators in the accountability age.

Carol Fletcher is the assessment and evaluation coordinator for the Texas Regional Collaborative for Excellence in Science Teaching, a statewide science teacher professional development program housed at the University of Texas at Austin.

Michael Fullan is the former dean of the Ontario Institute for Studies in Education (OISE) of the University of Toronto. He is recognized as an international authority of educational reform, and he is engaged in training, consulting, and evaluating projects around the world. Fullan led the evaluation team for the assessment of the National Literacy and Numeracy Strategy in England from 1998-2003, and in 2004 he was appointed special advisor to the premier and minister of education in Ontario. He is the author of a number of widely acclaimed books, including the *Change Forces Trilogy*, *Leading in a Culture of Change* (2003 Book of the Year Award, National Staff Development Council), and *Leadership and Sustainability: Systems Thinkers in Action* (2005).

Robert Gasparello is now the principal of Grimsley High School in Greensboro, NC. He was the principal at Hunter Elementary School for the first 8 years of partnership with the University of North Carolina at Greensboro. He received numerous local, state, and national awards for his leadership at Hunter.

Suzanne Horn is the director of the Secondary Education Program at Spring Hill College in Mobile, Alabama. Her research interests include K-12 literacy improvement, teacher development, and student improvement using self-regulation strategies.

Shera Johnson-Clark serves as program associate for custom solutions at the Center for Creative leadership, a global nonprofit provider of leadership development to business, education, and nonprofit executives.

Judith Langer, distinguished professor at the University at Albany, State University of New York, is director of the Center on English Learning and Achievement (CELA) and the Albany Institute for Research in Education (AIRE). She is an internationally known scholar in literacy and education. Her most recent book is *Getting to Excellent: How to Create Better Schools.*

Mark L'Esperance is an associate professor in the Department of Curriculum & Instruction at East Carolina University. His research interests include transformative school change and social class and school achievement.

Ann Lieberman is emeritus professor at Teachers College, Columbia University and currently a senior scholar at the Carnegie Foundation for the Advancement of Teaching. She is known for her work and writing on teacher development and leadership; networks, coalitions and professional communities and the culture of schools.

Jennifer Mangrum is coordinator of the elementary education initiative at North Carolina State University. Her research focuses on professional development, change initiatives, the development, function and impact of professional learning communities in elementary schools, and the use of the Paedeia method in instruction and organizational learning.

Jennifer Martineau serves as director of the design and evaluation center at the Center for Creative Leadership, a global nonprofit provider of leadership development to business, education, and non-profit executives.

L. Stephen Mazingo is the superintendent of Greene County Public Schools, North Carolina. His research interests include leadership development and school reform.

Monette C. McIver is a senior consultant with Mid-continent Research for Education and Learning (McREL). She was a research assistant on the CRESST KERA research project. Her areas of specialization are systemic school reform and writing instruction.

Sue Mercier is the curriculum coordinator at Hunter Elementary School and an adjunct lecturer at the University of North Carolina at Greensboro. She provided the on-site leadership for the partnership with UNCG, and she was responsible for many of the elements of reading instruction and teacher development associated with this partnership.

Sam Miller is professor and chair of the Department of Curriculum and Instruction at the University of North Carolina at Greensboro. He has worked with colleagues and practitioners in the schools to develop and implement the Professional Development School model as central to the UNCG teacher education program. His research interests include topics related to student cognition and motivation.

Joy Phillips is assistant professor, Department of Educational Leadership and Cultural Studies, College of Education, University of Houston.

Gerald Ponder is associate dean for academic affairs in the College of Education at North Carolina State University. His research and teaching interests include school reform, school culture, collaboration and partnerships, curriculum, and leadership.

Kathleen M. Ponder is a senior associate in the Design and Evaluation Center at the Center for Creative Leadership, a global nonprofit provider of leadership development to business, education, and nonprofit executives.

Pedro Reyes is associate vice chancellor for planning for the University of Texas System. Prior to this appointment, he was associate dean of graduate education and professor of education policy at the University of Texas at Austin. His research interests include the social organization of schools, the conditions of high academic achievement for children of poverty, and the stratification of learning opportunities for children of color.

Jean Rohr is an instructor at the University of North Carolina at Greensboro. Her research interests focus on the development of visioning in preservice teachers and how their visions for teaching develop during their preservice education.

David Strahan is the Taft B. Botner Distinguished Professor in Elementary and Middle Grades Education at Western Carolina University. His areas of specialization include middle level curriculum and instruction, teacher development, and school improvement.

Anita Ware is a school administrator in Charlotte, North Carolina. Prior to becoming an administrator she was a faculty member at the Principals' Executive Program in Chapel Hill, North Carolina. Her research interests include school reform in poverty settings, instructional leadership and district efficacy.

Sandra Webb is currently a doctoral candidate and literacy team leader at the University of North Carolina at Greensboro. She was a teacher n the Winston-Salem/Forsyth County (NC) schools, and a model clinical teacher, teacher in residence, and instructor in the Education Department at Salem College. Her research focuses on language, literacy, teaching practice, and school culture.

Shelby Wolf is a professor in the School of Education at the University of Colorado at Boulder, and she was coprincipal investigator of this CRESST project. Her research centers on children's language and learning through engagement in literature and collaborative as well as creative modes of expression-discussion, writing, the visual arts, and drama. Her most recent book, *Interpreting Literature With Children* (2004) portrays her close work with teachers as co-researchers in the study of children's literary learning.

LIST OF CONTRIBUTORS

Hilda Borko	School of Education University of Colorado at Boulder hilda.borko@colorado.edu
Cheryl J. Craig	Department of Curriculum and Instruction University of Houston ccraig@uh.edu
Heidi Carlone	Department of Curriculum and Instruction The University of North Carolina at Greensboro h_carlone@uncg.edu
Fern Dallas	Lenoir-Rhyne College Hickory, NC ferndallas@aol.com
Gerald G. Duffy	Department of Curriculum and Instruction The University of North Carolina at Greensboro ggduffy@uncg.edu
Karen Dyer	Center for Creative Leadership Greensboro, NC dyerk@leaders.ccl.org
Rebekah Elliott	Seattle, WA joriott@comcast.net
Vernon Farrington	Department of Educational Leadership East Carolina University farringtonv@mail.ecu.edu
Carol Fletcher	Center for Science and Mathematics Education The University of Texas at Austin carol.fletcher@mail.utexas.edu
Michael Fullan	OISE/University of Toronto mfullan@oise.utoronto.ca
Robert Gasparello	Guilford County, NC, Public Schools Greensboro, NC gasparellor@guilford.k12.nc.us
Suzanne Horn	Spring Hill College Mobile, AL shorn@axalea.shc.edu
Shera Johnson	Center for Creative Leadership Greensboro, NC johnsons@leaders.ccl.org

Judith A. Langer
Director, Center for English Learning and Achievement
University of Albany, SUNY
jlanger@uamail.albany.edu

Mark L'Esperance
Department of Curriculum and Instruction
East Carolina University
lesperancem@mail.ecu.edu

Ann Lieberman
Carnegie Foundation for the Advancement of Teaching
Stanford, CA
lieberman@carnegiefoundation.org

Jennifer Mangrum
Coordinator of the Elementary Education Initiative
North Carolina State University
Jennifer_mangrum@ncsu.edu

Jennifer Martineau
Center for Creative Leadership
Greensboro, NC
martineauj@leaders.ccl.org

L. Stephen Mazingo
Superintendent, Greene County Schools
Snow Hill, NC
steve@greene.k12.nc.us

Monette McIver
Mid-Continent Research for Education and Learning (McREL)
Aurora, CO
mmciver@mcrel.org

Sue Mercier
Guilford County, NC, Public Schools
Greensboro, NC

Samuel Miller
Department of Curriculum and Instruction
The University of North Carolina at Greensboro
sam_miller@uncg.edu

Joy C. Phillips
Department of Educational Leadership and Cultural Studies
University of Houston
jphillips@mail.coe.uh.edu

Gerald Ponder
College of Education
North Carolina State University
gerald_ponder@ncsu.edu

Kathleen Ponder
Center for Creative Leadership
Greensboro, NC
ponderk@leaders.ccl.org

Pedro Reyes	Associate Vice Chancellor for Planning The University of Texas System preyes@mail.utexas.edu
Jean Rohr	Department of Curriculum and Instruction The University of North Carolina at Greensboro j_rohr@uncg.edu
David Strahan	Department of B-K, Elementary, and Middle Grades Education Western Carolina University strahan@email.wcu.edu
Anita Ware	Druid Hills Elementary Charlotte, NC anitafaye.ware@cms.k12.nc.us
Sandra M. Webb	Department of Curriculum and Instruction The University of North Carolina at Greensboro swebb@triad.rr.com
Shelby A. Wolf	University of Colorado at Boulder School of Education shelby.wolf@colorado.edu

Printed in the United States
39499LVS00001B/124-174

9 781593 111892